THE ECONOMIC LEGACY 1979-1992

Edited by Jonathan Michie

Fellow and Lecturer in Economics, St Catharine's College;
Director of Studies and Lecturer in Economics, Newnham College;
Cambridge University, UK

ACADEMIC PRESS
Harcourt Brace Jovanovich, Publishers
London – San Diego – New York – Boston –
Sydney – Tokyo – Toronto

ACADEMIC PRESS LTD
Harcourt Brace Jovanovich, Publishers
24–28 Oval Road,
London NW1 7DX

United States Edition published by
ACADEMIC PRESS, INC.
San Diego, CA 92101

ISBN   0–12–494060–9
        0–12–494061–7 (pbk)

Typeset by Photo·graphics, Honiton, Devon
Printed and bound in Great Britain by Mackays of Chatham, PLC,
Chatham, Kent

THE
ECONOMIC
LEGACY
1979-1992

'This book should be compulsory reading for anyone who may imagine that the simultaneous achievement of European free trade, full employment in all countries, and a single fixed currency is possible without very considerable pain and difficulty.'

Professor Sir Austin Robinson, *University of Cambridge*

'This important book shows why the simple economic certainties of the Thatcher government aggravated the UK's long-term problems instead of curing them. It will be invaluable to serious students of the British economy.'

William Keegan, *The Observer*

'This is a timely collection by some of our finest political economists who, together, analyse current problems and their radical solutions.'

Professor Lord Meghnad Desai, *The London School of Economics and Political Science*

'This book exposes the evils of Thatcher's divided Britain. Her excesses meant the rich really did get richer during a decade of decline when the poor and powerless were penalised. It is a legacy of failure which has left a permanent scar on the nation's economic outlook.'

Rodney Bickerstaffe, *Chair, Trades Union Congress Economic Committee, and General Secretary of the National Union of Public Employees*

'...invaluable for those (not least lawyers) who want to assess the impact of the social policies of the last decade.'

Professor Lord Wedderburn QC FBA, *London School of Economics and Political Science*

THE ECONOMIC LEGACY 1979-1992

Contents

List of Figures   viii

List of Tables   x

List of Contributors   xiii

Preface and Acknowledgements   xv

Foreword   *Brian Reddaway*   xvii

Introduction   *Jonathan Michie*   1

PART I.   THE GLOBAL CONTEXT   9

1.   Britain, The United States and the World Debt Crisis   11
     John Toye
              Comment: The Political Economy of Growth   33
              Ajit Singh

2.   Financial Globalisation and Deregulation   37
     Jerry Coakley and Laurence Harris
              Comment: UK Monetary Policy in the 1980s   57
              Mića Panić

3.   Does Britain's Balance of Payments Matter Any More?   60
     Ken Coutts and Wynne Godley
              Comment: The Re-emergence of the Balance of
              Payments Constraint   68
              John McCombie and Tony Thirlwall

PART II.   GOVERNMENT POLICY AND STRUCTURAL CHANGE   75

4.   The 'Productivity Miracle', Profits and Investment   77
     Andrew Glyn
              Comment: A Legacy of Capital Shortage   88
              Ciaran Driver

5.   Thatcherism and the UK Defence Industry   91
     Paul Dunne and Ron Smith

Comment: Conversion and Economic Restructuring   112
John Lovering

6. Taking on the Inner Cities   115
    Barry Moore
        Comment: The Legacy in the Inner Cities   137
        Iain Begg

7. The Regional Legacy   140
    Ron Martin and Peter Tyler
        Comment: Market Failure in the Regions   168
        Michael Chisholm

PART III. THE CHANGING LABOUR MARKET   171

8. Labour Law and Industrial Relations   173
    Simon Deakin
        Comment: Collective Rights   191
        William Brown

9. Inflation Policy and the Restructuring of Labour Markets   195
    Jonathan Michie and Frank Wilkinson
        Comment: Demoralisation and Mobilisation   218
        Roger Tarling

10. Changes in the Labour Market and the Psychological
    Health of the Nation   220
    Brendan Burchell
        Comment: Public Welfare   234
        Ray Jobling

11. The Legacy for Women's Employment: Integration,
    Differentiation and Polarisation   236
    Jane Humphries and Jill Rubery
        Comment: Cause for Optimism?   255
        Francis Green

PART IV. THE ECONOMIC AND POLITICAL LEGACY   259

12. Government Spending and Taxation in the Thatcher Era   261
    Bob Rowthorn
        Comment: Government Policy and Company
        Profitability   293
        Paul Ormerod

13. Big Business, Small Business and the 'Enterprise Culture'   296
    Alan Hughes
        Comment: Enterprise Culture—Two Visions   312
        Michael H. Best

14. Industrial Prospects in the Light of Privatisation   315
    Ben Fine and Clara Poletti
           Comment: The Industrial Policy Legacy   330
    Malcolm Sawyer

15. The Development of Labour Policy, 1979–92   333
    John Eatwell
           Comment: An Agenda for the 1990s   340
    Will Hutton

Notes   343

References   347

Index   358

List of Figures

3.1.	The current account and its main components 1965–1991.	63
3A.1.	The economic growth–balance of payments trade-off 1968–1989.	69
4.1.	Manufacturing productivity and output in OECD countries 1979–1989.	78
4.2.	UK and OECD wage share in manufacturing 1973–1987.	83
4.3.	Manufacturing investment and profits in OECD countries 1979–1988.	86
4.4.	Percentage increases in investment by sector in OECD countries 1979–1989.	87
4A.1.	Real unit labour costs, capital productivity and profitability in Europe 1960–1990.	89
5.1.	UK military spending as a share of GDP 1975–1989.	94
5.2.	Military spending as a share of GDP for five countries 1980–1990.	95
5.3.	Defence share price relative to FT All Shares Index 1981–1991.	100
5.4.	Defence share price of individual companies relative to FT All Shares Index 1981–1991.	101
5.5.	Profits/sales ratios for defence companies and for all companies 1981–1990.	102
6.1.	Changes in population of working age grouped by type of area 1951–1981.	118
6.2.	Changes in total employment by type of area 1951–1981.	119
6.3.	Unemployment rates by type of area 1951–1981.	119
6.4.	The process of cumulative decline in the inner city.	122
6.5.	Inner city policy in the 1980s.	124
6.6.	Public expenditure on main DoE inner city programmes 1979–1980 to 1992–1993.	127
6.7.	Public expenditure on urban and regional/industrial policies 1979–1980 to 1992–1993.	128
7.1.	The map of regional aid 1934–1988.	145
7.2.	Regional and urban policy expenditures 1945–1946 to 1990–1991.	150
7.3.	The changing strength of regional policy: IDC refusals as a percentage of approvals plus refusals in the Midlands and South East 1950–1980 in terms of associated employment.	151
7.4.	Investment incentives 1950–1988.	151

7.5.   The Regional Employment Premium: index of real value   152
        of payments 1950–1977.
7.6.   Wages and cost of living in the South relative to the North   155
        of the UK 1979–1989.
7.7.   Manufacturing investment in the Development Areas as a   157
        percentage of UK investment 1951–1988.
7.8.   Employment in the South East as a proportion of UK   162
        employment 1965–1990.
7.9.   Location of new and growing sectors in the UK.   164
7.10.   Actual minus expected employment in the North   165
        1950–1989.
7.11.   Growth of employment in the North relative to UK   166
        employment growth 1951–1990.
7.12.   Regional unemployment disparities in the UK 1965–1990.   167
9.1.   Annual increases in earnings, prices and in prices and   196
        taxes 1975–1990.
9.2.   UK unemployment and percentage change in nominal   203
        earnings 1975–1990.
9.3.   UK unemployment and percentage change in real earnings   203
        1975–1990.
9.4.   UK unemployment and percentage change in net real   204
        earnings 1975–1990.
9.5.   Percentage changes in UK manufacturing productivity,   207
        product wages and real unit wage costs 1977–1990.
9.6.   Earnings and retail prices January 1990–July 1991.   216
12.1.   OECD general government outlays as a percentage of   262
        GDP 1969–1989.
12.2.   General government outlays in the European Community   263
        as a percentage of GDP 1969–1989.
12.3.   UK general government expenditure and revenue as a   264
        percentage of GDP 1965–1990.
12.4.   UK long-term pre-tax interest rates 1973–1979.   265
12.5.   UK consumption and gross domestic product 1970–1990.   269
12.6.   UK government and private consumption 1970–1990.   270
12.7.   Gross domestic UK capital formation 1979–1990.   271
12.8.   Top marginal OECD income tax rates 1988–1989.   281
12.9.   UK direct taxes and Social Security contributions as a   283
        percentage of personal income 1988.
12.10   General UK government outlays and GDP per head in   290
        1989.
12A.1. Profits (net of stock appreciation) as a percentage of GDP   294
        1963–1979.

List of Tables

1.1.	Terms of trade 1979–1990.	19
1.2.	Developing countries' external debt and debt service payments.	25
1.3.	Developing countries' external debt by type of creditor.	26
1.4.	Developing countries' ratios of external debt to exports and GDP.	27
1.5.	Developing countries' ratios of debt service payments to exports of goods and services.	28
2.1.	Banking centres' shares of international lending 1975–1990.	46
2.2.	Market share in international lending from London in 1990.	47
2.3.	Foreign exchange turnover in 1986 and 1989 in London, New York and Tokyo.	47
2.4.	Major stock exchanges' equity turnover in 1990.	48
4.1.	Labour productivity growth 1960–1989.	78
4.2.	Distribution of UK manufacturing productivity growth 1979–1989.	80
4.3.	Gains and losses from restructuring of UK manufacturing industry.	82
4.4.	Distribution of UK deep-mined coal productivity growth 1982–1990.	84
4.5.	UK investment and capital stock growth 1979–1989 (% increases, 1985 prices).	85
5.1.	Performance of a sample of 17 defence companies in 1986.	100
5.2.	Sales of major European arms producers in 1988.	104
6.1.	Inner city decline: population, employment and unemployment 1951–1981.	117
6.2.	Sectoral employment change in inner cities 1951–1981.	120
6.3.	Targeted public expenditure on inner cities 1989–1990 and 1990–1991.	126
6.4.	Cost/benefit ratios: package of benefits accruing from £10 000 of net additional public sector expenditure on Task Force projects.	133
7.1.	Relative job shortfall, migration and unemployment 1951–1981.	142
7.2.	Government expenditure on regional industrial policy 1961–1962 to 1992–1994.	149
7.3.	Regional indices of unit labour costs 1974–1988.	157
7.4.	Estimates of regional balance of payments in 1980 and 1987.	157

7.5.	Regional trends in self-employment 1979–1989.	159
7.6.	Business formation by region 1981–1989.	160
7.7.	The 'North–South divide' in employment growth 1979–1990.	162
7.8.	The importance of industrial structure in manufacturing employment growth in Development Areas 1952–1989.	164
8.1.	Strikes and industrial stoppages in the UK 1960–1990.	176
8.2.	International comparisons of strike activity 1978–1987.	177
8.3.	Trade union membership and density in the UK 1979–1989.	180
8.4.	International comparisons of trade union density 1970–1988.	181
8.5.	Annual growth in compensation per employee in selected OECD countries 1977–1992.	184
8.6.	Annual growth in unit labour costs (business sector) in selected OECD countries 1977–1992.	185
8.7.	Labour productivity in the UK 1980–1991.	185
8.8.	Unemployment rates in selected OECD countries 1980–1990.	187
8.9.	Employment growth in selected OECD countries 1980–1992.	189
9.1.	Manufacturing, materials and fuels, and import prices 1978–1990.	206
9.2.	Annual rates of growth of earnings at different points in the earnings distribution for manual and nonmanual workers 1979–1989.	209
9.3.	Average annual rates of growth of earnings in selected sectors 1980–1990.	210
9.4.	Shifting 'internal terms of trade' in manufacturing and in finance and insurance 1980–1990: ratio of wages to those in distribution, hotels and catering.	213
10.1.	Percentage of job transitions involving moves to less-skilled jobs by whether the transition was contiguous or involved a period without employment.	233
11.1.	Private household population by economic status in Great Britain 1983–1990.	238
11.2.	Contributions to changes in employment by sex and marital status 1983–1990.	239
11.3.	Percentage of women of working age working full time, part time and unemployed 1983–1988.	240
11.4.	UK employees in selected industries, June 1983 and September 1989.	242
12.1.	UK public sector net financial liabilities 1975–1989.	265
12.2.	UK general government consumption 1979–1990.	268
12.3.	Percentage earnings changes of selected groups 1972–1990.	273
12.4.	Education and health: real *per capita* spending in the European Community.	274
12.5.	Employment in the National Health Service 1971–1989.	275
12.6.	Selected education statistics for the public and private sectors 1971–1989.	275
12.7.	Selected UK Social Security benefits 1964–1991.	278

12.8.	UK government revenue 1979–1990.	280
12.9.	Pre- and post-transfer economic distance poverty rates at the end of the 1970s.	283
12.10.	Percentage of persons in households in bottom quintile of UK equivalised disposable income 1979–1988.	284
12.11.	Percentage shares of original, disposable and post-tax income by quintile groups of households 1979–1988.	285
12.12.	Hypothetical general government expenditure in 1990.	287
13.1.	Industrial support and support for small and medium-sized enterprises in selected countries 1986.	300
13.2.	Support for small and medium-sized enterprises in the UK and Germany 1988–1989.	301
13.3.	Unemployment and self-employment in Britain; businesses registered for VAT in the UK; 1979–1989.	302
13.4.	Changes in the employment size distribution of UK businesses 1979–1986.	304
13.5.	Number of enterprises and shares of output and employment by size of enterprise for UK manufacturing 1979–1988.	306
13.6	Employment, net output and net output per head by size of enterprise for UK manufacturing 1979–1988.	307
13.7.	Employment and output shares by size of enterprise in UK manufacturing 1935–1988.	308
13.8.	Acquisitions and mergers by UK industrial and commercial companies 1969–1989.	310

List of Contributors

Iain Begg	Senior Research Officer, Department of Applied Economics, Cambridge
Michael H. Best	Professor of Economics, University of Massachusetts, Amherst, USA
William Brown	Professor of Industrial Relations, Faculty of Economics, Cambridge
Brendan Burchell	Lecturer in Social and Political Sciences, Cambridge and Fellow of Magdalen College
Michael Chisholm	Professor of Geography, St Catharine's College, Cambridge
Jerry Coakley	Senior Lecturer in Economics, City Polytechnic, London
Ken Coutts	Assistant Director of Research, Faculty of Economics, Cambridge
Simon Deakin	Fellow and Lecturer in Law, Peterhouse, Cambridge
Ciaran Driver	Imperial College Management School, London
Paul Dunne	Lecturer in Economics, University of Leeds
John Eatwell	Fellow and Lecturer in Economics, Trinity College, Cambridge
Ben Fine	Professor of Economics, Birkbeck College, London
Andrew Glyn	Fellow and Tutor in Economics, Corpus Christi College, Oxford
Wynne Godley	Professor of Economics, Kings College, Cambridge
Francis Green	Reader in Economics, University of Leicester
Laurence Harris	Professor of Economics, School of Oriental and African Studies, London
Alan Hughes	Director, Small Business Research Centre, Department of Applied Economics, Cambridge

Jane Humphries	Fellow and Lecturer in Economics, Newnham College, Cambridge
Will Hutton	Economics Editor, *The Guardian* newspaper
Ray Jobling	Fellow and Lecturer in Sociology, St John's College, Cambridge
John Lovering	Senior Research Fellow, School for Advanced Urban Studies, University of Bristol
John McCombie	Fellow and Lecturer in Land Economy, Downing College, Cambridge
Ron Martin	Fellow and Lecturer in Geography, St Catharine's College, Cambridge
Jonathan Michie	Fellow and Lecturer in Economics, St Catharine's College, Cambridge
Barry Moore	Fellow and Lecturer in Land Economy, Downing College, Cambridge
Paul Ormerod	Henley Centre for Forecasting, London
Mića Panić	Fellow and Bursar, Selwyn College, Cambridge
Clara Poletti	Department of Economics, Birkbeck College, London
Brian Reddaway	Professor of Economics Emeritus, Department of Applied Economics, Cambridge
Bob Rowthorn	Professor of Economics, Kings College, Cambridge
Jill Rubery	Lecturer in Labour Economics, University of Manchester Institute of Science and Technology
Malcolm Sawyer	Professor of Economics, University of Leeds
Ajit Singh	University Reader in Economics and Fellow of Queens College, Cambridge
Ron Smith	Professor of Economics, Birkbeck College, London
Roger Tarling	Cambridge Economic Consultants
Tony Thirlwall	Professor of Applied Economics, University of Kent at Canterbury
John Toye	Professor and Director of the Institute of Development Studies, Sussex University
Peter Tyler	Fellow and Lecturer in Land Economy, St Catharine's College, Cambridge
Frank Wilkinson	Senior Research Officer, Department of Applied Economics, Cambridge

Preface and Acknowledgements

The background to this book is discussed in more detail in the Introduction, but in brief it sets out to evaluate the economic legacy of the three Conservative governments from 1979–1992: the end of Britain's relative economic decline, or a wasted decade? It aims also to analyse the prospects and possibilities facing the British economy in the 1990s and beyond.

All the chapters were commissioned specifically for this book and draft versions were discussed at a working conference in October 1991 convened by the *Cambridge Journal of Economics*. Thanks for their comments go to Daniele Archibugi, Ha-Joon Chang, John Grieve Smith, G.C. Harcourt, Anatole Kaletsky, Mike Kitson, Sir Austin Robinson, Alister Sutherland and Susan Willett. We are particularly grateful for presentations made by Professor Christopher Freeman and Professor Stan Metcalf. The book should not, of course, be seen as attempting to represent any collective view, neither of the *Cambridge Journal of Economics,* nor the conference participants, nor even of the authors. It aims only to report the work of experts in various fields, albeit on a common theme.

My personal thanks go to all the contributors for the speedy incorporation of points made on their draft chapters and chapter comments in October 1991; to the Editors of the *Cambridge Journal of Economics* for commissioning the work reported in this book and in particular to Ann Newton, the Managing Editor, for all her efforts; Jane Humphries and Alan Hughes who along with myself constituted the organising group for the project; Geoff Harcourt and Professor Metcalf for chairing the sessions at the October conference; Frank Wilkinson for his assistance in organising the publication; Jennifer Pegg and Carol Parr of Academic Press for the speedy turnround of the manuscript; Betty Clifton and Caroline Lewis for help with typing; Professor Brian Reddaway for his wide-ranging comments on several of the chapters as well as for contributing the Foreword; Mike Best, Geoff Harcourt, Jane Humphries and Ajit Singh for comments on an earlier version of the Introduction; and Susan Michie and Carolyn Downs for comments on drafts of various chapters. As always I am

indebted to my wife Carolyn Downs for all her support and help and
to our two-year old Alex for his good humour.

JONATHAN MICHIE

Foreword

Brian Reddaway

Having taken no part in organising this book, I would like to start by saying that it seems to me a thoroughly good idea to examine the legacy which will come to future UK governments—whatever their political character—after 13 years of Tory rule. There are, however, a number of problems associated with such a review and my main object in this Foreword is to write about *general* issues in a way that would be inappropriate in a chapter dealing with a single topic.

Multiple Objectives

It is apparent that a government (or the community which it governs) has a whole host of different objectives, and these may frequently conflict with one another. One cannot judge the quality of the legacy without surveying the whole field.

Thus high production, low inflation, reasonably stable exchange rates, a sound balance of payments, freedom from serious pollution, a satisfactory distribution of income and opportunities are all desirable (along with many other things), but none of them can be given overriding priority; and different people attach different weights to them, so that it is impossible to find a single measure which will please everybody as an overall guide to performance.

Worse still, within some of these fields different people have different views about what constitutes (for example) a satisfactory distribution of post-tax income. Mrs Thatcher considered it vitally important to reduce the level of income tax, so that people would retain as large a proportion as possible of 'their' income—though a big rise in *indirect* tax rates was imposed under her premiership and considered acceptable. She also considered that welfare payments should, in general, be reduced in relation to the average level of income, so as to encourage self-reliance—and should in many cases be made subject to a means test, so as to 'avoid wasting tax payers' money on paying child benefit to the Rothschild family'. Others, however, consider it perfectly proper to have a progressive income tax (whilst usually admitting that the high top rates which Mrs Thatcher inherited were absurd—running up to 98% on unearned income—and gave a ridiculous stimulus to tax avoidance and evasion); they also consider that many benefits should be paid without any means test to preserve the dignity of the recipients and to reduce administrative costs. In these spheres the authors can only analyse what *has* happened, and perhaps indicate their personal attitude to it. Each reader must then form his or her own assessment of the merits of what has been done.

A further complication arises when (for example) the position in 1992 seems relatively satisfactory, but the prospects for future change look rather grim: thus the level of personal consumption may be considered good, but this may have been achieved by low saving, low internal investment (which prejudices future growth) and a large deficit on the balance of payments (which will have to be eliminated). Different people may well take different views about a legacy of this kind.

What Standards Should One Apply?

The *simplest* test to apply is whether the item in question—say personal consumption—was higher in 1992 than in 1979. This naive test has been used by the government on many occasions, when claiming that (say) real expenditure on health and education is at a record level. There is, indeed, something to be said for reminding ourselves that we are better off than our ancestors, but it is in no sense whatever a satisfactory way of assessing the legacy from 13 years of Tory rule.[1]

The fallacy in this simplistic approach lies in the fact that real income per head of population has risen in virtually every year for which we have figures, unless the later one showed a much higher level of unemployment (or possibly a disastrous strike). The basic reason is that capital accumulation and technical progress are raising productivity year after year, and the resultant rise in real incomes makes possible an improvement in virtually everything to which the community attaches importance. Mrs Thatcher's claim that the 30 years before she came to power were years of wasted opportunities, has to be judged against the simple fact that *real* incomes rose *much* more in those 30 years than in any other 30-year period for which figures are available.

The ideal test would be to assess whether progress was better than was to be expected, given the 'exogenous' factors which made progress easier (for example, the development of North Sea oil) or more difficult (for example, the Gulf War). Making allowance for all such special factors is, however, very difficult. We might *like* to have a measure of the effects of Tory rule by comparing what actually happened with what might have been expected to happen with some other kind of government, but this is usually impossible and we have to start from the historical record of what *did* happen, and compare this with the progress achieved in earlier periods: if we feel ambitious we may try to add a note about the possible effects of some very special factors (such as North Sea oil).

This immediately raises the problem of *which* past period(s) to choose. The less scrupulous defenders of the Tory performance tend to chose 1973–1979, on the grounds that this is the immediately preceding period, and runs 'from peak to peak'. Personally I regard this as an attempt at deliberate deception, for these reasons: first, it was a very difficult period, largely because of the oil price explosion and its aftermath; second, 1973 was a quite exceptionally active year, so that the comparison runs from an exceptional peak to a year which had few of the true characteristics of a peak (*1972*–1979 compares much more similar years, and shows a very different picture, especially on productivity); and third, it is a very *short* period to use as a base for historical comparisons, so that cyclical (or other) disturbances have a much bigger influence on the outcome than they would over a longer period, when the basic trend would predominate.

Personally, in teaching applied statistics I use the 19-year period 1960–1979 as my historical yardstick for comparison with recent performance. It covers favourable years as well as the difficult late 1970s, and the terminal years are broadly comparable; moreover, a number of important statistics in the *Economic Trends Annual Supplement* start in 1960. All the years are within the period about which Mrs Thatcher was so contemptuous.

Output, Productivity and Employment

Two important yardsticks which emerge on the above basis for the economy as a whole are:

Annual growth rate of GDP (in real terms)	2.61%
Annual growth rate of output per person employed (including self-employed)	2.10%

One might compare this with the rate over the twelve years 1979–1991, but this might be regarded as unfair because 1991 is a year of slump (though in my view the 1991 recession is explainable primarily by government action). Leaning over backwards to avoid accusations of anti-Tory bias, we can take the ten years 1979–1989, ending with the 'unsustainable boom'. The results are:

Ten years growth of GDP at the historic rate	29.4%
Actual growth of GDP, 1979–1989	24.8%

So the 'Thatcher miracle' produced a level of output at the top of its boom which was *3.6% lower* than the yardstick.

As concerns output per person employed (including self-employed), the ten years' advance was actually 20.5% against a 'standard' of 23.1%. So despite the big growth in unemployment, final year productivity of those still in work was 2% *below* the yardstick. This result is not at all consistent with the government's claim that the growth in recorded unemployment reflects the dismissal of superfluous workers from the payroll; such action would have caused the rise in recorded productivity to be *above* the historic rate.[2]

Government Policies 1979–1992

Government policies have been greatly influenced by Thatcherite ideologies, but also by the views taken of how the economy works (on which economists are far from being unanimous). The constant feature has been to attach great importance to reducing (or even 'eliminating') inflation, with little consideration of the effects which the policies adopted to achieve this would have on other objectives (such as the level of employment, at least in the short-run). This seems to have been accompanied by a facile view that once inflation has been eliminated, a good rate of economic growth will follow *without* leading to a resurgence of inflation (this economic growth, it has been emphasised, will follow essentially from *private sector* actions for which the government can only set the stage).

In 1979 the rather simple-minded policy was to announce, with all the authority of a newly elected Tory government, that the growth of the money supply (assumed to be under government control) would become progressively lower over the next 5 years. All market operators (such as wage bargainers) were expected to believe that these targets really would be hit (unlike some targets announced by the Labour government), and that the rate of inflation would fall as a result: hence they would act 'responsibly' and reduce the rate at which money wages would rise—thereby helping to lower future inflation. The government even seemed to imply that the big rise in VAT would not cause a corresponding rise in prices—perhaps because the wage negotiators would recognise that workers would gain from the accompanying fall in income tax rates (which included a cut in the basic rates, as well as a big reduction in the unrealistic higher rates), and so would agree on a correspondingly smaller rise in money wages.

This policy was soon exposed as ludicrously oversimplified and overoptimistic. In a progressively deregulated economy, prices and money wages showed an accelerating increase which raised the demand for credit to cover working capital needs; and the government had no power to keep the rise in the money supply (M3) down to the target pace, despite the pretence that this had been 'carved in stone'. The only instrument which the government was prepared to use to keep down the rise in M3 was a progressive rise in interest rates, which were pushed up to unprecedented heights: the effect of this on M3 was more than offset by the endogenous rise in the demand for credit.

The failure to keep the rise in M3 down to anywhere near the target levels clearly made nonsense of the hope that wage bargainers would be guided by the falling M3 targets into correspondingly 'realistic' wage settlements. Prices actually rose faster than the rate which the oversimplified monetarist analysis would have predicted to accompany the *actual* rise in M3. Meanwhile, the fall in output and employment, which government statements had implicitly treated as of negligible importance, were really serious—largely because the high interest rates (and other factors) had driven the exchange rate up to a quite unrealistic level, at which many manufacturers were unable to compete effectively with foreign producers in home and export markets.[3]

The government's inability to hit its monetary targets in a deregulated world, and the dubious effects of the size of the money supply which *did* emerge, left the government without any clear and intelligible policy, despite attempts to preserve the appearance of a medium-term financial strategy. The final decision to join the Exchange Rate Mechanism of the European Monetary System can perhaps be regarded as a method of providing a clear objective which would strengthen people's faith that a 'responsible' policy against inflation would be followed—so that hopefully wage bargainers would reach 'realistically low' settlements on money wage rates, rather than blandly assuming that immoderate ones would be covered by a downward movement of the exchange rate.

What does emerge from the events of the last year or two is the government's continued priority for a reduction in inflation over any other objective, and its simple-minded faith in the power of high interest rates to achieve this (even if they produce other undesirable results). 'Interest rates will remain as high as is necessary for as long as is necessary to overcome inflation' is the clear signal of these two beliefs. The implication seems to be that even though inflation has been exorcised at the cost of a sustained period of low activity and high unemployment, it is worthwhile because non-inflationary growth will then follow, and will be sufficient to raise output and lower unemployment to acceptable standards, *without* restarting inflation.

This implication is one which I regard as quite unjustified. Economic life is a great deal more complicated, and 'so we lived happily ever after' has no place in it.

The Balance of Payments

Part of the legacy from 13 years of Tory rule is the UK's substantial adverse balance of payments on current account, *despite* the fact that the high level of unemployment and low level of activity are reducing the demand for imports. I regard this as a very serious weakness, since a rise in activity to a satisfactory level would raise imports substantially. If the motivating force producing such a rise in activity were to be a big rise in UK exports, the position might be acceptable; but if it was a rise in internal demand, whether for consumption goods or for machinery, the position would deteriorate, so that such a rise in internal demand would have to be kept to a low level.

Government spokesmen, however, have said on a number of occasions that they regard an adverse balance of payments as of little importance unless its origin is unsound government finance: the private sector can be relied on to behave 'responsibly', and will only have an excess of investment over savings if there is a real justification for doing so. It would then be perfectly simple, in a largely deregulated world, for the excess to be covered by borrowing abroad.

The weakness in this analysis can be seen by *disaggregating* the private sector into the relevant components, and pursuing the analysis through a period of years instead of looking only at a single one. A simple example will show the point.

Suppose (as indeed happened in the 1980s) that the balance of payments deficit had arisen through a reduction in (net) personal saving, with private investment at a rather low level. This in fact largely came about through some people incurring substantial debts, mainly through large borrowings on mortgage from banks and building societies: the sellers of the houses which they bought may be visualised as depositing much of the proceeds in building societies, but spending some of the capital profit which they had realised. Between them these people had done some dis-saving, but they might all have been behaving with financial prudence. The building societies might have lent more than they received in new deposits, but in a deregulated market they could prudently cover this by borrowing in the wholesale money market.

These borrowings in the wholesale money market would attract funds from abroad, lent on a very short-term basis ('hot money'). The British institutions would not worry about the short-term basis of the capital inflow, because they would expect to borrow from another lender (whether British or foreign) if the initial loan were called.

This procedure would not set in motion any process to reverse it, and could quite 'properly' continue indefinitely. The result would be a steady build-up of short-term debts to foreigners, matching an increase in UK long-term assets. Nobody in the UK would be under any incentive to take action, unless *the government* (which should take a wider view of its responsibilities than would be suggested by contemplating its own balance sheet) decided that the growing amount of hot money lent to the UK was becoming dangerous.

What would the danger be? The foreign lenders might become alarmed at the weakness of the UK's collective balance sheet, and start a run on sterling. The disruptive consequences might take many forms, but clearly they would be unpleasant. So although a moderate balance of payments deficit in a single year may not be a matter of any concern, the government needs to ensure that there is not a succession of deficits, unless the counterpart is a build-up of assets in the UK which will raise future exports or replace imports. The series of deficits which emerged in the late 1980s, whose counterpart was a high level of consumption based on debt creation, means that a serious weakness is included in the legacy from 13 years of Tory rule.[4]

Introduction

Jonathan Michie

The 1950s culminated with the British people being told that they had 'never had it so good', and returning a third Conservative government in 1959. The 1960s began with Labour's promise to unleash the 'white heat of technology', but instead were dogged by the long-standing burdens of military spending and balance of payments problems, with the Gnomes of Zurich being blamed for having blown Harold Wilson's government off course. The election defeat in 1970 came days after the announcement of unexpectedly bad balance of payments figures. The 1970s was the decade of U-turns, with Edward Heath at first promising to unleash market forces Thatcher-style, and then reverting to expansionary policies when unemployment hit the politically unacceptable level of one million. Labour was elected in 1974 on interventionist policies which were replaced after the 1976 turn to the IMF, leaving Labour to implement spending cuts and incomes policies, sometimes in collaboration with the Liberals in government, until Thatcher's 1979 victory. What of the 1980s and 1990s? This book is a critical economic history of the 'Thatcher era' or, more accurately, the period covered by the three Conservative administrations from 1979–1992. However, the aim is to be forward-looking, by considering what legacy the policies of 1979–1992 have left for the remainder of the 1990s and beyond.

An overview of the economic record of the three Conservative administrations from 1979–1992 is given in Professor Reddaway's Foreword. As Director of Cambridge University's Department of Applied Economics through the 1950s and 1960s, Brian Reddaway earned a reputation for having a keen interest in how economies work, and how they can be made to work better, as well as a reputation for attention to detail, preferring real data to unrealistic assumptions. His Foreword goes beyond the statistical record of output, productivity and other performance measures, to set out why we need to be concerned; especially important are his views on the balance of payments, where there have been attempts to argue that, no matter how bad the record appears, the situation need not concern us since it is simply the result of private individuals' preferences; governments need not get involved. Reddaway demonstrates that factors such as the balance of payments should indeed be treated seriously, and that on a range of important issues the legacy of 1979–1992 is a disappointing one.

Part I. The Global Context

It is ironic that the decade which ended with the collapse of the socialist countries was not one of great economic success for capitalism. The 1980s saw (according to World Bank figures) the majority of people living under capitalism become poorer over the decade. The 1980s also saw a net transfer of wealth from the poor countries to the rich. In the advanced capitalist world itself, the previous dominance of the USA began to give way to a three-way rivalry between North America, the European Community and the Pacific rim, dominated by Japan, with the emergence also of the 'four tigers' of South Korea, Hong Kong, Singapore and Taiwan. It is perhaps a sign of the times that a representative of the CIA told a US Congressional Committee that the work of the Agency would have to continue undiminished despite the end of the Cold War, with resources switching away from military reconnaissance of the Soviet Union to industrial reconnaissance of Japan.

These issues of trade, aid and debt are analysed by John Toye, who concludes that the domestic economic policies of the Thatcher and Reagan governments were pursued at great cost to the Third World; this, rather than aid, was the dominant economic factor (Professor Toye does of course document Britain's record on overseas aid during the 1980s, showing that it declined as a proportion of national income). Ajit Singh suggests that these detrimental effects of the West's economic policies were more than just an unfortunate spin-off. Keeping the Third World in a relatively depressed state has certain advantages for the advanced capitalist countries in terms of low raw material and fuel prices, as well as weakening trade unions at home. Reversing these policies of slow growth may therefore prove far more difficult than imagined.

The role of the City of London in the transfer of wealth from poor to rich is included in Jerry Coakley and Laurence Harris's analysis of the Thatcher governments' attempts to change the role of money and finance in the economy and to strengthen the position of the financial sector—attempts which failed even in their own terms. Mića Panić, agreeing with this thesis, argues that the conduct of monetary policy from 1979–1991 will become a textbook example of how such policies should *not* be pursued.

Britain's economic relations with the rest of the world show up most dramatically in the balance of payments, and here the long-term problems experienced by Britain are shown by Ken Coutts and Wynne Godley to have continued throughout the 1980s despite the benefits of North Sea oil. Indeed, the legacy post-1992 is worse than in 1979. John McCombie and Tony Thirlwall show not only that the balance of payments trade-off with other economic objectives deteriorated in the 1980s, but also that Economic and Monetary Union would translate this into a far worse regional problem.

Part II. Government Policy and Structural Change

The output performance of the advanced capitalist countries as a whole is considered by Andrew Glyn, placing the British record in context. The British performance itself is marked by its relatively regressive distributional outcome, with the productivity gains in manufacturing being dissipated through high profits and dividend payments rather than lower output prices and improved competitiveness. Ciaran Driver discusses the resulting inadequate capital stock, and the role of economic uncertainty in the 1980s in weakening investment.

Paul Dunne and Ron Smith's chapter points out that the high level of military spending by the first Thatcher government—an annual increase in real terms of 3% a year—was merely honouring a commitment made by the Callaghan government. The legacy left by the Labour governments of the 1970s was one of high military spending. Ironically, after honouring those commitments for a while, the Thatcher governments actually reduced military spending in real terms. They go on to argue not only that military spending is bound to fall further through the 1990s but also, controversially, that the Thatcher policy of allowing redundancies and bankruptcies is the best way to proceed. Policies of defence conversion and diversification tend to get captured by the defence firms themselves: better to let them go to the wall and use the resources for useful purposes elsewhere. John Lovering counters that such an argument depends on an overly optimistic view of market mechanisms and an overly pessimistic view of the possibilities for government restructuring: in his view, conversion policies meet an economic, industrial and political need.

Inner city riots presented one of the more dramatic images from the 1980s but behind the flashpoints lay a decade of inner city blight and decay, poverty and homelessness. Barry Moore analyses the Thatcher governments' attempts at taking on the inner cities, concluding that the scale and nature of the problem faced in economic regeneration and restructuring require more emphases on social and community policies, as well as a sustained and coordinated programme of infrastructure renewal. Iain Begg recalls Mrs Thatcher's remark following her third general election victory that 'we have a big job to do in some of those inner cities', but suggests that in many areas the problems were simply decanted to other districts.

The 'North–South' divide became part of the common vocabulary during the Thatcher years. Ron Martin and Peter Tyler consider to what extent the new regional policy approach post-1979 managed to tackle the problems, concluding that whatever successes policy had in terms of cost accounting, the imbalances remain as a legacy, and that the government's 1991 spending plans on regional policies into the 1990s would not really be up to the serious task that has to be faced. As for future policy, Michael Chisholm sees two prerequisites for success: first, better coordination, possibly through extending the principle of regional development corporations; and second, encouragement of local authorities to assist in the necessary local transformations.

Part III. The Changing Labour Market

Simon Deakin reports on the almost continuous legislation on industrial relations, trade unions and the labour market more generally over the three administrations, concluding that claims of an improvement in industrial relations have to be seen in the context of policies of deregulation and labour intensification which undermine productivity improvements required to maintain international competitiveness. William Brown argues the need for institutions to assist in such dynamic productivity improvements through cooperation rather than fostering competitive static cost-cutting.

Jonathan Michie and Frank Wilkinson track inflation and theories of inflation through the 1980s. The early claims that monetarist policies could and would eliminate inflation did not live up to their promise. Nominal wage increases remained steady at around 8% a year through most of the 1980s, with increases in real wages preventing upward pressure on nominal wages. Within this average, however, many sections did badly, and previous work suggests that this represents an inflationary legacy through a catch-up phase reasserting itself. However, Roger Tarling questions whether previous patterns will be replicated, or whether the relatively disadvantaged were not so weakened during the 1980s that they will remain a badly paid underclass, finding it more difficult than in previous eras to mobilise to improve their situation.

Brendan Burchell reports evidence that psychological health is undermined not just by unemployment, but more widely by the various forms of insecurity fostered during the 1980s, including the insecurity which rising unemployment spreads amongst people fearing for their jobs as well as those who actually do lose them. Continuing high unemployment in the 1990s should be generating far more urgent concern than is the case. Ray Jobling agrees on the evidence from psychological and sociological research, concluding that future governments must respond to these issues if they are truly to aspire to improving welfare. Jane Humphries and Jill Rubery suggest that the legacy for women's employment is mixed. While increasingly integrated into the wage economy, women's employment continues to be differentiated from that of men, and there was increased polarisation within the female labour force itself. As Britain became a more unequal society, some women benefited but many lost; in analysing employment experience, the categories of class and of gender both remain necessary. Francis Green describes the way in which training perpetuates the sexist division of employment, and highlights the importance, if the legacy of continued differentiation is to be overcome, of women's training not being concentrated on what is commonly thought of as 'women's work', as well as the importance of other policies such as a statutory national minimum wage.

Part IV. The Economic and Political Legacy

Bob Rowthorn's chapter demonstrates that to overcome the legacy of 13 years of Conservative underspending on pensions and other social welfare, as well as on education and health, any future government would have to increase taxation. How this is done will depend on what is thought politically feasible; perhaps wasteful private health schemes will be promoted to raise money without an explicit tax increase. There are other possibilities, such as a far more dramatic cut in military spending than advocated by any of the political parties. Or the income tax cuts for middle earners could be reversed. Unless these or other revenue-raising measures are introduced, we will be left with the legacy of underfunding. Paul Ormerod asks how things could have been different, suggesting that the economic situation at the end of the 1970s was not sustainable and that at least the shock of Thatcherite policies restored profitability. He argues, however, that for the 1990s a more positive approach based upon cooperation and not conflict is called for.

Alan Hughes documents the rise of the 1980s 'enterprise culture': a genuine turn by the British people toward initiative, self-employment and entrepreneurship? Or the industrial equivalent of Sherlock Holmes's dog that didn't bark in the night? Michael Best questions the meaning of an 'enterprise culture', arguing that it is perfectly possible to have an explosion of *unenterprising* small firms, particularly if they are in non-traded goods sectors. However, even in traded goods sectors they may just be continuing the British tradition of arms-length contact with the firm ordering from them, producing in the old wasteful ways. What is needed to overcome this legacy are networks between firms cooperating in a genuinely enterprising way.

Ben Fine and Clara Poletti assess the legacy for industrial policy in the 1990s, particularly for the steel and energy sectors privatised in the 1980s. They suggest that in many ways the policies of the 1980s represented a culmination of the past, continuing the absence of any policy coordination within or between sectors, the lack of industrial leadership from government or anywhere else, the overseas orientation of a significant section of industrial capital, and the continued short-term perspective from the City: all reinforcing Britain's position as a low-wage, low-investment, low-productivity economy. They argue that the Labour Party currently offers solutions little different from those which have been tried and have failed in the past. Britain's problem remains the creation, not the picking, of winners and this requires a far-reaching restructuring of economic and political power. Malcolm Sawyer concludes that there is an increasing appreciation of the need for a developmental role for the State. Yet while laying the basis for this realisation through the failure of her market forces approach, Mrs Thatcher also made its implementation more difficult by privatising industries and undermining developmental institutions.

John Eatwell argues that one of the major shifts in the Labour Party's economic thinking since 1979 is the abandonment of the idea that we can have Keynesianism in one country. The European Community, on the other hand, is a relatively closed economic entity within which traditional Keynesian demand management could work. Will Hutton's postscript on the agenda for the 1990s suggests that Labour's retreat from macroeconomic policy has gone too far, but that their welcome emphasis on industrial policy points in the right direction for the coming decade, which will require serious attempts at reindustrialisation.

Conclusions

A number of the chapters comment on Britain's international competitiveness and several of the authors focus on the need for a modern, expanding traded goods sector based on a renewal of manufacturing investment and enterprise. The competitive performance of a country is measured in terms of its overseas and domestic market shares. The only measure of success along both these dimensions is the behaviour of total ouptut. For manufacturing, which is the crucial sector in terms of international competitiveness, particularly for Britain as North Sea oil output declines, UK output rose by 6% over 1979–1991 compared with the OECD average (excluding the UK) of 35% with the UK coming in *twentieth* out of 21 OECD countries. The UK's share of total OECD manufacturing output fell from 6.5% in 1979 to 5.2% in 1991 (calculations by John Wells of Cambridge University's Economics Faculty).

As for the future, the political goal of Britain converging towards a modern European state along the lines of France, Germany or Sweden is commonly cited. The 1980s saw these countries experiencing historically low economic growth, so that Britain's performance was at least compatible with becoming more like these economies. However, even that chance was not taken. The British economy in 1992 is just as peculiar as it was in 1979 in terms of the bloated role played by the City of London, short-termism regarding productive investment, the relatively high burden of military spending, the disproportionate share of research and development which goes on military rather than civil purposes, and the relatively high proportion of investment directed overseas. This is the legacy of decades previous to the 1980s. However, added to this dismal inheritance, the figures reported in Rowthorn's chapter show that spending on public services and infrastructure fell away from European levels during the 1980s.

So much is well documented in the following chapters. The big questions for the future are what measures would be needed to overcome this legacy, to reduce military spending to the European average, to overcome the drag of the City of London, and deal with the backlog of infrastructural investment and training. Added to the specific problems of overcoming the legacy left by the British governments of the 1980s is the need for concerted Europe-wide action to reduce what has been a scourge of unemployment across the European Community. This book does not provide complete answers to these questions. Yet there is a common theme: the legacy from the decade of North Sea oil falls short of reasonable hopes; Britain is now a more divided and polarised society; our public services and infrastructure have deteriorated; and with unemployment set to remain above two million for the foreseeable future, something must be done.

PART I

The Global Context

1

Britain, the United States and the World Debt Crisis

John Toye

In 1982, it was finally recognised that much of the lending to developing countries that US and UK banks had undertaken since the 1973 oil shock could not be serviced or repaid on the terms that had been agreed. The realisation came in August 1982, when Mexico suspended payment on its debt. This international economic crisis, which soon changed the long-standing positive net flow of financial resources from the developed to the developing countries into a negative net flow, still in the early 1990s blights the economic prospects of many developing countries, and thus the prospects for world economic development in general.

In the UK the period of the emergence of the debt crisis and 8 years of its continuation coincide with the three administrations led by Mrs Margaret Thatcher, those of 1979–1983, 1983–1987 and 1987–1990. This coincidence poses two questions for economic historians of the recent past. Firstly, how far were British policies responsible for the state of affairs revealed by Mexico's suspension of debt service in mid-1982? And, secondly, how far were British policies during the years after 1982 helpful in alleviating the economic problems of indebted developing countries?

Before these two questions are addressed, it is necessary to establish the general background of policy against which the world debt crisis unfolded. This is attempted in the following two sections, which concentrate on the foreign policy background and on the economic policy background, respectively. It is important to highlight the interactions between the conduct of economic and of foreign policy, and to examine with this in mind, the crucial issue of the Anglo-American 'special relationship'. This is a complex matter, consisting not merely of personal and ideological affinities but also of structural features and partly divergent interests. It is necessary to understand these complexities before assessing the contribution of British policy both to the onset of the debt crisis and its agonisingly slow alleviation.

Mrs Thatcher, the Third World and the US Special Relationship

Mrs Thatcher was a thoroughly insular politician in 1975. When, almost by happenstance, she was elected as Leader of the Conservative Party, she knew little about foreign affairs and had rarely travelled abroad on official business. In the next few years before she became Prime Minister, she started to travel widely to Europe and also visited the Middle East and China. She also established her strong anti-Communist credentials with the speech which brought her the Soviet soubriquet of 'the Iron Lady'. Despite these preparations, however, her political trajectory remained largely a domestic one, and foreign affairs provided an unwelcome distraction from her self-imposed mission of economic and institutional reform within Britain.

As a result, the foreign policy of her 1979–1983 government had to rely heavily on the diplomatic finesse of her Foreign Secretary, Lord Carrington, and the traditional skills of the Foreign Office. It was these that led her early to her only constructive encounter with a developing country: she played a major role in successfully fashioning an independence settlement for Rhodesia/Zimbabwe. Under Carrington's guidance, she managed to do this despite her scarcely disguised contempt for black nationalism, the institution of the Commonwealth and, indeed, the Third World in general. However, this unpredicted triumph did not presage more of the same.

Apart from her 1979 visit to Zambia, her early trips to developing countries were either ceremonial or commercial, or a combination of the two. Her presence at the North–South summit at Cancun produced nothing but some British aid for an ill-conceived Mexican steel project. Her Middle East visit in the same year (1981) produced more British arms contracts with Saudi Arabia and the Gulf States, and much personal publicity. On more productive kinds of international relations, she was insensitive. The raising of overseas students' fees in 1981 caused great dismay in Malaysia and Singapore, from where many overseas students came to Britain. Nothing was done to soften the blow for these countries until eventually Malaysia decided to run a 'Buy British Last' campaign.

A significant change in Britain's relations with developing countries occurred after the Falkland Islands were recaptured from Argentina, with US logistic support, in mid-1982. The impact of the 'Falklands factor' in securing Mrs Thatcher's re-election in 1983 began to be appreciated in the US. This led to a revival of US gunboat diplomacy with British acquiescence and/or assistance. Shortly after 241 US marines were massacred in Lebanon, the US invaded Grenada (October 1983) and Britain acquiesced in this violation of international law. Britain permitted the US to use its air bases in the UK to bomb Tripoli in Libya (April 1986), and supported the US invasion of Panama (December 1989). These incidents yielded a regular supply of easy victories against some of the more obnoxious of Third World leaders, while little was achieved towards stabilising the major sources of international turbulence, the Arab–Israel problem and its interconnections with Islamic fundamentalism.

It is surely evident that Thatcher's dismissive attitudes and punitive actions towards many developing countries were underpinned by the keystone of her foreign policy—the UK's 'special relationship' with the US. She was an Atlanticist by conviction, in sharp contrast with those she placed in charge of her Treasury and Foreign Office—Geoffrey Howe and Nigel Lawson—who remained convinced Europeans. She was fortunate in that the US President for most of her time in office was someone who sincerely shared her simple conservative beliefs and her populist style of politics. She created assiduously out of these affinities a strong personal alliance that withstood several sharp disputes about policy. She was much more doubtful about US military action in Grenada and Libya than she ever admitted in public, for example. In short, there *was* something special in her political and personal relations with President Reagan.

Although she undoubtedly personalised the 'special relationship', Thatcher was also recognising one of the most robust features of Britain's position in the mid-twentieth century world—its fundamental dependence on the US. Every British government (except one) since 1945 has cooperated extremely closely indeed with the US Administrations of the time. Eden's government of 1955–1957 did not, and came to grief when Eisenhower aborted the Anglo-French Suez invasion of 1956. Some, like Wilson's government of 1964–1970, preferred to keep their overarching strategic and financial understandings with the US hidden from public view. Others, like Macmillan's, preferred to flaunt and dramatise them. Thatcher followed the Macmillan route, making a spectacular virtue of this basic Cold War necessity.

The Fruits of Insular Monetarism

The economic significance of Mrs Thatcher was as a pioneer of the application of monetarist economic doctrines to economic policy. The first of the Western conservative leaders to secure power in mid-1979, her government's initial decisions in the field of economic management were viewed widely as a crucial experiment to test the validity of monetarist doctrines in practice. Here 'monetarism' is defined simply as the three propositions that control of inflation is the supreme economic objective, that control of the money supply is both a necessary and sufficient condition for the control of inflation, and that governments can indeed control the money supply exogenously.

Monetarism in this sense had been very much a minority opinion among academic macroeconomists until the mid-1970s. Then a series of rapid 'conversions' ensued, among economists, journalists and lastly among politicians; Kaldor compared these conversions unflatteringly with the periodic outbreaks of mass hysteria in the Middle Ages (Kaldor, 1989, p. 178). The beliefs of many monetarists were ideological in character, and the beliefs of many others were politically opportunistic. Mrs Thatcher herself was one of these recent converts to monetarism, while her Chancellor (Geoffrey Howe) and Financial Secretary (Nigel Lawson) were even more recent converts—in Lawson's case, from Keynesian views extensively developed in the course of financial journalism.

One crucial appeal of monetarism was its apparent simplification of the task of economic management, through the downgrading of past policy objectives such as full employment and exchange rate stability, and the discarding of past policy instruments such as fiscal fine-tuning for demand management, and the official regulation of credit and incomes policies to control wage inflation. Instead, the new Thatcher government committed itself to what has been called 'insular monetarism' (Keegan, 1989, p. 173). The one overriding objective of policy was defined as the reduction of inflation, and the sole instrument to achieve this was the control of the money supply, money for this purpose being 'broad money' or M3. It was believed that the government could control the money supply by reducing the public sector's borrowing requirement (PSBR). This would be done by reducing public expenditure until it equalled tax revenue. Sound money and lower direct tax rates were seen as the right incentives to create growth in output and employment. The foreign exchange rate would continue to float according to market pressures, all attention and effort being focused on the domestic monetary front. This was the basic programme of insular monetarism.

Many professional economists at the time were sceptical, not to say incredulous, of this programme (the mood was captured by the 364 economists who criticised the 1981 budget in a letter to *The Times*). Some scepticism was fuelled no doubt by dislike of the social implications of the retreat from consensus objectives, but it was also based on a judgement that so many simplicities were not likely all to come right at once. Can governments really control the money supply, especially when central banks function as the lender of last resort, or when the government is deregulating the supply of credit? Are changes in the PSBR well correlated with changes in the money supply? Does an excess supply of money necessarily generate excess demand for a given supply of goods and services, and thus cause inflation? What about rising import prices and labour costs? Do these not cause inflation, to which the money supply has to accommodate itself? What about

Goodhart's law, that any stable monetary function collapses as soon as the dependent variable in it is made into a policy target? This catalogue of doubts could easily be extended.

Inflation quickly rose from an annual rate of 14.5% in 1979 to 19.9% in 1980 (GNP deflator). This catastrophic start to the anti-inflation crusade was important because it subsequently influenced the thinking of the 'supply-siders' in the Reagan administration. They came to believe in 1981 that Thatcherite monetarism had 'failed', and failed because taxes had been increased (VAT was almost doubled). UK inflation did gradually fall from its 1980 peak, and reached 4.6% by 1983. This appears to have been achieved by means of fiscal contraction throughout 1980–1982, including the strongly deflationary budget of 1981. The anti-inflationary impact of fiscal policy was assisted by the dramatic overvaluation of the pound, which peaked in early 1981 and was gradually corrected, by the rise in oil prices and by the fall in commodity prices induced by recession in the OECD world. Falling inflation allowed a gradual decline in nominal interest rates between 1981 and 1985. However, the real rate of interest increased rapidly, moving from negative in 1980 to 3% in 1981 and 4% by 1982.

The Origins of the Debt Crisis

The first seeds of the world debt crisis were sown after the first oil shock in 1973. The sudden, huge redistribution of income to OPEC oil exporters brought about by the oil price rise was not matched by an equally rapid increase in OPEC consumption. OPEC's huge new surpluses were, to a large extent, placed as bank deposits, and then on-lent by the commercial banks to other borrowers. The industrial countries adjusted their economies to the first oil shock surprisingly well, and thus generated rather little demand for OPEC savings. This put downward pressure on world interest rates. Many developing countries, particularly in Latin America, did not adjust their economies to the oil price shock but instead borrowed at what seemed (and indeed were at the time) favourable rates of interest—and without any accompanying policy conditions.

The increased instability of interest rates and exchange rates which followed the collapse of the Bretton Woods framework of international finance was, during the 1970s, maturing new departures in the methods of international finance. Depositors sought protection against adverse interest and exchange rate changes, and the commercial banks increasingly switched their terms from fixed-rate to variable-rate interest, usually denominated in US dollars. Neither developing country borrowers, nor the banks themselves seemed to understand the implications of this change. The commercial banks appeared to believe that sovereign debt would, by definition, necessarily be repaid. The developing country governments did not anticipate the financial upsets which would later be caused by Western governments dedicated to disinflation. Even without variable interest rates, severe disinflation would have squeezed borrowers who had borrowed at nominal rates of, say, 10% in the mid-1970s. Disinflation plus variable interest rates, however, made the squeeze quite insupportable.

The first 18 months of the Thatcher government had seen UK long-term interest rates rise to 15%, but inflation had risen rather than fallen. The real squeeze was to come in 1981. Not only was the UK deflating strongly, but additionally President Reagan and his new economic team were determined to apply supply-side doctrines to what was still the largest economy in the world. Supply-side economics differs from monetarism in its focus, because US monetary policy is in the hands of the Federal Reserve Board, rather than the US government. Supply-side theorists argued that fiscal policy should be geared around the incentive effects of taxation, rather than around tax revenue as a regulator of aggregate demand. Their basic proposition was that cutting tax rates can have such strong incentive effects that tax revenues can rise rather than fall when tax rates are cut.

Two tax-cut proposals based on supply-side logic had been part of Reagan's election platform. One was the Kemp–Roth reduction of 30% in personal income tax rates. The other was Barber Conable's plan to liberalise corporate depreciation allowances, to allow faster capital asset writedowns and thereby to reduce corporate taxes. Because of the doctrine that tax rate cuts produce revenue increases, the expenditure implications of the Republican tax plans for the US budget deficit were never properly explored in advance. Such calculations as were attempted were vitiated by inconsistent assumptions about future growth and inflation, which initially made the required spending cuts seem manageable. As it gradually became clearer in early 1981 that massive expenditure savings would be required if the budget was to be balanced, it also became clearer that they simply could not be found. This was partly because of the huge build-up of defence expenditure that was gathering momentum, and partly because Reagan ring-fenced Social Security spending.

Why did the Reagan economic team not abandon its tax plan, or at least raise taxes other than those specified in the plan, to neutralise partly the expected loss of revenue? Politically, Reagan decided it was better to 'win' on the tax cuts, even if he were defeated on spending cuts, because half of a political loaf seemed better than no loaf at all. In addition, Mrs Thatcher's experiences of 1979–1980 were taken as an awful warning. Her 1979 decision to double VAT was read as the cause of her subsequent failure (by 1981) to stop inflation and interest rates rising. The Reagan team simply ruled out all tax increases of any kind, for whatever reason. It is hardly surprising that the US quickly found itself with a structural budget deficit: expenditures were 24% of GNP by 1984, while revenues were only 19%.

The Federal Reserve Board exercised a quite tight control over growth in monetary aggregates and this had the effect of pushing nominal interest rates higher. The tax cuts neutralised the effects of higher interest rates on the demand for investment, which was maintained despite the monetary squeeze. The need to finance the very large government budget deficit and the simultaneously emerging large current account deficit, plus strong investor demand for finance, implied a large call by the US on foreign savings. Indeed, the World Bank calculated that the increase of $162 billion in the US government budget deficit represented some 8% of total world savings in 1979 (World Bank, 1985, p. 37). There is little doubt that budgetary movements of this size would have had a significant effect in increasing real interest rates and, given the structural nature of the deficit, keeping them high throughout the 1980s.

The disastrous impact on heavily indebted developing countries was soon felt. The dramatic rise in nominal interest rates in the strongly inflationary conditions at the end of the 1970s, and the failure of these historically high nominal rates to fall back very much once recession took hold of the developed economies in 1981–1982, not only raised the cost of new borrowing by developing countries, but also raised the cost of servicing all old debt with variable interest-rate terms. Since none of the developing country borrowers had ever imagined that real interest rates could move to the then prevailing levels, and since none of the responsible international financial institutions had ever warned them of such a development, they were caught in a classic debt trap.

The world debt crisis which erupted in mid-1982 was something over which the developing countries had precious little control. They might have foreseen that favourable terms of borrowing would not last. They might have resisted the lenders' transfer to them of the risks of interest rate variation. However, along with everybody else, they lacked the vision for the former; in July 1982, just one month before the Mexican moratorium, the IMF published a document which concluded that 'over the medium-term the rate of growth of international bank assets (on loans to LDCs) can be expected to remain high' (Griffith-Jones, 1991, p. 102). And they lacked the bargaining strength for the latter. It is also true that much of what was borrowed was invested unwisely by developing countries. However, what turned a drama into a crisis was the sudden leap in real interest rates and the effect that this had in leading to a rapid accumulation of indebtedness which was no longer within the borrower's control.

The other major consequence of the deflationary macroeconomic policies pursued by the US, the UK and other Western governments was the dramatic collapse of world commodity prices—including that of oil after 1981. The explanation for the failure of the international financial institutions to anticipate the debt crisis lies, at least in part, in their consistent forecasts of strong commodity prices, and hence of the manageability of the rapid accumulation of commercial debt in government hands. However, the heavily indebted developing countries experienced a strong terms of trade shock in 1981–1983, and (after a brief reversal in 1984) deterioration in their terms of trade continued from 1985–1988 (Table 1.1). These unfavourable movements were associated with a slackening of demand for industrial raw materials during the 1981–1983 recession in OECD countries, with slow recovery thereafter, with reduced demand for commodity stockholding at higher interest rates and with adjustment policies which neglected the cumulative effect of export supply increases on world market prices.

A country that is caught in a debt trap—with accumulating liabilities and diminishing ability to pay—soon begins to experience other strong destabilising forces. There is nothing novel in this; the process was lucidly described by Ricardo:

> A country which has accumulated a large debt, is placed in a most artificial situation; and although the amount of taxes, and the increased price of labour may not, and I believe does not, place it under any other disadvantage with respect to foreign countries, except the unavoidable one of paying those taxes, yet it becomes the interest of every contributor to withdraw his shoulder from the burthen, and to shift this payment from himself to another; and the temptation to remove himself and his capital to another country, where he will be exempted from such burthens, becomes at last irresistible. . . (Ricardo, *Principles of Political Economy and Taxation*.)

Capital flight from heavily indebted countries, despite exchange controls, usually grows very rapidly once a repayments crisis is acknowledged, both for Ricardo's reason of escaping additional taxes, and because it becomes attractive to speculate on the depreciation of the country's real exchange rate. Capital flight can quickly exceed the inflow of new foreign borrowing, both the quantity and the quality of investment can decline, and it becomes impossible to grow out of the debt crisis.

The economic policy of the Thatcher government pushed up UK nominal interest rates between 1979–1981, and thereby contributed to the emerging debt crisis. From spring 1981, UK nominal rates began to fall. However, as disinflation was now starting in earnest, real rates were rising. Developments in the UK alone would not have been weighty enough to trigger a major crisis. The Federal Reserve Board in the US was allowing the US prime rate to rise to unprecedented heights from 1979 onwards, in the attempt to control inflation. What 'Reaganomics' achieved between 1981 and 1985 was the persistence of high nominal interest rates, once recession had brought inflation down, and a severely weakened demand for developing countries' exports. The content of Reaganomics differed from that of insular monetarism,

Table 1.1. Terms of trade 1979–1990 (annual changes, percent).[a]

	1979	1980	1981	1982	1983	1984	1985	1986	1987	1988	1989	1990
Developing countries	9.5	16.6	2.9	-1.5	-3.6	1.4	-2.0	-16.3	1.5	-3.4	1.9	0.2
Africa	8.1	17.0	0.1	-8.0	-2.0	0.3	-0.8	-25.2	0.7	-5.2	0.2	-1.8
Asia	1.8	-1.4	-0.8	0.6	0.8	1.8	-0.5	-3.6	1.2	0.8	0.8	-1.0
Europe	-3.8	-5.6	0.4	1.1	-1.7	-0.9	-0.6	2.2	0.0	1.7	0.4	-2.1
Middle East	23.9	41.5	11.7	2.1	-8.4	0.3	-3.7	-44.3	8.6	-19.0	9.6	8.6
Western Hemisphere	5.6	7.4	-5.7	-7.8	-4.7	5.1	-5.2	-10.5	-3.2	-2.5	0.4	-1.5
Heavily indebted countries[b]	9.3	13.7	-3.9	-6.8	-4.3	4.6	-5.5	-14.5	-1.6	-3.0	1.1	-1.7
Industrial countries	-2.9	-7.3	-1.6	1.6	1.8	0.3	0.6	9.0	0.8	1.2	-0.2	-0.5
United States	-3.9	-13.4	1.9	3.0	3.3	1.9	-2.2	-0.3	-6.9	2.0	1.0	-1.9
United Kingdom	4.3	4.7	0.8	-0.5	0.4	-0.3	0.9	-5.1	2.0	1.1	3.1	2.5

Source: *IMF World Economic Outlook 1987–1991.*
[a]
[b]Argentina, Bolivia, Brazil, Chile, Colombia, Cote d'Ivoire, Ecuador, Mexico, Morocco, Nigeria, Peru, Philippines, Uruguay, Venezuela, Yugoslavia.

and it was incompetence as much as doctrine which produced the US government's structural deficit. The US–UK special relationship, as reinterpreted by Thatcher, required a blurring of differences on economic doctrine and a prolonged collusion with incompetence, at the expense of indebted developing countries.

Undoubtedly some developing countries had spent unwisely what they had borrowed. Many had indulged in lavish rearmament. In doing so they had had strong personal encouragement from Mrs Thatcher, who used her visits to developing countries to ensure that British companies gained important arms contracts. Subsequent criticism of debt-distressed countries for unproductive spending of loans ignored, no doubt deliberately, Mrs Thatcher's role in the governmental promotion of British arms exports.

The Aftermath: the Evolution of British Policy on Debt

British government policy towards the indebtedness of developing countries did not begin with the August 1982 Mexican suspension of debt repayment, which marks the start of the period of debt crisis. Already at the start of the 1980s, the officials concerned at the Treasury and the Bank of England seemed to have had some apprehension that all was not entirely well with the process of recycling petro-dollars by means of commercial bank lending to the Third World. At the same time, too public an acknowledgement of impending problems might have precipitated the crisis which they hoped to avoid. In retrospect, it is difficult to be sure how many of the emollient official statements on developing country indebtedness were genuinely complacent, and how many were merely tactically complacent.

The underlying anxiety which showed through most strongly was that commercial lending might be inappropriate for supporting the balance of payments of indebted countries, in the absence of an IMF stabilisation programme. By implication, the commercial banks might be willing to go on financing a balance of payments gap which was fast becoming unsustainable, whereas the IMF would be able to identify the point at which the macroeconomy had to be stabilised. Much confidence was publicly expressed that the IMF, its quotas recently increased, was adequate to this task, amidst the provision of a range of statistics which were interpreted to show that the LDC indebtedness problem was becoming less acute. This was in June and July 1982, just before the crisis finally broke. No-one seems to have spotted the implications of falling oil prices for heavily indebted oil-exporting countries like Mexico.

It was evidently difficult for the financial officials of a government so ideologically commited to the beneficence of freely operating market forces to suggest, even in the face of real interest rates that were rapidly rising to unusual heights, that danger might be at hand. The only market imperfection that was conceded was that the banks may have lacked all the information that they needed to assess the creditworthiness of individual developing countries. Even this problem was said to be greatly improved. Apart from maintaining good information flows, nothing else needed to be done by the authorities—no contingency planning, no identification of a lender of last resort, no increase in the banks' bad debt provisioning other than what they freely chose for themselves—and which the Treasury regarded as 'very satisfactory'.

Once Mexico's moratorium revealed the true seriousness of the indebtedness problem, a different tone was evident in British government pronouncements. Early in 1983, the Chancellor (Geoffrey Howe) admitted that the scale of the problem 'at times threatened to overwhelm the international financial and banking system'. He also acknowledged the 'huge changes being made in the pattern of poverty (in Mexico). . . because they have not got the institutions we have in the industrial countries which cushion us against the consequences' of massive macroeconomic stabilisation programmes. Despite the sympathy for Mexico, it is clear that minimising the self-inflicted damage to the international banking system was the government's primary policy objective. That could be attained by a mixture of cautious debt rescheduling, to be accompanied by an IMF stabilisation package, and encouragement of the commercial banks to continue lending to debt-distressed countries.

The provision of so-called 'new lending' by banks was (and remained) the most problematic element in this survival recipe. Having lent well beyond the limit of creditworthiness, the banks were reluctant to recycle any of the debt repayments which they received back to the debtors in the form of 'new' loans. In a classic illustration of Sen's isolation paradox, each bank wanted to minimise its *own* exposure, without regard to the effects of all banks behaving in this way on every bank's exposure. Just as the authorities had steered clear of giving directions on maximum lending, so now they avoided giving formal directions on minimum levels of continued lending, even through the mediation of the IMF. Nevertheless, behind the scenes, considerable pressures to continue lending were put on creditor banks in 1982–1983.

As for the plight of the debt-distressed developing countries, the time had come for grasping at straws. Howe recognised the role of the US federal government deficit in pushing up interest rates (and thereby precipitating the crisis). His only response was to talk vaguely and wishfully about the possibility that, by controlling its deficit, the US government might 'give a contribution as substantial but different in quality as that made by the establishment of Marshall Aid'. In the same wonderfully hopeful vein, he admonished industrial countries against protectionism. Avoiding protectionism to help the payments prospects of debtor countries was the ultimate counsel of perfection in the 1980s. The US relied on large Japanese and German payment surpluses to finance their own current account deficit. Such surpluses required ready access to the US goods markets: this in turn spurred protectionist sentiment and action in the US. Finally, the renewal of world economic growth would assist the debtors by pulling up commodity prices. Although growth did resume in developed countries after 1982 for 7 years, it was never vigorous enough to stop the general deterioration in the terms of trade of developing countries (see Table 1.1). In the highly indebted countries themselves, despite some growth between 1984 and 1987, real GDP growth before the 1990s was slight or negative. They were not enabled to grow out of debt.

Underlying this first phase of policy response was the posture that the debt crisis was no more than a temporary liquidity problem with which developing countries were faced. Comfort was derived from the proposition that sovereign nations do not, like firms, go bankrupt, but on the contrary have strong incentives (connected with the retention of creditworthiness) never to default. Many of the indebted countries had considerable untapped natural resources, so it was concluded that eventually both principal and interest would be repaid. The perception that, on the contrary, heavily indebted countries faced a fundamental structural problem in servicing their debt, because the debt service burden itself undermines the possibility of economic growth, and thus of emerging from the debt crisis, was slow to penetrate official thinking (Keynes' efforts to persuade the establishment that World War I reparations would place Germany in this same impossible position present a strong historical parallel).

During this phase, the commercial banks followed various strategies of self-protection. One was to make use of the secondary market in sovereign debt, to allow small players to exit at a price, and larger players to rearrange their exposure according to their assessment of risk by country. The debtors, too, used the heavy discounts in this market to make various kinds of debt buybacks and debt-equity swaps. The value of secondary market transactions rose from very little in 1984 to $50 billion in 1989. The banks also protected themselves by increasing their capital, to reduce their exposure ratios, and by increasing their provisions against bad debts. The nine largest US commercial banks increased their capital from $29 billion (1982) to $55.8 billion (1988), thereby reducing their exposure to capital ratio for developing country loans from 288% to 108%. By these means, the vulnerability of the US and UK banking systems, which was substantial in 1982, was gradually decreased.

The success of these self-protective measures by the banks in repairing the viability of the international banking system—which was seen as the primary objective of debt policy—seemed to validate the leave-it-alone, do-nothing philosophy of the UK government. Once he had become Chancellor of the Exchequer after the 1983 election, Nigel Lawson made felt his distrust of all attempts to solve the debt crisis, which he regarded as 'grandiose' and likely to be counterproductive. His instinctive preference was for the case-by-case, step-by-step, pragmatically reactive approach.

Nevertheless, the pressures of the Anglo-American special relationship led to the public endorsement by the UK of two major US initiatives intended to make progress in resolving the debt crisis. One was the Baker Plan, announced by Treasury Secretary James Baker in Seoul in September 1985. The other was the Brady Plan, announced by Treasury Secretary Nicholas Brady in March 1989. The Baker Plan was aimed at 15 highly indebted countries, mostly in Latin America but also including the Philippines, Ivory Coast, Morocco, Nigeria and Yugoslavia. The intention was to encourage an increase in new commercial bank lending by proposing complementary increases in lending by the World Bank and the IMF, to be accompanied by structural adjustment programmes. The Baker Plan achieved little progress, because it had no way of overcoming the banks' continuing unwillingness to supply 'new money' to countries still evidently in the grip of a debt crisis. The international financial institutions (IFIs) also failed to lend up to the Baker targets, fearing that the increase of their exposures when the banks were not increasing theirs meant that they were shouldering more of the risk, and thus bailing out the banks with public sector money, and possibly putting their own credit in jeopardy. The UK continued to give formal support to the Baker Plan throughout 1985–1989, even when its credibility had rather swiftly ebbed away.

The Brady Plan of 1989 broke new ground by recognising that formal, negotiated debt reduction would be necessary to end the debt crisis and by allowing the IFIs to provide partial guarantees of the value of the paper which embodied the new, discounted debt. Both of these departures from past practice were made in a renewed attempt to persuade the banks to come forward with more 'new money'. Both were unwelcome to Chancellor Lawson. The first implied that participating banks would, for the first time, accept losses arising on their developing country loans, and not merely put aside provisions against losses. The second formalised the use of public sector money to make that process less risky than it would otherwise be, and thus constituted a partial bail-out for the banks at the tax-payers' ultimate expense. Lawson disliked the latter feature of the Brady Plan both because of its implications for public expenditure and because he believed that the banks alone should be left to cope with the consequences of debts which were 'negotiated freely' by them with the debtors (House of Commons, 1990, pp. 4–5).[5]

Why then did Lawson publicly endorse the Brady Plan, despite its breach of a principle which he strongly supported? Why had he supported the earlier Baker Plan, despite his dislike of 'grandiose solutions' in general? One can only speculate, but part of the explanation may lie in the sterling crisis of January 1985. The fact that the pound fell almost to one dollar, and that the government proved unwilling in the event to see that psychological barrier broken, finally disposed of the insularity component of the policy of insular monetarism. International cooperation to regulate the movement of exchange rates was put back on the policy agenda and quickly embodied in the Plaza Agreement of September 1985. Britain had turned out to need international help to overcome the strength of the US dollar. It is reasonable to suggest that the UK was willing to reciprocate by giving public support for other plans of international cooperation which were devised by James Baker, and his successor, to address the debt crisis, whatever private reservations were felt about their substance. Such willingness would be eased by the fact that these plans concentrated on countries of major geopolitical importance to the US. The only country among the Baker 15 of which this is not true is the Ivory Coast: the 10 Latin American countries fall under the Monroe Doctrine; the US has bases in the Philippines, and large commercial and military interests in Morocco; Nigeria is the economic giant of sub-Saharan Africa, and Yugoslavia was pivotal in Cold War policies.

The major independent British move to ease the position of debtor countries came in April 1987. It was a plan to relieve the pressure of official (not commercial) debts for poor debtor countries in sub-Saharan Africa (SSA). This came as a considerable surprise to public opinion, because the Chancellor who proposed it to the IMF in Washington was not well known either as a friend of SSA countries or a sympathiser with those developing countries burdened by debt. He adhered to the view that the problem of excessive indebtedness was caused 'primarily by the mistaken policies' of the debtor countries themselves—the standard neo-liberal view (Griffith-Jones, 1991, p. 108). When Energy Secretary, he had intervened in North Sea oil production to cut back supply and slow down the rate of fall in the oil price. However, this was not out of concern for debtors. Rather, it was a response to OPEC pressure and the result of anxieties about aggravating the banking crisis. In the same year (1983), Lawson had shown little sympathy for African debtors at the Commonwealth Finance Ministers' meeting in Trinidad, leaving New Zealand to plead the African cause unaided.

A minor British initiative to help debtors was unveiled at the autumn IMF meeting in 1984. It consisted of waiving the rule that rescheduling debts automatically disqualified the country from export credit cover. This was helpful to debtors, but almost inevitable given the massive increase in debt rescheduling through the Paris Club after 1982. The 1987 Lawson plan represented a recognition that the official debt of SSA countries was unlikely ever to be repaid, plus a desire to steal a march on President Mitterrand who was contemplating a similar plan. The Lawson plan, and the later Mitterrand initiative, both became options of the 'Toronto terms', which effectively allow about one-third debt service relief on Paris Club debt for certain poor developing countries (mainly African) who undertake to implement IMF stabilisation programmes. By 1990, 13 eligible countries had benefited from the Toronto terms. Just before Mrs Thatcher's fall from power, Lawson's successor as Chancellor, John Major, proposed that debt relief possibilities be raised to two-thirds. These 'Trinidad terms' have yet to be universally agreed by OECD countries (although the UK decided in October 1991 to implement the Trinidad terms unilaterally, despite US opposition).

Despite substantial activity in debt reduction and conversion, both for commercial and for official debt, the absolute size of developing countries' external debt (not counting liabilities to the IMF) continued to rise, mainly as a result of the effective capitalisation of interest that could not be paid. In 1983, the figure was $880 billion; by 1990, it had risen to $1306.4 billion. Debt service payments rose from $120.6 billion in 1983 to $161.8 billion in 1990. As Table 1.2 shows, the situation of Latin America and the Caribbean—which in 1983 had the largest external debt and debt service payments—had improved somewhat relative to other regions by 1990. The indebtedness of Africa, Asia, Europe and the Middle East increased rapidly between 1983 and 1990, although not enough to displace Latin America from its position as (still) the largest debtor region with the heaviest debt service payments. The composition of developing country debt during this period shifted somewhat away from commercial and towards official debt (Table 1.3). This reflects the impact of the Baker and Brady plans, which had more influence over the actions of the official sector than over those of the commercial banks.

Table 1.2. Developing countries' external debt and debt service payments ($ bn).[a]

	External debt		Debt service payments	
	1983	1990	1983	1990
Africa	126.9	226.4	17.3	25.4
Asia	207.5	361.7	26.6	47.4
Europe	84.8	136.0	11.5	16.6
Middle East	125.4	163.5	14.7	24.3
Western Hemisphere	344.5	418.7	50.5	48.1
Total	889.0	1306.4	120.6	161.8
Heavily indebted countries[b]	394.7	495.3	56.0	55.8

[a]Source: *IMF World Economic Outlook 1991*. Excludes debt owed to the IMF.
[b]Argentina, Bolivia, Brazil, Chile, Colombia, Cote d'Ivoire, Ecuador, Mexico, Morocco, Nigeria, Peru, Philippines, Uruguay, Venezuela, Yugoslavia.

Table 1.3. Developing countries' external debt by type of creditor ($ bn).

	1982	1983	1984	1985	1986	1987	1988	1989	1990
Official	249.4	279.9	303.7	353.5	409.2	488.7	496.7	526.3	575.7
Commercial banks	433.7	461.5	471.5	487.1	507.4	545.0	532.2	515.5	517.9
Other private	156.1	147.5	154.8	163.9	179.7	182.2	194.8	192.3	212.7
Total	839.2	889.0	930.0	1004.5	1096.3	1216.0	1223.7	1234.1	1306.4

Source: IMF World Economic Outlook 1990, 1991.

It is more useful, in gauging the continuing impact of the debt crisis on developing countries, to look at external debt and debt service in relation to GDP and export earnings rather than simply to record the absolute figures. Tables 1.4 and 1.5 show external debt and debt service payments in relation to GDP and to exports, both for developing countries as a whole and for the 'Baker 15' heavily indebted countries. These indicate that, since the debt crisis erupted in 1982, the ratios of total external debt to exports, and to GDP, worsened through the mid-1980s and then returned to their 1982 levels by 1990. These were, of course, considerably above those of 1979. Little difference is evident between all developing countries and the heavy indebted group in this regard. The ratios of debt service payments to exports tell a somewhat different story. For all developing countries, the ratio did fall after 1982, from 19.6% to 15.5% in 1990. Also, the ratio declined relatively more for the highly indebted countries, from 51.5% to 27.9% (1982–1990). This reflects both debt rescheduling and the decline in total external debt that began after 1986.

The improvement in the debt service ratio, especially after 1987, was reflected in the size of current account imbalances in developing countries. Although still substantial, the average absolute deficits of the late 1980s were smaller than in 1981–1987 for developing countries as

Table 1.4. Developing countries' ratios of total external debt to exports and GDP (percent).[a]

	Total developing countries		Heavily indebted countries[b]	
	Debt/exports	Debt/GDP	Debt/exports	Debt/GDP
1979	90.9	24.2	183.7	31.0
1980	81.8	24.3	168.0	32.8
1981	95.0	27.7	202.6	37.6
1982	120.8	31.1	266.6	41.0
1983	135.6	33.0	288.9	46.0
1984	134.9	34.0	269.4	46.6
1985	152.0	35.9	284.3	45.5
1986	173.7	37.9	344.8	44.9
1987	162.1	37.6	339.3	44.4
1988	143.3	34.9	295.0	40.2
1989	129.3	32.3	264.1	38.9
1990	124.8	31.4	247.7	37.8

[a]Source: *IMF World Economic Outlook 1987–1991*. Excludes debt owed to the IMF.
[b]Argentina, Bolivia, Brazil, Chile, Colombia, Cote d'Ivoire, Ecuador, Mexico, Morocco, Nigeria, Peru, Philippines, Uruguay, Venezuela, Yugoslavia.

Table 1.5. Developing countries' ratios of debt service payments to exports of goods and services (percent).[a]

	Total developing countries		Heavily indebted countries[b]	
	Total service	Interest	Total service	Interest
1979	14.3	6.1	35.0	14.7
1980	13.2	6.6	29.4	16.0
1981	16.1	8.7	40.9	22.6
1982	19.6	11.1	51.5	31.1
1983	18.4	11.0	41.0	29.2
1984	19.7	11.7	40.8	28.9
1985	21.3	11.9	40.0	28.1
1986	22.7	12.1	44.0	28.7
1987	20.5	9.4	38.0	21.1
1988	20.0	9.6	44.8	24.9
1989	16.8	8.2	32.2	18.5
1990	15.5	7.6	27.9	15.6

[a]Source: *IMF World Economic Outlook 1987-1991*. Excludes debt service to the IMF.
[b]Argentina, Bolivia, Brazil, Chile, Colombia, Cote d'Ivoire, Ecuador, Mexico, Morocco, Nigeria, Peru, Philippines, Uruguay, Venezuela, Yugoslavia.

a whole, and for the highly indebted countries. Nevertheless, it is not clear that the 1980s have laid the foundations for subsequent sustainable growth. Growth in the developing countries in the 1980s was markedly slower than for the whole period 1965-1980: the heavily indebted countries would need to raise their current GDP by 45% to reach the levels that would have prevailed if the average growth rate of 1965-1980 had continued. There was no sign of any rising tempo of growth as the decade proceeded, either in developing countries as a whole, or among the highly indebted.

By 1991, some chinks of light among the general gloom were visible. A number of Latin American countries have benefited from negotiations completed under the Brady Plan—Mexico (February 1990), Costa Rica (May 1990), Venezuela (August 1990). The Philippines has also had a Brady deal. Some evidence also exists that positive net transfers of resources resumed in Latin America and the Caribbean from the creditor countries in 1990, although as yet only a few countries of the region have benefited, essentially Mexico, Chile, Columbia and Venezuela (Griffith-Jones and Gottschalk, 1991).

The position of SSA economies remains dire, despite the reliefs offered under the G7 plans. These remain small relative both to debt service obligations and to the size of debt service payments actually being made. While obligations exceed $20 billion per year, of which less than half is currently being paid, the additional relief provided by the Toronto terms is in the region of $0.1 billion. By themselves, these terms do not reduce the stock of debt, although both the US and France promised in 1989 to forgive the debt owed to them by low-income countries with adjustment programmes. The British efforts to implement the Trinidad terms in late 1991, unilaterally if necessary, were welcome in this context.

The Role of Aid

As the debt crisis turned off the flow of 'new money' from the commercial banks to the developing countries during the 1980s, nothing else took its place. The aid budgets of the industrialised economies did not expand to replace the commercial money, which by and large ceased once the debt crisis broke (except when coerced by the IFIs). Total flows of official development assistance ('aid') to developing countries were remarkably stable. Within the total of aid receipts, there was some substitution of DAC (Development Assistance Committee of the OECD) aid for non-DAC aid. This resulted from the impact of the falling oil price on OPEC donors and the disarray of the Soviet and East European economies in the latter half of the 1980s. However, for total aid flows, the failure to expand in real terms was unmistakable. The period around 1979–1980 seems to have been a transition point when aid donors decided that they could go thus far and no further (despite many unfulfilled pledges to raise the share of aid in GNP). This understanding seems to have been crucial in shifting the responsibility for adjustment from the shoulders of the industrialised nations onto the shoulders of the developing countries themselves. The prospect of evolving a new international economic order more favourable to developing countries vanished. Adjustment to whatever circumstances the international economy threw up now became the task of each individual developing country.

However, this apparent collective aid fatigue of the 1980s clearly affected some countries much more than others. Most of the OECD countries actually increased their net disbursements of aid, in real terms, during the decade. This was true of Denmark, Finland, France, Germany, Italy, Japan, the Netherlands, Norway, Sweden and Switzerland. A minority did seem genuinely fatigued and were unable to make any greater effort at resource transfer: such countries were Australia, Austria, Belgium, Canada and Ireland. Three countries reduced their aid effort over the decade: New Zealand (a minor donor), the US and the UK. It was the behaviour of the US and the UK, in particular, which prevented DAC aid flows from rising to meet some of the financial needs which emerged in the wake of the debt crisis.

In 1986, one of Britain's aid ministers wrote to his successor that, while Mrs Thatcher had many qualities, 'over-enthusiasm for the aid budget' was not one of them. Her lack of enthusiasm was most evident in the early 1980s: between 1981–1982 and 1986–1987, the volume of British aid declined by 2.8% a year in real terms. After this long decline, a small increase in the aid/GNP ratio was finally achieved by Christopher Patten, as minister responsible, in 1988.

If the 1979 aid/GNP ratio is taken as the norm, a cumulative shortfall of aid resources equal to 1.43% of UK GNP had occurred by 1988. Using the UN target of 0.7% of GNP as the norm would increase this shortfall to 3.33%. Along with this loss of resources, the British aid programme was damaged in other ways. An explicit commitment to 'give greater weight to political, industrial and commercial considerations' in the allocation of aid had mixed results. On the one hand, it permitted the development of an intelligent strategy for post-apartheid Southern Africa, centred around Mozambique. On the other hand, it permitted an expansion of low-quality export-related aid within a budget that was already shrinking in real terms (Toye, 1991).

One other loss which the British aid programme suffered in the 1980s was in the skills required for an independent critical perspective on the activities of the IFIs. The deep cuts of the early 1980s affected ODA staff and not merely the projects and programmes which they were administering. The capability to formulate a different adjustment strategy from that proposed by the IMF and the World Bank, or to criticise what was proposed reasonably knowledgeably, gradually decreased as the administration of aid was made leaner in terms of middle- and high-level personnel. Nor was what was lost in this way made good in other departments of government. The Treasury's international finance divisions also lack the skills and supporting staff of a typical IMF mission. A naïve attitude to the efficacy of IMF and World Bank conditionalities is a characteristic of many of the public statements of British officials on the debt crisis.

This state of affairs (to some extent mitigated by the financing of academic research on these questions) could produce some over-rigid attitudes about what is to be done as the debt crisis era is about to go into double figures. Brady-type debt reduction programmes need to be accompanied by sound adjustment programmes. Independent input into the design of such programmes is vital. If the IMF/World Bank adjustment programmes prescribed for indebted countries are taken to be unquestionably right, the persistence of the crisis is very easily ascribed to the debtors themselves, for having failed to do the right thing. In some cases this intransigence will be justified, because of poor programme design. A more discriminating approach could also be the approach which leads to new opportunities for aid expansion.

Conclusions

Mrs Thatcher's first words on taking office were 'where there is discord, may we bring harmony. . . where there is despair, may we bring hope'. For the developing countries of the world, these pious words must now have a somewhat hollow ring. Apart from Zimbabwean independence, her constructive encounters with developing countries were few. In the early 1980s, her policy objectives for them were largely commercial, especially in the securing of large contracts for British arms manufacturers. After the Falklands episode, British and US foreign policy regressed to that of an earlier era of frequent military intervention, with scant respect for international law, against developing country regimes which were, often with good reason, disliked.

The basis for sustaining this antagonistic extra-European posture was a reinvigorated 'special relationship' between the UK and the US. Building on shared political attitudes, Thatcher managed this relationship in a way which distracted attention from Britain's continuing structural dependence on the US and thus kept the intrinsic sources of friction tightly under control. In public, she made a fetish of her role as the unswervingly loyal ally of the US, absorbing the political damage which this periodically did to her and her government at home. As a result, she may have exercised more political influence in Washington than had been common for British Prime Ministers. Her popularity there was certainly much greater.

In the economic field, the effort at collusion was more difficult. Interpretations of the requirements of the 'new monetarism' differed among the converts on either side of the Atlantic (not to mention the differences between those on the same side). The institutions for the execution of economic policy also differed. In addition, the Reagan camp tried hard to learn the lessons of the 'Thatcher experiment' in advance of their own advent to power. In the event, UK inflation was gradually controlled after 1981 by fiscal contraction. In the US, monetary policy was more effectively used by the Federal Reserve Board against inflation. However, massive tax cutting created a large structural deficit for the US government. Nominal interest rates in both countries reached unprecedented levels and, when inflation decreased, real interest rates rose to, and remained at, roughly double their average level of the previous three decades (4% as against 2% for 1950–1980).

This rise in real interest rates in the early 1980s as a result of UK, and particularly US, policies put a major squeeze on those developing economies that had borrowed in the 1970s, at the behest of industrialised country governments and the IFIs. The new feature of variable interest rates had made them vulnerable to sudden changes in the international financial regime. The fragility of this recycling mechanism was finally revealed when falling oil prices forced Mexico to declare a debt moratorium in August 1982. From this point onwards, commercial banks were very reluctant to continue lending on the normal voluntary basis. This precipitated a widespread crisis in the developing world, in which debt obligations spiralled by the power of compound interest, and a whole range of ingenious remedial measures were not able to prevent the debt overhang from growing.

The British government did hint in public that it would be nice if the US could control its budget deficit, to help alleviate the debtors' plight. When that hint fell on deaf ears in Washington, nothing else was to be done. The real priority was the deflection of any further threats to the international banking system, allowing individual banks time to take countermeasures against the consequences of future outright defaults. Once such threats—for example, the emergence of a well-organised debtors cartel—had receded, the British government had little interest in taking major actions to ease the plight of debtor countries. The markets should be allowed to dictate the eventual outcome, it was strongly believed. The idea that governments should intervene to arrange a settling of accounts between creditors and debtors, to allow a fresh start on the international financial scene, was regarded as anathema (cf. Marcel and Palma, 1988, pp. 392–5).

Nevertheless, more modest plans by the US government to ease the plight of countries with heavy commercial debts were supported in public (but not in private) by the UK in 1985 and 1989. Britain's formal support, despite reservations about the principles involved, resulted partly from its need for international economic cooperation after the sterling crisis of January 1985 and partly from unwillingness to interfere with the US's pursuit of its own geopolitical interests. Britain's own debt initiatives have been more modest, to help African low-income countries with a burden of official debt. These proposals have been helpful, and are to be welcomed, but their cost, and the relief they gave, was still small by 1990.

The aid performance of both the UK and the US over the decade of the debt crisis has been one of steadily declining effort. The US volume of official development assistance fell in real terms between 1980–1981 and 1988–1989, and as a percentage of GNP from 0.27% to 0.18%. The UK volume of aid also fell in real terms between the same years, and as a percentage of GNP from 0.39% to 0.32%. These performances were markedly worse than for almost all other OECD aid donors. In Britain's case, the running down of the aid budget in the early 1980s had the additional unfortunate result that economic expertise on schemes of structural adjustment was impaired.

In 1991 some hopeful signs appeared, both of the initial successes of the Brady Plan, and of increased vigour in implementing debt reduction schemes for the least developed countries. However, many developing countries still had their debts treated much less favourably than terms granted to Poland and Egypt, whose geopolitical significance requires no underlining. They are still having to extract themselves unaided from the aftermath of the 1970s recycling of petrodollars. They have not had their despair replaced by hope. Nevertheless, they would very probably endorse Mrs Thatcher's final words on losing power: 'It is a funny old world'.

Acknowledgements

The author wishes to acknowledge very helpful initial discussions with Mike Faber, documentary materials supplied by Stephany Griffith-Jones and the excellent research assistance of Ian McKendry and Ana Marr. Both Mike Faber and Hans Singer commented on the original version of this chapter. The usual disclaimer applies.

Comment

The Political Economy of Growth

Ajit Singh

Professor Toye's chapter presents an elegant and sophisticated analysis of the UK's relationship with the Third World during the Thatcher era. UK aid fell in real terms between 1979 and 1988; moreover, as a proportion of GDP, it was considerably lower at the end of the Thatcher period than at the beginning. This reduction in aid was peculiar to the US and the UK (and New Zealand, a small aid giver)—many other OECD countries increased their aid in real terms in the 1980s.

John Toye notes the linkage between aid and armaments purchases and other commercial considerations which were emphasised in the Thatcher era. Instead of the aid question, however, the chapter rightly in my view concentrates on the political economy of the special relationship between the US and the UK and its impact on the rich countries' policies towards the international debt problem. I agree with much of the analysis but I would like to put forward a somewhat different interpretation on the events of the last decade and comment on its implications for the future.

Professor Toye's basic argument is that the inept policies of different kinds of monetarism followed by Reagan and Thatcher were responsible for the cataclysmic changes in world economic conditions which occurred in the early 1980s. In particular, the ensuing demand shock, the real interest rate and terms of trade shocks—and to that I would add the 'capital supply' shock—were directly responsible for the Third World debt crisis. I agree that the international financial institutions' handling of the crisis has been manifestly unsuccessful, in view of the sharp fall in trend growth rates which has occurred particularly in the heavily indebted countries of Latin America. Where I would differ is in characterising the Reagan–Thatcher policies as being inept.

These policies—Thatcher's monetarism and Reagan's supply-side measures—may have been inept in their execution, although opinions differ on this issue. Their consequences were certainly extremely unfortunate for many people since, in an increasingly integrated world economy, they reduced economic growth and caused high rates of unemployment and sharp reductions in real wages in large parts of the world. However, the central point I would like to make is that from the point of view of the North's Conservative governments, such policies were far from inept but served to further interests outlined in the following brief discussion (based on Glyn *et al.*, 1990; and Singh, 1990).

In sharp contrast to the previous pattern of development—the Keynesian model which prevailed during the Golden Age of 1950–1973 and with which to a greater or a smaller degree leading OECD governments still tried to persist in the period between the two oil shocks (1974–1978)—the Reagan–Thatcher supply-side and monetarist policies represented a different approach which emphasised the control of inflation (as opposed to an expansion of employment or full employment) as a primary objective, together with market expansion, privatisation, deregulation and so on. Although this market-oriented path of development, which was instituted in the US and the UK and which spread to different degrees to other OECD countries in the 1980s, has not yet won general acceptance, it would be a mistake not to recognise the 'achievements' of this model *from the perspective of Conservative governments in the North.*

First, there has been a major change in the balance of power, both internationally and internally. Internationally, the collapse of commodity prices, the extremely high real interest rates, and the reduction of capital flows have greatly weakened the economic and political power of developing countries. In the mid-1970s, these countries were vociferously demanding a new international economic order; today, most of them (particularly in Africa and Latin America) are severely constrained by their balance of payments, heavily in debt and in the position of being supplicants before the IMF and the World Bank. The latter two institutions are only willing to provide much-needed foreign exchange if these countries carry out 'structural reforms' which usually follow the same pattern of denationalisation, deregulation and internal and external liberalisation of markets, which are the hallmark of changes in the industrialised countries. Similarly, in the latter, the bargaining position of the trade unions, and of the working class in general, has been weakened both at the workplace and at the macroeconomic level. The second main success of the emerging new system has been an improvement in terms of inflationary performance, compared with the mid-1970s. Instead of the stagflation (low growth and high inflation) of those years, the 1980s have been characterised by low growth and low inflation. This is of course directly related to the weakened bargaining power of the unions and the fall in commodity prices that accompanied the changing internal and international balance of power.

There are, however, significant weaknesses in the 1980s record. First, although unemployment rates in the North can be expected to come down to some degree in the mid-1990s, as the rate of growth of the labour force declines as a result of demographic factors, they look set to remain exceptionally high in most European countries. Only an underlying increase in the rate of growth of world economic activity can offer the prospect of any improvement before then. Second, despite nearly a decade of IMF/World Bank management, the Third World debt problem is far from being resolved. Many heavily indebted countries in Latin America and Africa are no closer to resuming their previous growth rates even though they have suffered for several years the enormous economic and social costs of 'adjustment'. Third, there are extremely large payment imbalances in the international economy, which have become a source of major instability on the world's currency and stock markets.

Nevertheless, as long as high unemployment rates in the advanced countries remain politically acceptable, the balance of advantage (from the standpoint of Conservative governments in the leading OECD countries) lies in continuing with the current macroeconomic pattern of low growth and low inflation: if expansionary policies were followed and the world rate of economic growth rose on a sustained basis to anywhere near its 1950–1973 level, this would lead to a tighter labour market and therefore to an increase in the power of the unions, and more significantly, there would be a sharp rise in commodity prices, including oil. All of these factors would rekindle inflation. For conservative policy-makers, the only perceived benefit of an increase in the rate of growth of the world economy would be that it would greatly help towards solving the debt problem of developing countries. However, they fear that this would be at the expense of rising commodity prices, inflation and adverse changes in the economic and political balance of power. Since there are a variety of other ways of ameliorating the debt problem (such as write-offs or interest capping), it is unlikely that the leading OECD countries will seek to expand the world economy for this purpose alone.

To be sure, there is a great deal of discussion about policy coordination among the leading industrial countries to revive the world economy. However, it is important to note that the central objective of that policy coordination is *not* to bring about an overall increase in the rate of growth of world demand, but rather to redistribute the current level of demand among the leading countries in a way which will reduce their huge payments imbalances, and thus help restore stability in the currency and financial markets.

If the above considerations are combined with the expected deceleration in the rate of population growth, and the structural shifts already occurring in these economies towards service sectors with low productivity growth, the prospect for the OECD countries (and hence for the world economy) must be at best one of continued slow growth. This perspective assumes that the policy coordination currently being pursued by the leading OECD countries is wholly successful; if it is not, the world economy is likely to grow at a still slower rate, and then the possibility of a serious slump in the short term cannot be ruled out. Long ago, the Italian Marxist thinker, Gramsci, talked about the pessimism of the intellect and the optimism of the spirit. The above pessimistic scenario is probably the most likely outcome for the world economy in the medium term.

In principle, the resumption of 1950–1973 growth rates is not impossible but it would require, among other things, an explicit abandonment of the Thatcher–Reagan pattern of development of the 1980s and a commitment to a rather different economic and social order. However, for that to happen would require in turn a very specific political conjuncture in the leading OECD countries. I have serious doubts about the possibility of such a conjuncture materialising in the near future.

2

Financial Globalisation and Deregulation

Jerry Coakley and Laurence Harris

The strategy of the Thatcher administrations between 1979 and 1990 affected the whole of the economy: both industry—manufacturing, energy, construction—and services, including financial and business services, were transformed. In the process, labour's position was radically altered everywhere, with redundancies, changed working and bargaining conditions in manufacturing, and a further sharp twist to the upward trend of employment in services. A central pillar of the whole Thatcher enterprise was action to change the role of money and finance and to strengthen the position of the financial sector; whatever happened to manufacturing, the City was intended to flourish. The rise of the 'yuppie' in the popular imagery of the decade reflects the apparent initial success of that policy. In fact, however, the financial policies of the Thatcher decade were a failure, and the City has emerged without the real gains that were heralded.

If one or another section of British capital could be identified as being at the forefront of Mrs Thatcher's political constituency it was undoubtedly financial capital—its bankers, brokers, dealers, analysts and consultants. In terms of the theses of Perry Anderson and Tom Nairn on the historical origins of the British state, the centrality of finance in the polity of Mrs Thatcher's governments reflects a continuity since the beginnings of the modern British state. Irrespective of whether Thatcher's political base represents a continuation of an old coalition (and there are grounds for rejecting the general Anderson–Nairn thesis) or a new political development, there can be no doubt that, from the point of view of economic affairs, the strategy was seen as an attempt to promote the financial sector while transforming it to enable the City to take the lead in a financial world that was fast changing under the impact of internationalisation and new technology. In this chapter we examine that project and argue that if Thatcher's legacy includes the enfeeblement of British industry, it also includes a failure to rebuild the financial system on a sound basis. Surprisingly, the policies of Thatcher's governments failed even the City.

Our evaluation of Thatcher's strategy for finance is mainly in terms of its own goals, not the popular criterion of whether the City provides appropriate finance for industry. The strategy had three rather different central aims which were, in part, mutually incompatible. One goal, which gave the name 'monetarism' to the era, was to make control over financial variables the key to macroeconomic discipline. At different times this was conceived as targeting either some measure of the money supply or the exchange rate, and in each case interest rates were used as the instrument. A second goal was to promote the international competitiveness of the City as a global financial centre. The purpose behind this was to boost the profitability of the City and to create employment in an expanded financial services sector centred on South East England; to achieve this, deregulation was employed as the instrument. A third goal was to change the financial system to effect a shift of national wealth away from public ownership to the private sector. The main instrument in this case was privatisation but regulatory and taxation measures affecting housing, pensions and particular types of savings such as PEP schemes also played their part.

The greatest inconsistency within this set of goals was between the monetarist policy of attempting to control finance and the competitive goal of deregulation, but other inconsistencies are also apparent. For example, Mrs Thatcher's general antagonism towards the European Community and her continued opposition to monetary union ran counter to her objective of promoting the international competitiveness of the City. The upshot of such incompatibility of objectives was that the Thatcherite strategy for finance was pursued unevenly and several changes of policy occurred. The most remarkable was the formal abandonment of broad money-supply targets in 1985 and their replacement by a policy of shadowing the Deutschmark (a policy sharply contested in Downing Street).

We argue in the following sections that the overall results of the Thatcherite finance project can largely be judged a failure even when appraised on its own terms.[6] The origins and logic of the strategy and the reasons for its failure were not simply matters of policy formulation and execution, since the strategy was conditioned by underlying trends: in addition to the influence of history (the legacy of the City's past at the centre of the British Empire), changes were underway both internationally and domestically which influenced the conditions under which finance could operate and be transformed. This chapter begins with an outline of these exogenous trends, especially the phenomenon of the internationalisation of finance. This is followed by an examination of the way the strategy addressed each of its three goals: the pursuit of macroeconomic discipline through financial instruments, promotion of the City's international competitiveness through deregulation, and promotion of the shift from public to private ownership of assets. We argue that Thatcher's financial policy was a qualified failure in terms of these three goals in addition to its failure to address the faults of Britain's financial system from the point of view of manufacturing industry. Both dimensions are relevant for Britain's prospects in a more integrated, post-1992 Europe and we also examine the position of Britain's financial sector in Europe.

The Internationalisation of Finance

One difficulty in discussing government strategy towards finance since 1979 is disentangling government policy's specific contribution from developments already underway within international financial markets. To simplify, Mrs Thatcher attempted to channel and redirect these trends to her constituency's own advantage and towards the attainment of her specific goals for finance. Her administrations' strategy towards finance was conditioned principally by the trend towards internationalisation in which financial intermediaries and markets everywhere, but especially in the advanced capitalist countries, participated.

Internationalisation was far from being a new phenomenon but it assumed new forms in the 1970s—marked by the growth of the euromarkets in bank credit and bonds, by the adoption of (more or less) floating exchange rates, and by an expansion of multinational banks—and its character altered again in the 1980s. Perhaps the main development of the 1980s was the growth of international markets in bonds (including short- and medium-term notes) and equities, and the growth of cross-border dealing in derivative instruments such as options, futures and swaps. These new developments in the internationalisation of finance were the context for each aspect of Thatcher's financial policy.

Most directly, trends in the internationalisation of finance shaped the goal of strengthening the City's international competitiveness. Stemming from roots that can be traced back to its imperial position in the late nineteenth century, the City entered the 1970s as the leading centre for international banking and other financial services such as eurobonds and specialist insurance. During the 1970s it improved the crucial element of that lead, its banking strength, by consolidating its position as the world centre for the new forms of eurocurrency banking. The surpluses accumulated by many oil-exporting countries following the 1973 oil price rise were largely placed in bank deposits (as against long-term assets), and London-based banks succeeded in attracting the majority of those eurodollar deposits. London was the centre through which the banks on-lent these funds in the relatively new forms of syndicated, variable-rate loans to sovereign borrowers including Third World and East European states; the process was misleadingly dubbed 'the recycling of petrodollars'.

The defining characteristic of the euromarkets based in London was that they were relatively unregulated by the Bank of England. This freedom from regulation was especially important because their transactions—intermediating between the worldwide surpluses and deficits of dollar capital—were not subject to the exchange controls that still restricted exports of capital from Britain. The oil exporters' petrodollars were largely deposited in London rather than New York because, while American banks were initially subject to restrictions on the interest rates they could pay, the London banks were not.

The euromarkets were a rupture of the nexus between financial markets and national systems of regulation. They were 'offshore' markets in the sense that they did not fall within the remit of national systems of financial regulation. Indeed, as time went on the problems associated with the eurobanking markets established the need for international regulation. The Basle Concordat in 1975, which was updated following the collapse of Banco Ambrosiano in 1983, was an early example of the new approach to the international coordination of financial regulation. The new forms of international regulation concentrated on the adequacy of banks' own capital and on allocating to different authorities the tasks of supervising international banks but, significantly, the eurobanking business remains free from national interest-rate controls or credit controls.

In the context of these changes, London's international banking position was strengthened during the 1970s but at the end of the decade it was clear that the City's relative supremacy could not be taken for granted. British-based financial intermediaries such as pension funds and insurance companies were fettered by exchange controls on the export of capital, and the London Stock Exchange operated on the arcane basis of an exclusive gentlemen's club rather than as a competitive market. A consequence of the latter was that international securities business was bypassing London and was being siphoned off to the newly deregulated New York Stock Exchange. Thus both the abolition of exchange controls and the deregulation of the Stock Exchange—two key Thatcherite policies in the next decade—had strong driving interests and it is doubtful whether a Labour administration could have ignored the pressure from the City, reinforced by the structural changes underway internationally, unless it were prepared to change the City by forcing a historical turn towards supporting industrial regeneration. Mrs Thatcher's contribution was to bring forward the timing of the policy, to leave her laissez-faire stamp on its form, and to promote the continued international ambitions of the City at the expense of industry.

The internationalisation of finance received an impetus from developments in information and communications technology and from financial innovation throughout the 1980s, a decade which Schor (1990) has dubbed 'the era of global neoclassicism'. For instance, the development of computerised, screen-based trading systems facilitated the cross-border linking of banking, securities and derivatives markets. The euromarkets based in London continued to evolve and develop in new directions. Examples include the provision of multiple option facilities in place of syndicated loans, and the rise of the euronotes market and of the equity warrants sector of the eurobond market. The techniques of distribution within the eurobond market were applied to new equity issues and this market became known as the euroequities market.

The global trends in international finance had effects on each of the three goals of Thatcher's financial strategy. They gave urgency to the need to strengthen the City's international position in comparison to New York, Tokyo and other world cities, for although London ended the 1970s as the leading international banking centre there was no certainty that this could be maintained. Moreover, since the London Stock Exchange lagged behind its competitors, major steps were required if it was to gain a strong position in a rapidly developing international system. With regard to financial policy and macroeconomic discipline, it was believed that developments in the internationalisation of finance prevented the continuing use of direct controls over credit and other traditional, Keynesian instruments of macroeconomic policy. Further, the policy of shifting assets from the public to the private sector was partly effected through the new, internationalised equity markets: the euroequities new issues market was used for the sale of shares to overseas investors in the larger privatisations carried out by the later Thatcher administrations.

Financial Instruments and Macroeconomic Discipline

Developments in UK monetary policy by the Thatcher administrations in the 1980s occurred within the broader context of a changing international system of monetary relations—a system that had been increasingly unregulated and volatile since 1971. When floating exchange rates reintroduced a more full-blooded price mechanism to the foreign exchange markets in 1973 they were hailed as a panacea for the problems of the Keynesian Bretton Woods system. By the end of the 1980s the wheel had come full circle and economists of various persuasions were advocating a return to some type of fixed-rate regime once again. Moreover, within the European Community proposals were gathering momentum for Economic and Monetary Union, in which fixed exchange rates featured centrally. Monetary policy and macroeconomic discipline face different conditions when there are fixed exchange rates (and exchange controls) between currencies from those they face under a system of unregulated foreign exchange markets, so the problems confronted by Thatcher's macroeconomic strategy changed as the international system itself changed.

One of the innovations of the first Thatcher administration was the promulgation by Chancellor Howe of the medium-term financial strategy (MTFS), whose central feature was target bands for money supply and government debt/GDP. The MTFS was the brainchild of Howe's deputy, Nigel Lawson, who was then Financial Secretary to the Treasury. It was supposed to signify the end of Keynesian fiscal fine-tuning and was founded on two beliefs—that the money supply is the key instrument for controlling inflation without a slump (founded on a simplistic belief in the Quantity Theory), and that floating exchange rates would give the government effective control over the money supply. As became apparent in later years, the belief that flexible exchange rates are essential for national control over the money supply was an article of faith in Mrs Thatcher's own definition of sovereignty, and informed her opposition to European monetary union.

The MTFS was a failure. The authorities failed to achieve control over the rate of growth of the money supply (which consistently exceeded the top of the target bands) and the targets themselves were frequently revised upward, thereby destroying the rationale of the strategy—its claim to provide a stable framework. The attempt to use high interest rates to reduce the growth of the money supply led to a sharp rise in sterling exchange rates under the floating-rate system. The combination of high interest rates and an overvalued pound induced the historical rise in unemployment and shrinkage of Britain's manufacturing industry of 1980–1982, as is well documented. Since control over the money supply could not be achieved, the Quantity Theory targets lost their primacy in macroeconomic policy in the mid-1980s. In fact, when broad money supply (£M3) targets had to be abandoned in 1985, the authorities then identified M0, a questionable category, as an indicator of macroeconomic conditions rather than as an instrument for controlling inflation.

The failure to achieve money supply targets indicates a contradiction at the heart of Thatcher's financial policy, since it resulted partly from Tory policies that deregulated the financial sector. Broad money-supply movements are closely related to changes in bank lending and other forms of credit. Deregulation encouraged competition between financial intermediaries (notably between banks and building societies) both for the expansion of deposits and for the supply of credit and, as margins were squeezed, profitability could be maintained only by increased lending at finer margins. Similarly, the Tories' deregulation of foreign exchange flows to strengthen the City's international position (in the context of trends toward increased internationalisation) led the government to believe that it could not control the money supply by old methods. Credit controls would be evaded by inflows of foreign credit, and Bank of England influence on banks' balance sheets would penalise London banks and thereby weaken the City's competitiveness against foreign centres.

After abandoning the MTFS, government policies in the second half of the 1980s were dominated by exchange-rate considerations. From the mid-1980s the idea of sovereignty over the money supply as the mechanism for macroeconomic discipline was replaced (in a halting and politically unstable manner) by the strategy of having a relatively stable exchange rate as the regulator. Once again, interest rates were the main instrument for attempting to ensure that the targets were met. The context of these moves towards stable exchange rates was the progress being made within the European Monetary System (EMS) and proposals for moves towards Economic and Monetary Union within the European Community. The Tories were confronted with the issue of membership of the Exchange Rate Mechanism of the EMS, entry into which had been advocated by the Governor of the Bank of England as early as 1984. The issue was sidestepped, unresolved and rumbled on until 1990.

In the meantime, Nigel Lawson as Chancellor resorted to an unofficial policy of shadowing the Deutschmark as a means of stabilising the exchange rate. Now interest rates were being employed explicitly as an instrument to achieve exchange-rate targets. Although stabilisation of the exchange rate has frequently meant high interest rates in order to maintain a high exchange rate, in 1987–1988 Lawson maintained low interest rates partly to keep the pound under DM 3.00 and partly as a response to the October 1987 stock market crash. This helped fuel what has since become known as the Lawson boom, which was characterised by credit expansion and rapid inflation of real estate prices—it marked the peak of the financial system's expansion in the Thatcher era and represented a fundamentally unsustainable misalignment of the role of finance. Entry to the Exchange Rate Mechanism in October 1990 at an overvalued exchange rate consolidated the new role of exchange-rate targets, and macroeconomic policy returned to the use of systematically high interest rates to achieve exchange-rate policy at the cost of recession. However, the return to high interest rates also ensured the collapse of the boom in real estate values, on which much of the City's credit expansion had been based, and it precipitated a severe crisis for the financial system, the end of which is not yet in sight.

Enhancement of the City's International Competitiveness

The start of the Thatcher era coincided with a widespread shift in concepts of Britain's place in the international division of labour, and many commentators saw the destruction of manufacturing industry wrought between 1980 and 1982 as an inevitable, even desirable shift towards a new age when the service sector would become the country's leading edge. Indeed, Thatcher's own policy was to promote the growth of services, and especially financial and business services. There is no need to view this as an inexorable development in a post-Fordist sense: in reality it represented a strategic economic choice and served the

City's broadly defined interests of promoting London in competition
for business against New York and other financial centres. The principal
instrument used was deregulation, a series of measures designed to
remove existing restrictions on financial markets.

The first measure, and in some ways the most important, was the
abolition in 1979 of exchange controls over capital movements, which
gave all UK companies and individuals a licence to export capital. In
particular, it permitted UK financial intermediaries to invest freely in
deposits, bonds and shares abroad—a process termed 'overseas portfolio
investment' or 'international portfolio diversification'—and it had a
marked effect on the export of capital by pension funds, insurance
companies, banks and investment and unit trusts. In the first 6 months
of 1980, pension funds and insurance companies invested four times as
much in overseas equities as they did in the first half of 1979 before
controls were lifted. In subsequent years the outflow of funds from
Britain into portfolio investment overseas continued on a strong upward
trend, interrupted temporarily only by the 'homing' tendency consequent
upon the 1987 crash of global stock markets, so that in 1989 the annual
gross outflow reached an astonishing level of some £33.1 billion (or
£52.8 billion if overseas direct investment is included). At the same
time, the inflow of portfolio investment also rose steadily, albeit at
lower levels.

The abolition of exchange controls also encouraged UK-based
multinationals further to internationalise their operations through the
process of overseas direct investment. The latter received a fillip from
the boom in cross-border mergers and acquisitions which swept the
advanced capitalist economies in the late 1980s; the funds the City had
channelled into some Third World and socialist countries in the 1970s
were poured into financing giant takeover battles in the US and
elsewhere after the debt crisis broke in 1982.

Deregulation did benefit the City in two ways in the short term.
First, the large cumulative net outflow of capital increased net receipts
of foreign interest, profit and dividends (IPD). Government ministers
presented these increases in national terms and argued that the
accumulation of foreign assets should be seen as a prudent investment
that would provide future IPD income for the country as a whole to
compensate for the loss of Britain's manufacturing base. The data
reveal, however, that net IPD receipts peaked in 1986 at £5.1 million
and that they have been sustained in recent years mainly by net earnings
on direct rather than portfolio investment. Second, the two-way but
unequal flow of both portfolio and direct investment was an aspect of
the internationalisation of the City's business that generated increased
profits from fees, commissions and charges.

Whatever the short-term benefits, the promotion of London as an
international centre, boosted by the 1979 deregulation of capital
movements, did not in fact succeed in the long term. Revised statistics

published in the 1991 *Pink Book* reveal that the policy has not succeeded in building Britain's net overseas assets on a sustained basis in the manner envisaged. Although the lifting of controls did initially lead to a rush to invest overseas, by the end of 1990 the value of net overseas assets, at £29.6 billion, was lower than its 1981 level of £32.6 billion. The significant point is that these assets had risen in the intervening years and had reached a peak of £103.6 billion in 1986. Their fall back to £30 billion reflects partly the bearish trends in world equity markets and adverse currency movements, but it also reflects a sharp increase in net overseas borrowing by UK banks in particular. Similarly, the net value of IPD receipts fell at the start of the 1990s to show a deficit (of almost £800 million) in the first half of 1991 for the first time since 1980. In brief, the City had not invested British savings abroad in assets that would provide a secure alternative to the wealth being run down in the industrial areas of Britain.

The second major act of deregulation was the set of reforms known as 'Big Bang', initiated in 1983 and implemented by the London Stock Exchange in 1986. The reforms were, above all, aimed at increasing the exchange's international role. 'Big Bang' had three major components: it liberalised entry to the exchange, it abolished fixed commissions for services, and it abolished the old established division of labour between single-capacity brokers and jobbers (dealers). This effectively made the old floor-trading system redundant and it was replaced by a computerised system of screen-based trading. The prices of 750 multinational stocks are displayed electronically on a price dissemination system called SEAQ International, although only about 200 stocks are actively traded. Again this gave London a first-mover technological advantage over its major rivals, especially other European exchanges, and turnover on international equities in London since then has far exceeded that of its rivals.

The reforms permitted commercial bank subsidiaries to enter the equity markets on the London Stock Exchange and prompted a wave of takeovers as banks bought existing Stock Exchange firms (at inflated prices) to form securities houses with a central role in equity and bond markets. This was particularly important because it seemed to give a competitive edge to London compared to New York and Tokyo, where commercial banks faced restrictions on equity-related activities under the 1933 *Glass–Steagall Act* in the US and *Article 65* (which was modelled on that Act) in Japan after World War II. However, this growth in the banks' stock market business did not prove sustainable. It was obvious at the time of 'Big Bang' that excess capacity in security dealing had been created and, in the wake of the October 1987 stock market crash and the subsequent bear market, heavy losses and market overcapacity forced many banks to reduce their securities business or even to leave the securities market.

A third aspect of deregulation impinged on banks and building societies. As well as removing controls over bank balance sheets that had previously been used (and failed) in attempts to control the growth of bank credit and the money supply (such as the 'corset' controls on bank liability expansion), these measures focused on removing laws and regulations that segmented the financial markets. In retail commercial banking, Tory reforms effectively abolished the principal distinctions between banks and building societies: the latter were enabled to offer deposit, payment, personal credit and investment advisory services similar to those of banks, and indeed to convert to commercial banks, as in the case of Abbey National. Meanwhile, the commercial banks were permitted to expand their mortgage lending.

These measures of deregulation which, as indicated above, made the monetarist ideal so difficult to attain in macroeconomic policy, were intended to strengthen the City's international competitiveness but that goal was not achieved. In fact, the international standing of the City deteriorated in some respects during the 1980s despite Thatcher's best deregulatory efforts. Why did this occur? It can be explained partly by competitive deregulation: London had no monopoly over deregulation and its rivals followed its lead in progressively liberalising their own financial markets; further, in some cases, they avoided London's mistakes, which are outlined below.

In 1980 London appeared to have an unassailable lead in international banking markets (Table 2.1) and its 27% share of the total was more than double that of its nearest rival, New York, and more than five times that of Tokyo. During the 1980s both New York and Tokyo, which had been losing out to offshore financial centres in the eurocurrency markets, permitted the establishment of eurocurrency facilities onshore. In the US these were introduced in 1981 as 'international banking facilities' which are a separate set of banking accounts not subject to domestic US banking regulations. Their Japanese counterpart was established in 1985 and is known as the Japanese offshore market (although physically onshore). Partly as a result of these developments and partly for other reasons (such as the strength of the real economy in Japan during the 1980s), by 1988 London had lost its primacy in international banking and was second to Tokyo in

Table 2.1. Banking centres' shares of international lending 1975–1990 (%).[a]

	1975	1980	1985	1987	1988	1990
UK (London)	27.1	27.0	25.4	22.1	20.9	18.4
Japan (Tokyo)	4.6	5.0	10.8	18.7	21.0	19.3
US (New York)	13.5	13.4	13.3	9.9	10.1	7.7
Offshore centres	11.6	10.7	18.5	18.0	18.5	18.2

[a]Source: Bank of England.

Table 2.2. Market share in international lending from London in 1990 (£ bn).[a]

Japanese	US	Other overseas	UK retail	Other UK	Total
182.5	68.9	148.6	43.1	30.6	473.7
(38%)	(15%)	(31%)	(9%)	(7%)	

[a]Source: Bank of England.

the volume of its international bank lending business: London's share of international bank lending was only 18.4% in September 1990, compared with the 19.3% booked in Tokyo at that time. Despite this, London still retains some vestiges of a leading role: it can boast of the presence of the largest number of branches or subsidiaries of overseas banking firms and of the largest foreign exchange turnover. However, the former is also one of London's weaknesses, since so much of 'London's' banking business is in the hands of Japanese, American and other foreign banks located there. This renders it vulnerable to business being transferred to Tokyo and, to a lesser extent, New York and other European centres (Tables 2.2 and 2.3).

In the capital markets, Europe's other stock exchanges—notably Paris, Madrid, Amsterdam and, to a lesser extent, Frankfurt—have been implementing their own deregulatory reforms but have avoided London's overinvestment in trading facilities. Thus, whereas London (and South East England) have experienced large redundancies in securities houses that overexpanded to take advantage of the growth expected to follow 'Big Bang' and subsequently paid the price in the wake of the October 1987 stock market crash, other financial centres have enjoyed steadier growth. The future shape of stock exchanges within Europe is bound up with competing proposals relating to the 1992 reforms, as indicated below. Currently, London's ISE (International Stock Exchange) ranks third behind Tokyo and New York in terms of the ISE's published data on equity turnover but the available data inflate London's lead: about one-half of London's reported foreign

Table 2.3. Foreign exchange turnover in 1986 and 1989 in London, New York and Tokyo.[a]

	London	New York	Tokyo
1986 ($ billion)	90	58	48
1989 ($ billion)	187	129	115
Change 1986–1989	108%	120%	140%

[a]Source: Bank of England.

equity turnover is off-exchange but the available data for competing centres do not include this category of trading. London is currently the leading exchange for turnover of foreign equities but this is due in part to the lack of progress in deregulation on competing European exchanges. Frankfurt is beginning to challenge London and its turnover in domestic equities has exceeded that of London since 1989, while adjusted total turnover figures (Table 2.4) place it ahead of London in 1990. London remains the leading eurobond centre but Thatcher's fiscal rigour has sharply undermined the status of the domestic UK gilt-edged market.

In derivative markets (futures and options), London ranks about equal fourth with Paris after the two Chicago exchanges and Tokyo, but its share of total turnover is only 8%. Paris, Amsterdam and, more recently, Frankfurt have followed London's lead in establishing computerised exchanges dealing in futures and options. The Paris exchange became so successful within the European time zone within such a short time that the Bank of England has felt obliged to expedite the merger of the two London exchanges: the London International Financial Exchange (LIFFE) and the London Traded Options Market (LTOM). The challenge by MATIF, the Paris futures exchange, for leadership within Europe is likely to intensify, since it has linked up with the two Chicago exchanges by means of GLOBEX, their new electronic trading system devised by Reuters.

London's future prospects in other financial markets and activities look no brighter. Specialist insurance, in which London was formerly an international leader, has also registered a decline. In 1990 the insurance sector's net foreign earnings were, at £2.2 billion, below their 1983 level and well short of the peak of £4.9 billion attained in 1986. Estimates of London's share of international insurance business suggest a decline from 50% in 1976 to some 25% now. Total funds (such as pension and life assurance funds) under portfolio management in the UK fall some distance

Table 2.4. Major stock exchanges' equity turnover in 1990 (£ bn).[a]

	Domestic	Foreign	Total turnover
New York	—	—	749
Tokyo	730	8	738
Frankfurt[b]	281	6	289
NASDAQ	243	16	259
London[c]	158	74	232

[a]Source: *ISE Quality of Markets Quarterly.*
[b]Frankfurt denotes the Federation of German Exchanges.
[c]Foreign turnover has been adjusted downward for data consistency with other exchanges.

short of the equivalent totals managed in both Tokyo and New York but, reflecting London's propensity to export capital, they appear to contain a higher proportion of international investment.

In sum, the international standing of the City has deteriorated in the course of the 1980s. This has occurred despite the best efforts of successive Thatcher administrations to promote its interests at the expense of other sectors of the economy. It could be objected that the external challenges to the City resulted from exogenous factors beyond Mrs Thatcher's control, such as deregulation in competing financial centres. However, this merely underlines the point that Mrs Thatcher had no special prerogative in relation to the deregulation of financial markets and illustrates the fragility and short-term benefits of a financial strategy based on free-market principles.

Shift to Private Ownership of Assets

The development over the 1980s of Tory policies on privatisation illustrates the opportunism of policy formulation in this area as events and proposals were rationalised after they occurred and presented as a coherent whole. Nevertheless, privatisation did have a basis in Thatcherite ideology as a whole and, in particular, it fitted well with the government's strategy for boosting the City.

Two of the main aims served by the privatisation of publicly owned wealth were 'the rolling back of the state' (which took a financial form in the drive to reduce the Public Sector Borrowing Requirement (PSBR) through the sale of assets), and the creation of a belief that property ownership was being extended (supporting the confused ideology of a property-owning democracy). These notions have been much discussed but a third objective of privatisation, which was in some ways the most important, was to fuel the expansion and profitability of the financial sector's business.

Privatisation encompassed a range of policies but, from the point of view of its relation to the financial system, its most important elements were, first, the sale of shareholdings in public enterprises ranging from British Telecom to water utilities and, second, the sale of municipal housing to former tenants. The key to their significance for the City was the process we call 'financialisation', without which privatisation could not occur. In order to transfer publicly owned enterprises and their physical assets to private ownership it was necessary to create and market forms of equity that could be owned and traded as financial assets. Similarly, for municipal housing, titles had to be created that could be valued, traded and, above all, used as collateral for mortgages and other credit. Thus, both types of privatisation required the financialisation of real assets. Financialisation has some parallels with securitisation in the US, in which pools of relatively illiquid bank and other loans are resold to investors as debt securities. In both cases a class of assets is made more liquid by the creation of new securities so that both involve the sale of asset-backed securities. Both permit an indirect expansion of credit facilities through the creation of new financial assets. However, the financialisation that accompanied British privatisation is a more fundamental conversion than securitisation since the underlying assets were formerly publicly owned real assets rather than relatively illiquid, private financial assets.

As privatisation continued through the 1980s Mrs Thatcher linked it to an ideology of 'popular capitalism' in which the broadening of share ownership featured centrally. How successful has this been? First, it failed to curb the upward trend in the growth of institutional shareholding (by pension funds and insurance companies): the proportion of shares owned by individuals continued to decline throughout the 1980s, falling from 28% of the total in 1981 to 21% in 1989. This has occurred despite the rise in the number of individual shareholders from 3 million in 1980 to 11 million in 1990—one in four of the population aged 16 or over—but it is estimated that 54% own shares in one company only and a further 20% in two companies only. Owners of shares in the new Abbey National and the Trustee Savings Bank (TSB share owners are especially numerous in Scotland) probably account for over one-half of the new shareholders and these institutions were already owned by their members (in practice, the people who then came to own their quoted shares) rather than by the state. The data also confirm that the profile of individual shareholders is heavily skewed in the direction of Mrs Thatcher's political constituency: some 41% of all individual shareholders live in the South East, and 31% of the total are members of socioeconomic groups A and B compared with 17% of the population overall. As an illustration of the continuing inequality among share owners it is estimated that 80% of the market value of individual shareholdings is accounted for by wealthier individuals who own portfolios worth £50 000 or more.

The process of financialisation of real assets and their transfer to private ownership had a significant impact on the City's business. The potential benefits to the City were the short-term fee revenue from handling the transfer of assets, the profitability of shares in privatised industries, the expansion of interest-generating loans made possible by the enlarged base of private financial assets, and the strengthening of the process of internationalisation. Privatisation of enterprises provided fee income for the merchant banks, stockbrokers and lawyers employed to handle the exercise. In large 'popular' sales like British Gas and British Telecom, a further large source of fee revenue was tapped by the banks and brokers that handled resales by investors taking a quick profit. A major, controversial source of income was the fee paid to institutions which acted as underwriters in situations where the risk borne was minimal. The profitability of newly privatised shares had a short-term component arising from the underpricing of the offers for sale, so that many experienced quick capital gains. Several of these sources of profit within the financial system—viewed as costs to the government of privatisation—have been calculated in a number of ways and criticised as too high by financial economists. One example is the sale of £3 863 million of shares in British Telecom where, according to the National Audit Office, the amount of such expenses was £263 million (6.8% of the total). Some estimates place the average benefits of the whole programme to the City higher, with underpricing accounting for some 14% of the value of the sales and fees accounting for a further 5%.

The other, less direct and longer-term benefits to the City have been no less significant. The profitability of shares obtained through privatisation has a long-term component arising from the fact that privatised industries have frequently been shaped so that they remain monopolistic and are able to obtain a high rate of profit in future years. Those high profits have accrued on the shares held by capital market institutions such as pension funds and insurance funds. Moreover, before the City would regard them as suitable financial investments the enterprises' balance sheets were restructured by the state writing-off some £15 billion of debt to the Exchequer. Lastly, other elements that could place future profits at risk, such as the electricity industry's nuclear programme, were removed from privatisation packages.

Another long-term structural effect of privatisation was on international finance. The conversion of national, state-run assets into private, financial assets contributed to the internationalisation of finance because shares in privatised utilities companies were designed to attract foreign investors: shares in the largest privatised enterprises are traded on stock exchanges around the globe. One or two privatisations (British Aerospace and British Airways) involved restrictions on the proportion of shares foreign investors could own but these were rather anachronistic exceptions, since privatisation has otherwise been an important element in stimulating international movements of capital and strengthening the City as an international centre.

The sale of municipal housing provided a different type of long-term contribution to the financial system from that made by the City's dealing in the shares of formerly public enterprises. Perhaps more than in other countries the British credit system rests on collateral in the form of real estate, so the privatisation of quantities of publicly owned housing released a significant volume of real assets that could act as the long-term basis for an expansion of financial business. As a result of the 1980 *Housing Act* and subsequent legislation that gave municipal tenants the 'right to buy' their residences (at discounts which in some cases were up to 70% of the notional market price), almost 1.5 million dwellings were sold during the 1980s. The financial dimension of this privatisation of public assets was an expansion of mortgage lending to fund individuals' purchases. This formed part of the growth of personal debt that has marked the transformation of the financial system and the institutions' attempts to profit from the interest on personal retail credit (similar to the growth of credit-card debt and personal loans of various types). Mortgages for the purchase of 1.5 million privatised dwellings contributed significantly to the growth in the total number of mortgages from 5.5 million in 1981 to 8.0 million in 1990.

We noted above that the financialisation of assets in order to transfer them from public to private ownership did appear to achieve an expansion of private ownership of equities and real estate, although the expansion of share ownership was more apparent than real. To assess the success or failure of the strategy in broad terms it is necessary to examine the increase in both assets and debt and not just the gross acquisition of private assets. Alongside the much publicised growth in private assets, Thatcher's deregulation strategy actively conspired to increase private-sector debt by fomenting competition between lenders, while the financialisation and privatisation of public assets increased private-sector debt to finance their purchase (especially in the form of mortgages to buy the municipal housing). The rapid expansion of debt has introduced a new element of fragility and potential instability into British economic affairs. For example, the net borrowings of industrial and commercial companies increased almost four-fold between the year ends of 1982 and 1990, and this has been a strong contributory factor to the recent spate of record insolvencies. The starkest illustration of the growth of personal-sector debt is the increase in the number of repossessions of people's homes by creditors following the privatisation of public-sector housing. Repossessions of all properties by building societies rose from 6000 in 1982 to 23000 in 1990, and mortgage lenders expect to repossess as many as 80000 in 1991. This expansion of debt greatly increases the risks borne by firms and individuals, irrespective of whether it is called high gearing or overborrowing. If the financialisation and privatisation of national wealth has aimed to create a 'property-owning democracy', equally deregulation has ensured that it is one based on the systematic insecurity that high gearing invariably generates. In the long term, that gearing has weakened the foundations of the financial system itself, especially since its collateral is based upon unsustainable real estate values.

What were the effects of this sale of the family silver? It did roll back the state to a significant extent but that is not the same as fulfilling the claims made for private ownership, since the privatised enterprises have been protected from the full force of competition. This is true even with respect to capital market discipline, since the managements of privatised enterprises have not been subjected to the threat of takeover or shareholder revolts. Privatisation has not succeeded in creating a stable expansion of property ownership but rather has contributed significantly to the increased inequality in wealth distribution that has marked the Thatcher era. However, the third objective of privatisation, benefiting the City, was realised in the short term although the long-term benefits are less secure.

The International Position and Prospects in Post-1992 Europe

We have shown that the Thatcher governments' economic strategy had the interests of finance at its core and, within that, the City's aim of strengthening its international position in competition with other financial centres had special prominence. We have shown that the Tories' strategy for finance failed to achieve their goals, including the latter one: surprisingly, London has failed to attain a secure lead over its rivals and has even lost its leading position in international banking. As a result, London begins the 1990s as a regional, European financial centre rather than as the leading world financial centre. Even within the European Community it reigns supreme only in banking markets, for it now faces stiff challenges from both Paris and Frankfurt in derivatives, securities and even some insurance markets. The real test of Thatcher's policies to strengthen the City will lie in Europe and especially in post-1992 Europe. What are the prospects for London under the 1992 European Financial Area (EFA) proposals?

The 1992 programme involves perhaps the most fundamental set of deregulatory proposals ever formulated for a group of advanced economies. Like internationalisation, it is a major exogenous development that has to be considered in any discussion of the future role of global finance and the City's position within the European time zone. Essentially, the major purpose of the 1992 proposals is to increase the internationalisation and centralisation of capital within the European Community so that EC-based capital can compete with its US and Japanese counterparts (although other objectives such as increasing consumer choice are emphasised in the official documents). Mrs Thatcher's financial policies (abolition of exchange controls, deregulation and privatisation) in fact prefigured many of the major 1992 proposals and have neatly dovetailed into the EFA programme. The aim of the EFA proposals is to create a common market in financial services by 1992 by means of basic harmonisation of the rules and operations of financial intermediaries and markets. They are being implemented by means of EC Directives addressed to member states which are obliged to adapt their national systems of legislation accordingly. About 50 of the 300 Directives relating to 1992 concern financial services and about one-half of these had been implemented by early 1991.

The idea of basic harmonisation is that market forces will compel member states to deregulate their supervisory systems down to the basic EC level, since firms and business will gravitate towards the least regulated regimes. In practice, harmonisation is designed to operate on the basis of the two principles of mutual recognition and home-country supervision. The first means that national authorisations and controls over financial intermediaries would be mutually recognised by all the member states, while the second implies that the supervisory authority of an intermediary's domicile would have controlling competence throughout the EC.

Although the major impact of the 1992 programme will be felt mainly during the 1990s, the programme has already started with the abolition of exchange controls in most member states and the approval of some Directives. The Second Banking Directive (SBD), adopted by the EC Council in December 1989, aims to harmonise laws and rules for the free operation of credit institutions across the Community. It establishes the 'single licence' principle: once a credit institution is authorised by its home supervisor it can internationalise across the Community on either a services basis—it has freedom to export its services to all EC member states—or an establishment basis—it can branch freely throughout the Community. It operates on the basis of a weak version of reciprocity: non-EC banks are allowed to establish in the EC on the basis of some access to their (non-EC) markets. It defines legitimate banking activities in line with the universal banking model by allowing a broad range of activities as practiced by German banks and first analysed by Hilferding. This is likely to give German banks a competitive edge over their rivals in the 1990s, especially since their business finance record appears to make them potentially attractive to business customers.

The banking Directives have led to increased international centralisation of banking capital which thus far has assumed the form of cross-participations within the European Community rather than cross-border mergers. The takeover of Morgan Grenfell by Deutsche Bank is an exception but it met with Tory approval as another instance of the market mechanism in operation. The banking Directives have increased links between banks and insurance companies, especially on the continent. This has been called *allfinanz* in Germany (for example, the cross-participations between the largest insurer, Allianz, and the second bank, Dresdner) and *bancassurance* in France. The overall effect is that the Directives are likely to increase concentration in the top echelons of banking and insurance. One of the imponderables is how UK-based banks and insurance companies will compete in this new environment, since their internationalisation strategies within Europe in the past have a relatively poor track record.

Another threat to London as the leading EC centre for international banking comes from a contradiction within Thatcher's overall financial project. On one hand, the antagonism of successive Thatcher administrations towards Europe undermined their goal of enhancing the City's international competitiveness. Mrs Thatcher's opposition to Economic and Monetary Union and her misguided conception of British sovereignty have undermined the City's chances of being the location for a future

European central bank. The siting of this central bank, together with its influence on the operation of European monetary policy in future, is likely to be crucial in determining the preeminence of financial centres within the Community in the 1990s. On the other hand, Mrs Thatcher's deregulatory policies did give London a first-mover advantage in several respects. Unfortunately, from the City's point of view, the 1992 programme seems likely to hasten the process of competitive deregulation and thereby undermine London's competitive edge in some European markets. This illustrates the short-term and fragile nature of the benefits that accrued to the British economy from the application of Thatcherite deregulation to financial markets.

The future shape of securities markets within Europe is much more uncertain, partly due to competitive deregulation as London's rivals follow its 'Big Bang' lead and partly due to a basic conflict of interest between London and its continental rivals over the appropriate future trading structure within Europe. London is pushing for a single licence in securities markets based on the SBD and for the extension of its SEAQ International trading system to other European exchanges, which would consolidate its post-'Big Bang' lead in securities markets (the delays in implementing its electronic settlements system (TAURUS) notwithstanding). The Paris Bourse and some other continental exchanges had been advocating an alternative strategy consisting of a linked network of national exchanges in which each exchange would have a Euro-tier for quoting the stock prices of leading European multinational companies. If adopted, this strategy would undermine the SEAQ International system and give continental exchanges a better chance of competing with London on a more equal footing. At the end of 1991, however, stalemate has been reached and the integration of European stock exchanges remains some distance away.

Finance, Economic Decline and Alternatives

We have argued that the Thatcherite financial strategy can by and large be judged a failure. Monetary discipline through control of the money supply failed dismally, and the long struggle to replace it with a discipline based on exchange-rate targets caused instability and problems that still persist. With regard to the financialisation of national wealth to enable a growth in private wealth ownership, there has been a major shift of assets out of public ownership but the structure of private-sector net wealth has not strengthened. The problem is indicated by the growth of personal and corporate debt, the low personal savings ratio and the dependence of private-sector wealth on unsustainable valuation of real estate. At the outset of the Thatcher era the City had already established itself as the leading international centre for banking, eurobonds and international insurance. Deregulation intially served to enhance the

City's lead but as the decade proceeded other centres began to challenge the City's supremacy in several markets; although London currently remains Europe's leading financial centre, even that regional lead is under threat in several categories of business. The losses being incurred by British banks and insurers, the redundancies in financial firms of all types, the collapse of the real-estate market upon which much of the asset base of Britain's financial system depends, all suggest that Thatcher has not succeeded in putting the City in the favourable position it might have desired to meet that challenge.

However, the overall judgment on financial policy has to be much broader than whether it achieved the goals the Tories set themselves, for those goals were in line with the City's own views and interests; they, themselves, have to be put in the context of the economy as a whole. From that perspective, the fundamental issue facing financial policy at the end of the 1970s was whether Britain's system could be restructured to create a framework in which the financial institutions and markets would contribute to a transformation of the economy's productive base. Over previous years the view had gained support that Britain's financiers used criteria that were too short term, that they were concerned with asset valuations at the expense of production conditions and with the liquidation value of collateral rather than the going-concern value of a firm, that they were unwilling to fund research and development, and that their historical interest in international portfolio investment and government debt had distorted the criteria they used for industrial financing. The financial strategy adopted by the Thatcher administrations did not seriously attempt to address those problems but instead, by adopting the City's own objectives, reinforced the effective separation between the City and industrial regeneration.

However, right-wing ideologists could claim that the three main elements of the financial strategy would assist industrial restructuring as well as meeting the financial objectives we have examined. The monetary rule of the MTFS was claimed to be industry-friendly because it would provide a climate of predictable financial stability to replace the stop–go cycle; deregulation would strengthen industry through increasing international competition for capital; and privatisation would strengthen the economy by introducing efficiency criteria into privatised utilities. In fact, however, those policies, introduced because of the City's objectives, had harmful rather than beneficial effects on industry. The tight money of the MTFS contributed to the dismantling of a large part of manufacturing industry instead of its regeneration; financial deregulation fuelled both a credit boom and an increase in international finance that, between them, created a high level of company indebtedness without a change in the markets' and banks' short-termism and lack of interest in production development; and privatisation of utilities has not led to a planned improvement of the infrastructure.

To what extent was the unhappy experience of the past decade due to Tory policies? Would a Labour government have made any difference or were the policies the inevitable result of underlying trends? As noted above, the underlying trends of internationalisation made some form of deregulation inevitable if the City was to maintain its international role; but a radical reforming government could have chosen the quite different, domestically oriented, path of restructuring finance so that it worked in partnership with private and public enterprises to finance a long-term regeneration of production. The financialisation and privatisation of public assets was not inevitable; instead, a Labour government could have built a new industrial strategy on the basis of a revitalised public sector. And, although Labour governments in 1967 and 1976 had adopted early, limited forms of monetarism, the attempt to use financial and monetary policy alone to achieve macroeconomic balance was a specifically Tory policy linked to their complete rejection of corporatist and Keynesian arrangements. Thatcher's policies for finance, therefore, were not inevitable, but by adopting them the Conservatives both prolonged industry's problems and, to a significant extent, failed to achieve their own aims, the objectives of the City itself.

Comment

UK Monetary Policy in the 1980s

Mića Panić

No UK government since World War II has attached so much importance to monetary policy as the Conservative governments led by Mrs Thatcher. Unfortunately, no other government has pursued it with such a combination of dogmatism, ignorance and downright incompetence. Nothing illustrates this better than the three extraordinary policy blunders in the 1980s.

First, one of the most important policy decisions taken by the Thatcher government, within months of taking office, was to abolish all exchange controls in October 1979. The wisdom of this decision can be argued. What is indisputable, however, is the fact that its most important consequence was to establish an even closer link between UK and foreign financial policies and behaviour. This meant two things: the country lost the ability to pursue an independent monetary policy, and quantitative monetary aggregates became even less reliable as an indicator of the government's macroeconomic policy stance than before (Panić, 1982). Yet 6 months after abolishing exchange controls the government proudly unveiled its medium-term financial strategy (MTFS) which proclaimed its determination to follow an independent monetary policy irrespective of the policies pursued by other major industrial countries. Moreover, success was to be judged according to the containment of money-supply growth within rigidly defined targets.

The result was the biggest slump in output and increase in unemployment since the 1930s, with the fall in output at the beginning of the 1980s exceeding that during the Great Depression. Monetary and fiscal policies were tightened to bring money-supply growth within the predetermined targets. However, the more this was done, the more the money supply expanded above its target, as foreign funds moved into sterling to profit from high interest rates in the UK relative to those prevailing in other countries. With the exchange rate appreciating and domestic demand stagnant, tens of thousands of enterprises folded, especially in the manufacturing sector, and hundreds of thousands of people lost their jobs—many of them permanently. The economy has yet to make up for the loss of its productive potential during this period.

The Government played down these developments by arguing that this was nothing more than the effect of an important structural adjustment in the economy: from manufacturing to services, especially financial services, in which the UK enjoyed important comparative advantages. Yet as Coakley and Harris's chapter points out, the relative importance of London as a financial centre also declined during the 1980s. This is hardly surprising as, historically, great financial centres have always been located in the most successful, dominant economies of their time—moving from country to country with the passing of economic supremacy. The reason for this is quite simply that there is a strong interdependence between the real and financial sectors of any economy. A large, highly competitive and rapidly growing real sector not only generates a large volume of savings but also requires a large financial sector to intermediate between savers and investors, as well as to satisfy their growing diversity of needs and preferences. Hence, by destroying a far from insignificant part of the real sector, the Government's policies also weakened the UK financial sector and, thus, the City of London.

Second, it is impossible to have a genuinely single market in Europe if there are a number of independently managed floating currencies. Even with no barriers to trade or factor movements, the risk and uncertainties would be too high for the market to be truly unified (Panić, 1991). Yet Mrs Thatcher's governments were consistently opposed to the idea of European Monetary Union, refusing even to join the European Exchange Rate Mechanism (ERM) until October 1990. In this the government not only jeopardised the creation of a single European market, which it supported strongly, but also risked serious losses in UK economic welfare, as the uncertainty about sterling's position relative to that of other EC currencies made it more attractive for firms—both in manufacturing and in services—to expand and modernise their operations in Community countries other than the UK.

Finally, when the Government was forced by the business community to recognise the potential cost of its insistence on an imaginary monetary independence and join the ERM in October 1990 it did so at what was clearly too high an exchange rate. The pound was fixed to the Deutschemark at the rate prevailing at the time, which reflected neither the relative competitive strength of the two economies nor the real purchasing power of the two currencies, but rather the fact that UK monetary policy was much tighter—because of its high rate of inflation—than those of other major industrial countries. Moreover, given the weakness of the UK economy compared with that of Germany, this rate could be sustained only by persisting with high interest rates to cover the risk premium, attract foreign capital and thus prevent a devaluation of sterling. The result was the second old-fashioned economic slump in 10 years—something no other major country has experienced.

For all these reasons, the extraordinary tale of UK monetary policy from 1979–1992 is likely to be recounted in economic textbooks for years to come as a classic example of how not to pursue such a policy.

3

Does Britain's Balance of Payments Matter Any More?

Ken Coutts and Wynne Godley

Over the past 20 years we have in many articles pointed to the deep-seated problem of Britain's poor international competitiveness, which has increasingly constrained the long-term growth of the economy and the ability to maintain high levels of employment. We believe that these warnings have been fully vindicated by subsequent events. Since 1979 the average growth of GDP has been the lowest in the postwar period, characterised by two recessions and one boom, and unemployment has increased by over a million. Yet the lesson of poor trade performance has not been learned and public discussion of macroeconomic policy tends to ignore the balance of payments altogether. With free capital movements current account deficits are considered of little importance, and (it is sometimes supposed) when we have a common currency it will entirely cease to matter.

We believe that these arguments are profoundly wrong. No matter what the system of capital movements or the currency regime, the prosperity of any district, region or nation depends ultimately upon exports rising fast enough to pay for the imports it requires.

In this chapter we discuss the performance of the balance of payments since 1979 and examine the arguments put forward by government ministers and others that it ceased to be an effective constraint on the conduct of policy during this period. We argue that notwithstanding the apparent strength of our external payments and balance sheet, the situation worsened markedly during the 1980s, so that any recovery from 1992 fast enough to reverse and subsequently bring down unemployment will be accompanied by unsustainable deficits unless policies are addressed to the problem of poor competitiveness in home markets and abroad.

Economic Policy since 1979

The Conservative government which took office in 1979 had ambitious plans to improve Britain's economic performance by a combination of macroeconomic and microeconomic policies. The reduction of inflation to a low and sustainable rate was the first priority of macroeconomic policy. At first this was expressed in quantitative monetary targets as part of the medium-term financial strategy (MTFS) but after 1981 this policy was gradually abandoned after conspicuous failure to meet the announced money-supply targets. Expenditure, taxation and interest-rate decisions were taken instead to manage aggregate demand with the objective of low and stable inflation, although for the period as a whole with only temporary success. The state was to be rolled back by selling public-sector assets, waste was to be eliminated in public spending, and public expenditure as a share of GDP was to be progressively reduced. The burden of taxation was to be shifted from direct to indirect taxes.

Prominent among microeconomic policies was the government's trade union legislation to weaken the effective use of strikes as a bargaining weapon in pay disputes, to make dismissal easier and to give management more authority to reorganise working practices. Incentives were to be provided by reductions in personal and corporate taxation, by the encouragement of small businesses and self-employment, and generally by promoting an 'enterprise culture' to stimulate competitiveness. The strong anti-inflationary stance which induced the post-1979 recession and real exchange-rate appreciation introduced a tougher competitive atmosphere, particularly for manufacturing firms exposed to foreign competition. A massive shake-out of labour resulted: many firms were forced to close and much capacity was scrapped. After the 17% fall in manufacturing production between the second quarter of 1979 and the first quarter of 1981, output began a long, slow recovery, while labour productivity began to grow unusually rapidly from 1981. The government emphasised that from a smaller base manufacturing was becoming more efficient and better able to compete internationally.

When the surplus of trade in manufactures continued to dwindle and turned negative in 1983, an alternative argument became fashionable, that manufacturing was becoming less important to Britain's external trade. With the removal of exchange controls and the deregulation of financial markets, trade in financial services were supposed to be the dynamic and buoyant sector of growth during the 1980s. However, earnings from financial services, although they increased sharply between 1979 and 1986, have since been a relatively stagnant component of net foreign exchange earnings.

According to many economists the balance of payments ceased to be a constraint, actual or potential, on macroeconomic policy during the 1980s. The current account went firmly into surplus after 1979 because

of the rapid build-up of North Sea oil revenues and a sharp drop in
the demand for imports induced by the 2-year drop in GDP. It remained
in surplus until after 1986 although output began to recover in the
second half of 1981, at first sluggishly, and unemployment continued
to rise until the second quarter of 1986. Were it not, according to this
sanguine view, for mistakes in macroeconomic policy—the notorious
Lawson 'blip'—the balance of payments would not have been a problem
at all. Even the large deficits of 1989–1990 were easily accommodated
without pressure on the exchange rate. The government's concern was
the rise in the inflation rate back towards 10%, which brought the
return of tough monetary policy begun by Mr Lawson and continued
by Mr Major. In the government's view the onset of the second recession
in 10 years with unemployment back above 2 million and rising towards
3 million in 1992, is the necessary cost of reducing inflation by six
percentage points. The current account deficits were the complementary
symptoms of a boom which had become excessive, but were not
important in their own right.

We believe that this interpretation of the balance of payments position
in the last decade is profoundly mistaken. In our view there are two
principles of fundamental importance to economies which are highly
integrated into international trade and these must be clearly understood.
First, in the medium term the warranted growth rate of the economy
depends on the growth rate of exports relative to the share of imports
in home demand; growth of output at the warranted rate in the medium
term will imply that exports (and other net income) are paying for
imports. Second, if the growth rate of the economy necessary to
maintain employment in the medium term is greater than the rate
warranted by foreign trade performance, then growing trade deficits
will be generated which will be unsustainable because they will lead
inexorably to a rising ratio of debt to GDP; at some stage the rising
burden of servicing the debt will require the economy to generate large
trade surpluses so that a net transfer of resources pays the interest on
accumulated borrowing. Alternatively, the economy will be trapped in
a syndrome of slow growth and unemployment will rise from one
business cycle to the next.

It is widely believed that the British economy experienced a major
supply-side improvement during the 1980s, and that the emergence of
large balance of payments deficits in 1988 and 1989 was the result of a
failure to control aggregate demand. We take the view that so far as
trade performance is concerned, any growth of output over the 1980s
which was high enough to bring unemployment down to the levels of
1979, would have caused the balance of payments to go into deficit
with roughly the same effect on the balance of trade as actually occurred.
While undoubtedly demand grew too fast after 1987, a steady growth
of demand no higher than productive potential would not have avoided
large external deficits.

As Figure 3.1 indicates, while the overall current account was in surplus until after 1986 with the oil balance making an important contribution, this masked a steady but progressive deterioration in the balance of trade on manufactures through the whole period. In 1979 the manufacturing balance was in surplus by 1.5% of GDP; by 1989 it was in deficit by 3.5% of GDP. The manufacturing balance has deteriorated almost continuously over the past 30 years. In times of recession, as in 1979 and 1991, the ratio of imports to home demand has slowed, but the trend of imports has continued to be faster than that of exports.

There is some econometric evidence that export performance was better, given relative prices and world demand, during the 1980s than in the 1960s or 1970s (Landesmann and Snell, 1989). The manufacturing export firms which survived the 1979–1981 recession may have emerged with more competitive determination to expand export markets. Some sectors of manufacturing, such as chemicals, pharmaceuticals and aerospace, continued to be strong in international trade. As manufactur-

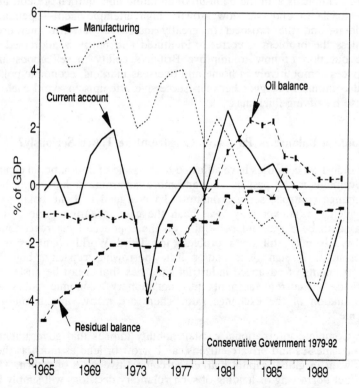

Figure 3.1. The current account and its main components 1965–1991.

ing output recovered slowly, some part of their sales and those of new entrants would be devoted to exports. However, any discernable improvement in export performance appears to have been counter-balanced by the continued rapid growth of imports in home markets, so that the balance of trade in manufactures continued to decline. The record of investment, training and expenditure on research and development in manufacturing during the 1980s was poor. When demand began to expand rapidly in 1987 and manufacturing output increased sharply, serious shortages of capacity and in skills emerged in 1989. Where supply-side policies should have had some discernable macroeconomic effect on manufacturing performance, the effects seem to have been insufficient to reverse the long-standing decline.

Although the scale of the 1991 recession has cut the manufacturing deficit (and there was a well-publicised surplus in July 1991), when the economy begins to make a modest recovery in output, it will do so this time from a position of a deficit in manufactures and an overall current account deficit of almost £5 billion, compared with a surplus of an equivalent magnitude in 1981. We are between the Charybdis of chronic external deficits with the build-up of an intolerable burden of debt, and the Scylla of endemic slow growth, high unemployment—open and hidden—and the prospect of greatly increased outward migration. Unless the problem is correctly identified and policy is addressed to the question of how to improve Britain's ability to sell goods and services competitively in home and overseas markets, economic policy will continue to stagger between successive attempts to avoid each of these horrifying dilemmas.

Should a Balance of Payments Constraint be Taken Seriously?

As industrial countries have adjusted to the scale of international capital movements in the past decade, and more governments have abolished exchange controls, some economists have argued that the balance of payments, whatever may have been the case in earlier periods, has ceased to be a relevant constraint on the conduct of macroeconomic policy. It may still be a problem for Third World countries with substantial foreign debt and/or little borrowing capacity, but the governments of advanced industrial countries should not be misled by deficits on current account into deflationary economic policy or devaluation of the exchange rate. There are many variants on this theme.

(1) Complete international capital mobility implies that governments, businesses and private citizens can borrow or lend as much as they want in global capital markets at competitive rates of return. The net borrowing or lending of such voluntary decisions will simply be the counterpart of any current account deficit or surplus.

(2) A corollary of (1) above is that governments should limit their concern to public-sector borrowing. An external deficit is the business of private firms and citizens who wish to undertake transactions in borrowing or lending. It matters to them that interest and capital will have to be repaid. If they make excessive overseas borrowing they may suffer the fate of insolvency, but the process is self-correcting and does not concern governments or other private citizens. This view was argued forcefully by Nigel Lawson in 1989 when the public-sector accounts were in surplus but the current account was over £20 billion in deficit.

(3) The current account deficits after 1986 are the temporary consequences of changes in private saving behaviour which are self-correcting. For UK consumers the deregulation of credit markets for housing and personal finance provided an opportunity to relax a liquidity constraint. Rational consumers were able to redistribute the intertemporal pattern of their expenditure and this led to a fall in the savings ratio. Since rational consumers know that additional borrowing will have to be repaid, the future savings ratio will increase and with it the external deficits will fall.

(4) A current account deficit is the incidental consequence of inward investment seeking a higher or safer return on capital. It is a sign of the strength of underlying profitable investment opportunities, not of weakness in foreign trade.

(5) There is no important difference in trade between Sussex and Normandy, and between Sussex and more distant Yorkshire, except that foreign trade may involve a foreign exchange risk. Since no-one worries about trade between regions within a common currency (or even attempts to measure it), once the UK joins a full monetary union with its EC partners, the 'problem' will disappear entirely.

It is indeed the case that capital mobility makes much more flexible the finance of temporary external payments deficits, in the sense that governments do not have to arrange explicit loans with central banks or negotiate standby loans with the IMF. It will be sufficient, should the government wish to maintain a steady exchange rate, for it to adjust domestic interest rates so as to attract an inflow of capital commensurate with the current account deficit. The private firms or citizens involved in such borrowing will have been motivated by relative rates of return, relative risk and so on, and not with the financing of a trade deficit.

However, while a sustained trade deficit may at some stage put downward pressure on the exchange rate or cause domestic interest rates to rise, it is the need to service the accumulating debt which remains the effective constraint on the ability to run deficits. While it may be banal to state that debt cannot grow indefinitely relative to income, whether of a private citizen or of a nation, at some point action must be taken to stabilise the debt. At this stage *the trade balance* will have to move into surplus, to provide the real resource transfer with which to service the interest on the debt and if possible repay capital. For a nation in this situation the cost falls on its citizens in terms of lost output and unemployment, not just on private agents who may have undertaken risky borrowing. If this argument is accepted, the force of points (1) and (2) above is lost. The ultimate 'self-correcting' mechanism for excessive borrowing will be all the more costly for private citizens, the longer trade deficits are ignored.

Point (3) is slightly different because it argues that the emergence of the trade deficit in 1986 was a temporary consequence of a stock adjustment where consumers were satisfying their intertemporal budget by merely reallocating the time profile of consumption: when the adjustment is complete, the trade deficit will be reversed. Although the financial deregulation and rapid growth in the demand for credit which followed may be characterised as a largely temporary reduction in personal savings, which certainly made a major contribution to the rapid growth of demand, this does not, of itself, have to imply any particular deterioration of the trade balance. If consumers devoted all of their increased expenditure to domestically produced goods, or exports increased in line with consumers' appetite for imported goods, the financial balances of the corporate sector and the government would rise by the extent of the fall in personal savings, and would leave national savings unchanged. The strategic question remains whether a growth of demand, *however this came about*, which was large enough to reduce unemployment, would have caused a large deficit to emerge in the second half of the 1980s. Our view remains that given the poor underlying performance of manufacturing and the lack of alternative buoyant overseas earnings growth, an unsustainable deficit would have emerged.

The argument that the huge deficits of 1988–1990 were a reflection of the strong confidence of the international community in profitable capital formation is difficult to believe. There are some examples of direct investment in the UK, such as by Japanese car manufacturers, which will be of long-term importance for employment and trade with our EC partners. However, UK firms also invested heavily overseas and the balance of portfolio investment during the 1980s was heavily outward. Most inward capital flows were in response to the rise in UK interest rates. In general, nations may gain long-term benefits from a period of direct inward investment, in building up their productive capacity, and will in the interim run counterpart current account deficits. However, such investments will have to be profitable and eventually generate enough exports to pay for the amortisation, profits and interest associated with the investment.

What finally of the argument that a region within a common currency area cannot have a balance of payments problem? (Mr Samuel Brittan is a well-known exponent of the essential irrelevance of the balance of payments as a guide to macroeconomic policy; see *Financial Times*, 12 September 1991.) One significant difference between regional trade and international trade is that within a national economy a region's trade deficit can be automatically financed by fiscal transfers. Central government provision of common services in health, education, social security, transport and so on helps to ameliorate the problems of a region with a chronic tendency to import more tradeables than it can export to other regions or abroad. Were it not for such transfers, a region with poor trade performance which could not improve its competitiveness would experience high unemployment and migration of its population to more prosperous areas. The UK will cease to have an explicit balance of payments to finance when it enters full monetary union, but it will not thereby have disposed of its balance of payments problem, because its prosperity will continue to depend upon the ability to trade goods and services successfully, both within the single European market and to the world. It is for this reason that governments which are concerned to see economic prosperity widely dispersed throughout the EC should take steps to promote regional policy and should encourage the development of fiscal equalisation at the EC level.

Conclusions

During the 1980s the government claimed that it had successfully implemented a supply-side programme of measures to encourage an efficient and competitive economy. By the end of the decade, that claim stood in sharp contrast to the rise in unemployment of over one million—despite a deterioration in the balance of payments—with only a modest reduction in inflation to show by way of macroeconomic achievement. Trade performance in home and overseas markets is of crucial importance to Britain's prosperity in the 1990s and this must not be veiled by claims that trade deficits can be allowed to persist without serious consequence, or that they are self-correcting without the 'nanny state' interfering. There are by now enough examples, both in the Third World and amongst advanced industrial economies, of nations which are paying a heavy price for ignoring the warnings.

Comment

The Re-emergence of the Balance of Payments Constraint

John McCombie and Tony Thirlwall

Governments generally set themselves at least four macroeconomic goals by which economic performance is then judged: low levels of unemployment; fast growth; stable prices; and balance of payments equilibrium on current account, which is regarded as an intermediate objective or a necessary condition for the attainment of the other three. Balance of payments deficits typically put downward pressure on exchange rates, which is inflationary, and require high interest rates to finance them, which leads to slower growth and rising unemployment. These objectives may conflict: low unemployment conflicts with stable prices because it brings wage pressures; fast growth and low unemployment conflict with balance of payments equilibrium because increasing pressure of demand leads *pari passu* to a rising level of imports, while exports are determined largely exogenously by the level of world activity. In the UK these trade-offs are worse than at any time since 1950. This is the economic legacy of the Thatcher years.

First, the unemployment–inflation trade-off is worse. Four per cent inflation was compatible with less than 250 000 unemployed in the 1950s; 500 000 in the late 1960s; 1.5 million in the 1970s; and today it requires close to 3 million.

Second, the unemployment–balance of payments trade-off is worse. In the 1950s and 1960s, balance of payments equilibrium was compatible with roughly 500 000 unemployed. In the 1970s, 1 million unemployed were required. Today the position is so weak that equilibrium probably requires at least 3 million unemployed.

Third, the economic growth–balance of payments trade-off is worse, which is illustrated in Figure 3A.1, measuring the balance of payments position (as a percentage of GDP) on the vertical axis and the growth of output (GDP) on the horizontal axis. Before 1968, there was a well-defined trade-off so that above approximately 3% growth the balance of payments deteriorated, and below that a surplus developed. Since then, the relationship has steadily worsened and drifted towards the

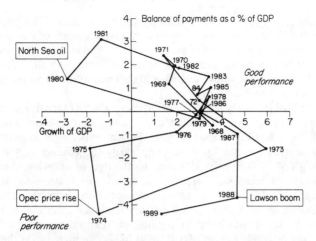

Figure 3A.1. The economic growth–balance of payments trade-off 1968–1989. Growth of GDP plotted against balance of payments as a percentage of GDP.

bottom left of the graph. There was a short-lived improvement in the trade-off after the 1967 devaluation; it then deteriorated when oil prices quadrupled in the early 1970s, and improved again when Britain became a net oil exporter in the early 1980s.

Unfortunately, during the early 1980s, the increased growth potential was not realised with the exchange rate kept high by a tight fiscal and monetary policy, so that between 1979 and 1981 investment contracted by 28% and manufacturing output by 15%. The contraction in domestic demand during this period, together with the coming onstream of substantial oil revenues, gave the UK a large balance of payments surplus, so that there was a temptation to consider balance of payments problems a thing of the past. However, with the subsequent Lawson boom, a current account deficit of about 1% of GDP re-emerged in 1987. This reached nearly 4% in 1989 before the severe recession that commenced in 1989 began to reduce it. The UK is once again in the grip of a balance of payments constraint that plagued it throughout the 1950s, 1960s and 1970s.

We mean by the term 'balance of payments constraint' that a country's performance in external markets, and the response of the world financial markets to this performance, constrain the growth of the economy to a rate which is below that which internal conditions (such as the rate of unemployment and capacity utilisation) would warrant. In the 1950s and 1960s this was expressed in 'stop–go' policies when consumption-led booms were brought to an abrupt end by balance of payments crises. Consequently, the trend rate of growth of output was largely determined by the performance of exports and was arguably below the maximum growth of potential GDP during these years. (The maximum growth potential is not an exogenously given datum but is partly a function of the actual growth rate. This is because a faster growth of output leads to a faster growth of productivity through the 'Verdoorn effect' which is caused *inter alia* by a higher rate of induced investment and of induced technical progress.)

For much of the early postwar period there was an extensive discussion as to whether or not the balance of payments constraint could be relieved by a flexible exchange rate. Recent experience suggests that while a devaluation can improve temporarily the balance of payments *for any given growth rate*, it seems ineffective in allowing the trend growth rate to increase. There are a number of reasons for this. In particular, it is difficult for a nominal depreciation to be converted into a real depreciation if there is inflationary feedback from higher import prices to higher domestic prices because of 'real wage resistance'. This is a distinct possibility especially if, as is likely, an increase in the trend rate of growth requires a *continuous* depreciation of the currency.

The 1980s saw swings in effective exchange rates of a number of countries that made the devaluations of the 1960s and early 1970s seem small by comparison. Nevertheless, such variations in effective exchange rates had little effect on the real economies; the large surpluses and deficits persisted despite large changes in exchange rates. This is because relative price changes and price elasticities of demand have become less important in determining trade patterns and the balance of payments. Manufactured goods have become more differentiated and nonprice competition has become the most important factor in determining a country's success in overseas markets. Exporting firms which operate in oligopolistic markets 'price to the market' and maintain their relative prices constant in overseas markets in the face of exchange rate changes. Firms are also unlikely to increase their exports if they believe that the depreciation of the currency is likely to be short-lived. The large swings in exchange rates in the 1980s are more likely to have been interpreted as the temporary consequences of short-term capital flows or speculative bubbles than were earlier, smaller exchange rate changes.

David Turner (1988) of the Warwick University Macroeconomic Modelling Bureau used the NIESR and LBS forecasting models to determine the UK's present growth rate consistent with balance of payments equilibrium. He found that 'on plausible assumptions, principally concerning how fast world trade is likely to expand, and on the further critical assumption that there is no change in the competitiveness of exports or imports, the LBS and NIESR models both suggest that UK growth can average no more than 1% per annum over the medium term if there is to be no further deterioration in the current account'. Turner also considered the extent to which the balance of payments equilibrium growth could be raised through a devaluation. He showed that, in order for the growth rate to be raised by approximately one percentage point to 2% per annum for a 5-year period, there would have to be a devaluation of sterling of 20–30% (after 5 years, the price advantage obtained by the devaluation would have been largely eroded by the resulting domestic inflation). A corollary of this is that for the trend growth rate to be raised above 1% per annum, there would have to be a sustained depreciation of the exchange rate by several per cent per annum, which is incompatible with membership of the Exchange Rate Mechanism.

An interesting question, not examined by Turner, is the extent to which the balance of payments constraint could be relaxed if there were some form of incomes policy that prevented domestic costs eventually increasing to offset the initial devaluation. We are not sanguine that this would provide a *long-term* solution to the UK's balance of payments problems. There is increasing evidence that it is nonprice competition that matters in international trade. As Posner and Steer (1979) concluded in their survey of competition in international trade:

> Historically there is no doubt that nonprice influences have dominated—the proportion of the total change they 'explain' is an order of magnitude greater than the explanatory power of price competitiveness.

An improvement in price competitiveness may provide the UK with a temporary breathing space. However, there is the danger that this would remove the incentive for British managers to improve nonprice competitiveness and to develop the high-technology products for which world demand is growing most rapidly, i.e. for which there is a high world income elasticity of demand for exports. Moreover, to the extent that price elasticities are higher for the more basic homogenous commodities, a decline in the growth of relative unit labour costs may actually induce British manufacturers to trade downmarket even more than at present—i.e. to produce those goods that are subject to increasing competition from the low-cost newly industrialising countries.

The worsening trade-off between sustainable growth and the balance of payments is, in our view, a direct result of the policy of benign neglect towards both manufacturing industry and the state of the balance of payments. Manufacturing's crucial importance is that its output is potentially tradeable, whereas a large proportion of service output is not. As we argue in a forthcoming book (McCombie and Thirlwall, 1992), the UK's basic problem is that the income elasticity of demand for exports is very low, and the income elasticity of demand for manufactured imports is high. Both factors are symptoms of the same disease—weak nonprice competition in terms of the characteristics of goods produced and traded: their quality, sophistication, reliability and marketing. It is a serious indictment of Mrs Thatcher's period of office that, far from an economic transformation having taken place which would allow faster growth on a sustainable basis, the achievable growth rate has actually fallen because the balance of payments millstone weighs even more heavily. To improve Britain's growth prospects, which would also contribute to full employment with less inflationary pressure (at least from the exchange rate or high interest rates), requires urgent attention to Britain's tradeable goods sector. There is some evidence that the world income elasticity of demand for UK exports has risen since the early 1980s and this indicates that there may have been some improvement in the nonprice competitiveness of British exports (Landesmann and Snell, 1989). If this is correct, it suggests that the UK's balance of payments equilibrium growth rate may have risen to about 2% per annum (part of the increase in income elasticity may have been due to exceptional boom conditions in the US, where UK exports do particularly well). On the other hand, Turner (1988) found no evidence of an increase. Moreover, the balance of payments equilibrium growth rate will be reduced to the extent that the income elasticity of demand for imports may also have increased.

It has been argued by some commentators that there is no need to be concerned about the current account deficit, since the level of overseas borrowing is now determined by the private sector on the basis of commercial calculations about the costs and benefits of such a course of action. The only difference between borrowing domestically and abroad is that a risk premium is attached to the latter because of the volatility of the exchange rate. Any excessive borrowing overseas will be self-correcting as the cost of borrowing rises, with an increasing risk premium as the deficit grows. The problem with this argument is that the resulting adjustments are neither smooth nor gradual. As the ratio of overseas debt to GDP increases, the world financial markets become increasingly nervous about a collapse in the exchange rate and the consequent capital losses; once the exchange rate starts to fall, speculative actions are likely to be destabilising and would lead to a rapid fall in sterling, with the possibility of a vicious circle of inflation–depreciation occurring. The use of high interest rates to defend sterling has an externality effect of pushing the domestic economy into recession with adverse effects on investment and employment, even when there is existing unemployment. The period of floating exchange rates has seen a number of spectacular examples of the balance of payments constraining domestic macroeconomic policies. The sterling crisis of 1976 comes readily to mind, when the Labour government's attempt to reduce unemployment in the face of excess capacity foundered on the balance of payments deficit and the collapse of sterling. Between early March and early June 1976, the effective value of sterling fell by a little over 12%. Nevertheless, the government tried to keep interest rates low to encourage an expected increase in investment. As a result, sterling fell by a further 9% between early September and mid-November. The fall in the exchange rate eventually caused a *volte-face* in economic policy; the minimum lending rate was raised from 9% in April to 15% in November 1976 and severe cuts in the PSBR were agreed with the IMF. Other examples include the failure of the 'Mitterand experiment' in 1982 to boost growth and the problems of the Italian economy during 1980–1981. The 1980s have also shown that even the US is not immune from pressures engendered by a balance of payments deficit.

What of the argument that if Britain were to join a European Monetary Union with a single currency its balance of payments difficulties would vanish overnight? This is the view of Samuel Brittan:

> . . . the ability to dump the balance of payments problem once and for all is among the greatest but least emphasised advantages of Emu. (*Financial Times*, 27 June 1991.)

With a single currency, it is certainly true that there can be no 'foreign' exchange problem in the normal sense and no exchange rate to defend, but there would still be imbalances between exports and imports which would not be naturally or easily compensated for by private lending and investment, or, for that matter, by interregional fiscal transfers in a federal union. Those who say that balance of payments problems would disappear with a single currency draw the analogy with regions of a country that use a single currency. Certainly, we do not talk about balance of payments difficulties of Sussex, Yorkshire or even of Scotland or Wales. However, this does not mean that they do not exist. Any shortfall of a region's exports below its planned level of imports will be manifest in slow growth, high unemployment and depressed economic conditions in general. In other words, it is the level of income (and the rate of growth of output) that adjusts to bring the regional, as well as the national, balance of payments back into equilibrium. This is inevitable unless the structure of industry can be altered in the depressed regions to increase the share of high-technology industry for which the income elasticity of demand for exports is high; or price competitiveness is improved through subsidies or a fall in real wages; or the region receives capital inflows in the form of private-sector lending or government fiscal transfers. While it is true, therefore, that the movement from a multiple-currency system to a single currency does away with the outward manifestation of balance of payments difficulties because there is no exchange rate to defend and foreign currency reserves become irrelevant, the inward manifestation of balance of payments deficits remains.

In dismissing the importance of the balance of payments for the healthy functioning of the real economy, Samuel Brittan refers to the absurdity of treating trade between Sussex and Normandy entirely differently from trade between Sussex and the more distant Yorkshire when all three regions are supposed to be in a single market. However, there are good reasons for treating trade between Sussex and Normandy differently from trade between Sussex and Yorkshire. This would be the case if Britain as a nation state feels a responsibility for the residents of Sussex that it does not feel for Normandy, and is capable of dealing with disparities between Sussex and Yorkshire through its own internal fiscal system that could not be guaranteed if the viability of Sussex was being threatened by the superior competitiveness of Normandy within a monetary union using a single currency. In some circumstances, the exchange rate could be a useful, if limited, weapon for protecting the inhabitants of Sussex.

The issue of the balance of payments goes deeper, however, than the question of the exchange rate alone. The role of the balance of payments in accounting for intercountry differences in growth rates has been ignored for too long by orthodox economic theory, which in the pre-Keynesian days argued that the balance of payments, like everything else in the economic system, was self-adjusting through the price mechanism, and then in the 1950s analysed growth performance from the supply side with no reference to demand. The Keynesian revolution, paradoxically, did not help because Keynes's model was concerned with the short term and dealt for the most part with a closed economy. The emphasis on the imbalance between savings and investment diverted attention from the greater potential imbalance between exports and imports which in practice may be harder to rectify. A strong export performance relative to import demand is vital to the strength of aggregate demand in the system as a whole, single currency or not. Some economic sovereignty would be lost by movement to a single currency, but much more was lost when Britain joined the European Community in 1973. The ability to protect and encourage strategic industries has gone; the possibility of designing systems of managed trade to even out payments imbalances has gone; the ability to protect against certain countries with persistent surpluses has been taken away; and differential taxes which discriminate in favour of the tradeable goods sector fall foul of the Treaty of Rome.

Britain's balance of payments is chronically weak. High interest rates are required to finance deficits that now tend to arise when the country attempts to grow faster than only 1 or 2% per annum, which further damage the real economy. Three centuries ago the mercantilists recognised this dilemma with great clarity, and so did Keynes in his defence of mercantilism against the classical free-traders who treated the mercantilists as 'imbeciles', to use Keynes's word. As Keynes rightly recognised, the interest rate required for external balance (to finance current deficits) may be way out of line with that required for internal balance (in the sense of achieving fast growth and full employment). The problem does not go away in a single-currency area with depressed regions (or countries) competing for investment funds. Britain needs all the monetary and fiscal instruments it can muster to break the 40-year syndrome of weak balance of payments, slow growth, depressed demand, and deindustrialisation leading to further balance of payments weakness. This is as true today as it was before the putative Thatcher economic miracle.

PART II

Government Policy and Structural Change

4

The 'Productivity Miracle', Profits and Investment

Andrew Glyn

Rapid growth in productivity in UK manufacturing is widely believed to have been the outstanding economic achievement of the Thatcher decade. Whilst there has been a mass of valuable analysis of the processes behind this productivity improvement (see Feinstein and Matthews, 1990; Oulton, 1990; and the chapters by Hughes and by Deakin in this volume), there has been less discussion of how the benefits of this productivity increase were distributed. This chapter traces the extent to which the benefits were 'passed on' to consumers (via falls in the relative price of manufactured goods) or retained within the sector as increased real wages or profits. The rise in profits is then analysed and its reflection in higher dividends, share prices and investment examined. It is shown that while profits rose rapidly, investment by manufacturing industry did not; to the extent that manufacturing profits were reinvested this was predominantly in the service sectors, particularly finance. This left manufacturing industry unable to meet domestic demand in the later 1980s and ill-placed to meet international competition. Throughout, UK experience is situated in comparative international perspective, which sheds some light on its particular features.

Who Gained from the Productivity Miracle?

Between 1979 and 1989, when the Thatcher boom came to an end, hourly labour productivity in UK manufacturing industry rose by 4.7% per year. This could qualify as a 'miracle' in several respects. First of all, it represented a dramatic improvement over the years 1973–1979 when productivity rose by only 1.7% per year (Table 4.1). Productivity growth in the 1980s was not exceptional in comparison to the years before the general slowing of growth in 1974; over the period 1960–1973

Table 4.1. Labour productivity growth 1960–1989 (average annual percentage growth rates).[a]

Sector	USA	Japan	Europe[b]	UK
Business				
1960–1973	2.2	8.6	4.2	3.6
1973–1979	0.0	2.9	2.3	1.6
1979–1989	0.8	3.0	1.8	2.1
Manufacturing (hourly)				
1960–1973	3.3	10.3	6.1	4.2
1973–1979	1.4	5.5	4.0	1.7
1979–1989	3.6	5.5	3.1	4.7

[a]Sources: *OECD Economic Outlook*, June 1991, Table 43; *BLS Monthly Labour Review*, July 1991, Table 50.
[b]Unweighted average of growth rates for 9 countries.

it had averaged 4.2% per year. However, with somewhat sluggish productivity in the rest of Europe in the 1980s (averaging 3.1% growth per year), the advance in the UK put it second only to Belgium, rather than in its accustomed position at the bottom of such league tables (Figure 4.1). The dramatic improvement in UK productivity growth

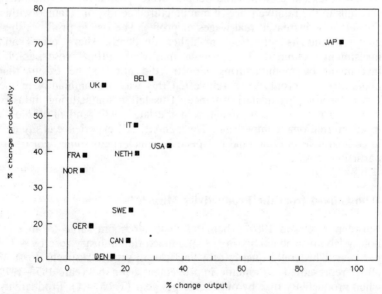

Figure 4.1. Manufacturing productivity and output in OECD countries 1979–1989.

was confined to manufacturing and mining. In the business sector as a whole the acceleration in UK labour productivity was much less marked (see Table 4.1), with performance in the 1980s hardly above the European average. The implication is that productivity growth in UK services was rather poor. This was indeed the case. To take two sectors whose performance is discussed later, in both distribution and in finance and business services, output per worker grew at less than 2% per year.

Confirmation that productivity performance in UK manufacturing was indeed a striking feature of the Thatcher years raises the question of who benefited. Table 4.2 examines how the rise in productivity was divided between increased output and reduced employment, the degree to which it was reflected in falling relative prices of manufacturing products, the relative gains of wages and profits, and where the rising profits were deployed. The most fundamental point is that the more than 50% rise in manufacturing productivity took the form mainly of reduced employment (down 26%), whilst output increased only by 12.2%. This was an uncommon pattern during the 1980s. Only France and Norway showed similarly rapid productivity growth through cuts in employment (Figure 4.1); most countries with substantial productivity growth achieved quite rapid output growth (Japan is the extreme example, and Belgium outstanding amongst European countries). Most countries with stagnant output growth tended to show low productivity growth. The UK pattern of productivity growth via cuts in employment has particular distributional implications; first the impact on prices is examined.

Total factor productivity in UK business rose 15.9% less than in manufacturing over the period 1979–1989 (Table 4.2, business/manufacturing productivity). This could have resulted in correspondingly sharp falls in the relative prices of manufactures. Total factor productivity (TFP) shows the extent to which output grows in excess of (a weighted average of) factor inputs. It thus shows the extent to which real incomes of the factors employed can rise, measured in terms of the sector's output. Thus if real incomes of factors in two sectors were to grow in line, measured in some common unit such as prices of consumer goods, then the relative prices of the two sectors should change in inverse proportion to their TFPs. However, the decline in relative manufacturing prices was much less than the relative rise in TFP (Table 4.2, manufacturing/business prices). This suggests that much of the extra productivity gains (on this calculation more than one-half) were kept within the manufacturing sector rather than being distributed to consumers through relatively cheaper manufactured goods.

Total real incomes in the manufacturing sector depend both on its output and on the evolution of the relative prices of manufacturing value-added and of consumer goods. Over the period 1979–1989, declining relative prices of manufactured goods offset the rise in manufacturing output so that manufacturing real incomes fell slightly.

Table 4.2. Distribution of UK manufacturing productivity growth 1979–1989.*a*

	1989 (relative to 1979=100)
Manufacturing sector output	
Output	112.2
Employment	74.0
Productivity*b*	151.6
Manufacturing compared to all business	
Manufacturing/business prices*c*	95.0
Business/manufacturing productivity*d*	84.1
Manufacturing income	
Real income*e*	104.3
Real profits*f*	143.9
Real wage income*g*	94.5
Real wages per head*h*	127.8
Real profits per unit of capital*i*	127.7
Use of manufacturing profits	
Investment*j*	112.8
Real dividends*k*	173.2
Real share prices*l*	224.8

*a*Sources: Calculated from CSO *UK National Accounts 1991*, Tables 1.7, 2.1, 2.4, 13.7, 17.1, plus 1979 data from CSO; *OECD Labour Force Statistics*, UK Tables III; IV; *IMF Financial Statistics; CSO Business Monitor P5* No. 21, Table 2 and No. 14.
*b*Manufacturing real value added per person employed.
*c*Manufacturing value-added deflator divided by business-sector (GDP less dwellings, public administration, health and education) deflator.
*d*Business-sector total factor productivity divided by manufacturing total factor productivity (with labour and capital stock inputs weighted by 1979 income shares).
*e*Manufacturing output divided by ratio of consumer prices to manufacturing prices, i.e. purchasing power (in terms of consumer goods) of manufacturing incomes.
*f*Manufacturing gross profits (including excess of self-employment incomes over average wage) deflated by consumer prices.
*g*Manufacturing income from employment, adjusted for self-employment, deflated by consumer prices.
*h*Real wage income divided by manufacturing employment.
*i*Real profits divided by manufacturing (gross) capital stock.
*j*Gross fixed capital formation including assets leased by manufacturers.
*k*Estimated from dividends in accounts of manufacturing companies operating mainly in UK, deflated by consumer prices.
*l*Industrial share prices deflated by consumer prices.

However, within this, total real profits rose sharply (44%) whereas aggregate real wage incomes fell by 5% (Table 4.2, manufacturing income). Those workers who kept their jobs, however, saw a substantial (28%) increase in their real wages, a very similar rate of increase to that of profits per unit of capital.[7] Much of the benefit from the rapid growth of manufacturing productivity, therefore, was retained within the manufacturing sector and a disproportionate part of that appropriated as profits. Despite this, manufacturing investment hardly grew at all. Part of the explanation was that dividend payments rose twice as fast as profits, and shareholders gained additionally from share prices which rose twice as fast as dividends (Table 4.2, use of manufacturing profits). Such increases dwarf, in relative terms, the benefits that accrued to consumers or to the workers whose reorganised, and often speeded-up, working practices lay behind the 'miracle'.

Such estimates of who gained are independent of whether all of the improvement in manufacturing productivity represented a net gain in output to society. Since less than one-quarter of the higher productivity was reflected in increased manufacturing output, the crucial question is whether all the labour 'freed' from manufacturing contributed to production elsewhere in the economy, and at what productivity level. Services employment grew faster after 1979 (2.1% per year for 1979–1989 as compared to 1.4% per year during 1973–1979), and no doubt the flood of ex-industrial workers contributed to this increase (as did the rise in women's participation rates). However, the fact that loss of industrial jobs is closely associated across countries with rising unemployment (Glyn and Rowthorn, 1988), the fact that registered unemployment was half a million higher in 1989 than in 1979 and the persuasive arguments as to the influence of hysteresis on the NAIRU (Layard and Nickell, 1987), all point to the probability that part of the labour rationalised out of manufacturing industry either found no replacement job or displaced other workers. Accordingly, by some margin the net gain from the productivity 'miracle' was less than the gross gain. The gains and losses from the restructuring of manufacturing industry are illustrated in Table 4.3.

Profits and Productivity in OECD Countries

The weak performance of manufacturing productivity in many other European countries after 1979 has already been stressed (in Germany, for example, it declined from 4.3% per year for 1973–1979 to 1.8% per year for 1979–1989). Despite such weak productivity growth, a recovery in manufacturing *profitability* was rather widespread, reversing the near universal profit squeeze from the mid-1960s up to 1979.

In contrast to the UK case, where real wage growth was maintained

82   *Andrew Glyn*

Table 4.3. Gains and losses from restructuring of UK manufacturing industry.

Sector	Gains	Losses
Shareholders	Dividend increases (73%), share price increases (125%)	
Consumers/taxpayers	Cheaper manufactured goods	Extra taxes to support unemployed
Manufacturing workers still with jobs	Wage increases (28%)	Higher intensity of work
Ex-manufacturing workers (26% of 1979 total)		Work in a lower-wage sector for many, unemployment for some

and profit recovery was derived from faster productivity growth, the usual pattern was for a drastic slow-down in (pre-tax) real wages which permitted a restoration of profit margins even when productivity growth declined. Figure 4.2 illustrates this by presenting a simple decomposition which shows how the manufacturing wage share declined after 1979 for the average of the 14 OECD countries for which data are available, together with the contrasting case of the UK.[8]

British Coal—An Extreme Case

Coal mining does not count as manufacturing; yet the increase in productivity in the UK coal industry was more remarkable still. In the wake of the 1984–1985 miners' strike there was a massive round of pit closures together with tremendous pressure to rationalise production and increase productivity at the continuing pits (for a detailed evaluation, see Glyn, 1988) and this has continued unabated. Over the period between 1982–1983 (the last year before the miners' action seriously affected production) and 1990–1991, productivity more than doubled (Table 4.4). Productivity was forced up nearly three times as fast as in manufacturing; given the sharp decline in output, this implied a fall in employment of over 70%. Coal faced a terrific squeeze on prices, as liberalisation of the coal market permitted competition from imported coal; the result was a halving of the purchasing power, in terms of consumer goods, of incomes generated within deep-mined coal. However, the extraordinary productivity increase permitted both the small losses of 1982–1983 to be turned into a gross profit, and real

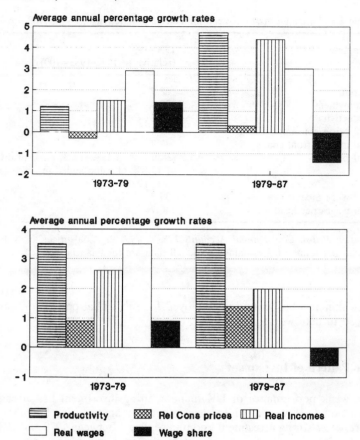

Figure 4.2. UK and OECD wage share in manufacturing 1973–1987
Sources: as for Tables 4.1 and 4.2, plus *OECD National Accounts* and Armstrong *et al.* (1991) for the wage share. Real wage data are hourly and pre-tax (including all social security contributions).

wages per head to rise sharply. Since most UK coal is sold to the electricity supply industry, the government gained not only from improved coal finances but also from the boost to electricity profits, as little of the rise in coal productivity was passed on to consumers. The ultimate beneficiaries were those taxpayers (disproportionately from the top income groups—see Rowthorn's chapter) whose tax cuts were 'justified' by the improved public sector borrowing requirement (PSBR) to which nationalised industries' surpluses, such as that in electricity, contributed. Apart from the miners who experienced much more intense work practices (but with sharp rises in average pay), the obvious losers

84   *Andrew Glyn*

Table 4.4. Distribution of UK deep-mined coal productivity growth, 1982–1990.[a]

Component	1990–1991 (relative to 1982–1983=100)
Output	68.7
Employment	27.9
Productivity	246.2
Coal prices/consumer prices	69.4
Real income from coal	47.7
Real profits	small loss in 1982–1983, gross profit of 13.8% of value added in 1990–1991
Real wage income	39.2
Real wages per head	140.7

[a]Source: *British Coal Annual Accounts 1983/4, 1990/91*. Coal prices are value added per tonne of deep-mined coal. All data are for financial years.

were miners who became unemployed for substantial periods or were forced to take worse-paid jobs.

The Pattern of Investment

The weak performance of UK manufacturing investment has already been noted. However, whilst investment in manufacturing languished there was a strong investment boom in services. Between 1979 and 1989 the level of investment carried out by the goods-producing sectors of the economy—agriculture and industry (a broader category than manufacturing as it includes mining, energy and construction)—rose by a mere 10.3%. Over the same period, investment in the services sectors (distribution, transport and communication, finance and business services and 'other') rose by 108.3%. Whilst in 1979 investment in these two broad categories was running at a very similar level, by 1989 investment in services was nearly twice investment in industry.

An even more dramatic comparison is between manufacturing on the one hand (of decisive importance for the UK's trade) and banking, finance, insurance and business services (accountancy, etc.) on the other (affected particularly by financial deregulation and the credit boom). Manufacturing investment (purchase of new machinery, factories, etc.) was 12.8% higher in 1989 than 1979, whereas investment by the financial and business services sector (new offices, computers, etc.) rose by 320.3% (see Table 4.5). In 1979, investment by the latter sector was around one-third of the level of investment in manufacturing; in 1989,

Table 4.5. UK investment and capital stock growth 1979–1989 (% increases, 1985 prices).[a]

	Investment	Capital stock
Agriculture	−16.0	4.1
Oil and gas	−28.1	66.6
Other energy and water	9.0	6.9
Manufacturing	12.8	12.0
Construction	1.7	7.8
Distribution, hotels and catering	60.8	58.2
Transport and communication	39.7	1.1
Banking, finance, insurance and business services	320.3	105.0
Other services	75.1	32.9
Dwellings	9.0	25.3
Total	45.0	25.6

[a]Source: CSO *UK National Accounts 1991*, Tables 13.7, 14.8. All leased assets are included in the sector of the user.

it was around one-third more than manufacturing investment (with finance investment alone over one-half that of manufacturing). Between 1979 and 1990 the total stock of capital in manufacturing industry rose by some £34 billion (1985 prices). If all the extra investment in the financial and business services sector over and above the 1979 level, which took place during the years 1980–1990, had been channelled into manufacturing then its capital stock would have been risen two and a half times as fast as actually occurred.

The poor performance of UK manufacturing investment stands out not only in relation to services, but also in comparison to other countries. Figure 4.3 shows a significant shortfall in UK investment growth as compared to all countries other than the USA, despite the fact that the profit recovery was amongst the strongest. A number of countries (Belgium, Canada, Japan) generated rapid increases in manufacturing investment despite little change in profitability.[9] Certainly, weak output growth must have contributed to low UK manufacturing investment but in part it also reflected the low investment rate which left the sector incapable of meeting additional demand when the consumer boom came, culminating in the huge deficit on manufacturing trade at the end of the 1980s (see Coutts and Godley's chapter in this volume).

The pattern of investment away from manufacturing towards distribution and finance was apparent in even more extreme form in the USA. US manufacturing investment was stagnant between 1979 and 1988 whilst distribution investment doubled. Data for other countries suggest that such a disproportionate rise in distribution investment

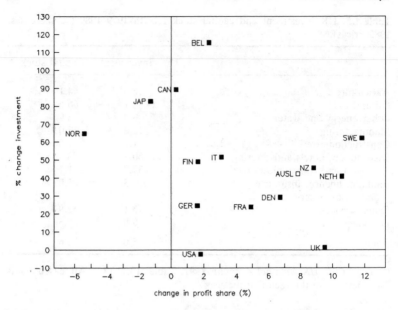

Figure 4.3. Manufacturing investment and profits in OECD countries 1979–1988.

occurred only in the US and UK.[10] Whilst investment in finance grew rapidly in many countries in the 1980s (Figure 4.4), even allowing for exaggeration due to the inclusion of leased assets, the contrast between booming financial investment and stagnant manufacturing investment occurred only in the US and UK. Finance investment was typically in the range of 10–15% of manufacturing investment in 1989 (and only 5% in Sweden)—nowhere near the (1988) UK level of 40% of manufacturing investment, even with leased assets excluded. It seems that the disproportionate investment in distribution and finance in the 1980s was a phenomenon particular to the US and UK.

Conclusions

This chapter has examined how the benefits and costs of the rapid increase in productivity in UK mining and manufacturing were distributed. The fact that the rise in productivity took place without a rapid increase in output implied huge job losses, and substantial costs for those made, and above all those remaining, unemployed. Workers who retained their jobs gained from rather substantial increases in real wages, though conditions of work were often more intense. A disproportionate part of the increased productivity accrued as higher profits, of which an increasing part was paid out as higher dividends,

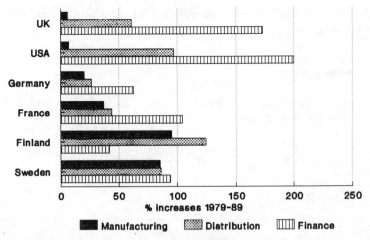

Figure 4.4. Percentage increases in investment by sector in OECD countries 1979–1989 (source: *OECD National Accounts*). Figures for Germany and the UK are for 1988.

contributing to even larger rises in share prices. Whilst manufacturing investment recovered in the later 1980s it barely exceeded its 1979 peak, leaving a meagre growth of capital stock over the decade as a whole. By contrast, those service sectors most closely linked to the consumer boom absorbed the major part of the rise in investment. Explanations for weak manufacturing investment in the face of sharply rising profitability include the damage to manufacturers' confidence caused by the recession of the early 1980s and subsequent slow recovery, uncertainty generated by the huge swings in competitiveness generated by sterling's fluctuations, stock-market pressures to raise dividends, and the financial attractions of growth via acquisition rather than new investment. The result of low manufacturing investment was that capacity was overstretched in 1989, even though output had grown a little more than 1% per year in the 1980s, culminating in a massive trade deficit. In the subsequent recession manufacturing productivity stagnated, with both output and employment falling some 6% between 1989 and the first half of 1991: manufacturing investment fell even more.

Much of the apparent prosperity of the 1980s came from redistribution, away from those made unemployed and from workers towards shareholders, rather than from increased production; such redistribution was complemented by changes in the tax and government expenditure systems (see Rowthorn's chapter), and papered over in the later 1980s by the illusions fostered by the credit boom. The market forces unleashed by the Thatcher government, and the rationalisation of

industry which resulted, most blatantly failed to provide a durable basis
for future growth.

Acknowledgements

The author is grateful to Wendy Carlin, Ciaran Driver and Bob
Rowthorn for their comments.

Comment

A Legacy of Capital Shortage

Ciaran Driver

One of the most durable legacies of economic activity is the size,
composition and quality of the capital stock. The adequacy of this has
implications not only for growth but also, through employment, for
distribution. Manufacturing capital stock grew very slowly in Britain
over the 1980s: net investment was negative for the first half of the
decade, following a period of unrecorded scrapping. The story for
business investment as a whole is no less important: the statistics appear
to indicate, despite fast growth for some years in some sectors, a general
failure of investment in most of Europe, but especially Britain. The
spectre of sustained 'capital-shortage' unemployment is not fanciful.

From the late 1960s the rate of growth of capital stock has roughly
halved both in Europe and in the UK, in line with rising capital output
ratios. The trend fall in capital productivity was arrested in the 1980s
in Europe. Since this coincided with a marked fall in the wage share,
the result was a steep rise in profitability (Figure 4A.1). The same
process occurred in Britain, although the falling wage share was
accompanied by higher real wage growth (than in the 1970s) for those
in work, while the rise in capital productivity may have begun earlier
than elsewhere.

Glyn's chapter points to a weak manufacturing investment response
to the profit recovery in Britain. Indeed, corporate sector savings

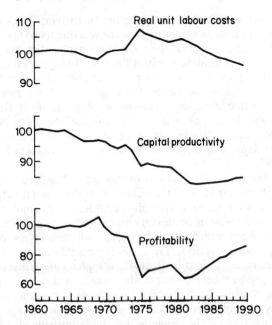

Figure 4A.1. Real unit labour costs, capital productivity and profitability in Europe 1960–1990 (source: *European Economy* 1989). Indexed to 1960 = 100.

exceeded investment for the whole period from 1982–1988. Investment responds to expectations of future profitability and to other influences such as current growth. The latter was strong enough to produce a short burst of high investment at the end of the 1980s, but this was not sufficiently sustained to affect significantly the capital stock. The story is similar for Europe, where investment responded to current growth but failed to reflect anticipations of a profit recovery.

Net ratios of investment to output for the business sector were lower in the 1980s than in the previous decade for all major European countries. For Britain, the ratio fell from 9.5% to under 7% (net ratios are appropriate because of the rising share of shorter-lived assets in the total which distorts the comparison of gross figures). British investment performance would look even worse were it not for the case of financial services; caution in respect of investment did not extend to this sector. The change in composition of investment is remarkable. In Britain in 1979 the combined share of chemicals, engineering and metal goods, food and motors amounted to 20.5%, twice that for financial services. By 1989 the ratio was reversed, with a 30% share for finance and half that for the industrial sectors.

Econometric equations of investment have not been very successful at explaining recent developments. To a certain extent, high real interest rates must have been a depressing factor. In Britain, the pressure for higher dividend ratios in response to perceived threats of takeover may also be responsible. However, the most likely explanation is that higher profitability has been achieved only at the cost of heightened uncertainty over future distribution and consumption patterns. This uncertainty has been complemented in Britain by the huge scale of the redistributive programme, by the changing composition of government and private expenditure and by the change in technical coefficients of production following from changes in labour processes. Evidence that uncertainly has a serious depressing effect on investment is provided in Driver and Morton (1992).

What are the policy implications of this legacy? Before overreacting it is important to bear in mind the qualification that capital output ratios probably have been permanently reduced, at least for manufacturing, in recent years as a result of costless increases in the quality of the capital stock (which are not recorded) and by higher utilisation levels consequent on changing labour practices. These developments suggest that a focus on fixed investment alone is inadequate: complementary investments in market and product developments also count. If demand uncertainty has been the chief factor depressing irreversible commitments, there is a fairly ready solution in policies to stabilise growth and in self-financing tax/subsidy packages. The remedy for underinvestment cannot be expected to work quickly but the experience of the financial services sector suggests that dramatic change is at least possible, if not always desirable.

5

Thatcherism and the UK Defence Industry

Paul Dunne and Ron Smith

In military terms, Mrs Thatcher's period of office opened with the 'New Cold War', the Soviet invasion of Afghanistan and Reagan's military build-up in the US. It closed with the 'End of the Cold War', planned cuts in military spending and the Iraqi invasion of Kuwait. She resigned before the Gulf War itself but that war seems unlikely to alter the established trend towards reduced military burdens. This chapter analyses the changes in defence policy and the defence industry that occurred during her period of office and evaluates the effect of the application of 'Thatcherism' to defence. First, it provides some evidence on Conservative policy towards defence in the 1980s. These facts are relatively uncontroversial but may be unfamiliar. Second, it provides an interpretation of this evidence. This interpretation, which may be surprising, is that despite Mrs Thatcher's image as a bellicose 'Iron Lady', Thatcherism, particularly after 1985, represented the most sustained attack on the British military–industrial complex since World War II. This was a result not of Mrs Thatcher's personal involvement but of the application of the economic ideology of Thatcherism. Third, we draw some tentative conclusions from our analysis about the contingent nature of the relationship between state and market. These suggest that in some areas, such as defence, even socialists—perhaps especially socialists—would want to encourage free markets and avoid public ownership.

The following section considers the nature of the concepts of Thatcherism and the military–industrial complex which form the focus of our analysis. The evolution of defence policy under Mrs Thatcher's governments is then reviewed, as are the effects of these policies on industry and the economy. The general role of the state in arms production is then discussed and lessons for the future development of policy considered. The final section draws some conclusions.

Thatcherism, Militarism and the Military–Industrial Complex

Although the concepts of Thatcherism and the military–industrial complex tend to be associated with left-wing analyses, neither need be partisan. For the purposes of this chapter we treat Thatcherism as the implementation of an economic ideology which emphasises reduction of state spending and the replacement of state intervention, such as industrial policy, by market forces. Market forces are promoted by policies such as privatisation and the introduction of competition. The ideology is a traditional one; what distinguishes Thatcherism is its determined implementation.

We limit our analysis to the economic effects of changes in defence policy, abstracting from the wider social and political impacts of militarism (see Smith (1983) for a discussion of these wider aspects). Edgerton (1991) provides a recent contribution to the debate over militarism and the UK state; he argues that Britain remains 'militant–industrial' and militaristic in the post-Cold War world, and describes the British as the 'high-tech Ghurkhas' of the Western World.

The term military–industrial complex (MIC), despite its current left-wing connotations, was introduced by Dwight Eisenhower, an ex-military Republican President of the USA. He had a very conservative concern: the danger that coalitions of vested interests could exploit the special nature of decision-making about military matters to shape choices against the national security interest in order to extract funds for their own purposes. These coalitions could include some members of the armed services, of the civilian defence bureaucracy, of the legislature, of the arms manufacturers and their workers. From the point of view of Eisenhower, this was a case where the interests of capitalism (discussed in Smith, 1977) might diverge from the interests of capitalist defence firms. Indeed, Schwarz (1990), in a detailed historical analysis of the development of the MIC, uses the term 'military–industrial–congressional complex' to emphasise the importance of political linkages. The nature of the MIC and the theoretical understanding of the relationship between military spending and economic development are important considerations, as they will condition the interpretation and expectations of the economic effects of reduced military budgets (see Dunne (1990) for a summary of the approaches).

It is important to recognise that the MIC can be a threat to a right-wing state. The development of the MIC in the US was linked to New Deal economics and its attempts to introduce economic planning. The Pentagon, with its planned economy, free health care, generous pension arrangements and so on, used to be described as the largest Socialist Society outside the Iron Curtain. In addition, if the state faces threats to its security and relies on the efficiency of the military and their equipment to maintain its viability, then military spending will certainly not be regarded as irrelevant waste to be used for economic purposes. The UK Conservative government had reason to be concerned about the efficiency of its military and their equipment. Prior to the accession of Gorbachev, it took the Soviet threat very seriously; it fought two high-intensity wars, in the Falklands/Malvinas and in the Gulf, and a continual low-intensity war in Northern Ireland. The last was a war where Prime Ministers were in the firing line: the IRA came very close to killing Mrs Thatcher at Brighton and Mr Major in Downing Street.

   MICs are not peculiar to capitalist economies, or to right-wing governments. Under Conservative and Socialist governments France has created a classic MIC, largely internalised within the state. Kolodziej (1987) described the tight symbiotic relationship that exists between the procurement agency, the Delegation Generale pour l'Armement (DGA), and the largely nationalised arms firms. The DGA has acted as a patron for the industry, using procurement and export promotion as part of a coherent industrial policy, developed over decades, in which defence firms, mainly state-owned, have considerable freedom to develop weapons they think will sell abroad. The armed forces and politicians are marginalised by technocrats trained at the Ecole Polytechnique who move between the DGA and the firms. The need to promote arms exports has meant that French foreign policy has often been driven by the requirement to sell arms and that equipment has been designed in the light of foreign not French military needs, prompting repeated complaints by the French armed services. Recently the collapse of export demand for arms, the integration of the European defence industry and deficiencies in the performance of French forces in the Gulf have thrown doubt on the viability of this traditional military–industrial strategy.

   The issues discussed below have an important European dimension. The pressures encouraging the evolution of a more coherent European defence identity have prompted debate over whether the British-style 'hands-off' free-market approach to the arms industry, or the French-style symbiosis between state and arms firms should provide the model for a multilateral organisation.

Thatcher's Defence Policies

During their first period of office, up to about 1985, apart from privatising the arms firms, Conservative defence policies broadly followed the trends of the previous Labour government. After 1985 defence spending was cut sharply and competition introduced into procurement. This change in direction was an important contributory factor in making military production less profitable and prompting a massive restructuring and internationalisation of the UK arms industry, a process which is continuing at a UK and European level.

The broad trends in spending are evident from Figure 5.1, which shows the shares of total military spending and spending on military equipment as a percentage of GDP. The break around 1985 is obvious. Until then the Conservative government had honoured the commitment to expand real defence spending by 3% a year. This commitment had been given to NATO by Mr Callaghan's Labour government as part of the Long-Term Defence Programme initiated in London in 1977, endorsed at the Washington summit of 1978 and described in the 1979 Labour *Statement on the Defence Estimates*. While it might be argued that the Labour promises should not have been taken seriously and that the commitment would not have been honoured, nonetheless it was the basis of subsequent Conservative policy. Figure 5.2 shows the international pattern over this period. Except for the US, the other NATO powers did not increase the share of defence expenditure in output in the early 1980s, although defence burdens generally declined in the late 1980s.

There were other elements of continuity. The large amount of preparatory work and planning done under the previous Labour government and passed on to the Conservatives, pointed to Trident as 'the only option' for the modernisation of the British nuclear deterrent. The only dissent from this, among those involved in planning, seems to have come from David Owen, who wanted cruise rather than ballistic missiles. The later change by the Conservatives from the C4 to D5 missile system was consistent with the emphasis on the importance of commonality with the US established by the Labour working groups. The cost of Trident at a time of increasing pressure on the defence budgets squeezed other categories of expenditure.

The Conservatives also maintained the four main commitments (independent deterrent, European ground and air forces, North Atlantic

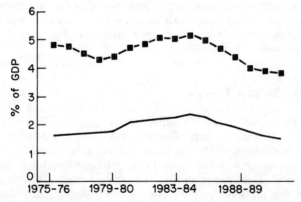

Figure 5.1. UK military spending as a share of GDP 1975–1989: –■–, military expenditure; —, equipment.

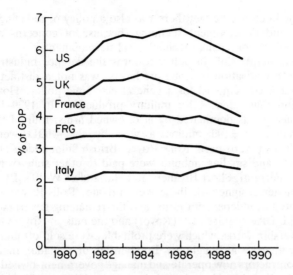

Figure 5.2. Military spending as a share of GDP for five countries 1980–1990.

maritime forces, and defence of the home base) inherited from Labour. John Nott's defence review of 1981, which had tried to reduce the role of the maritime forces, was pre-empted by the Falklands/Malvinas war of the following year. Within this general framework, the Conservatives introduced one minor, but important, change: they released more information about defence. This is clearly illustrated in a comparison of the amount of detail in Labour and Conservative *Statements on the Defence Estimates*, but it applied more generally, for example revealing the existence of the Chevaline project. Defence was a much less sensitive issue for the Conservatives and they could thus be more open about it.

For the first 5 years of the Conservative administration, defence was effectively shielded from the two major tenets of Thatcherism: control of public expenditure and exposure to market forces. Subsequently that protection was removed. In 1984–1985 the commitment to NATO of 3% growth in real military expenditure was ended and the policy of reducing public expenditure was finally applied to defence. The defence budget fell in real terms by 12% between 1985–1986 and 1990–1991, mostly prior to the ending of the Cold War. As a share of money GDP it moved from 4.5% under Labour to a peak of 5.2% and then fell to under 4%, so that in 1990 the share of national income devoted to defence was the lowest since the 1930s. The 1990 Autumn *Statement on Public Expenditure*, following the *Options for Change* defence review, anticipated the decline continuing by a further 6% in real terms by 1993–1994, leaving it at less than 3.5% of GDP. There is little evidence that the Gulf War will disturb the downward trend. Within a constrained defence budget there was also a policy of reducing defence research and development spending, because of concerns about its negative effects on civilian technological development.

The one major shift in policy towards the defence industry before 1985, the privatisation of arms producers, was not a distinct defence choice but a consequence of a general economic policy. However, it had major consequences for military production. In 1979–1980, the arms industry was dominated by state-owned firms: four of the seven firms paid over £100 million a year by the MOD were state-owned (British Aerospace, Rolls-Royce, British Shipbuilders and Royal Ordnance), and smaller amounts were paid to other state-owned firms (BP, BL, Ferranti, Short Brothers and Harland & Wolff). By the time Mrs Thatcher resigned all these were private. Rolls-Royce and BAe were floated as independent firms, and the remaining government stake in BP sold. BAe acquired BL (Rover) and the bulk of Royal Ordnance; the BS warship yards, which were profitable, were sold off individually; Short Brothers was bought by Bombardier of Canada. In addition, private contractors now operate and manage government-owned facilities such as the Royal Dockyards and the Atomic Weapons Establishment. With the partial exception of frigate production, the privatisations left all monopolies intact.

Initially the Conservatives continued the Labour policy of using cost-plus contracts and preferential purchasing to maintain a British defence industrial base. This policy was popular with both firms and unions but there were a number of occasions where the British system was purchased against stronger foreign competition and then performed badly. For instance, under the Labour government it had been decided to buy the UK Nimrod Airborne Early Warning (AEW) System from GEC rather than the US AWACS. Despite spending about one billion pounds on the system, it could not be made to work properly and the AWACS eventually had to be purchased. Until AWACS was delivered, British AEW was provided by Shackleton aircraft. The Shackletons were a development of the World War II Lancaster bomber and were well over 40 years old when they were retired in summer 1991 to be auctioned by Sotheby's as collectors' items for museums. Despite the rapid growth in spending up to 1985, resources were inadequate to meet commitments. Given the failure of John Nott's defence review of 1981, Michael Heseltine, the subsequent Minister of Defence, attempted to reconcile objectives and resources by efficiency savings. These were to be produced by the introduction of market forces and competition into defence procurement. This new procurement policy was implemented by Peter Levene, Chief of Defence Procurement from 1984. He had previously run a small defence firm, United Scientific Holdings, and had acted as an advisor to Heseltine. The new regime involved a marked change. There was competition for contracts, fixed prices rather than cost-plus, payments were tied to performance milestones, and risk was shifted onto the contractor. The share of contracts let competitively rose from about 30% in 1980 to over 60% in 1985–1986; and pure cost-plus contracts fell from about 16% to 4%. The share let competitively fell back somewhat after 1985–1986, because of a series of large projects where there was only a single possible producer, but then rose again. It was initially anticipated that this competition would only be notional, since most major weapons systems were produced by monopolies. To make competition effective required allowing foreign firms to compete, and this was perceived as politically unacceptable. This view was widely held outside the MOD, and even within the MOD concern was expressed in evidence on the initial attempt by GEC to acquire Plessey:

> Moreover the MOD suggested that if there was a monopolistic United Kingdom producer of equipment it could more effectively lobby to try to ensure that the MOD did not buy abroad and this would clearly be in the interests of such a producer. The MOD said it was a feature not only of the United Kingdom but of the United States and of all the countries in Western Europe that, in defence markets, if procurement authorities tried to move into a competitive international market they found that the domestic companies used their political influence and political pressure to restrict that possibility. (Monopolies and Merger Commission, 1986, p. 65.)

Despite strong political opposition from MPs of both parties, from trade unions and from domestic monopolies, the share of imports did rise significantly, and the cancellation of the GEC Nimrod AEW and the purchase of the Boeing AWACS was a very public signal of this greater willingness to buy abroad. Even in cases where British equipment was eventually purchased, having real competition from abroad appears to have driven down prices.

This shift was almost certainly beneficial. Evidence from a string of earlier decisions, where British weapons were bought for political reasons after substantial lobbying by domestic manufacturers, suggests that domestic preference in weapons is wasteful and expensive and has no benefits to the British economy or technology. The decisions include the original choice of Nimrod over the US AWACS, the choice of Marconi rather than US Gould torpedoes, and the choice of BAe ALARM over Texas Instruments HARM missiles. In each of these controversial procurements the choice to buy British, which Labour supported, proved wrong with hindsight. It is difficult to verify the savings from competition but the MOD has given a range of examples which in total saved many hundreds of millions, and in an investigation of these procurement initiatives, the National Audit Office (1991) concurred that the MOD has made significant progress in the search for value for money. Despite this, the policy has been widely criticised. Influential studies such as that by Taylor and Hayward (1989) have argued the need for support of the defence industrial base and have suggested that successful companies should not be endangered by heedless regard for a narrowly defined concept of 'value for money'. While significant, the changes were not universal and their effects varied across industries. Hilditch (1990) argues that the move to competitive procurement in shipbuilding was compromised by a concern for employment policy in the regions, despite the limited effectiveness of procurement as a means of maintaining employment. Lobbying, of course, continued on a large scale and it was probably a significant factor in the 1988 and 1991 decisions in favour of the British Challenger II tank over its foreign competitors.

The competitive procurement policy implemented by Peter Levene until his retirement shortly after Thatcher, was continued by Defence Ministers after Heseltine—George Younger and Tom King. The policy was promoted in Europe, and internationalisation of the industry encouraged. Reciprocal purchasing arrangements for smaller contracts were arranged with the French; the MOD put pressure on the Independent European Programme Group (IEPG), the organisation designed to coordinate European arms procurement, to promote competition; and more fixed-price contracts were introduced for collaborative projects such as the European Fighter Aircraft. The general aim of British policy was to create a free-trade area in arms within Europe, with procurement based on value for money after open competition. For instance, the MOD welcomed Siemens' involvement in the revised GEC bid for Plessey as being in tune with the impetus towards a more open and efficient European defence market (Monopolies and Mergers Commission, 1989, p. 43). Concern was expressed not by the MOD, but by what the Commission discretely referred to as 'other government departments', the intelligence agencies worried about foreign control of cryptographic capability.

The Conservatives argued that a strong European defence industry would arise as a result of the restructuring produced by free trade and market forces, not as the result of protection and specific industrial policies directed by European governments. Thus, not only was the government fairly relaxed about the acquisition of UK defence firms by foreign companies such as Siemens, but it opposed extension of the EC Common External Tariff to weapons and opposed EC policies which would restrict US ownership of European arms firms. Given the size of UK arms exports to the US, the dependence of the UK on imports from the US for its nuclear delivery systems, and the number of UK defence subsidiaries in the US, this position is understandable.

The Implications for Industry

In all but the smallest countries of the advanced capitalist world defence industries have been characterised by concentrated national capitals with close links to their national states, who have protected them on strategic grounds. This symbiosis inhibited internationalisation of capital in the defence industry and cross-country division of labour. True multinationals characteristic of most other industries were conspicuously absent in the arms industry, despite large economies of scale. Fixed costs, particularly research and development, account for about one-third of total costs in military projects and there is a steep learning curve: thus the cost of a weapon is largely a function of the length of the production run. The consequence of national preference was short production runs, general excess capacity and higher prices for military equipment. There was also a particular set of relations of production which led to complex, expensive and impractical weapons. Rising development costs and falling defence budgets made this position unsustainable and provoked massive restructuring of the European industry. British firms restructured ahead of their European rivals under the impetus of the new procurement regime: Lovering (1990) and Smith (1990) have reviewed the market.

To provide some indication of the performance of the arms firms over the 1980s we have created a sample of 17 major defence contractors from the Datastream company databank. The sample used is given in Table 5.1 (p. 100), taken from ACOST (1989) where, unusually, information on the share of turnover which was defence-related is reported. Figure 5.3 shows the ratio of the share prices of these companies relative to the FT All-Share Index. There is a general downward trend which shows a faster fall around 1985, with the introduction of the new regime which had higher risks and lower returns

Figure 5.3. Defence share price relative to FT All Shares Index 1981–1991.

100 Paul Dunne and Ron Smith

Table 5.1. Performance of a sample of 17 defence companies in 1986.[a]

Company	Turnover (£ m)	Civil	Defence	MOD
BAe	3137	24	76	32
Chloride	310	92	8	8
Dowty	520	58	42	19
Ferranti	485	36	64	48
GEC	5969	72	28	22
GKN	2200	95	5	5
Hunting Industries	233	48	52	52
Lucas Industries	1397	88	12	3
Pilkington	1214	91	9	4
Plessey	1461	59	41	26
Racal	1270	68	32	10
Rolls-Royce	1600	44	56	37
Short Bros	200	75	25	20
Smiths	389	77	23	14
Thorn–EMI	2735	88	12	9
Vickers	600	85	15	3
Westland	344	29	71	58

[a]Source: ACOST (1989, p. 55) and company accounting data for the cases where ACOST gives data for the defence division rather than the quoted company.

for UK arms producers. This is a simple unweighted average and does not reflect relative company sizes or differing degrees of defence exposure (many of the sample are large diversified companies). In addition, the composition of the stock market has changed and there is considerable variation in individual performance, as illustrated in Figure 5.4 (pp. 102–103).

Nonetheless, Thatcherism was associated with a large discount to the market for Britain's arms firms. In the case of one of them, Riley (1991) comments:

Go back to the Autumn of 1982, when the British economy was struggling out of its last slump. Then it was GEC which was reaching the peak of its fortunes; briefly it was Britain's most valuable company, because it appeared recession-proof and it enjoyed cost-plus pricing on much of its public sector business, especially defence contracts. But today GEC has slumped to 20th in the size rankings and is shrinking on many fronts: the one-time crown jewel of British industry seems doomed to become an offshoot of Siemens. Glamorous electrical stocks accounted for 8% of the All-Share Index in 1980, but about 2.5% today.

These glamorous electrical stocks were mainly also defence companies.

It is difficult to measure the degree of competition in the defence market because the MOD does not publish the relevant information, but one measure of competition (described in Smith, 1990) suggests that concentration increased substantially with the nationalisation of BAe and BS by the previous Labour government, remained roughly constant from 1980 until 1986–1987 and then fell sharply, remaining lower for the next 2 years. It is also difficult to measure profitability in defence production, given the uncertainties of accounting conventions and the multiproduct nature of many of the companies, but it seems to have been similar to the industrial average around 1985 and then fell somewhat relative to the average. Figure 5.5 shows the share of profits (published pre-tax) in total sales for the defence sample relative to all companies.

Although each measure has its inadequacies, stock market prices, concentration measures, reported profits and press comment all indicate a worsening of the relative environment for arms firms over the 1980s. Some firms responded to this increased competition and reduced profitability by diversifying out of defence, the most successful move being that of Racal into cellular telephones. Racal, Thorn–EMI and Philips all put their defence divisions up for sale; however, only Philips found a buyer. BAe, while it remains a major defence producer, diversified into property and car manufacture, largely through acquisition, and obtained a valuable—and undervalued—property portfolio through the purchase of Royal Ordnance. However, diversification by defence companies is difficult and dangerous, as BAe discovered. The skills required by the military and the commercial markets are quite distinct. The most important skill for a defence producer—the ability to persuade governments to give it money—does not provide a competitive edge in civilian markets. Racal was rather atypical, in that although very dependent on defence, it was primarily an exporter of military communications equipment and had a company policy of keeping its sales to the MOD below 20% of turnover. This export orientation gave it relevant technical, marketing and commercial skills which the other major contractors lacked. The others took a different route, attempting to monopolise and internationalise their defence activities. Monopolisation became a dialectical product of the policy to promote competition.

Moves designed to increase monopoly power included the purchase by Vickers, the only private tank producer, of Royal Ordnance's tank factories; the purchase by BAe of the rest of Royal Ordnance; and GEC's failed 1985 attempt to take over Plessey and subsequent successful attempt with Siemens. The internationalisation of the UK industry involved the purchase of US defence companies by GEC, Plessey and Ferranti among others; the expansion of exports of arms, particularly two large sales to Saudi Arabia under the Al Yamamah contracts, which earned BAe over £8bn in revenue; and various joint ventures

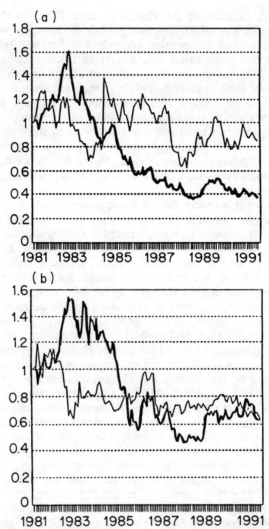

Figure 5.4. Defence share price of individual companies relative to FT All Shares Index 1981–1991. (a)⎯, BAe; ▬, GEC. (b) ⎯, GKN; ▬, Plessey. *Continued opposite.*

with European firms. In defence, there is a long tradition of politically negotiated collaborative ventures, such as those agreed between the UK, Germany and Italy to produce the Tornado. These arrangements tend to be unwieldy, bureaucratic, and suffer a considerable cost penalty. In the past, they have proved difficult to cancel once they have got underway, but cancellation has become more common. In response

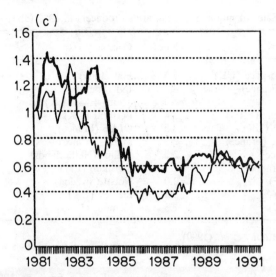

Figure 5.4. (*continued*). (c) ___, Racal; ▬, Thorn–EMI.

to these problems, the UK government has encouraged commercially, rather than politically, organised joint ventures. International linkages include extensive subcontracting, offset purchases, cross-holdings of shares, research cooperation and the like, often with US as well as European companies.

Figure 5.5. Profits/sales ratios for defence companies and for all industrial companies 1981–1990.

104   *Paul Dunne and Ron Smith*

Table 5.2. Sales of major European arms producers in 1988 ($bn).[a]

Company	Sales	Company	Sales
British Aerospace (UK)	5.5	Fiat (Italy)	1.5
Thomson (France)	4.5	INI (Spain)	1.3
GEC (UK)	4.3	Thorn–EMI (UK)	1.2
Daimler–Benz (FRG)	3.4	Ferranti (UK)	1.2
Rolls-Royce (UK)	2.5	GIAT (France)	1.2
Aerospatiale (France)	2.3	Matra (France)	1.2
DCN (France)	2.2	Philips (Netherlands)	1.0
Dassault (France)	2.1	Oerlikon (CH)	0.9
MBB (FRG)	2.0	Nobel (Sweden)	0.9
Lucas (UK)	1.8	Plessey (UK)	0.9
EFIM (Italy)	1.5	Siemens (FRG)	0.8

[a]Source: Anthony *et al.* (1990).

Table 5.2 shows the main European defence firms in 1988. These European national champions are quite small relative to American competitors: in 1988 the combined arms sales of the 100 top European companies were about the same as those of the top 10 US companies. In world terms the largest European company, BAe, ranked 7th. The table is already out of date, since the European arms industry followed the British in restructuring. Examples of the changes include the formation of Deutsche Aerospace by the Daimler–Benz acquisition of MBB; the acquisition of Plessey by GEC & Siemens; the merging of Aerospatiale's avionics interests into Thomson–CSF; the proposed but postponed merger of Thomson–BAe missile interests; the sale of most of Philips' defence interests to other majors such as Thomson; the sale by Ferranti, after massive losses at its US subsidiary, ISC, of a large part of its defence interests to GEC; the proposed formation of Eurocopter from the merger of MBB's and Aerospatiale's helicopter interests; and the acquisition of many smaller companies such as FN in Belgium and Heckler–Koch in Germany by foreign majors. The general expectation is that the market will soon comprise a few large players and a periphery of specialist niche producers. Internationalisation is inevitable, since national production of major weapons systems is no longer viable except, perhaps, in the US.

The world defence industry faces major problems because of falling real defence budgets, falling demand for arms exports, rising development costs and increased competition. A French DGA official describes the European position as follows:

. . .probably 30% excess in production, too many competing players on the supply side, too many disagreeing members on the demand side, domestic markets closed to the tune of 90% or so, and maybe worse things to come: domestic armaments budgets are being reduced and disarmament will spur a technological race, increasing the need for R&D while decreasing production. (Roger, 1991.)

The UK Monopolies and Mergers Commission concurs:

. . .falling demand and growing overcapacity; increasingly sophisticated and expensive technologies; breakdown of national markets and internationalisation of procurement through consortia. (Monopolies and Mergers Commission, 1991.)

There is no doubt that the economic forces to which the industry is subject will produce changes in the international division of labour, massive restructuring and a new relation between the arms producers and individual national states. This might be done on a European or global basis, by market forces or by negotiation between governments. European defence multinationals could come in many forms: national companies with subsidiaries in other European countries; true transnationals such as Shell and Unilever produced by merger; multinational subsidiaries of national companies, as proposed by BAe and Thomson; consortia for specific products such as Airbus and Panavia (which makes Tornado). Although change is inevitable, the direction of change is less clear because of uncertainties about demand (how many weapons of what sort will be needed in the new strategic climate), technology (how they will operate) and supply (who will create comparative advantage). Given these uncertainties and the lack of appropriate political mechanisms, planned restructuring of the industry on a European level is likely to be almost impossible. Even if it were possible, such planned restructuring might not be desirable. Given the balance of forces and the power of the MIC, the end result of such planning would probably be a 'tank mountain' produced by a Common Armaments Policy to join the 'butter mountain' produced by the Common Agricultural policy. As discussed below, this is not a general case against planning, for instance to aid restructuring in hard-hit regions, but a recognition that the lobbying power of the MIC may enable it to capture the planning process and use it to its own ends. The European policy dimension is discussed at more length by Fontanel and Smith (1991): here we examine the national policy dimension.

Issues

The central issue is the relationship between the state and military industry. This relationship differs substantially within Europe. By applying Thatcherism, Britain adopted a more commercial, free-market approach. Arms producers have been privatised, competitive tendering for fixed-price contracts has become the norm, contracts have been awarded to foreign suppliers, and the MOD insists that it has no industrial policy for the defence industrial base. The MOD takes no responsibility for industrial sponsorship or for technologies unrelated to immediate defence needs; the very few exemptions are for quite specific needs such as nuclear weapons production and cryptoanalysis, where it is felt that allies cannot be trusted. This represents a sharp break from the historical, more dirigiste tradition in defence production.

The French have maintained dirigisme and have created a partnership between state and industry within a coherent industrial policy which emphasises the export of arms and the development of technological leadership. The contrast between the British and French processes brings out two related issues: whether the state should own the arms firms, and whether procurement should have military value for money as its prime objective or should rather be part of a general industrial policy.

State ownership and control

The state-owned UK defence companies were sold not for any particular defence reason but as part of a general policy of privatisation: the Conservative government privatised anything that was profitable enough, or could be made to look profitable enough, to find a buyer. There is a large literature on privatisation, though none of it addresses the particular problems of defence. However, to provide a context for a discussion of defence issues it is necessary to consider more general issues in the comparison of state and private ownership.

The literature tends to focus on the relative merits of state and market. This is too undifferentiated. Before we can judge the effect of a change from public to private ownership we must assess the character of the particular state and the particular market. To assess the character of the state we need to know its specific objectives, the political and economic constraints under which it operates, the quality and honesty of its agents, and its power to implement and monitor policies. Similarly, to assess the character of a market we need to know the specific nature of production, competition and internationalisation: who are the owners, the customers, the suppliers, the workers, the sources of capital? State ownership can vary from, at one extreme, merely holding the majority of shares in an enterprise to, at the other extreme, complete integration within the state where the employees of the enterprise are civil servants, as was the case with Royal Ordnance. Private ownership also takes a variety of different forms and the success of National Freight, one of the earliest privatisations, seems to have owed a lot to the fact that it was owned by its employees. Posing the question in this way would lead us to expect that the experiences of nationalisation and privatisation would be very differentiated, contingent on the specific character of state and market, and this is exactly what is found.

Consider one market, steel. Under private ownership the UK steel industry was notorious for its inefficiency and slow adoption of new technology, and remained marginally profitable only as a result of protection and cartelisation. Steel was renationalised in 1967; during the 1970s the nationalised industry (BSC) conducted a massive investment programme but productivity improved little and it made large losses. During the 1980s, under state ownership, the new investment was exploited more efficiently, the unions were crushed, and there were mass redundancies and productivity improvements which transformed BSC from the highest- to the lowest-cost producer in the world. It could be privatised at the end of 1988 only as a result of their transformation in efficiency which occurred under state ownership. Looking across the world, the private US steel industry failed to restructure and adopt new technology, while its most rapidly growing competitor was the nationalised Korean company Posco, run by a retired General. Generalisations about private ownership in steel are not necessarily transferable to other markets because the cost and production structures differ. Generalisations about state ownership under a Thatcher or Korean military government are not transferable to state ownership under say a French or Italian government because the political structures differ.

In defence, the point is well illustrated by the contrast between BAe and Thomson–CSF, two aggressive, acquisitive, internationalising arms firms. The details are described in the Monopolies and Mergers Commission (1991) study of the proposed merger of their missile interests: the Commission approved the merger but the firms abandoned it. Thomson was a French family firm, which was nationalised, and the French government now owns the majority (though not all) of the shares in what has become a very successful nationalised multinational. It comprises 65 companies, 43 in France and 22 overseas, and is the third largest defence electronics company in the UK. The Monopolies and Mergers Commission described the evolution of the company as follows:

> We were told that at the time of nationalisation in 1982 Thomson–CSF was on the verge of a major crisis. Whilst in the private sector, the company had acquired businesses that proved to be loss-making. It was very highly geared and in 1982 it reported a loss of FF 2,051 million. Since then the company has undergone far-reaching rationalisation affecting the scope and organisation of its various businesses, its capital structure and its profitability. It has focussed its activities on its core business and divesting loss-making businesses, restructuring its industrial sites and improving cash management, while sustaining research and development and capital investment. (Monopolies and Mergers Commission, 1991, para 2.16.)

GIAT, the French nationalised ordnance producer, is undergoing a similar process of rationalisation and foreign acquisition; the difference is that its history was as a loss-making public arsenal, rather than as a private organisation. British Aerospace was formed in 1977 by the nationalisation of BAC, Hawker–Siddeley and Scottish Aviation. The Conservative government converted it into a public limited company in

1981, when half the shares were sold, the remainder being sold in 1985. Even though it held half the shares, the government does not seem to have intervened in BAe beyond restricting foreign holding of its shares. BAe subsequently bought Royal Ordnance and British Leyland (the Rover Group) which had previously been government-owned. The main effect of nationalisation was rationalisation of the competing airframe and missile makers, but there had already been substantial prior rationalisation of the airframe industry. Even without public ownership, earlier governments had been able to force rationalisation and shape the policies of the industry, because they were the major customer for military aircraft and provided launch aid for civil aircraft.

Ownership matters in that it confers specific rights, but the mere fact that one of the companies was nationalised and one privatised, does not distinguish the two, because it does not indicate how the rights of ownership were used. This illustrates the argument that it is not state or private ownership itself that is important, but the character of the ownership, the constraints and the policies followed. Two characteristics of the defence market are important. The first is obvious: the bulk of its products are bought by government. The second is the fundamental uncertainty and asymmetry of information associated with military matters. Strategic and technological uncertainty about needs, costs and performance are inherent to weapons. The secrecy endemic to military matters and the specialised experience of the armed forces and the defence contractors give them considerable control over information. This raises what economists call 'moral hazard' problems: the danger pointed out by General Eisenhower in his warnings about the MIC that defence manufacturers, perhaps in conjunction with the armed services, can use this uncertainty and asymmetry in information to capture and exploit government purchasing in their own interest rather than in some notional national interest.

How can such exploitation be minimised? Should arms companies be kept private, at a distance, so that the government has no responsibility for their profitability, production and employment and thus is less open to lobbying and leverage? Or is it better for the state to own them, under the direct control of the government, to stop such exploitation? If it is believed that exploitation is a direct result of capitalist firms' drive for profits, then public ownership appears more attractive; if, however, allowance is made for a more general concept of surplus or rents which can be extracted by state employees, this is not the case. Nationalised arms firms tend to be as expansionist and acquisitive as private ones. Within a state the transfers of surplus tend to be less obvious and it can be difficult to identify the true cost of military activity. Within a market the transfers are somewhat more transparent.

Public ownership internalises the substantial externalities and risks which are associated with defence procurement and allows the state to have direct control over the enterprise, rather than having to bargain with an independent and powerful firm. This can be thought of as the 'first-best', unconstrained solution. However, it may not be the best solution given the constraints imposed by the lobbying power of the MIC. Once it is well established within government the MIC can make the state the captive rather than the master of the military industry, forcing the state to shape national policy so as to underwrite the activities of the arms firms. The second-best solution, keeping the arms firms at arm's length through the market, may be preferable. Which organisational structure makes it more likely that the state controls the MIC, rather than the MIC controlling the state, is clearly contingent on the specific nature of the state and the MIC. We would suggest that the MIC has more leverage when it gets inside the state apparatus than when it is kept at arm's length through market relations. If the state is seen as a neutral instrument of government then public ownership may appear attractive, but if it is seen as an arena of conflict, giving the MIC an established defensive position within the arena appears dangerous.

Industrial policy

The question as concerns industrial policy is whether the state should choose which weapons it purchases merely on the basis of which product—domestic or foreign—best meets the military need at the least cost, or whether it should take into account wider industrial implications. The latter might include employment and balance of payments consequences, the spin-offs from military technology and the long-term health of the domestic defence industrial base. This issue is discussed at greater length in Smith (1990). The issues are very similar to those involved in state ownership. In principle, there are large externalities which profit-maximising firms may ignore and such market failure creates an *a priori* presumption for state intervention through industrial policy. In practice, any industrial policy is liable to be captured by rent-seeking defence interests, creating the danger of government failure worse than the market failure it was designed to correct.

Two empirical issues are relevant to judge the size of the externalities. First, how large are the technological spin-offs from defence production to the civil sector? The evidence, reviewed in ACOST (1989), suggests that such technological spin-offs are rather small. Second, how strong are the security arguments for a domestic weapons production capability? Given the prolonged lead-times required to produce weapons, the strategic value of national production capacity seems rather small compared to the alternatives. The alternatives include promoting standardisation to allow resupply from allies, ensuring maintenance and conversion rather than production capacity and keeping adequate levels of inventories. Finally, if direct externalities (from employment, savings on the balance of payments, tax revenue, etc.) are important, they should be taken account of more generally, not just in defence. Given the lobbying powers of the defence companies, they tend to be able to get treated as a special case, as the MOD emphasised in their evidence quoted above.

To offset special pleading, it is important to apply general economic rules to defence, and this is reinforced by the fact that while the MOD have some expertise in judging military needs, there is no reason to expect them to be good at judging industrial implications. Nor is an *a priori* case for some industrial policy sufficient: a case has to be made for some specific industrial policy. This would almost certainly have to be implemented on at least a European level. National markets are too small to support viable producers, and promotion of national champions is a heavily negative-sum game. The political difficulties in determining a specific policy are illustrated by the conflict over Westland, the small UK helicopter producer which ran into financial difficulties. The excess capacity was obvious: Europe had four helicopter producers for 2 800 military helicopters, while the US had four helicopter producers for over 10 000 military helicopters. However, resolution of Westland's position split the Conservative Party and provoked the resignation of two Cabinet Ministers, Michael Heseltine and Leon Brittan, before the final solution, in which a US company took a stake, was decided by the stock market.

Policies for adjusting to lower military spending

The general argument that industrial policies for defence firms should be based on general economic principles—applied across the board rather than being tailored to defence needs—applies to the issue of conversion. The Thatcher cuts in military spending relied on market forces, commercial initiatives and macroeconomic policy to effect the adjustment. Now that the world is facing a situation of declining military expenditures, the conversion of military industry has attracted considerable attention. Historical experience and econometric evidence suggest that the transition to lower military budgets will create few problems at the national level as long as there are sensible macroeconomic policies (see Barker *et al.*, 1991). However, individual industries and regions will face problems of adjustment within national economies. There is thus a role for some form of planning to overcome regional and local adjustment problems, and to take account of wider issues such as the environmental impact. However, these should be general policies for regional and industrial adjustment and should not be tailored to defence companies.

Conclusions

The option of continuing Thatcherite defence policy might, in principle if not in political practice, be attractive to Socialist governments. First, it would involve continuing the present policy of cuts in defence spending; this is desirable given the other pressing needs for public expenditure and the damage the military burden has done to the UK economy. Second, it would involve continuing to publish at least as much material on defence budgets and procurement as at present. Third, it would leave the arms firms private: public ownership gives the arms firms a privileged position within the state to press for their projects. Fourth, it would maintain fixed-price competitive procurement based on value for money rather than national preference: this provides those weapons that are necessary at the lowest cost, reduces the political leverage of the military lobby, and increases the incentive for the arms firms to diversify out of defence. It should certainly not be a Socialist objective to seek to create a dominant position for the British military–industrial complex in a protected European market. That is a prescription for higher defence budgets, further cost escalation on ineffective weapons, and the creation of an even more powerful pressure group with an interest in international tension.

This is not to say that planning is not important. The transition to lower military budgets while creating no likely macroeconomic problems will create problems within national economies. It will be necessary to provide some form of planning to overcome regional and local adjustment problems and to achieve economic benefit from the 'peace dividend'.

Acknowledgements

We are grateful to Joyce Wheeler for assistance in accessing the Datastream company databank, and to John Lovering and Francis Green for comments.

Comment

Conversion and Economic Restructuring

John Lovering

Paul Dunne and Ron Smith's chapter argues that Thatcherism represented 'the most sustained attack since the war' on Britain's cancerous military–industrial complex and that an incoming government could do worse than continue current policy towards the defence industry, although this should ideally be complemented by 'sensible' macroeconomic policy. Their argument is provocative but misleading: it misconstrues Thatcherism, oversimplifies developments in the British defence industry and thereby arrives at dangerous policy recommendations.

Thatcherism was both more and less than the 'determined implementation' of neo-liberal economic policy. It was also Atlanticist (or 'Churchillian') geopolitics, aiming to reinforce the US alliance and the military superiority of the US and NATO. The government's intentions towards Britain's bloated defence industry—where they were thought out at all—were less to run it down than to shed 'fat' and find new ways of propping up the remaining core. Things could not have carried on as before in the defence industry whatever government was in power. However, the particular solution stumbled upon by the Thatcher governments hastened its restructuring, whilst giving it an economically and socially malign twist. Through increased reliance on market forces (in reality, politically constructed market forces) it was to become an ancillary to the US defence industry, especially via a European defence complex, and to increase its general presence in export markets.

Companies fed for years on easy contracts from Whitehall could not be reborn as dynamic, aggressive international competitors without a degree of supportive government intervention and this was unthinkable to the government. So Thatcherism resulted in a rather chaotic and incomplete modernisation in the leading defence companies and there were many casualties amongst the lower ranks. The drift was towards a more internationalised arms industry—in terms of corporate alliances, markets and even (embyronically) in production—together with concentration on a favoured core of national champions (above all, BAe and GEC). Against a background of few opportunities in Britain's tottering non-defence sectors, leading firms had little option but to 'dig deeper' and attempt to build up their comparative advantage in military market niches (Lovering, 1990).

The short-term benefits were confined to modest savings in defence equipment costs. The longer-term costs include massive job loss, which may soon total one-third of a million, and the collapse of the industrial core in several defence-dependent localities. This is not a straightforward matter of a contraction of the defence industry leading to a transfer of resources into civilian industries. The restructuring was much more perverse. While growing more dependent on sales to a few overseas buyers (notably Saudi Arabia), the defence sector continued to take a relatively large share of the elite professional labour market (at least until the 'planning blight' phase of 1991) in order to compete more aggressively. However, it used an even smaller proportion of this scarce labour for 'blue skies' research which might be potentially beneficial for the non-defence economy. More was devoted to short-term military development work such as customising equipment for foreign armed services (Lovering, 1991). So Thatcherism was less an 'attack on the military–industrial complex' than on workers and communities which had come to rely on the industry. At the same time it gave a boost (albeit a rather incoherent one) to the attempt by leading companies to construct the infrastructure of a new military–industrial complex on the international level.

Dunne and Smith oppose any 'special policy' which might throw money at defence companies. Their policy argument rests on two key assumptions but neither is spelled out sufficiently to clinch the case. The first is a gloomy pessimism about the ability of governments to influence management strategies in firms. This is far too fatalistic— taken seriously it would forbid any attempt to construct even the mildest social democratic economic policy. The second is a cheery optimism about governments' ability to bring forth new companies and new industries simply by creating the right macroeconomic environment. This is economically implausible. The experience of the 1980s gives little indication that the British non-defence economy has the capacity to generate jobs and wealth on the scale required to soak up jobs lost in defence, let alone to meet wider objectives. By concentrating on the defence sector, Dunne and Smith either ignore the appalling state of the rest of industry or falsely blame this entirely on defence spending. However, the British defence industry *per se* is not the prime mover of national deindustrialisation (although this is not to deny that a militarist bias in government policy over many decades has been bound up with the economic malaise).

If 'Thatcherite' policy were to continue, the likelihood is that by the late 1990s the arms industry would still be overrepresented in Britain, although it would generate very few jobs and benefits. The 'peace dividend' would have been frittered away, just as North Sea oil revenues were in the 1980s. If the historic opportunities which now present themselves are to be grasped, much more attention should be given to the ways in which defence companies—which remain at the commanding heights of British manufacturing, high technology and exports—might be redirected towards more generally productive strategies. In other words, there is a strong case for exploring a conversion strategy. This should be an integral part of the industrial, technological and regional innovations which would be needed to translate any new macroeconomic policy into an enduring improvement.

There is also a political dimension here. In effect, Dunne and Smith ask defence workers and communities simply to accept job losses and await deliverance from above, courtesy of a 'sensible macroeconomic policy' the likes of which no-one has actually experienced and in which few non-economists believe. The denial of the chance of participation is surely not an aspect of Thatcherism they would wish to advocate. At a time when the groundswell of enthusiasm for arms conversion is at an unprecedented level (see IPMS, MSF, TGWU, 1990), Dunne and Smith's advocacy of market forces neglects both economic realities and political–ideological opportunities. More serious attention to conversion would not only engage key questions about economic restructuring, it would also challenge the top-down bias of policy formation (and especially the antidemocratic avoidance of any debate on defence and industrial planning in the Labour Party).

6

Taking on the Inner Cities

Barry Moore

When the Conservative government took office in 1979, a major shift in the direction of urban policy and more specifically inner city policy was already taking place. The 1977 White Paper, *Policy for the Inner Cities*, marked a watershed in post-War urban policy. For the first time, the government emphasised the weakening economic base of the inner cities as the critically important factor underlying their physical deterioration and as being responsible for creating the conditions in which large concentrations of unemployed and socially disadvantaged people lived. Hitherto, successive governments had seen the plight of many of these people as primarily the outcome of their own personal inadequacies, difficult family circumstances or racial intolerance. It was also increasingly recognised that the physical deterioration manifest in the inner cities of the major conurbations reflected their economic decline and their failure to attract investment for property redevelopment and urban renewal. The new and growing sectors of the UK economy were choosing New Town and overspill locations in the hinterlands of the conurbations and carrying in their wake investment in infrastructure and the built environment so desperately needed in the inner cities. At the same time, population dispersal was steering an increasing share of new housing and social investment away from the large conurbations and their inner areas to smaller and more rapidly growing towns.

As the 1970s came to an end it was also increasingly apparent that a major spatial restructuring of the UK economy was in progress in which the conurbations and larger cities were not only sharing the traumas of national deindustrialisation, but also experiencing an absolute decline in economic activity and population on an unprecedented scale. In this process of national and urban restructuring, the weaker and more vulnerable groups in society inevitably experienced the most severe problems of adaptation as competition for jobs in circumstances of persistently high national and regional unemployment intensified. The predicament of these disadvantaged groups in the inner areas (particularly in those cities outside the more prosperous regions, and heavily dependent on manufacturing industry) was further exacerbated by a narrowing economic base in which to compete for jobs. Subsequent analysis of the 1981 *Census of Population* lent strong support to this view (Begg *et al.*, 1986).

Throughout the 1980s, Conservative administrations accepted the fundamental argument of the 1977 White Paper of the need for the economic regeneration of the inner cities. However, although key policies inherited in 1979 were retained, notably the Urban Programme and curtailment of New Town policies, subsequent policy developments in the 1980s were quite radical and inevitably reflected views on the causes of relatively weak economic performance in the UK economy more generally. This chapter reviews inner city policy developments in the 1980s and the main themes that underpin the plethora of inner city initiatives introduced.

The first section presents a brief overview of the economic predicament of the inner cities at the beginning of the 1980s and shows the deep-seated nature of inner city problems and their relationship to long-term trends in industrial and spatial restructuring in the UK economy. It is argued that inner city problems are not problems of decline *per se* as economic activity and population decant to suburbs and hinterland towns, but rather that they arise from the unbalanced nature of decline, whereby concentrations of unemployed and other disadvantaged groups are trapped in decaying inner city areas with severely limited opportunities to leave should they so wish. Moreover, although such concentrations have tended to occur in inner city areas where private low-cost rented accommodation and Local Authority housing are available, other parts of conurbations, notably some peripheral Local Authority estates, have also experienced above-average concentrations of deprivation.

The second part of the chapter describes the changing stance of inner city policies in the 1980s and shows the complexity of the policy response with its panoply of new programmes, initiatives and 'experiments'. It is shown that to a significant extent policy developed in an *ad hoc*, piecemeal fashion with little or no attempt to approach inner city problems with a strategically guided policy package. The total public expenditure devoted specifically to resolving inner city problems (as opposed to public expenditure which impinges coincidentally on inner city areas) is less than one-third of the £3bn claimed to be associated with the Conservatives' *Actions for Cities* programme. It is also shown that if other geographically differentiated public policy programmes are taken into account, such as regional policy (which is focused primarily on the major conurbations of the North and Scotland), then public expenditure committed to the economic regeneration of inner city areas may well have fallen rather than increased since 1979.

The third section reviews recent evaluations of the effectiveness of inner city programmes. It is shown that policies are making some progress in removing inner city physical dereliction and in securing economic regeneration, but that these achievements fall far short of what is required to improve significantly the economic opportunities that confront the inner city unemployed and disadvantaged.

The final section considers future policy development and argues for a more strategic and coordinated approach to inner city problems, focused on the critical issues of 'unbalanced decline' and the need to place much more emphasis on improving the competitive position in the labour market of those who live in inner city areas or depressed peripheral estates.

The Decline of Britain's Inner Cities

At the beginning of the 1980s Britain's inner city population of working age had experienced three decades of uninterrupted decline, from just under 5 million to about 3.3 million. Similarly, employment of inner city residents had also fallen relentlessly in this period from 3.8 million to 2.2 million (Table 6.1). In the same period, the number of unemployed inner city residents had risen by 269 000 and their unemployment rate was some 50% above the national average. Thus, not only was there a problem of persistently higher unemployment rates among inner city residents stretching back over 30 years, but this problem was steadily intensifying.

The economic predicament of the inner cities at the beginning of the 1980s is also brought out very clearly when comparisons are made

Table 6.1. Inner city decline: population, employment and unemployment, 1951–1981.[a]

	1951	1961	1971	1981
Population (000s)	4982	4720	3946	3346
Employment (000s)	4826	4886	4170	3586
Commuters (000s)	997	1223	1259	1391
Inner city residents (000s)	3829	3663	2911	2195
Unemployed residents (000s)	111	146	237	380
Unemployed residents (%)	2.8	3.8	7.5	14.8
Total unemployed (%)	2.2	2.9	5.4	9.6
Unemployment rate of residents relative to UK=100	133	136	144	151

[a]Source: Begg *et al.* (1986).

with other areas. Figures 6.1–6.3 show populations of working age, employment and residential unemployment rates for inner cities, outer cities, free-standing cities, small towns and rural areas for 1951–1981. There is a particularly sharp contrast between the decline of the inner cities and their worsening unemployment position and the growth of the smaller towns and rural communities and their improving unemployment position.

Much of the absolute loss of economic activity in the inner cities was associated with the decline of manufacturing activity. This in turn created many of the problems of physical dereliction associated with vacant sites and derelict buildings formerly occupied by manufacturing industry. Table 6.2 shows that over 1 million manufacturing jobs were lost in the inner city areas between 1951 and 1981, and over one-quarter of a million service-sector jobs. By contrast, the smaller towns and rural areas gained some 225 000 manufacturing jobs and 3 million service-sector jobs.

The restructuring of the national economy away from manufacturing employment to service employment, combined with an urban–rural shift of economic activity in the period up to 1981, therefore had profound consequences for the economies of inner cities in Britain. Moreover, in contrast to the economy more generally, the decline in manufacturing employment in the inner cities was not offset by a growth of employment opportunities in service activities.

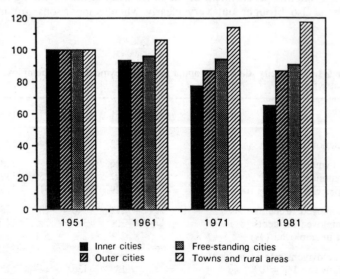

Figure 6.1. Changes in population of working age grouped by type of area 1951–1981 (relative to UK = 100).

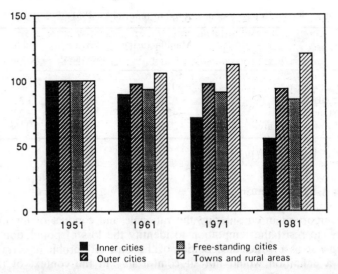

Figure 6.2. Changes in total employment by type of area 1951–1981 (relative to UK = 100).

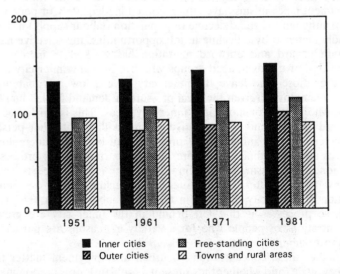

Figure 6.3. Unemployment rates by type of area 1951–1981 (relative to UK = 100).

Table 6.2. Sectoral employment change in inner cities 1951–1981 (000s).[a]

	Manufacturing	Private services	Public services
Inner city areas	−1018	−210	−40
Outer city areas	−613	+372	+326
Free-standing cities	−425	+212	+201
Small towns/rural areas	+225	+1854	+1158

[a]Source: Begg *et al.* (1986).

Inner City Problems

It is important in considering the rationale and conduct of inner city policy, to resist the temptation to identify the loss of population and jobs *per se* as a sufficient definition of the inner city problem: certainly, such a definition would not sit comfortably in the context of three decades of post-War urban policy designed explicitly to decant population and economic activity away from major conurbations and their inner cities. Insofar as problems have emerged as a result of the economic decline of the inner cities, it is primarily because such decline has been socially and economically unbalanced and at the same time market adjustment mechanisms have either worked inadequately or perversely. Thus, although the trend decline of population (labour supply) has been broadly matched by a decline in job opportunities, the selective nature of both inward and outward migration has worked to increase the proportion of disadvantaged groups who live in many inner city areas. Many of those who leave the inner city have a lower probability of being unemployed (given the local pressure of demand for labour) than those who remain or move into inner city areas. This is partly because outward movers tend to be relatively more skilled, but other personal characteristics that influence the probability of becoming unemployed, such as age and ethnic origin, are not unimportant in this process. In addition, an increasing proportion of inner city jobs have been secured by inward commuters, which suggests a decline in the competitive position of inner city residents in the local labour market. The result of these processes is that left behind in the inner city are growing concentrations of people who for a variety of reasons are particularly prone to unemployment.

Whether these concentrations of urban unemployment matter from a policy angle (and whether they present a problem) turns predominantly on the view taken of the social consequences. So long as there is generalised unemployment in the country, the majority of those unemployed in the inner cities are likely to be unemployed somewhere and, insofar as they do secure a job through effective inner city policies, many will do so at the expense of others elsewhere. There is no clear-cut case on economic grounds for diluting concentrations of urban unemployed, although it must be recognised that selected skill shortages in certain areas could be relieved in this way, and that should national unemployment fall significantly, then economic benefits could flow from carefully designed redistributive initiatives. It should also be recognised that considerations relating to the efficiency of public service delivery and infrastructure provision may also provide an economic justification for slowing down or stabilising economic and demographic decline.

From a policy perspective it is also important to understand how the housing market has interacted with the processes of urban decline both to create concentrations of unemployed and socially disadvantaged in the inner city and to encourage selective inward and outward migration of population. There is a clear tendency for an above-average proportion of the unemployed and other disadvantaged groups to live in Local Authority or low-cost rented segments of the housing market. Thus inner city concentrations of disadvantaged groups are often closely associated with geographical concentrations of Local Authority and low-cost privately rented housing in inner cities. Moreover, given that a large proportion of new building investment outside the inner cities in the 1960s and 1970s was in the owner-occupied sector, households in these rented tenures could enjoy improved opportunities for outward migration only if they could enter the owner-occupied segment of the labour market. Those in the unfurnished rented sector have been particularly prone to being trapped in the inner city. The halt in the New Town programme at the end of the 1970s and the heavy concentration of the rented sector in the major conurbations and larger cities also did little to enhance the potential mobility of disadvantaged groups living in the inner cities. Most of the population loss from the inner urban areas is attributable to housing market factors, rather than responses to environmental conditions or even employment opportunities, although the latter seem to be important in cities in the north of the UK.

If the operation of the housing market has been critical in the spatial allocation of the unemployed and disadvantaged, the commercial property market has also proved inadequate to the task of redevelopment in the wake of disinvestment in the inner city. In part, this reflects the pervasiveness of external diseconomies, as empty factories and derelict sites have emerged as industry has left the inner city. It also reflects the inevitably increasing uncertainty of inner city properties as sound investments in the context of economic decline, and their doubtful potential for achieving returns compared with properties located in more dynamic areas.

In this process of economic and demographic decline, the public sector is important in respect of its role not only as landlord and land owner but also as a provider of public services. Local authorities experience a fiscal squeeze as tax yields fall relatively and the *per capita* cost of service provision rises relatively. At the same time, unbalanced social decline raises the proportion of the local population dependent on locally provided public services. If provision of public services falls short of needs relative to other areas, this further worsens the plight of the disadvantaged and encourages dispersal of economic activity and of the population of deprived groups. This suggests that the processes of decline in the major concentrations and larger cities of the UK may be cumulative and reinforcing rather than self-equilibrating (Figure 6.4).

Inner City Policy Objectives in the 1980s

The central objective of inner city policy embodied in the 1977 White Paper was the economic regeneration of the inner cities and the slowing down of the large-scale loss (dispersal) of population and jobs. Significantly, these key objectives were largely retained by the new government. Although subject to modification, notably with respect to the balance between economic and social services and community projects, the 1988 Urban Programme, for example, differed little from the revamped Urban Programme inherited from the Labour government in 1979. The objectives of Conservative inner city policy in the 1980s

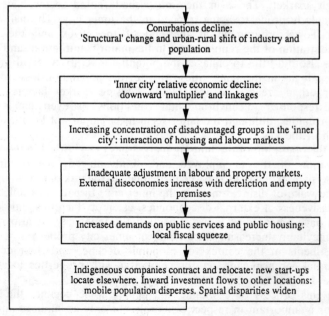

Figure 6.4. The process of cumulative decline in the inner city.

are perhaps best summarised in *Action for Cities* (1988): first, to encourage enterprise and new business, and help existing businesses to grow stronger; second, to improve people's job prospects, their motivations and skills; third, to make inner city areas attractive to residents and to businesses by tackling dereliction, bringing buildings into use, preparing sites and encouraging development, and improving the quality of housing; and fourth, to reduce crime and make inner cities attractive places in which to live and work.

These four broad objectives not only overlap but also contain within them a number of related objectives. The first objective, for example, includes new firm formation as well as retention and improvement of indigenous inner city firms. The third objective includes removal of physical dereliction, infrastructure improvement, housing development and site preparation for economic development. It is also apparent that objectives such as preparing sites and bringing buildings into use are very much intermediate objectives necessary to secure economic regeneration and jobs. Although the emphasis has been very much on the regeneration of the built environment, *People in Cities* (1990) indicates a shift in policy in the late 1980s towards partnership and the role of people in the inner cities. *Getting People in Jobs* and *Targeting Urban Employment*, both published by the Department of the Environment (DoE) in 1990, reinforce the new emphasis on people and partnerships at a time when the development task is severely hampered by a property market in deep recession.

Two other points should be made when discussing the government's inner city policy objectives. Firstly, within the variety of programmes and initiatives that fall within the scope of the *Action for Cities* programme, there exists a raft of specific programme objectives relating to, for example, the Urban Programme, Enterprise Zones, Urban Development Corporations and Safer Cities Schemes. Secondly, a number of national programmes have been 'bent' towards inner city areas and might sensibly have been included in the *Action for Cities* programme. To these should be added the programmes and objectives of relevant Local Authorities, other agencies and the private sector.

Programmes, initiatives and public expenditure

The period after 1979 has witnessed a proliferation of programmes and initiatives concerned with inner city regeneration. This is brought out in Figure 6.5 which shows six central government Departments responsible for some 30 inner city initiatives and programmes encompassed within *Action for Cities*. The DoE is the dominant Department for inner city policy and has several key programmes that are specifically targeted on the inner cities: these include the Urban Programme, Urban Development Corporations, City Grants and City Action Teams. Ten of the 26 Enterprise Zones are located in inner city areas, as are two

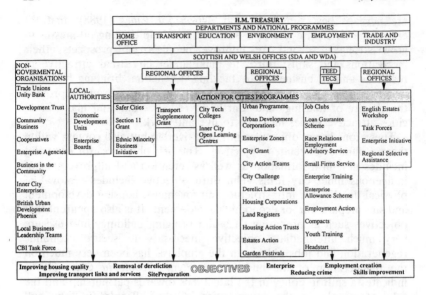

Figure 6.5. Inner city policy in the 1980s.

of the Garden Festivals, and may reasonably be regarded as targeted on inner cities, but the incidence of Derelict Land Grant and other DoE programmes is coincidental. The most recent initiative has been the City Challenge, which involves 'top-slicing' of £82.5m a year of housing and inner city programme funding. Competitive bids from Urban Programme authorities are required and there is a responsibility to develop a strategy that encompasses the local area and the wider city economy and includes a wide range of local organisations. Two Department of Trade and Industry (DTI) programmes are targeted specifically on inner cities—the English Estates Managed Workshop Programme and the 16 Inner City Task Forces. The incidence of the Enterprise Initiative and Regional Selective Assistance in inner cities is again coincidental. The two Department of Education and Science (DES) initiatives impact mainly on the inner cities but only the Inner City Open Learning Centres and Headstart are focused specifically on inner cities, although the activities of the Race Relations Employment Advisory Service are almost entirely concentrated in inner city areas. The severely diminished role of the Home Office in the post-1977 White Paper period is indicated by the paucity of initiatives of which only Safer Cities is 100% targeted, although the Ethnic Minorities Business Initiative impinges mainly on inner city areas.

The total public expenditure associated with the *Action for Cities* programme is approximately £3bn (1989–1990), of which the DoE accounts for £1130m, the Department of Employment for £1120m, the

DTI for £220m, the Department of Transport for £250m and the Scottish and Welsh Offices together for about £300m. However, this level of public expenditure is a poor guide to the Conservative government's commitment to inner city regeneration through specifically targeted policies. Inner city targeted public expenditure by central government Departments is shown in Table 6.3.

Of the £3bn public expenditure that benefits inner city areas, less than £1bn is differentiated specifically in favour of inner cities—i.e. areas outside inner cities do not in general benefit from the associated programmes. If programmes with a high incidence in inner cities are also included, differentiated expenditure rises to approximately £1.3bn. It should be pointed out that the latter enhanced totals of public expenditure are accounted for largely by Enterprise Zones, which are being phased out in the early 1990s. What also stands out from Table 6.3 is confirmation of the dominance of the DoE, which is responsible for approximately 90% of inner-city specific expenditure.

Local Authorities have also played an active role in supporting inner city economic regeneration and the intensity of economic development initiatives increased sharply in the late 1970s and early 1980s. A survey of local authorities in 1986 revealed that significant resources were devoted to economic development (£145m of capital spending by 161 authorities and £77m of revenue expenditure by 177 councils). By the end of the 1980s over 200 authorities were engaged in economic development (Audit Commission, 1991). The Widdicombe Committee Report estimated local government expenditure on economic development to be about £220m in 1986–1987, equal to about 1% of total local government expenditure. These resources devoted to economic development are quite small and it should be remembered that such expenditures were not associated only with inner city authorities. Moreover, there is evidence that switches in Rate Support Grant away from inner city Local Authorities in the 1980s and cuts in housing subsidies more than offset increased resources devoted to economic development.

Enterprise Boards were set up in the early 1980s by a number of Local Authorities, to stimulate the local economy by investing in firms either to ensure their survival or to help them expand and create jobs. Funded initially through Section 137 of the *Local Government Act 1972* which permitted a 2p rate call to fund activities beneficial to local residents, Enterprise Boards were established in the major conurbations of London (GLEB), Merseyside (MEB), the West Midlands (WMEB) and West Yorkshire (WYEB). Lancashire Enterprise was set up by the County Council. By 1986 accumulated investments by the Enterprise Boards amounted to £50–60m.

The remaining group of initiatives in Figure 6.5 are delivered by a rather mixed bag of non-government organisations ranging from Cooperatives and Development Trusts concerned with employment

Table 6.3. Targeted public expenditure on inner cities 1989–1990 and 1990–1991 (current prices).

Government Department	Expenditure (£m)	
	1989–1990	1990–1991
Department of Environment: inner-city specific		
Urban Programme	241	245
Urban Development Corporations	439	542
City Grants	35	49
City Action Teams	4	8
Total	719	844
Other high incidence:		
Enterprise Zones (est.)	200	200
Estates Action (est.)	150	150
Home Office: inner-city specific		
Safer Cities	4	N/A
Other high incidence:		
Ethnic Minorities Business		
Initiative	N/A	N/A
Department of Education and Science: inner-city specific		
Inner City Open Learning Centres	N/A	1.3
Other high incidence:		
City Technology Colleges (est.)	28	36
Department of Trade and Industry: inner-city specific		
Inner City Task Forces	18	23
English Estates Managed Workshop		
Programme	N/A	N/A
Department of Employment: inner-city specific		
Compacts	19	31
Headstart	N/A	N/A
Other high incidence:		
Job Clubs	10	15
Race Relations Employment		
Advisory Service	N/A	N/A
Overall totals		
Inner-city specific	760 (est.)	900
High incidence	388 (est.)	401

and social objectives, to Inner City Enterprises and British Urban Development concerned primarily with urban renewal. Public expenditure support for these initiatives is limited and may often come from a variety of sources. For example, Local Enterprise Agencies are supported by DTI grants and Local Authorities. A number of these initiatives have a specific inner city focus but attract only limited financial support by comparison with the major central government programmes. In this context it is also important to recognise the growing importance of inner city partnerships in the process of securing urban regeneration. In Glasgow and Birmingham in particular, but also in a number of other cities, strategic partnerships between the private sector and Local Authorities are ensuring that the private sector makes an important contribution to urban regeneration in the inner city. Birmingham Heartlands, for example, is a long-term strategic urban renewal partnership between the City Council, the Chamber of Industry and Commerce and five private sector development companies. Other initiatives in Birmingham include the Ten Company Group Equal Opportunity Project, and the Birmingham Action Team. Private sector participation in urban regeneration has also been encouraged by local Business Leadership Teams—The Newcastle Initiative, The Wearside Opportunity and The Bristol Initiative are only three examples of some 15 such initiatives in the UK.

Although there are difficulties in piecing together comprehensive information on the public sector resources committed to inner cities in the 1980s, the information assembled above demonstrates that public expenditure on a relatively narrow range of DoE programmes has been and remains overwhelmingly important. This is particularly the case if only those policies that address the inner city specifically are considered. Thus trends in public expenditure on inner city policy can be judged broadly by examining expenditure on these programmes (Figure 6.6).

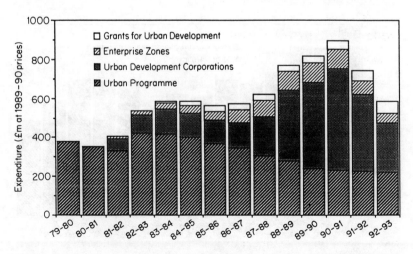

Figure 6.6. Public expenditure on main DoE inner city programmes 1979–1980 to 1992–1993 (source: Government expenditure plans 1990–1991).

128   *Barry Moore*

In total, public expenditure on inner cities has risen from just under
£400m in 1979–1980 to about £800m in 1989–1990, although it is
projected to fall sharply in the period from 1990–1992 to 1992–1993.
Within the total, Urban Programme expenditure has about halved from
around £400m in 1979–1980 to around £200m at the beginning of the
1990s. This reduction in the Urban Programme has been offset
by growing commitments to the Urban Development Corporation
programme, Enterprise Zone expenditures (which include here local
rates foregone) and grants for urban development.

However, the moderately encouraging trend of public sector support
for inner city economic regeneration in Figure 6.6 has to be set not
only against reductions in Rate Support Grant to inner city Local
Authorities referred to above, but also against reductions in expenditure
by the DTI on regional development policies which are targeted mainly
on encouraging economic development in the major conurbations of
Merseyside, Tyneside, Strathclyde and the West Midlands. Figure 6.7
shows a falling trend in the combined total of DoE urban policy and
DTI regional policy expenditure in the period from 1979–1980 to
1989–1990, as increased expenditure on urban policy has been more
than offset by falling expenditure on regional policy.

Main policy themes

Six major themes have underpinned the Conservatives' approach to
inner city policy and the wide range of government programmes and
initiatives that made up their radical policy package in the 1980s. Firstly,

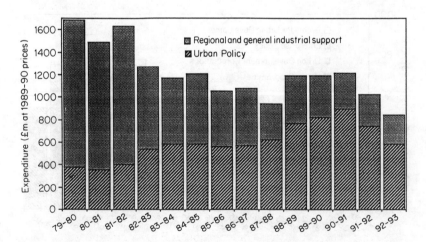

Figure 6.7. Public expenditure on urban and regional/industrial policies
1979–1980 to 1992–1993 (source: Government expenditure plans 1990–1991).

there was a strong belief that many of the problems faced by the inner city unemployed and socially disadvantaged could ultimately be solved only by the economic regeneration of the inner cities. Closely linked to the theme of economic regeneration was the theme of inner city 'containment' and the acceptance that post-War dispersal policies had to be attenuated. Thirdly, there was the anticollectivist theme that argued that the observed weakness of inner city economies was a consequence mainly of supply-side failures related to limited enterprise development, inadequate and inappropriate skills and poorly functioning labour and property markets. Fourthly, there was the recognition that the private sector had to be mobilised to support the substantial resources required to secure inner city economic regeneration. This theme emerged partly because of pressures to reduce public expenditure but also because of a belief that Local Authorities had been singularly unsuccessful in achieving inner city regeneration. Ideally, public funds were to be used to lever private sector resources into inner cities. A fifth theme relates to increasing control by central government and loss of control by Local Authorities in key policy areas such as housing, education and transport which are of critical importance in securing inner city renewal. The final theme relates to what Lawless (1988) has called 'the search for coordination'. Indeed, it has been argued that *Action for Cities* launched by the Prime Minister in 1988 contained no new policies and was entirely concerned with integration.

The above themes are reflected in the range of policy initiatives introduced in the 1980s (see Figure 6.5) and also in the gradually changing balance of the Urban Programme in favour of 'economic' projects. Perhaps the most controversial of these new initiatives have been the Urban Development Corporations (UDCs). If New Town Development Corporations could successfully acquire and develop land and foster some of the most economically dynamic areas of the UK, why should UDCs not play a similar role in inner cities? UDCs would concentrate on land reclamation and public infrastructure, using public funds as catalytic money to encourage private sector development. Following the establishment of the London Docklands Development Corporation and the Merseyside Development Corporations in the early 1980s, five 'second-generation' UDCs were set up in 1987 and four 'third-generation' UDCs were established during 1988 and 1989. To achieve their objectives UDCs were given major statutory powers to acquire land at values that took no account of potential development gains, to determine planning applications or deem themselves planning permission. UDCs were also given substantial public funds and in terms of public expenditure commitments UDCs are now the main programme for inner city economic regeneration.

The Urban Programme is the other major DoE inner cities programme. It has four main objectives: improvement of employment prospects, reduction in derelict sites, strengthening of the social fabric and encouragement of self-help, and reduction in the number of people in acute housing stress. Nearly three-quarters of expenditure is on economic and environmental projects with the remainder on social and housing projects. The Urban Programme is coordinated and administered directly through Local Authorities.

Enterprise Zones represent another major policy initiative of the first Conservative government and were introduced in 1981. The main inspiration for Enterprise Zones came from Professor Peter Hall (currently Urban Policy adviser to Michael Heseltine, who was responsible for the initiative in 1981). Hall argued that the crisis in Britain's inner cities had reached the point where an entirely new and unorthodox approach should be adopted. This Enterprise Zone 'experiment', as it became known, established geographical enclaves in which there existed minimal government bureaucracy, a relaxed and liberalised planning regime and where the burden of taxation was reduced compared with other areas. Some 25 Enterprise Zones were designated in the early 1980s each with a life of 10 years (the first Zones established in 1981 have recently been de-designated and two new Zones have been announced). The primary objective was to encourage industrial and commercial activity in areas where physical decay and economic distress were particularly severe and also to stimulate property development through the use of capital allowances for construction and relief from Local Authority rates.

In the same year (1981) that Enterprise Zones were introduced, Michael Heseltine created the Merseyside Task Force in response to the 1981 riots in Toxteth. The Task Force initiated a number of major projects to 'lever' private sector investment into Merseyside but no strategic vision was established. The five City Action Teams were announced in 1985, with the central objective of coordinating central government activity within the major conurbations, and in 1988 two other City Action Teams in Leeds and Nottingham were established. *Action for Cities* (1988) further emphasised the government's intention to improve coordination; however, the Urban Programme and Partnership remain a major vehicle for attempts to bring together different tiers of government and different government departments.

The Inner City Task Forces of the DTI have four main objectives: to create jobs by removing constraints on recruitment and local enterprise development, to facilitate and encourage enterprise by local people through training, financial and managerial assistance, to improve employability through training programmes and to support environmental and community initiatives. In addition, there are 'cross-cutting' objectives such as pump-priming of private sector investment, improving coordination between government programmes, local capacity building, targeting the employment needs of specifically disadvantaged groups and developing innovative approaches to local problems.

A striking feature of the main inner city programmes noted above is their emphasis on property-led economic development. Thus UDCs, Enterprise Zones and a significant proportion of the Urban Programme are concerned with facilitating and encouraging business development in the inner cities through the removal of dereliction, land reclamation and encouragement of property development. Disadvantaged or unemployed inner city residents benefit from such policies largely indirectly through so-called 'trickle-down' effects of increased inner city economic activity.

It should perhaps also be pointed out that the approach adopted in Scotland through the Scottish Development Agency has arguably been much more oriented towards the development of a coherent strategy towards urban deprivation and decline. In particular, it is claimed that more balance has been achieved between property development, direct support for economic development, housing renewal and rehabilitation, and that cooperation and support from Local Authorities and the private sector has been achieved to a greater extent than in many other parts of the UK.

Effectiveness of Inner City Policies

Several evaluations of urban policies have now been carried out and indeed, recognition of the desirability of setting up monitoring systems when a programme starts and carrying out subsequent evaluations is an encouraging development of the 1980s. It must be said at the outset, however, that the Departments' (and the Treasury's) concern with cost-effectiveness measures (such as cost per job) is an excessively narrow view of a policy's achievements, even if it does permit comparison of programmes within and across Departments: there is a real danger that Departments may end up doing the wrong thing very efficiently. There was undoubtedly also an attempt in the 1980s to borrow from the private sector business and managerial techniques thought to embody good practice, such as value-for-money audits, monitoring and evaluation. It also became apparent in the 1980s that, in addition to traditional measures of policy performance such as economy, efficiency and effectiveness, attention also had to be paid to the notion of 'leverage', a concept more familiar in the United States. Here performance was judged according to the ratio of public to private sector funds directed at the policy or programme objectives. This spirit of good business practice was also strongly reinforced by the Treasury with its Financial Management Initiative launched in the early 1980s.

The primary purpose of evaluation is to assess the degree to which policy, programme and project objectives are being secured and to assess how effectively, efficiently and economically they are being achieved. Critical to the success of the evaluation process is an unambiguous statement of policy objectives or intended outcomes by the Departments concerned. In practice, objectives for inner city policy have rarely been specified clearly let alone quantified in terms of jobs to be created or hectares of derelict land and premises to be removed. There have also been difficult and still unresolved questions relating to programmes with multiple objectives. However, it is fair to say that considerable progress has been made conceptually, if not always in practice, in establishing a framework of evaluation which emphasises additionality, deadweight, displacement and indirect local linkage and multiplier effects.

What then has inner city policy achieved in the 1980s? In brief, it is apparent that the policy has been effective in encouraging property development in inner city areas which would not otherwise have occurred or would have occurred much more slowly and in a more piecemeal manner. Although no major evaluation of UDCs has yet been published, their achievements in terms of physical regeneration are familiar and well known. The London Docklands Development Corporation has removed over 2 square miles of dereliction, Canary Wharf is a reality, nearly 9000 housing units are in place and, with three-quarters of the budget devoted to land reclamation and infrastructure improvement, the physical environment has undoubtedly been upgraded and improved. Moreover, leverage has been significant: £½bn public expenditure has attracted £3bn private sector investment. In Merseyside, the property development achievements have, not surprisingly, been more modest but are nevertheless apparent. The absence of a detailed and comprehensive evaluation makes it impossible to judge how much of this development is deadweight, but it is difficult to doubt that at the very minimum the inner city redevelopment process was accelerated by the UDC initiatives. However, it is important to recognise that 'many of the regeneration success stories of the 1980s derived from, and were dependent upon, a buoyant property market which provided the stimulus and impetus for physical redevelopment' (Audit Commission, 1991).

Jobs have also been generated in inner cities by the UDCs but in the absence of a detailed and rigorous evaluation it is not possible to assess the net additional impact on employment opportunities and the local labour market more generally. The Docklands Consultative Committee (1988) suggests that only about one-fifth of the 20 000 jobs attracted to London's Docklands by 1987 can be regarded as genuinely additional. The persistently high unemployment rate for Docklands suggests that the effects of new economic activity and job creation have benefited mainly commuters rather than local unemployed residents. Only relatively recently has the London Docklands Development Corporation recognised the importance of training and is now allocating more resources to it. However, relatively little has been done to improve the skills of local unemployed and minority groups or to improve their competitive position in the local labour market.

An interim evaluation of the Enterprise Zone initiative has been carried out (PA Cambridge Economic Consultants, 1987) and a final evaluation is in progress. The evaluation indicates that Enterprise Zone policy instruments have effectively stimulated the physical regeneration of a number of inner city areas even when allowance is made for displacement effects on neighbouring areas. By the end of the 1980s the majority of Enterprise Zone designated areas had been upgraded significantly in terms of removal of dereliction, land reclamation and property development.

The impact of Enterprise Zone policy on job creation has also been positive even after allowing for deadweight and displacement. By the mid-1980s a total of 35 100 additional jobs had been created in Enterprise Zones and, after allowing for displacement, some 13 000 jobs could be attributed to the policy (200–300 jobs per annum). The cost per job was estimated at £23 000. However, the criticisms raised above with respect to UDCs are equally applicable to Enterprise Zones.

A similar methodological approach to that used to evaluate Enterprise Zones was used to evaluate the DTI's Inner City Task Force Programme (PA Cambridge Economic Consultants, 1991). Here the approach attempted to go beyond job creation to assess the impact on enterprise generation, employability and training and environmental improvement. Table 6.4 shows the results for the three Task Force areas of Handsworth, Rochdale and Doncaster. The evaluation study concluded favourably on the cost-effectiveness of the programme and argued that it created significant multiple benefits. However, it was also clear that significant variations in cost-effectiveness existed between the three Task Force areas.

Evaluations of the Urban Programme have also been carried out and, as in the case of the Task Force programme, the benefits are very

Table 6.4. Cost/benefit ratios: package of benefits accruing from £10 000 of net additional public sector expenditure on Task Force projects.[a]

Unit of cost	Benefits
Every £10K of net public expenditure	1 job (2 job-years) 2 training places (1.3 training-place years) 40.6 small firms advised/assisted 12.0 residents receiving community benefits 0.75 sites improved environmentally £3.8K spend on improving the physical environment

[a]Department of Trade and Industry, report prepared by PA Cambridge Economic Consultants (1991).

diverse. Each year some 20000 jobs are alleged to be created or saved but these estimates do not allow for additionality and displacement. If the adjustments for the latter are similar to those found in Enterprise Zone or Task Forces, the net additional job creation would be 5000–7000 jobs per annum.

In summary, the review of major programme evaluations suggests significant but limited success in the removal of dereliction, land reclamation and environmental improvement. However, the geographical focus of such achievements has been narrow and, in relation to the scale of the problem, there is a strong presumption that achievements fall a long way short of what is required. Jobs have been created and 'enterprise development' has been secured but although evaluations of all programmes have yet to be completed, it is clear that achievements here also fall far short of what is required significantly to reduce unemployment disparities between inner city areas and other areas in the UK. There is also relatively little research on who gets new jobs created in inner city areas. However, the absence of specific attempts to target jobs on unemployed inner city residents in the majority of programmes, suggests that many of the jobs created go to people who live outside the inner city areas, i.e. to commuters. Housing remains a major problem in inner city areas and continues to act as a mechanism for concentrating disadvantaged groups. The private sector has been mobilised in a number of ways, notably in property development, but leverage is still low outside London. There is also a genuine and legitimate concern that economic regeneration led by the private sector may be dominated by redevelopment to the disadvantage of local residents, particularly the more disadvantaged groups. Coordination has proved difficult, although recent experience of the European Commission Community Support Framework suggests that potential benefits can be secured if coordination is attempted within a strategic planning framework.

Future Policy Development

Inner city policy in the 1980s was based on a number of assumptions concerning the problems being addressed and, arguably more importantly, their causes. Guiding inner city policy was the view that at the heart of the problem was the weakness of the inner city economy. To overcome this weakness required a range of essentially supply-side policies designed to relax constraints on business development and to stabilise the dispersal of economic activity and population. Targeting was mainly geographical and policy was aimed at improving the physical environment and providing premises rather than people-based. Improved job opportunities in the inner city would benefit the unemployed and disadvantaged groups indirectly through so-called 'trickle-down' effects.

It was recognised that inner city problems were multifaceted and required coordination of a complex range of programmes and initiatives.

Several points arise from this perception. Firstly, it is questionable whether policy can reverse the net outward movement of population and economic activity. A great variety of factors underpin these trends and policy inevitably can have only a limited effect in offsetting these factors. If decentralisation cannot be reversed the role of policy must be to ensure that all groups have the opportunity to move, should they so choose, and that suitable job and housing opportunities exist for those who remain in the inner city. It may therefore be necessary to accept that inner city regeneration may have to occur within the context of declining conurbations and major cities.

Secondly, there can be no presumption that property-led economic regeneration, with minimal regard to the competitiveness of inner city residents in the local labour market, will succeed in improving the job prospects of the less skilled, the long-term unemployed, minority groups and disadvantaged groups. Policy must recognise that a degree of 'targeting' is necessary and that inner city economic regeneration should pay careful regard not only to the business development needs of inner city companies but also to the economic, housing and social needs of inner city residents.

An important implication of this is that what is required for effective inner city economic (and physical) regeneration is a strategic approach which recognises that inner city areas are integral parts of an inner city economy, which in turn is linked closely with the wider conurbation and its regional hinterland. Thus, as indicated earlier, the majority of inner city population loss is to the hinterland and determined very much by housing and residential preferences. Equally, much of the outward movement of economic activity is to the regional hinterland. This suggests that inner city strategy should be formulated not at the level of the inner city Local Authority but at the appropriate regional level. A regional tier would be better placed to secure both vertical coordination between central and local government and horizontal coordination between the programmes of different government departments.

If inner city strategy were to be formulated within the wider context of the regional economy it would necessitate careful reconsideration of the potential for securing more balanced outward movement of population and industry. In particular, the focus of attention would switch more towards issues that relate to housing conditions and housing choice as being central not only in their own right, but also in improving job prospects for certain inner city residents. Equally, a more strategic approach would continue to recognise the problems posed for economic regeneration by dereliction and physical decay in inner areas (and in some of the peripheral estates). The experience of the 1980s suggests that policy can successfully stimulate physical redevelopment, given the right property market conditions, but it must do so whilst recognising the preferences, aspirations and needs of local residents and local businesses.

The experience of the many policy initiatives introduced in the 1980s also demonstrates that some policies are more effective than others in creating new job opportunities and in securing multiple objectives. The DTI Inner City Task Force Programme is an example of a programme that could be usefully expanded (currently this programme attracts about £23m per annum) within the context of a more coherent strategy. However, tinkering and fine-tuning of existing policies will do little to secure the degree of restructuring and economic redevelopment of inner cities necessary to tackle the deep-seated problems of long-term unemployment and disadvantage. It must be recognised that only a major and concerted strategy, funded and resourced by central government in partnership with Local Authorities and the private sector, can adequately address the problems of inner cities. 'Flagship' projects and *ad hoc* developments must be replaced by coordinated infrastructure renewal which supports the development of new sectors and ensures that established businesses are retained and supported in their expansion. The infrastructure renewal programme must accept that current disparities in infrastructure provision in transport, housing, environmental improvement and other social overhead capital between inner city areas and other more prosperous areas, necessitate a major diversion of resources to the inner city across a wide range of public expenditure capital programmes. A sustained and coordinated programme of infrastructure renewal will require not only adequate resources from central government but also increased flexibility in the use of local resources of both the public and private sectors.

Equally, only a radical restructuring of training and employment policies can tackle the critically important question of improving the competitive position of the long-term unemployed, ethnic minority groups and other disadvantaged groups in local inner city labour markets. Training programme resources must increasingly be allocated to individual TECs on the basis of a thorough and rigorous assessment of the labour market needs of both local area residents as well as local businesses. Allocation based on 'needs assessment' would help to ensure that resources would flow to the areas of greatest need and it could also be structured in a way that takes account of differences in the unit input costs of training and enterprise development support between areas and for different client groups. However, if training and employment policies are to reach the most disadvantaged, difficult and demanding inner city groups, practical mechanisms must be set up to target these groups specifically and to avoid the current situation whereby resources flow largely to low-cost, high-volume training because TECs are bound to output-related funding.

If policy-makers accept the scale and nature of the problems faced in tackling the economic regeneration and restructuring of inner cities and the problems associated with the growing concentrations of unemployment, poverty and deprivation, they must also recognise that these problems will take many years to resolve and adjustments will be neither painless nor easy. This suggests that a strategy to address inner city problems must focus not only on the fundamental causes of the problems but also on the symptoms. Much more emphasis must therefore be placed on social and community policies. This requires a willingness to encourage real participation of local residents and businesses not only in implementing policies but also in articulating the overall local area strategy. It is, of course, these groups that are the ultimate 'clients' of policy. In this respect Local Authorities have a critically important role to play in identifying local needs and implementing and delivering policy. To do this requires re-establishing a fiscal framework within which local authorities can feel secure and acquire the necessary financial resources to permit a genuine partnership with central government and the private sector.

Comment

The Legacy in the Inner Cities

Iain Begg

The inner cities posed a particularly uncomfortable challenge to the government in the 1980s. Inner city economic decline had persisted over several decades, indicating a long-term loss of competitive advantage across a broad range of economic activities and implying a need for large-scale intervention to assist regeneration. The inner cities also constituted a political and institutional challenge. Virtually all the Local Authorities concerned were Labour controlled and many became involved in legal and political battles with central government. This meant that there was little consensus about how to approach regeneration, with the result that the institutional framework for the formulation and delivery of policy lacked coherence. When, following her third general election victory, Mrs Thatcher made her well-publicised remark that

'On Monday, we have a big job to do in some of those inner cities', she was articulating both an economic imperative and a political clarion-call.

The 1981 riots had highlighted the plight of the inner cities, as had a succession of reports and analyses in the 1970s and 1980s (see Robson, 1988, for a summary). Although there were inevitable differences of opinion on the weight to attach to different causes, the nature of the decline was evident. For various reasons, cities have become less attractive to manufacturers, while expanding service sectors have tended not to absorb factors of production made redundant by the decline of manufacturing. Derelict land, crumbling infrastructure and concentrations of deprivation associated with high unemployment testified to a cumulation of economic and social problems. Essentially, the decline of the inner cities has to be seen as a form of market failure in which the opportunities for the employment of indigenous factors of production in these areas are inadequate. These structural effects were compounded by fiscal pressure on Local Authorities that arose partly from the increasing gap between public spending needs and a dwindling tax base, and partly from budgetary pressure from a central government anxious to reduce aggregate public expenditure as part of macroeconomic policy.

In addressing the predicament of the inner cities, it can be argued that three basic approaches are possible. The first would be to manage decline so that it does not give rise to unacceptable social costs. This, to a degree, had been implicit in past urban policy, with the creation of New Towns, but had broadly ceased by the 1980s. A second would be to create mechanisms to provide income support for those left behind. The social security system and transfers from central to local government based on assessments of 'need' do provide such support in the UK, but came under attack in the 1980s with cuts in both. Indeed, political conflict between central and local government often led to substantial cuts in flows from the Exchequer to some of the most deprived inner areas, so that policy exacerbated rather than helped to diminish deprivation.

The third approach is to adopt initiatives to support regeneration and the 1980s saw a proliferation of such schemes, as the chapter by Moore shows. These have been predominantly property-led and may have aimed as much at changing the character of urban economies as at providing new opportunities for unemployed residents. Retail developments which promote the image of the city as a place of consumption, and offices intended to accommodate commuters were seen as more important than job creation. By contrast, only limited efforts were made to improve the job prospects of individuals through training or other schemes, highlighting the fact that social objectives were largely neglected.

Although the notion of recreating urban economies in the mould of those of the past is manifestly far-fetched, serious doubts have to be raised about whether policy in the 1980s was well conceived. The evidence suggests that a lack of coherence in the policy package diminished its overall effectiveness. As the Audit Commission observed in an appraisal of urban policy, 'it is hard to escape the conclusion that at the level of the individual city there can be programme overkill within a strategic vacuum' (1989, p. 32). The emphasis on property and the low level of funding of many schemes has, arguably, shown a lack of balance in neglecting other factors of production.

However, the doubts about policy are not confined to questions about whether individual schemes were sensible in their own right. The key question is whether, as a policy package, they provided an adequate basis for the transformation of urban economies. Certainly, the weight of evidence suggests that in today's economic environment, the agglomeration economies of cities are more suited to segments of the service sector such as financial and business services and so-called 'information' sector activities. However, it also has to be recognised that aggregate demand for such activities is limited: just as it is implausible for all localities to develop science parks, there is only room for a finite number of financial centres or major retail outlets. What remains to be confronted is the question of how policy should seek to reshape cities which are left behind.

Thus, although urban policy in the 1980s undoubtedly succeeded in transforming *parts* of some cities, it is not clear how such policies will affect entire conurbations or the country's urban system as a whole (Begg and Moore, 1990). In many urban areas, regeneration in the inner city has simply decanted problems to other districts. Indeed, the unrest seen in many peripheral estates in recent months may herald the next generation of 'urban problems'. If so, the legacy of 1980s inner city policy may be that problems, far from being solved, have just been swept under the carpet.

7

The Regional Legacy

Ron Martin and Peter Tyler

With the late-1980s' euphoria in certain quarters over the performance of the UK economy went a corresponding optimism that the higher rate of national growth, aided by the Government's attempts to liberalise market forces, would trickle down to the nation's depressed regions and help reduce the long-standing divide between the prosperous South and the lagging North of the country. It even became fashionable to argue that not only were regional policies ineffectual as compared to market forces in bringing about regional convergence in economic prosperity, but that such policies could in fact frustrate the process of regional economic regeneration and adjustment.

This chapter assesses the impact of the Thatcher years on the traditional 'North–South divide' in the UK. That the divide widened markedly during the course of the 1980s has been fully documented elsewhere (see Martin, 1988). The specific aim here is to examine this widening of regional disparities in terms of the dramatic changes to regional policy that also occurred under the Thatcher governments. We begin by outlining the nature of the regional problem in the UK, in terms of how it is conventionally defined for regional policy purposes. The subsequent section then documents the changes in the form, instruments and strength of regional policy that have taken place since 1979. We then attempt to assess the achievements of regional policy under Thatcher, relative to the impact that regional policy had in previous periods. We conclude by outlining the likely future prospects of the regions and the 'North–South divide' in the light of the policy legacy of the Thatcher years.

The Nature and Scale of Regional Problems

The nature of the regional problem facing the UK can be described in many ways, although the most frequently used definition has been in terms of labour market imbalance, and within this context typically in terms of unemployment disparities. In principle, problems of economic development between regions within any nation, or for that matter between nations within an entity such as the European Community, can be conceived as problems of imbalance between supply and demand, the crucial distinction being that the degree of imbalance varies between the regions concerned. Thus, taking the labour market as one major dimension, unemployment is the physical manifestation of imbalance between the number of people looking for work and the number of job opportunities available to them. This is currently a problem at the national level in the UK. What makes it into a regional problem is that the degree of unemployment varies quite dramatically across the different regions of the country and that this disequilibrium has persisted for a very long time.

Two other ways of conceptualising the regional problem are worth mentioning. The first relates to geographical differences in infrastructure and services. For example, poor-quality housing and poor communications are both manifestations of inadequate infrastructure in relation to need. The second relates to what is commonly referred to as fiscal stress, where the fiscal capacity of an area through the local tax base is inadequate to meet its public expenditure needs. These further types of geographical imbalance are usually more prevalent in urban regions and are helpful in conceptualising the problems of congestion and deprivation. Throughout, however, the labour market remains of central importance because the movements of people and jobs influence the scale of the problem, or imbalance, which exists.

The nature and scale of the regional problem from a labour market perspective can be summarised with the help of the labour market balance sheets presented in Table 7.1, which are derived from Moore *et al.* (1986). For a given region, the change in the labour force which arises through natural increase and changes in participation is compared with the actual growth in job opportunities which occurred. The difference between the growth of the labour force and the growth of employment equals the employment shortfall in the region concerned. This shortfall manifests itself in either net migration from the region and/or an increase in the numbers seeking work—the unemployed in the region. The absolute job shortfall in the region gives a preliminary indication of the scale of the problem, although it is important to realise that the growth of labour demand and supply in a region are interdependent and are separated in the labour market accounts merely for analytical convenience.

Table 7.1 shows the labour market balance sheets for two groups of regions, one containing the four traditional Development Area regions of Scotland, Wales, the Northern region of England and Northern Ireland, and the other the remainder. The inability of the economic base of the Development Areas to generate sufficient job opportunities

Table 7.1. Relative job shortfall, migration and unemployment 1951–1981.[a]

	Four Development Area regions[b]			All other regions			United Kingdom		
	1951–1961	1961–1971	1971–1981	1951–1961	1961–1971	1971–1981	1951–1961	1961–1971	1971–1981
Natural increase in labour force	131	162	159	177	124	350	308	286	509
	(2.5)	(3.0)	(3.0)	(1.0)	(0.6)	(1.7)	(1.4)	(1.2)	(2.0)
Plus: Increase in participation	120	259	73	1848	634	144	1968	893	217
	(2.3)	(4.8)	(1.3)	(11.0)	(3.3)	(0.7)	(8.9)	(3.6)	(0.8)
Less: Increase in employment	−12	42	−131	2173	373	−336	2161	416	−467
	(−0.2)	(0.8)	(−2.4)	(12.9)	(1.9)	(−1.7)	(9.7)	(1.7)	(−1.8)
Employment shortfall	263	378	363	−148	385	830	115	763	193
	(5.0)	(7.0)	(6.5)	(−0.9)	(2.0)	(4.1)	(0.5)	(3.1)	(4.7)
Net migration of labour force	201	229	102	−312	−80	82	−111	149	184
	(3.8)	(4.3)	(1.8)	(−1.8)	(−0.4)	(0.4)	(−0.5)	(0.6)	(0.7)
Increase in numbers seeking work (unemployed)	62	149	261	164	465	748	226	614	1009
	(1.2)	(2.8)	(4.7)	(1.0)	(2.4)	(3.7)	(1.0)	(2.5)	(3.9)
Relative job shortfall[c]	224	250	140	−387	−179	31			
	(4.2)	(4.7)	(2.5)	(−2.3)	(−0.9)	(0.2)			

[a]Source: Moore et al. (1986). All figures in parentheses are percentages of the actual labour force in the base year of each period.
[b]Scotland, Wales, Northern Ireland and the Northern region of England.
[c]The relative job shortfall is calculated by standardising the absolute job shortfall for changes in the national pressure of demand.

is clear. In the 1950s the Development Area group of regions had an employment shortfall of some 263 000 jobs, whilst the Southern regions had a surplus of 148 000, indicating that the Southern employment base generated more employment opportunities than it could fill from increases in its own labour force. The basic pattern of a greater relative job shortfall in the North compared to the South was repeated in the 1960s and 1970s.

The balance sheet approach shows that the traditional response to the employment shortfall in the Development Areas has been net outward migration. This peaked in the 1960s and fell in the 1970s as job opportunities became less available throughout the UK. The unemployment rate remained at a higher level in the Development Areas than in the more prosperous Southern regions for the whole 1951–1981 period. In fact, absolute differences in unemployment rates between the two groups of regions widened (although relativities narrowed as unemployment rose).

If the effects of rising national unemployment are allowed for in the accounts, as provided by the relative job shortfall indicator, in both the 1950s and 1960s net outward migration accounted for about 90% of the relative job shortfall in the Development Areas. In the 1970s the figure fell to approximately 70% as less job opportunities were available elsewhere in the UK to potential migrants from the depressed regions. As a consequence, unemployment in the Development Areas began to bear more of the imbalance effect. It is clear from the accounts that net outward migration has been a major relief valve in the traditional depressed regions.

This mechanism is in accordance with the orthodox neoclassical theory of interregional economic equilibration, and tends to emphasise the importance of a flexible quantity response (migration). Substantial migration cannot, however, be particularly welcomed as a solution to the regional problem, even in relatively prosperous times such as the 1950s and 1960s. The extent to which workers in depressed regions should have to migrate to find work over many decades relative to workers in more prosperous regions raises questions of equity, and provokes fierce debates about the whole concept of involuntary migration. Even putting this rather thorny issue to one side, it has also become clear that there are efficiency arguments for not relying too heavily on a migration response to 'solve' the problems of depressed regions. Substantial migration between regions in the UK has imposed severe pressures on services and infrastructure in relatively prosperous areas and especially on housing, and this has led to inflationary effects that have had implications for the nation as a whole (Martin and Tyler, 1990). Moreover, the migrants from the depressed regions inevitably tend to be the better educated, younger and frequently more enterprising individuals, and this in itself exacerbates the problems that face the economies of the depressed areas as they try to regenerate.

Ultimately, a more satisfactory alternative to substantial net outward migration from the depressed regions of the UK appears to be the restoration of a sound economic base within these areas which is capable of generating a satisfactory level of income and thus job opportunities for their inhabitants. This in itself, given the relatively open nature of regional economies, necessitates the generation of sufficient exports to finance the desired level of income. In this sense the regional problem has been the result of a failure to arrest the structural decline of the old industrial regions and to promote the growth of new industries and employment opportunities. It is within this context that it is necessary to consider the role given to post-War regional policies and the changes in approach between successive governments, most notably since 1979.

The Thatcher Approach to Regional Policy

Throughout its post-War history, traditional regional policy had been conducted as a form of spatial Keynesianism and had been based on three main premises. First, the problem of the economically depressed areas was interpreted as being primarily structural in nature, due to localised deficiencies of demand. This view was very much a legacy of the inter-War experience of the depressed areas and the collapse of the basic export and staple industries during that period. Second, the case for intervention was justified both on social grounds, in terms of reducing regional imbalances in employment opportunities, and on economic grounds, in terms of bringing national efficiency gains by utilizing the unemployed labour in the depressed areas and thus allowing the macroeconomy to achieve a higher rate of noninflationary growth. Third, it was assumed that the solution to the regional problem was to redistribute industry from the low-unemployment growth regions to the high-unemployment depressed areas, and that this was best achieved through a system of substantial investment controls in the former and capital grants and labour subsidies in the latter. This general policy model was accepted to a greater or lesser extent by all post-War governments up to the end of the 1970s, and its main features can be summarised as follows. In the immediate post-War years regional policy assistance focused on the old industrial districts that had been designated as Special Areas in the 1930s (Figure 7.1). By the mid-1960s nearly 17% of the UK's working population was in districts covered by Assisted Area status. In 1966 new Development Areas were defined which embraced the whole of Scotland, the Northern region, Merseyside and large parts of Wales and the South West. Within these regions a number of localities having particularly high rates of unemployment were designated as Special Development Areas. In the early 1970s further expansion to the map of regional aid occurred, involving a new category of Intermediate Areas. By the close of the decade the Assisted Areas contained almost 50% of the UK's working population.

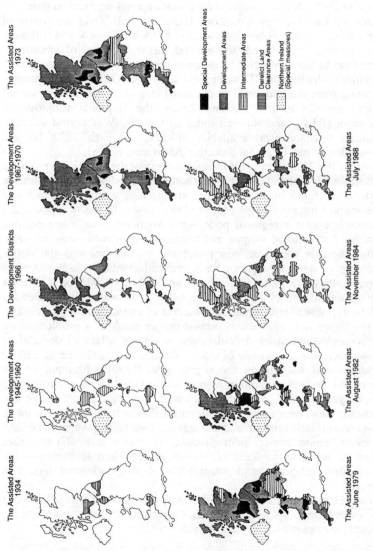

Figure 7.1. The map of regional aid 1934–1988.

The Assisted Areas 1973

The Development Areas 1967-1970

The Development Districts 1966

The Development Areas 1945-1960

The Assisted Areas 1934

The Assisted Areas July 1988

The Assisted Areas November 1984

The Assisted Areas August 1982

The Assisted Areas June 1979

Special Development Areas

Development Areas

Intermediate Areas

Derelict Land Clearance Areas

Northern Ireland (Special measures)

During the early post-War years, regional policy assistance took the form of Government Advanced Factory Building and the reclamation of derelict land. This system was backed up by a system of constraints on new factory building in the prosperous areas of the South East and Midlands. Initially this restraint consisted of a building licence system, but after 1947 this was replaced by a more formal mechanism based on Industrial Development Certificate (IDC) controls. Over the course of the 1960s, further policy instruments were introduced and although their precise form varied, the general thrust consisted of investment incentives to industry with a heavy emphasis on automatic capital grants, specifically the Regional Development Grant (RDG). For approximately 10 years from the mid-1960s to the mid-1970s, there was also a blanket labour subsidy in the Assisted Areas, the Regional Employment Premium (REP), and through much of the post-War period selective financial assistance was available, which in the early 1970s became consolidated into Regional Selective Assistance (RSA).

Under the Thatcher governments, all three of the traditional premises underpinning regional policy were thoroughly modified in line with the Thatcherite focus on monetary constraint, supply-side economics and free-market liberalism (see Martin, 1985, 1988). In the first place, the economic case for regional policy—the argument that it has positive benefits for national output and employment growth—was rejected: rather the case was to be 'now principally a social one with the aim of reducing, on a stable long term basis, regional imbalances in employment opportunities' (Department of Trade and Industry, 1983, para. 16). At the same time, the nature of the regional problem was given a somewhat different political interpretation. The lack of employment opportunities in the depressed regions was viewed not so much as a problem of an unfavourable industrial structure, nor as one of a lack of demand or public spending, but as one of microeconomic disequilibrium caused by rigidities and failures on the supply side. The predicament of the depressed regions, in other words, was attributed to a particularly severe geographical overconcentration of the problems that, in the Thatcher view, were responsible for national industrial decline: too much government intervention and assistance, insufficient wage flexibility, excessive union power, poor productivity and a lack of enterprise. These supply-side weaknesses, it was argued, had undermined the competitive efficiency and adaptability of the traditional industrial regions.

One element in this supply-side interpretation that was singled out for special emphasis by the Thatcher governments was labour market rigidity, and particularly wage inflexibility:

> Imbalances between areas in employment opportunities should in principle be corrected by the natural adjustment of labour markets. In the first place, this should be through lower wages and unit costs than comparable work commands elsewhere. . . The Government believe that wage

bargaining must become more responsive to the circumstances of the individual enterprise, including its location. (Department of Trade and Industry, 1983, paras 9–11.)

This focus on the failure of the labour market to function properly in depressed areas was in effect a return to the views of the pre-Keynesian economists of the 1920s and 1930s, such as Pigou, Cannan and Clay, who had advanced essentially the same argument at the time when the depressed regions had first begun to decline.

Another crucial supply-side weakness said by the Thatcher governments to be a basic cause of the problems of depressed regions is a lack of enterprise, particularly the low rate of new firm formation and technological innovation. In fact, by the late 1980s, Britain's industrial problem as a whole had been redefined in these terms, and both industrial policy and regional policy became subsumed under the government's new Enterprise Initiative. As far as the regions were concerned, the Enterprise Initiative meant a change in the balance of regional policy so that the main aims of the government's enterprise policies were properly reflected in the regions. Regional policy in effect became a regionally differentiated form of the overall enterprise strategy, intended to promote local business development.

As part of this shift in perspective and political ideology, the Thatcher governments also rejected the idea that the problems of the depressed regions would best be solved by an extensive system of investment subsidies and controls intended to redistribute industry from low- to high-unemployment areas. Instead, the aim was to 'encourage the development of indigenous potential within the Assisted Areas with the long term objective of generating self-sustaining growth in these areas'. This was to be achieved by a much more cost-effective and discretionary system of assistance, and one which was targeted especially at promoting new firm formation and business development in the depressed regions. It was in this context that the old regional policy package was dismantled and the new policy model put in place.

One of the most dramatic changes has been the rolling back of the map of regional aid. The first significant changes came in 1979 when Sir Keith Joseph as Secretary of State for Trade and Industry began a 3-year descheduling programme, summarised in Figure 7.1. In November 1984 the Government abolished the Special Areas and collapsed the three layers of Assisted Areas into two, comprising Development Areas and Intermediate Areas. Furthermore, the Development Areas eligible for regional assistance were reduced to some 15% of Britain's working population, heavily focused on the older conurbations, while the Intermediate Areas covered approximately 20% of the working population, including for the first time Birmingham and the West Midlands. Since 1984 further changes have been made (Figure 7.1). These changes have resulted in a highly fragmented and localised pattern of assisted areas, reminiscent of the system of Development Districts used briefly in the mid-1960s. In spatial terms, then, regional policy was made simpler and much more selective.

At the same time, the range of policy instruments deployed to tackle the regional problem was radically changed. First, at the beginning of the 1980s, the IDC system was withdrawn. RDGs were initially reduced to a uniform rate of 15% in the new Development Areas, with replacement investment no longer eligible, and, with the exception of firms with less than 200 employees, investment projects were subject to a cost per job limit of £10 000 for each new job created. The scheme also incorporated a job grant, at a rate of £3000 for each new job created as an option instead of the straight capital grant. The scheme was also expanded to cover certain service sectors. In 1988, however, the RDG was completely abolished, marking the end of nearly 30 years of regional policy assistance in this form. RSA and Government Advanced Factory Building were retained and, as part of the 1988 Enterprise Initiative, supplemented by new Regional Enterprise Grants and regionally differentiated Business Consultancy Initiatives.

The changing strength of regional policy

The changing volume of government expenditure on each component of regional policy over the post-War period is shown in Table 7.2. The overall constant price expenditure on regional policy is also summarised in Figure 7.2 where the average real annual expenditure on regional policy is shown for the different governments over the post-War years.

A number of key features emerge from Table 7.2 and Figure 7.2. Real expenditure on regional policy measures was extremely low during the 1950s, as described in the previous section. The position began to improve in the early 1960s and expenditure increased steadily throughout the decade to reach a post-War peak by the end of that period. Overall expenditure remained high until the mid-1970s. Thereafter expenditure fell, first under Labour and then under Thatcher, until by 1985–1986 real expenditure on regional policy measures was barely more than 10% of its post-War peak. During the late 1980s the annual rate of expenditure stabilised at less than £250 million (1989 prices) per annum, and is planned to fall towards £200 million per annum over the early 1990s. In contrast to regional policy, expenditure on urban policy measures has risen in real terms since the beginning of the 1980s, to some 300% more than regional policy expenditure by 1990–1991. Table 7.2 indicates that during the period 1964–1965 to 1971–1972 when policy expenditure was growing fairly rapidly, approximately 30% was on the REP, nearly 38% on investment grants, nearly 19% on grants and other loans and approximately 6% on Government Advanced Factory Building and land reclamation. In the early 1970s the balance changed somewhat, with 33% on the REP, nearly 45% on investment grants, 7% on RSA and 4% on Government Advanced Factory Building.

Table 7.2. Government expenditure on regional industrial policy, 1950–1951 to 1992–1994 (average annual expenditure).

Incentive	1950–1951 to 1960–1961	1961–1962 to 1963–1964	1964–1965 to 1971–1972	1972–1973 to 1975–1976	1976–1977 to 1978–1979	1979–1980 to 1984–1985	1985–1986 to 1990–1991	Planned 1991–1992 to 1993–1994
Investment incentives								
1. Investment grants, Regional Development Grants and regionally free depreciation	7	—	71	193	518	473	74	18
2. Regional Selective Assistance	—	—		32	39	57	84	115
3. Government Advanced Factory Building and land reclamation and provision		8	12	17	51	118	53	65
4. Other grants and loans		12	35	34	—	—	—	—
Labour subsidies								
5. Regional Employment Premium			57	143	73	—	—	—
6. Other labour subsidies			9	8	13	1	—	—
7. Other assistance		1	3	6	20	4	—	—
Regional business development incentives								
8. Regional Enterprise Grants							1	12
9. Business Consultancy Initiative							10	55
Total cost								
Current prices	7	21	187	433	714	653	222	265
Constant 1989–1990 prices	80	194	1355	1843	1835	989	242	221*

*Based on the Government's estimates of inflation over this period.

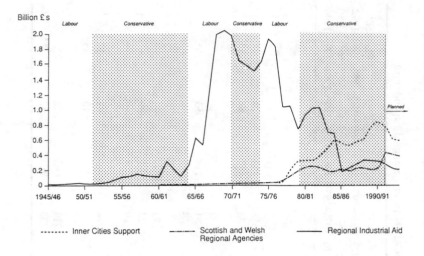

Figure 7.2. Regional and urban policy expenditures 1945–1946 to 1990–1991 (at constant 1989–1990 prices).

By the late 1970s the REP had been cancelled and investment grants represented some 73% of the overall expenditure. However, by the end of the 1980s, with the abolition of the RDG, investment incentives accounted for only one-third of total assistance. Of an annual expenditure of just over £200 million in real terms on regional policy by the end of the decade, nearly one-quarter was going to Government Advanced Factory Building and a similar amount to other 'supply-side measures' such as Regional Enterprise Grants and Business Consultancy advice.

The rise and fall of government spending summarised in Table 7.2 and Figure 7.2 provides only a partial indication of the strength of the regional policy package and how this has changed. The patterns of expenditure provide no indication of how the IDC control has varied in intensity. Some indications of the strength of this important restraining element of regional policy can be assessed by expressing expected employment associated with refusals as a percentage of employment associated with approvals plus refusals in the prosperous regions of the South East and Midlands (Figure 7.3): in the 1950s approximately 5% of applications for IDCs were turned down each year, and this increased to between 20% and 30% in the 1960s. During the 1970s, however, the percentage of applications refused in the prosperous regions began to fall, averaging 10%, and by the beginning of the 1980s the IDC policy had been phased out completely.

Expenditure on the investment incentives component of the regional policy package does not indicate the relative effect of these incentives

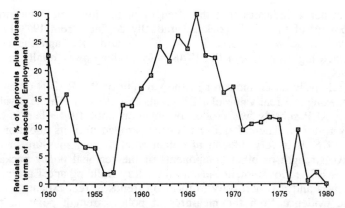

Figure 7.3. The changing strength of regional policy: IDC refusals as a percentage of approvals plus refusals in the Midlands and South East 1950–1980 in terms of associated employment.

on company decisions. The average expenditure is a reflection of take-up and does not indicate the unit strength of the instrument. Also, the nature of the incentive has varied between grant and tax allowance. For these reasons, it is better to calculate the discounted present value of the various incentives in order to measure their value in a consistent manner. This approach allows quantification of changes in amount of cash grant paid and favourable tax regimes (for example, free depreciation) into one index. Present values are calculated separately for buildings and for plant and machinery and the two series combined using appropriate weights relating to capital expenditure on the two types of expenditure in the UK. A 10% discount rate is used, along with the appropriate effective tax rate on retained profits in the year concerned. The present value series derived is shown in Figure 7.4.

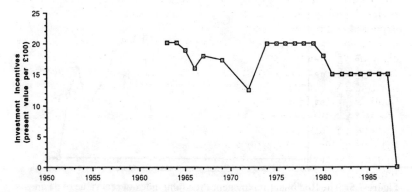

Figure 7.4. Investment incentives 1950–1988.

The evidence indicates that the strength of the investment incentive component of the policy package gradually declined from 1963–1970. Its 1963 value was restored in the 1972 *Industry Act* and the level remained high throughout the 1970s before falling away totally in the 1980s.

A relatively crude indicator of the strength of the REP is obtained by indexing the real value of REP grants (Figure 7.5). The real value of the REP subsidy was eroded by inflation until 1974 when it was partly restored. Thereafter it was further eroded until its abolition in 1975–1976. It is very difficult to obtain a satisfactory measure of the relative strength of other components of the regional policy package such as RSA, Government Advanced Factory Building and Enterprise Initiatives and it is necessary to focus on trends in real expenditure.

The evidence from the measures of policy strength point to the following broad phases. An active post-War phase (1945–1951) was followed by regional policy effectively in abeyance during the 1950s. There was a brief transition period in the early 1960s followed by an active policy phase from around 1963 to the mid-1970s. Thereafter, policy began to weaken with a return in the 1980s, in many respects, to the pattern of the 1950s.

The new regional policy model developed under the Thatcher governments can thus be summarised in the following way. First, it involved a distinct shift from a demand-side to a supply-side approach. Second, the rate and scale of regional support was dramatically reduced, both as measured by annual spending on regional assistance and in terms of the abandonment of what had previously been the main regional policy instruments (IDCs and RDGs). Third, the thrust of policy was shifted away from relatively large-scale capital investment in the regions to the promotion of indigenous enterprise, small firms and market competition in the depressed areas. Whether this new policy model represents a coherent strategy for the regions is questionable.

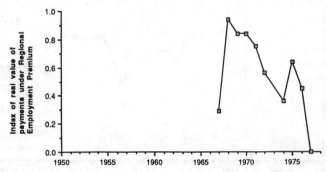

Figure 7.5. The Regional Employment Premium: index of real value of payments 1950–1977 (source: Moore *et al.*, 1986).

As with so much of Thatcherism, it is important to distinguish between what the Government claimed it was doing or intended to do and what it actually did. The difference between political rhetoric and actual policy was often significant. Indeed, there appear to have been some major differences of view about the importance of regional policy within the government itself. Thus, whereas Peter Walker, when Secretary of State for Wales, emphasised the positive contribution of an intervention-ist regional policy for the economic recovery of that region, David Young as Secretary of State for Trade and Industry did not speak of regional policy at all, but played up the role of market processes and the creation of business enterprise as the best way of closing the 'North–South divide'. At the same time, Young actively courted overseas (especially Japanese) investment to locate in the regions. By the end of the 1980s, official regional policy had in effect become marginalised. Only a few Conservatives, most notably Michael Heseltine, seem to have recognised the implications of this marginalisation for the depressed regions themselves.

Assessing the Achievements of Policy Under Thatcher

In evaluating the regional policy of the 1980s it is necessary to assess what the new policy measures were able to achieve, not only in relation to the nature and scale of the problem, but also in the context of past achievements of regional policy. Of course, assessing the impact of regional policy during the Thatcher period is far from straightforward. In the first instance there is no obvious or readily agreed counterfactual: we do not know what would have happened in the absence of the Thatcher policy regime. A number of factors might have changed, including the state of the national economy. It is for this reason that wherever possible when examining variables that might be expected *a priori* to be affected by regional policy, we examine them over as long a time period as possible and seek to discern cyclical and secular movements. This section focuses on four main areas of possible impact, namely, increased wage–price flexibility, improvements in competitiveness and investment, the encouragement of new enterprise formation and the creation of new jobs.

Increased wage–price flexibility

While the Thatcher governments acknowledged that it would be unrealistic to expect wage adjustment alone to eliminate regional unemployment disparities, nevertheless they appeared to believe that lower relative wages in regions of high unemployment would help to stimulate new jobs. No region-specific measures to 'deregulate' local labour markets were introduced. Instead, the Thatcher governments relied on the impact of their general policies of reforming industrial relations legislation, restricting the scope of employment protection, abolishing the Wages Councils, privatisation and limiting public-sector pay awards. They also called for radical changes in private-sector pay bargaining, and urged employers to break up national negotiations and to tie pay more closely to local labour market circumstances. Further, as part of the drive to force the pace of locally based wage determination, the third Thatcher government declared its intention to move away from national pay agreements for public sector employees.

Two issues are involved in assessing this aspect of the Thatcherite view of the regional problem: were regional wages actually as inflexible as they were claimed to be, and did the general labour market policies introduced under Thatcher actually increase the degree of regional wage–price flexibility? To evaluate these issues, we constructed wage and cost-of-living data, for both manual and nonmanual male workers, for the 62 counties of Britain annually for the period 1979–1989 (see Martin and Tyler (1990) for full details of these data series). These local areas were then grouped into two sets according to whether the local degree of collective wage bargaining coverage (in 1985) was greater or less than the national average. Local variations in the degree of collective bargaining coverage, which may be viewed as a proxy for 'union power', closely follow the spatial pattern of unemployment, so that the vast majority of the areas with high collective bargaining coverage are high-unemployment areas in the 'North' of the country, and those with below-average collective bargaining coverage are almost entirely low-unemployment areas in the 'South'. Trends in relative wages, cost of living and unemployment between these two groups of Northern and Southern labour markets are shown in Figure 7.6. Allowing for the effects of the recession in the early 1980s, the North experienced a marked deterioration in relative unemployment over the decade, and especially during the boom of the second half of the 1980s, reflecting the much slower recovery of this part of Britain in comparison to the South. This increase in relative unemployment in the North was associated with a decline in relative money wages for both manual and nonmanual workers, which suggests that some movements occurred in the interregional money wage structure in response to differential movements in regional labour demand and unemployment. However, this adjustment of the interregional money wage structure was out-weighed by markedly different relative cost-of-living movements between the two parts of the country. Nonhousing living costs varied only marginally across the country, and even by the end of the 1980s boom were only about 3% higher in the South than in the North (Figure 7.6). In contrast, housing costs in the South increased dramatically relative to those in the North during the 1980s, especially for nonmanual workers (house prices increased nearly three times faster in the South East than in Wales, Scotland and the Northern region). This differential housing

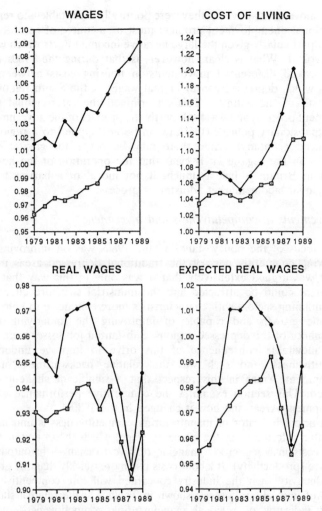

Figure 7.6. Wages and cost of living in the South relative to the North of the UK 1979–1989 (—□—, manual; —◆—, nonmanual).

cost inflation completely cancelled out the relative growth of money wages in the South. As a result, there was little overall response of the interregional real wage structure despite marked unemployment and wage growth differences between the two parts of the country.

There was, then, some relative *nominal* wage adjustment downwards in the North relative to the South but it might be argued that in a truly flexible Northern labour market very large relative movements would have been required to achieve labour market clearing. The adequacy of such movements—even if they were politically acceptable—to remove the regional unemployment problem must be a source of considerable debate, particularly given the large negative income effects which would be provoked. What is clear, however, is that during the 1980s there were marked differential movements in housing costs between the regions which depressed consumer real wages in the South relative to the North of the country. This undermined the interregional wage adjustment process, and was itself partly the product of the government's own expansionary policies (the Lawson boom) applied to a regionally imbalanced economy. While there may be scope for greater wage flexibility in the regions, it is clear that the operation of the housing market in Britain is just as much, if not more, of a barrier to the interregional labour market adjustment process.

Improvements in competitiveness and investment

A key focus of the policy stance in the 1980s was on improving the underlying competitiveness of the traditional depressed areas in the UK. It was argued extensively that it was only in this way that new investment could be attracted and the industrial structure altered to one containing sectors with characteristics more conducive to enhanced economic growth and capable of improving the underlying trade performance of the depressed regions. Substantial job losses were seen as an inevitable consequence of this drive to improve underlying competitiveness, and such was the relative backwardness of the Development Areas in this respect that a significant shakeout was expected. This section examines the competitive performance of the Development Areas and how it changed in the 1980s.

A principal indicator of manufacturing competitiveness is unit labour cost (often referred to as the efficiency wage) which shows how average labour costs in a region are changing relative to changes in output per employee (productivity). If labour costs rise more quickly than the growth of productivity then the industry concerned will lose competitiveness. Indices of unit labour cost are shown in Table 7.3; the relative stability of this indicator of regional manufacturing competitiveness over a substantial period is clear. It is difficult to see how the marginal improvements which occurred in manufacturing competitiveness in the North could bring about much by way of convergence in the growth of demand and thus output, nor, in themselves, lead to a substantial relative influx of new investment. This belief appears to be confirmed on examining what has happened to the regional balance of payments of the North in relation to the South (Table 7.4). Whilst the balance of payments in the South was broadly in balance, the North was persistently in severe deficit throughout the 1980s.

A further indicator that might be expected to respond to relative improvements in competitiveness is investment. Figure 7.7 indicates

Table 7.3. Regional indices of unit labour costs 1974–1988 (relative to UK=100).[a]

Region	1974	1979	1984	1987	1988
North	96	100	97	99	99
Yorkshire–Humberside	100	101	99	100	100
East Midlands	101	102	99	100	101
East Anglia	100	100	98	101	100
South East	101	99	100	100	101
South West	101	101	102	103	104
West Midlands	100	101	99	99	98
North West	98	98	98	98	97
Wales	101	102	100	96	95
Scotland	99	100	102	101	101
Northern Ireland	104	106	105	103	104
	100	100	100	100	100

[a]Source: Cameron *et al.* (1990).

Table 7.4. Estimates of regional balance of payments.[a]

Region	1980	1987
Southern	+1070	−900
Midlands	−90	+800
Northern	−7360	−6640

[a]Source: Cameron *et al.* (1990).

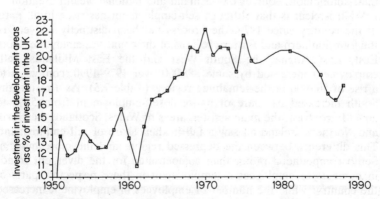

Figure 7.7. Manufacturing investment in the Development Areas as a percentage of UK investment 1951–1988.

what has happened to the proportion of UK total manufacturing investment being undertaken in the Northern region. Throughout the relatively passive phase of post-War regional policy, the Northern group had an average of 13% of total manufacturing investment in the UK per annum. By the end of the active regional policy phase from the early 1960s to the mid-1970s, this had reached over 20% per annum. During the 1980s the percentage fell back again.

The promotion of enterprise: new firm formation and self-employment

The two symbols most commonly invoked by Thatcherites as evidence of the new 'enterprise' Britain of the 1980s are self-employment and new firm formation. Available data suggest that the numbers of self-employed in Great Britain rose by some 1.45 million or 75% between 1979 and 1990. In fact, it was this increase in self-employment that constituted the so-called 'employment boom' that the Thatcher governments repeatedly claimed they had wrought: over the same period, the number of employees in employment actually *declined* by 326 000 (*Employment Gazette*, 1991). Although estimates of growth in self-employment do not reveal how much was part-time or secondary in character, there is no doubt that the 1980s saw a dramatic rise in self-employment. How far this upsurge in self-employment was a result of government policies is difficult to assess. Certainly the government made it easier for people to set up in business through its various tax allowances. Some of the increase, however, is likely to have been a by-product of the mass redundancies and unemployment of the 1980s. It is also important to consider that the vast bulk of self-employment is in building, construction and services, especially distribution, catering and personal services, all of which are crucially dependent on—rather than autonomous sources of—demand and national wealth creation.

What is clear is that although self-employment has risen in all parts of the country since 1979, the process has been distinctly uneven. In the four Southern and Eastern regions of the country, namely the South East, East Anglia, the South West and the East Midlands, self-employment increased by some 888 000 over 1979–1990, compared to a rise of 563 000 in the remaining regions (Table 7.5). As a result, the South increased its share of national self-employment from 52% to 56%. In contrast, the main assisted areas of Wales, Scotland, the North and Northern Ireland all saw a fall in their share of self-employment. This difference between the depressed regions and the more buoyant South compounded rather than compensated for the divergent trends in numbers of employees in employment in these respective parts of the country: while the number of employees in employment increased by some 461 000 in the four Southern regions over 1979–1990, in the rest of Britain the number actually fell by 787 000. As for the

Table 7.5. Regional trends in self-employment 1979–1989.[a]

Region	Self-employed					Changes in employees in employment 1979–1990
	1979		1990		Change 1979–1990	
	(000s)	(%)	(000s)	(%)	(000s)	(000s)
South East	651	34.2	1198	35.7	547	165
East Anglia	79	4.1	156	4.6	77	111
South West	146	7.7	306	9.1	160	173
East Midlands	116	6.0	220	6.5	104	12
South	992	52.1	1880	55.9	888	461
West Midlands	141	7.4	244	7.3	103	−144
Yorkshire–Humberside	134	7.0	271	8.1	137	−82
North West	214	11.2	326	9.7	112	−250
North	79	4.0	116	3.5	37	−133
Wales	124	6.5	199	5.9	75	−40
Scotland	160	8.4	247	7.4	87	−129
Northern Ireland	64	3.4	76	2.3	12	−9
North	916	47.9	1479	44.1	563	−787
United Kingdom	1908	100.0	3359	100.0	1451	−326

[a]Sources: Department of Employment; Daly (1991).

Development Areas themselves, although the growth in self-employment does appear to have compensated for the decline in employees in employment in Wales and Northern Ireland, it failed to do so in Scotland and the North.

It is, perhaps, as the champion of the small firm that Thatcherism is most frequently portrayed. The sharp rise in new business registrations since the early 1980s, from around 150 000 per annum to over 250 000 per annum by the end of the decade, caught the imagination of politicians and academics alike, to a degree that an image was created of small, innovative, flexible and dynamic enterprises rapidly replacing the old landscape of large, mature, inflexible firms. It is, however, a development whose importance is frequently exaggerated. In particular, the small new firm enterprise phenomenon was far from regionally uniform (Table 7.6). Since the beginning of the 1980s the rate of new firm formation has been consistently higher in the Southern half of the country, and especially in the South East, East Anglia and the South West (Mason, 1991; Keeble, 1990). Of the assisted regions only Wales achieved a new firm formation rate on a par with the national average. Of course, the small firm sector is notorious for its high death rate, and this too has been more favourable in the South and East. As a consequence, net business formation rates (registrations minus de-registrations) in the more prosperous South and East have been well

Table 7.6. Business formation by region 1981–1989.[a]

Region	New business registrations		Net change in stock of businesses	
	Number (000s)	Rate	Number (000s)	Rate
South East	698.3	96.1	152.1	20.9
East Anglia	70.9	104.1	13.9	20.4
South West	153.5	99.6	33.0	21.4
East Midlands	114.6	78.1	21.8	14.9
West Midlands	147.8	72.1	24.1	11.7
Yorkshire–Humberside	129.0	69.7	18.5	11.7
North West	170.2	69.0	17.7	7.2
North	62.9	56.1	8.6	7.7
Wales	75.9	80.8	12.2	12.9
Scotland	109.9	54.9	17.1	8.5
Northern Ireland	31.9	63.0	6.8	13.4
United Kingdom	1764.9	80.6	325.8	14.9

[a]Source: Central Statistical Office (1990). Rates calculated per 1000 employees in 1981.

above those in the North. In particular, all of the assisted regions have had rates below the national average.

On the evidence available, therefore, there is little indication that Thatcherism unleashed and fostered an enterprise revolution in the depressed regions of the country. The take-up of the government's general small business incentives (such as the Business Expansion Scheme and Enterprise Allowance) has been much greater in the South East of Britain than in the Northern regions (Martin, 1988), while the take-up of the new Regional Enterprise Grants and regionally differentiated Business Consultancy Initiatives in the Development Areas has thus far proved disappointingly low. To the extent that an enterprise revolution has occurred, it has been concentrated in the South and East. This is hardly surprising: both the formation and survival of new businesses are shaped in large part by local economic conditions, not only the relative buoyancy of demand but also the scale and quality of business support infrastructures, including access to finance. In all these respects the Northern regions of Britain, including the Development Areas, have been disadvantaged relative to the Southern part of the country. The regional components of the government's Enterprise Initiative have failed to rectify this disparity.

The creation of new jobs

The preceding sections have focused on identifying whether there was any significant improvement during the 1980s in some of the key economic variables upon which the new regional policy stance was targeted. The analysis is now extended to the creation of new employment opportunities because although the 1980s marked a change in the post-War emphasis given by governments to net job creation as the direct objective of regional policy, it remains the case that if unemployment disparities and sustained net outward migration from the North are to be removed then there must ultimately be an improvement in the rate of new job creation in the North relative to the South.

We begin by examining the overall record of employment change in the assisted regions of the UK relative to the Southern regions during the Thatcher years. Table 7.7 shows the growth of job opportunities (including those arising from increases in self-employment) over the period 1979–1990. The employment base of the South expanded significantly over the period, the result of an overall increase of over 1 440 000 service jobs which offset a loss of over 900 000 jobs in the production and construction industries. There was also an increase of nearly 890 000 in the self-employed in the South.

In contrast, employment in the Development Areas contracted by 311 000 jobs, with an expansion in service jobs of 325 000 offset by a loss of over 636 000 jobs in manufacturing. Whilst there was also an

Table 7.7. The 'North–South divide' in employment growth 1979–1990 (absolute changes, 000s).

Area	Employees			Self-employed	Overall change in job opportunities
	Production/ construction	Services	Total*a*		
South	−940	1442	461	888	1349
Assisted areas	−636	325	−311	211	−100

*a*Includes agriculture, forestry and fishing.

increase in self-employment of 211 000, it was not sufficient to offset the loss of employee jobs, so that there was an overall net loss of over 100 000 job opportunities in the Development Areas compared to the overall gain of over 1 349 000 in the South (Table 7.7). The plight of the Development Areas relative to the South in securing a share in the overall growth of jobs nationally is demonstrated in Figure 7.8. Throughout the 1970s the relative share of employment opportunities in the South East fell slightly, arguably in part the consequence of the relatively strong regional policy during this period, which diverted job opportunities from the South to the Development Areas. However, with the onset of the 1980s there was a significant turnaround. As the service sector in the South boomed and the rate of industrial job loss in the North accelerated, the South increased its supremacy, a position

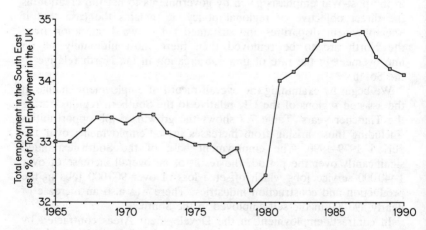

Figure 7.8. Employment in the South East as a proportion of UK employment 1965–1990 (source: Department of Employment).

which has only begun to alter somewhat with the onset of the 1990–1991 recession and its severe impact on the services sector in the South.

The relatively poor employment performance of the Development Areas in previous years was attributed largely to their poor industrial structure, with a relatively large concentration of labour resources in industries which nationally were growing relatively slowly or declining relatively rapidly. Changing this weak industrial structure such that sufficient net exports could be generated to ensure an acceptable rate of economic growth was an integral objective of all post-War regional policy. This was one area in which the policy stance of the 1980s was in agreement—hence its focus on enhancing underlying competitiveness as a route to encourage new inward and indigenous industry in order to change the structural base of the depressed regions. Table 7.8 presents evidence on how the relative structural disadvantage of the Assisted Areas changed throughout the post-War period according to the broad phases of regional policy. The stark contrast in the industrial structure of the assisted regions to that of the Southern grouping is apparent. During the 1950s the difference between the two was marked. By the early 1970s the relative structural disadvantage of the assisted regions had been reduced. However, it was quickly restored in the period of the late 1970s immediately after the oil crisis and was particularly pronounced throughout the 1980s. Further evidence of the continued failure of the assisted regions to alter their industrial structure in the 1980s through the attraction of new and growing industry is provided in Figure 7.9, where the evidence suggests that new and growing sectors continued in this period to concentrate in the prosperous South East.

Additional insight into the relatively disastrous employment performance of the Development Areas during the 1980s is provided by the 'differential' growth component isolated in Table 7.8. The differential employment growth series indicates those differences in employment change that occurred in the Development Areas after allowing for national growth and industrial structure effects. The differential series has been used extensively to isolate the impact of regional policy (see Moore *et al.*, 1986) and is helpful in allowing for other factors that affect employment growth. Table 7.8 indicates that differential employment growth in the Development Areas was negative during the 1950s, a period of passive regional policy, and then became positive in the periods when regional policy was strengthened. There was a slower differential growth in the late 1970s and a neutral change in the 1980s. The position is illustrated more clearly in Figure 7.10. The dramatic turnaround in differential employment growth in the Development Areas at the time of the strengthening of regional policy is apparent. The diversion of new growth opportunities into the Development Areas as a result of regional policy has been estimated to be of the order of 385 000 jobs in the period 1960–1981 (Moore *et al.*, 1986). In addition

Figure 7.9. Location of new and growing sectors in the UK.

Table 7.8. The importance of industrial structure in variations in manufacturing employment growth in the Development Areas 1952–1989.[a]

Period	Actual minus national	Contribution of industrial structure	Residual or differential
1952–1959	−2.7	−1.5	−1.2
1960–1965	0.0	−1.2	+1.2
1966–1971	+2.9	−1.3	+4.2
1972–1975	+3.0	−0.1	+3.1
1976–1981	−4.3	−1.8	−2.5
1981–1989	−2.0	−2.0	0.0

[a]As a percentage of base year employment in each period, i.e. 1952, 1960, 1966, 1972, 1976, 1981. Structural adjustment on a 1978 industry basis.

to these direct effects on manufacturing employment there were indirect effects on employment in the nonmanufacturing sector, which bring the total estimated effect of regional policy in these previous periods to some 540 000 jobs. However, what is perhaps most ominous about the differential employment series presented in Figure 7.10 is the relatively poor growth of the differential series in the 1970s, which appears to

Figure 7.10. Actual minus expected employment in the North 1950–1989.

begin as the regional policy measures were weakened. This pattern of relative decline continues throughout the changed policy regime period of the 1980s, and there is some indication that the pattern of differential growth resembles that which characterised the passive regional policy period of the 1950s, although it is difficult to know what the alternative position might have been.

The total extent of the relatively poor employment growth in the manufacturing sector of the Development Areas during the 1980s is demonstrated in Figure 7.11 which shows the difference in the growth of job opportunities in the Development Areas after allowing for the growth of jobs nationally over the period 1951–1990, thus putting the impact of alternative regimes of regional policy into perspective. The pattern of employment change in the Development Areas was extemely poor under the relatively passive regional policy of the 1950s and did not turn around until the relatively active policy of 1960–1976. The pattern during the 1980s again followed the 1950s position very closely.

The Regional Legacy

The past decade has witnessed a significant change in the coverage, type and volume of public expenditure on regional policy. In retrospect, some of these changes were clearly long overdue. Thus the move to greater selectivity by area and in the application of specific instruments meant that a policy package of a given strength was being operated more cost-effectively. In this respect, the evidence suggests that the UK

Figure 7.11. Growth of employment in the North relative to UK employment growth 1951–1990.

was amongst the first in Europe to improve the efficiency with which its regional policies were operated.

In a similar vein, emphasis on encouraging growth from within (the indigenous sector) relative to the post-War focus on encouraging growth from without (the immigrant sector) was an inevitable consequence of the relatively depressed time of the early 1980s. However, the Thatcher government, like all other post-War British governments, still managed to pull the stops out when it came to attracting a prized multinational investment like Nissan, and in these cases it is difficult, we believe, to distinguish between the Thatcher policy package and its predecessors. A further feature of regional policy during the Thatcher years was the extension of 'supply-side enterprise measures'. This focus on the liberalisation of markets to make them work more efficiently was not new; it was reminiscent of the pre-Keynesian orthodoxy of the 1920s. Quite what has been achieved by these supply-side measures will remain the subject of debate. We have found it difficult to detect much fundamental improvement in the underlying competitiveness of the Development Areas relative to the South, or in new firm formation. This is hardly surprising given the enormous competitive advantage long enjoyed by the South, and the immense regional inertia this represents. As our investigation with respect to regional wage flexibility suggests, there was *money* wage flexibility in the North. What was lacking was regional *real* wage flexibility, because of the differential movement of prices in regional housing markets.

Although there was a growth of self-employment in the Development Areas, this was well below that of the South. Moreover, the growth that occurred was woefully insufficient to compensate for the dramatic decline in jobs. The adverse industrial structure remains. The failure to generate sufficient job opportunities in the Development Areas, and the North more generally, relative to the South has inevitably been reflected in further net outward migration and a substantial widening in regional unemployment disparities, to an extent unprecedented in the post-War period (Figure 7.12).

In the light of the scale of the regional problem, whatever the achievements of regional policy during the Thatcher years, we cannot believe that the current volume of resources devoted to regional policy is adequate, however cost-effective that policy may now be. Whereas expenditure on urban policy in the UK has increased since the early 1980s, expenditure on regional policy has fallen dramatically. There is, therefore a pressing need for a coherent and well-resourced regional policy. This view is reinforced given the additional competitive pressures which are likely to face the Northern and Development regions in an integrated Europe.

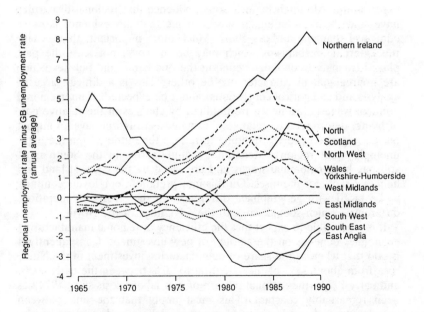

Figure 7.12. Regional unemployment disparities in the UK 1965–1990.

Comment

Market Failure in the Regions

Michael Chisholm

Britain's regional problems are deep-seated and intractable, a fact which
is well documented in the chapter by Ron Martin and Peter Tyler and
which is of critical importance in assessing our expectations concerning
the impact of the Thatcher years. It does seem clear that during the
1960s and 1970s there was some reduction in the scale of regional
disparities. Equally, this was a period of active regional policy. Since
then, there has indeed been a sharp reduction in regional policy
expenditure. Although there is some evidence that regional disparities
have since been widening, it seems to me that this evidence is more
equivocal than the authors allow. Much more important, though, are
the external mechanisms which may be at work, not least the part
played by macroeconomic events on the one hand, and policies which
are nonregional in character on the other. This is a difficult area of
analysis and categorical conclusions cannot be expected. If interregional
nominal wage adjustments are nullified by changes in the relative cost
of living, determined by relative housing costs, this will have an impact
on the migration process, tending to reduce the outflow from the high-
unemployment regions. Meantime, manufacturers in the South must
still pay higher nominal wages and are faced by the costs of land and
hence of rents for premises. On this interpretation, employers continue
to be faced with geographical differences in their costs of operation,
differences which should work to the advantage of the North.

It is reasonable to expect that the efficiency of regional manufacturing
economies depends on the amount of new investment. Consequently it
is odd that whereas the share of manufacturing investment in the North
rose from about 13% of the UK total to 20% between the early 1960s
and early 1970s, the regional pattern of unit labour costs since 1974 has
been remarkably constant. This must imply that the link between
investment and productivity changes is rather weak and calls into
question the value of attempts to shift the geographical pattern of
investment through incentives.

That the South has enjoyed faster growth in self-employment and a
higher rate of new firm formation than the North since 1979 cannot

reasonably be doubted. However, without comparable data for earlier periods, we cannot conclude that the North has suffered under the Thatcher policies. By comparison with the inter-War period, there has been a quite remarkable transformation in the geographical pattern of new firm formation; the North has sharply improved its relative performance. That there is still a sizeable differential may be testimony to the failure of recent policy, and may reflect the slowness with which regional differentials change. In any case, as the authors point out, the adverse effects of industrial structure in the North were more severe in the period 1981–1989 than in any period of comparable length since 1952. The hill up which the North has been climbing has clearly become much steeper in recent years, as staple industries have been decimated. Is it not remarkable, therefore, that unemployment and other differentials have not widened much more sharply?

The authors call for a coherent and well-resourced regional policy but do not define what such a package might be. Nor do they consider the possibility that it is measures which traditionally lie outside the scope of regional policy which may be equally important. For example, the capping of Local Authority expenditure has jeopardised the receipt of European Community funds which are conditional on the availability of matching funds locally provided.

One of the clearest failures of Thatcherite thinking is the limited attention given to the role of externalities—both positive and negative—in all aspects of economic life, including the regions. To emphasise the role of individuals and of firms, treated as atomistic units operating in 'markets', is to ignore the fact that many important markets can never work properly because there is no practicable way to charge or compensate in an appropriate way. As a result, a large amount of money is spent on individual programmes, each treated in isolation from the others, and without the strategic control which is necessary to gain the maximum benefit from externalities. The abolition of the metropolitan counties and failure to provide a suitable alternative framework is one example. Another is the accessibility crisis facing London's Docklands and a third is the failure so far to permit British Rail to capitalise on the Channel Tunnel in an effective way. Failures of this kind, endemic in government, have been exacerbated in recent years.

Finally, the history of regional policy in the post-War period contains a fundamental lesson which must be learned. Changes have been so frequent that no policy initiative has been given adequate time to prove itself before major alterations have been introduced. There can be little doubt that a lot of money has been wasted as a consequence. Whatever regional policy package is in place, two things need to be done as prerequisites. First, better ways to coordinate existing policies must be found, which may mean extending the principle of Regional Development Corporations. Second, the tendency to centralise economic and political power must be reversed, which implies loosening the constraints on Local Authorities and indeed positively encouraging them to assist in the necessary local transformations.

PART III

The Changing Labour Market

Part III

Employment Law and the
The Changing Labour Market

8

Labour Law and Industrial Relations

Simon Deakin

The Thatcher governments of the 1980s made reform of the labour market a central part of their economic programme. To this end, legislation curtailed the right to strike and subjected trade unions to an unprecedented degree of external regulation and supervision, while basic employment rights were eroded. Although incomes policies for the private sector were rejected, in the public sector established bargaining arrangements were undermined by deregulation and privatisation and by the imposition of cash limits on pay. Unions in the nationalised and public employment sectors suffered demoralising defeats in a series of set-piece strikes. The result was, in official eyes, a fundamental transformation of employment relations. Unsurprisingly, independent opinion on this claim is sharply divided. One line of thought identifies a decisive improvement in manufacturing productivity during the Thatcher years, brought about by a combination of high unemployment, greater competition in product markets, increased labour flexibility and the ending of state support for trade unionism (Metcalf, 1989). Against this are sceptical accounts which either cast doubt on the idea that changes in industrial relations law were motivated by any coherent economic strategy (Auerbach, 1991) or question whether government policies have produced any long-term change in the structure of the industrial relations system (Kelly, 1990). A further possibility is that structural changes did occur as a result of deregulation, most notably in terms of the intensification of labour and the deterioration of pay and conditions in certain sectors of the economy, but that far from paving the way for productivity improvements, these developments have impaired effective labour utilisation and competitiveness in product markets (Nolan, 1989).

The central issue to be examined in this chapter is the relationship between the formation of policy, the implementation of legislative change and the consequences in terms of economic performance. Although ostensibly committed to a neo-liberal ideal of limited government, the Thatcher governments, to a greater extent than any of their immediate predecessors, used legislation to restructure the industrial relations system and align it with what they saw as the needs of a competitive economy. If economics played a greater role than before in formulating labour relations policy, the impact of legislation upon labour market performance was, however, far less clear-cut.

The Influence of Economics on Legislative Policy

The move to liberalise the labour market can be seen as complementing the adoption of monetarism in macroeconomic policy and the abandonment of policies of full employment in the late 1970s (Wilkinson, 1987). Attention switched from management of the level of demand in the economy to supply-side explanations of unemployment, most notably the role of trade unions in regulating workplace practices and setting a floor to wages and conditions through sector-level collective bargaining. This policy received its clearest expression in the 1985 White Paper, *Employment: the Challenge for the Nation*, which was as much a justification and review of policies already in place as a programme for future reforms. The White Paper offered a 'sound' framework of economic policy based on control of the money supply; removal of obstacles to the creation of jobs in the form of labour market regulation; and, in exceptional cases, direct action in the form of training and make-work schemes for the long-term and young unemployed. Similar approaches to labour market reform were advocated in other countries at this time, most notably in the USA and Germany, but the degree of legislative change in these systems proved nowhere near as great as in the UK (Deakin, 1991).

The particular features of the British labour law and industrial relations system at the start of the 1980s presented an opportunity but also a difficulty for a strategy of deregulation. By international standards labour law regulation in Britain was comparatively weak. Although this made the task of deregulation easier, it also meant that new forms of legal intervention were necessary to address the issue of union power in the labour market, as the sources of union strength were largely extra-legal.

The traditionally limited role of labour law in the industrial relations system arose from the preference for voluntary collective bargaining over legislation as the principal source of pay determination and job regulation. Under this system of 'legal voluntarism', statute imposed no duty to bargain (except for a short period during the 1970s) and collective agreements were not, on the whole, capable of being enforced through actions for breach of contract. The Donovan Report affirmed this basic abstentionist approach by rejecting proposals for a tighter framework of legal controls in collective labour law, but it gave a limited endorsement to a greater role for individual employment law as part of the strategy for formalising and regularising plant-level industrial relations. Both Conservative and Labour governments of the 1970s pursued the policy of extending unfair dismissal and job security legislation, while in collective labour law the voluntarist consensus appeared to be confirmed by the failure of the Conservative government's *Industrial Relations Act* between 1971 and 1974.

It was partly because the advances made in employment and social security law in the 1960s and 1970s were so limited that they were vulnerable to being rolled back in the 1980s. They provided a thin layer of social protection in a system which remained essentially voluntarist. Redundancy compensation and earnings-related unemployment benefits dated only from 1965, unfair dismissal from 1971, and maternity protection from 1975. The exclusion from protection of part-time and temporary workers, which the Thatcher governments sought to extend by a series of changes to qualifying conditions, had been written into the legislation from the start. A fundamental weakness that affected the whole statutory framework of employment protection was the predominant role played by the common law of the contract of employment; this facilitated the process by which deregulating legislation carved out exceptions and derogations from minimum standards of job and income security.

In collective labour law, by contrast, this type of deregulation would not be effective, as the sources of trade union power did not depend on a formal statutory underpinning of positive rights. Some inroads were made by the rescission in the early 1980s of the Fair Wages Resolution and the Schedule 11 procedure for the extension of minimum terms and conditions laid down in sector-level collective agreements. The bulk of changes in trade union law, however, took the form of expanding, rather than diminishing, the role of the law. To this end, a series of Acts cut back the scope of immunities and so increased the scope of common law regulation of strike activity. The most important single measure was the *Employment Act* of 1982 which removed the blanket immunity of trade unions from liability in tort, narrowed down the 'trade dispute' formula which had previously protected most forms of industrial action, and strictly regulated the closed shop. The immunities were further narrowed down in the 1988 and 1990 Acts, which amongst other things imposed a general ban on secondary strike action. In addition, new forms of statutory regulation were introduced to complement the expanded role of the common law. The *Trade Union Act* of 1984, which was extended in 1988, made membership ballots compulsory prior to official strikes and imposed regular balloting requirements for the election of certain national officials and the establishment of union political funds. The *Employment Act* of 1988 provided individual members with a further set of rights against their unions, most notably by limiting the power of unions to discipline

members who refused to obey strike calls or similar instructions, and
the 1990 Act extended the range of union responsibility for 'unofficial'
strikes and increased employers' powers to dismiss strikers.

As a result of the above changes, Britain became practically alone
in western Europe in failing to legislate for a basic floor of rights to
terms and conditions (Deakin, 1990), while legislative interference with
trade union autonomy led to repeated condemnations of government
policy by various supervisory bodies of the International Labour
Organisation (Ewing, 1989).

The Economic and Social Impact of Legislative Change

Strikes and industrial conflict

The reduction in the incidence of strike activity in the 1980s is one of
the government's principal claims for the success of its labour law
policies. In terms of working days lost per year, the average in the
1980s was 7.2 million as opposed to 12.9 million in the 1970s and 3.5
million in the 1960s. A small number of large-scale strikes, in particular
the miners' strike of 1984–1985, swelled the total of working days lost
in the 1980s. In terms of the number of stoppages, the 1980s showed
a clearer improvement on both the 1960s and 1970s (Table 8.1).

The improvement is less impressive when placed in the context of

Table 8.1. Strikes and industrial stoppages in the UK 1960–1990.[a]

Year	Working days lost (000s)	Workers involved (000s)	Stoppages in progress
1980	11 964	834	1348
1981	4266	1513	1344
1982	5313	2103	1538
1983	3754	574	1364
1984	27 135	1464	1221
1985	6402	791	903
1986	1920	720	1074
1987	3546	887	1016
1988	3702	790	781
1989	4128	727	701
1990	1903	298	630
10-year averages:			
1960–1969	3555	1357	2462
1970–1979	12 870	1616	2631
1980–1989	7213	1040	1129

[a]Source: *Employment Gazette.*

international developments (Table 8.2). Most of the leading industrialised countries experienced a decline in strike activity in the 1980s. In Western Europe, small increases were recorded during this period in Norway, Denmark, Finland and Germany. All these countries still had a lower average number of working days lost than the UK even after its improvement. In the other countries strike activity fell: France, Sweden, Spain, Portugal, Greece, Italy, the Netherlands and Ireland all experienced a larger decline than Britain over the period 1978–1987.

Legislation made the environment less attractive for strikes in three main ways: by restricting the scope of immunities, by widening the range of sanctions which could be brought against trade unions and individual strikers, and by improsing upon unions a complex network of rules concerning ballots and the discipline of members. The changes to the immunities appear to have succeeded in restricting certain forms of strike action, in particular secondary boycotts and picketing.

The increased possibilities of winning damages and injunctions against trade unions following the *Employment Act* of 1982 also had an impact

Table 8.2. International comparisons of strike activity 1978–1987.[a]

Country	Working days lost per thousand employees in employment		
	1978–1982	1983–1987	1978–1987
UK	540	400	470
Australia	600	250	420
Austria	—	—	—
Canada	820	440	620
Denmark	120	250	190
Finland	300	520	420
France	120	50	80
Germany	40	50	50
Greece	950	590	760
Ireland	800	400	600
Italy	1160	510	840
Japan	20	10	10
Netherlands	30	10	10
New Zealand	350	550	450
Norway	60	140	100
Portugal	210	120	160
Spain	1120	560	850
Sweden	250	60	150
Switzerland	—	—	—
Uniited States	200	100	150

[a]Source: *Employment Gazette* (June 1989).

on union behaviour. The use of sequestration orders to enforce injunctions in the miners' strike of 1985 and the seamen's strike of 1988 in each case severely weakened the unions' capacity to pursue the dispute (although in the case of the miners' strike the courts' intervention was based on the general law of contract and not upon the changes made to union immunity and responsibility in 1982). In practice, the interlocutory injunction is an extremely effective means of stopping a strike in its tracks and gives employers an overwhelming tactical advantage in the conduct of a dispute. Even in a case where trade unions act within the scope of the remaining immunities—such as a 'primary' dispute over pay or jobs—court procedures can delay a strike beyond the point at which the union can usefully bring economic pressure to bear on the employer, as happened in the national docks strike of 1989.

By making unions formally responsible for a wide range of strikes, and by requiring membership ballots in the case of all strikes which are in law the union's responsibility, the *Trade Union Act* of 1984 strengthened the power of central union organisation over the rank and file, and reversed a trend towards fragmentation which had weakened unions in some areas. Although some strikes foundered owing to the failure of unions early on to observe the balloting requirements of the 1984 Act, where these requirements were applied they could be put to good effect to rally support for industrial action and to put pressure on employers in advance of the strike commencing. Over 90% of strike ballots under the 1984 Act resulted in votes for industrial action.

Conscious that the 1984 balloting laws had back-fired, the government introduced amendments in 1988 and 1990 which sought to diminish the effectiveness of ballots as a source of union negotiating strength. The 1988 Act narrowed the union's choice of the balloting constituency and limited the scope of ballots covering more than one workplace. The 1990 Act went several steps further by making the union responsible for a far wider range of strike action—including any industrial action authorised or encouraged by a shop steward, regardless of whether the union's own rules gave him or her such authority, subject only to a right to repudiate it by writing to all the members and employers concerned. Because a strike ballot must now precede an official strike for it to be lawful, the union can endorse pre-ballot industrial action only at the risk of incurring extensive legal liabilities. It must repudiate first, and then organise a ballot if it wishes to make the strike official. The practical difficulties in taking such a course are obvious. At the same time, workers who take part in any unofficial strike (as defined under the legislation) will be liable to selective dismissal by their employers.

These draconian provisions appear to have been designed to avoid a repeat of the successful strike action on the London Underground in 1989, which was organised by unofficial strike committees that operated independently of the union. They illustrate, however, a deepening confusion on the part of the government concerning the proper role of unions in controlling and limiting strikes. Extension of the legal responsibility of unions in this way is likely to result in unions trying to keep out of unofficial strike action at any cost, and will make the orderly settlement of disputes more difficult. However, unions will have every reason to pre-empt unofficial action by organising strikes on their own initiative, when discipline and control will be strengthened.

The overall impact of strike legislation was therefore to weaken certain traditional forms of industrial action, most notably secondary action, picketing and various forms of unofficial action, while paradoxically strengthening some others. The increased availability to firms of injunctions and related court interventions provided a powerful weapon which employers in some sectors used to limit union power. However, it is far from evident that these changes were responsible for the general decline in strike activity in the 1980s. High unemployment and the absence of an incomes policy more clearly distinguish the 1980s from the strike-prone 1970s. The rapid fall in unemployment after 1987 saw a sudden revival of strike activity over pay, with over 4.1 million working days lost in 1989. Most of these were in the public sector where the government was attempting to enforce a pay norm of 7%.

Collective bargaining, union membership and recognition

In contrast to the rapid growth during the 1970s, union membership declined in every year of the 1980s, falling from the post-war peak of 13.3 million in 1979 to 10.2 million in 1989, a decrease of 24%. If union density is taken to signify membership as a proportion of the total labour force, there was a decline from 51% in 1979 to 37% in 1989; if membership as a proportion of employees in employment is taken as the relevant measure of density, figures indicate a fall from a peak of over 58% in 1979 to below 46% in 1989 (Table 8.3). This represents a high figure internationally, although care must be taken in interpreting comparative data in this area as not only do methods of calculating density differ from country to country, but membership itself is not necessarily a good indicator of union strength. Britain remains in the middle order of OECD countries, with a density in terms of the labour force as a whole which is comparable to that of Italy and Germany and far higher than in France or the USA (Table 8.4). The highest density figures are those for the Scandinavian countries, in particular Sweden. In part these differences reflect the separate functions which union membership performs in various systems, including the degree to which access to the benefits of collective bargaining and social protection depends on union membership. A better means of assessing the significance of the decline in British membership is to compare it with trends in other countries over the 1980s. While density in Sweden and

180   *Simon Deakin*

Table 8.3. Trade union membership and density in Britain 1979–1989.[a]

Year	Total recorded membership (000s)	Density		
		Percentage of those employed[b]	Adjusted percentage of those employed[c]	Percentage of labour force[d]
1979	13 289	58.8	52.9	51.9
1980	12 947	57.7	51.9	50.3
1981	12 106	56.7	51.0	47.1
1982	11 593	55.5	49.9	45.2
1983	11 236	54.7	49.2	43.8
1984	10 994	53.0	47.7	41.6
1985	10 821	51.8	46.6	40.5
1986	10 539	50.5	45.4	39.3
1987	10 475	49.7	44.7	38.7
1988	10 376	47.8	43.0	38.0
1989	10 158	45.9	41.3	37.0

[a]Sources: trade union membership: Bird *et al.* (1991), Table 1; employees in employment and labour force: *Employment Gazette, Historical Supplement* No. 2 (November 1989), Table 1.1 (August 1991).
[b]Membership as a percentage of employees in employment (seasonally adjusted figures, June).
[c]Membership adjusted by 0.9 to take into account retired, unemployed and Irish members in recorded figures (see Bailey and Kelly, 1990).
[d]Membership as a percentage of the labour force (working population minus the armed forces; includes self-employed, unemployed and non-employed on government training schemes).

Norway actually grew between 1980 and 1988, it fell by over 30% in France, 29% in the Netherlands, 28% in the USA and 9% in Germany; the corresponding figure for the UK was 18%.

Explanations for the decline in British trade union membership have focused on the cyclical effects of high unemployment and economic recession, rather than the compositional effects associated with the decline of manufacturing industry relative to services. The rapid decline of manufacturing at the start of the 1980s and the resulting loss of full-time, male-dominated jobs certainly had an impact in terms of flows out of membership. However, union density fell in all sectors and not just in manufacturing. At any given time trade unions were recruiting large numbers of members and losing others; what has to be explained is the contrast to the 1970s, when density rose rapidly at a time of continuing decline in manufacturing employment and a rise in female employment. From this perspective, the critical factors in the 1980s are the inhibiting effect of high unemployment and the combination of

Table 8.4. International comparisons of trade union density 1970–1988.[a]

Country	Union density %[b]				Change in union density (%)	
	1970	1980	1985	1988	1970–1980	1980–1988
United Kingdom	49.7	56.3	50.5	46.1	13.3	−18.1
Australia	50.2	56.4	56.5	53.4	12.3	−5.3
Austria	70.4	65.3	60.8	58.2	−7.2	−10.9
Belgium	54.9	75.7	80.9	77.5	37.9	2.4
Canada	31.1	35.1	35.9	34.6	12.9	−1.4
Denmark	62.2	91.4	90.8	86.0	46.9	−5.9
Finland	58.8	85.8	86.6	90.0	45.9	4.9
France	22.3	19.0	16.3	12.0	−14.8	−36.8
Germany	37.9	42.9	44.0	40.1	13.2	−6.5
Greece	—	—	36.7	25.0	—	—
Iceland	—	68.1	—	78.3	—	15.0
Ireland	59.0	63.4	62.2	58.4	7.5	−8.2
Italy	40.8	60.5	59.6	62.7	48.3	3.6
Japan	35.1	31.1	28.9	26.8	−11.4	−13.8
Netherlands	40.5	39.9	34.1	30.2	−1.5	−24.3
New Zealand[c]	46.2	55.0	47.3	42.1	19.0	−23.5
Norway	58.1	65.3	65.4	67.7	12.4	3.7
Portugal	59.0	58.8	51.6	(30.0)	0.3	—
Spain	—	22.0	16.0	—	—	−27.3
Switzerland	34.2	34.5	32.6	30.0	0.9	−13.0
United States	30.0	24.7	18.0[d]	16.4[d]	−17.7	−28.7[d]

[a]Source: *OECD Employment Outlook* (1991), Table 4.1.
[b]Total recorded membership as a percentage of employees in employment, except where noted otherwise.
[c]Total membership in the private sector as percentage of private sector employees in employment.
[d]Total employed membership as a percentage of employees in employment.

relatively low inflation and the absence of an incomes policy, which produced rising real incomes for most private sector employees, in particular in those areas of the economy where collective bargaining remained strongly embedded.

Density, which is usually calculated on the basis of membership, is only one measure of union strength and influence; a more meaningful measure of the influence of trade union power in regulating terms and conditions of employment is the coverage of collective bargaining agreements. The coverage of collective agreements will be greater than union membership for a number of reasons. It is normal for terms and conditions laid down in agreements at either plant or sector level to be applied to union members and non-members alike in plants where unions are recognised, while in the past it has also been common for firms which do not recognise unions to follow sector-level agreements informally; in addition, the impact of statutory wages orders should be considered here as a substitute for collective bargaining which affected large numbers of non-unionised employees. ACAS estimates at the start of the 1980s suggested that the terms and conditions of over two-thirds of full-time employees in employment were affected in some way by a collective agreement, while the extensive influence of collective bargaining in manufacturing industry and the public sector was confirmed by the first *Workplace Industrial Relations Survey* (WIRS). One measure of the decline in the impact of collective bargaining in the early 1980s is derived from the findings of the two WIRS surveys which provide information on the numbers of employees employed in private sector establishments which recognised trade unions. This source provides only limited evidence of coverage in the wider sense, as it is unable to indicate the possible extent of the influence of sector-level agreements or statutory wages orders on terms and conditions; however, as both of these were becoming less important as sources of regulation of private sector employment during this period, their importance should not be exaggerated. On this definition of coverage, the WIRS data indicate a decline in percentage terms between 1980 and 1984 from 84% to 65% for manual workers and 62% to 49% for nonmanual workers (Beaumont and Harris, 1991). The principal cause was the higher rate of closure of unionised plants during this period, rather than derecognition. Apart from a few well-publicised examples such as the docks and national newspapers, derecognition as such was rare throughout the 1980s, despite the fact that there were very few legal obstacles to it.

However, this picture of relative stability in industrial relations procedures at firm level masks the continuing decline of national or sector-level bargaining, and the weakening of union power in the labour market which comes with the enforced decentralisation of bargaining levels. The decline of sector-level bargaining long predates the advent of the Thatcher governments; from the middle 1960s onwards national agreements in manufacturing were increasingly confined to setting a floor of minimum wages and conditions which were only directly relevant for employees without a recognised union to negotiate for them at plant or company level. In the 1980s even this floor was removed, firstly by the repeal in the early 1980s of 'fair wages legislation' which provided for the extension of sector-level agreements to non-union firms, and more recently by the break-up of national multi-employer bargaining in a number of sectors.

A number of means, direct and indirect, were used to undermine national bargaining. These included the ending of the statutory system of Industry Training Boards in most sectors in 1982 and the curtailment in 1986 of the powers of statutory Wages Councils which previously determined the pay and conditions of 2.75 million low-paid workers.

Following the *Wages Act*, Wages Councils were confined to setting single minimum wage rates for their sectors as opposed to rates for all grades of workers as previously. Changes to strike law also undermined national bargaining. In some sectors, including merchant shipping and newspapers, laws restricting picketing and secondary action limited the ability of unions to resist employer moves to break up or narrow the scope of national agreements. The 1982 Act made it difficult to conduct national disputes except as the aggregation of local disputes between employers and their own employees. This was partly responsible for the demise of the National Engineering Agreement in 1990, which followed a series of local settlements to the engineering unions' demands for reductions in working time.

Similar moves towards decentralisation occurred in the public sector. The enforced privatisation of many local services was accompanied by legislation that banned Local Authorities from using contract compliance to maintain union recognition and minimum terms and conditions for the privatised workforce; the earlier repeal of the Fair Wages Resolution and Schedule 11 procedure had eased the way to privatisation by removing legal powers to extend national collective agreements to all firms in particular sectors. Schools and hospitals which opt out of Local Authority control have been given powers to set their own pay and conditions. In the Civil Service, departments and divisions are being encouraged to make their own agreements outside the structure of central pay bargaining.

In both the private and the public sectors, competitive pressures on employers are cited as a major reason for decentralisation. In the private sector this has taken the form of the increasing use of divisional bargaining units within companies, reflecting the different product markets and cost constraints within which separate divisions operate. Decentralisation to take advantage of regional or local differences in labour market conditions has not been a principal factor behind change. In the public sector the process has been directly stimulated by government, seeking to reproduce what it takes to be the normal competitive pressures of private industry. In both cases, the extreme flexibility of the law of collective bargaining is an important factor facilitating change. In contrast to the highly juridified forms of bargaining which are found in continental labour law systems, British labour law makes no attempt to specify the level at which bargaining should take place (plant, division, company or sector), nor to regulate the relationship between agreements at different levels; nor does it provide any collective mechanism for the enforcement of terms agreed in bargaining.

The traditional absence of legal regulation of collective bargaining may in one sense have been a source of strength in the 1980s, since it limited the degree to which changes in the law could affect the core of trade union power. However, increased decentralisation and the absence

of a wider statutory floor of rights threaten the long-term viability of
collective bargaining. The combination of falling union density and
scattered bargaining units may produce a situation in which the
advantages of collective bargaining for firms increasingly outweigh the
costs in terms of the union mark-up on wages, precisely the pattern
which precipitated the large fall in US union density in the 1970s and
the 1980s.

Pay, performance and productivity

In the private sector, average pay increases more than kept pace with
retail price inflation, reflecting in part the continuing strength of
collective bargaining and the absence of any incomes policy or
mechanism for centralised pay coordination. This contradicted the
government's aim that competitive forces should act as a restraint on
pay. The rate of increase of nominal wages was high by international
standards and was only partly offset by the better than average increases
in productivity in the mid-1980s, so that the relative rise in unit labour
costs was again considerable; from 1987 the rate of productivity increase
tailed off as well (Tables 8.5–8.7).

In the public sector, where the government operated various informal
pay norms on a year-by-year basis, wage growth was more restricted.
After the last large-scale exercise in pay comparability with the private
sector in 1980, relative pay for the public sector steadily declined.
Groups with formal pay review bodies and other arrangements linking
them with private sector pay movements—in particular the medical

Table 8.5. Annual growth in compensation per employee in selected OECD
countries 1977–1992.[a]

Country	1977–1987	1988	1989	1990	1991[b]	1992[b]
United Kingdom	10.7	8.1	8.1	10.9	9.2	7.5
France	10.3	4.8	5.1	4.9	4.8	4.8
Germany	4.6	3.2	3.0	4.6	5.8	5.4
Italy	14.4	8.0	9.1	8.9	8.2	7.8
Japan	4.6	3.2	4.1	4.3	4.0	3.9
United States	6.2	4.8	2.8	3.4	4.2	4.3
OECD Europe	9.3	5.6	5.9	7.0	6.8	6.1
EEC	9.6	5.5	5.7	6.9	6.8	6.2
Total OECD	7.2	4.9	4.5	5.2	5.3	5.0

[a]Source: *OECD Employment Outlook* (1991), Table 1.5. Growth figures
(percentage changes from the previous period) calculated on the basis of 1987
values expressed in 1987 US dollars.
[b]Projected increases.

Table 8.6. Annual growth in unit labour costs (business sector) in selected OECD countries 1977–1992.[a]

Country	1977–1987	1988	1989	1990	1991[b]	1992[b]
United Kingdom	8.0	7.3	10.1	12.5	6.9	3.5
France	7.4	0.9	2.0	3.1	3.6	2.8
Germany	2.9	0.1	0.4	2.6	4.7	4.6
Italy	11.9	4.3	5.8	7.8	6.8	5.4
Japan	1.5	−1.4	1.1	0.5	1.9	1.7
United States	5.7	3.5	2.9	4.2	3.7	2.9
OECD Europe	7.0	2.8	3.8	5.9	5.3	3.9
EEC	7.2	2.6	3.6	5.7	5.2	3.9
Total OECD	5.4	2.4	3.1	4.3	4.0	3.0

[a]Source: *OECD Employment Outlook* (1991), Table 1.5. Growth figures (percentage changes from the previous period) calculated on the basis of 1987 values expressed in 1987 US dollars.
[b]Projected increases.

Table 8.7. Labour productivity in the UK 1980–1991.[a]

Year	Output per person employed (1985=100)		Output per person-hour in manufacturing
	Whole economy	Production industries	
1980	87.6	73.7	78.1
1981	89.2	77.8	82.2
1982	92.6	84.1	86.7
1983	96.7	92.1	92.1
1984	97.6	94.0	97.5
1985	100.0	100.0	100.0
1986	103.3	105.3	103.8
1987	106.1	110.1	109.6
1988	107.5	113.2	115.5
1989	107.2	113.7	120.8
1990	107.4	114.4	121.1
1991	107.0	114.4	

[a]Sources: *Employment Gazette, National Institute Economic Review.*

professions, nurses, judges and senior civil servants, and the police—maintained their position. Those who lost ground after the Clegg comparability exercise were the teachers, whose collective bargaining rights were suspended in 1986, health service ancillary workers and local government workers.

Qualitative evidence for the existence of a 'new climate' in industrial relations comes from the increased use by management of measures designed to increase employee participation in the enterprise, including profit-related pay and employee share ownership and consultative bodies on work organisation including quality circles. Interest in these developments has been generalised to the point at which a 'new industrial relations' is seen to be emerging, in which the collective bargaining relationship is less important than management strategies and specialised techniques for eliciting greater effort and involvement from individual employees. This implies a certain 'individualisation' of employment relationships. Flexibility in the form of the contract of employment was another focus of interest in the 1980s, but there was very little concrete evidence of systematic changes in recruitment strategies or in the arrangement of working time. Established methods of varying labour costs and inputs—the extensive use of overtime and shift work and the employment of part-time and subcontract labour—remained in use to a much greater extent than annualisation of hours, flexible shifts and variation of the basic working week for full-time workers (Horrell and Rubery, 1991).

Complete flexibility of work status and the individualisation of terms and conditions of employment were by and large restricted to those sectors which underwent varying degrees of deregulation and decollectivisation; in these areas flexibility was little more than a synonym for job insecurity (Turnbull, 1991; Evans, 1990). In the docks, following the abolition of the National Dock Labour Scheme in 1989, and in parts of construction, the removal of union influence has led to general intensification of work, longer hours, cuts in pay and employment benefits, loss of employee status and the ending of job classifications; similar developments have occurred in privatised services and in the cross-channel ferries following the failure of the 1988 strike. These are simply the most extreme examples of the effects of trade union influence being marginalised, as similar changes have been felt to a greater or lesser degree in large parts of the private and public sectors.

To the extent that competitive pressures in the private sector and government pressure in the public sector led simply to greater intensification of labour, the results may have been more profitable for firms and consumers (or taxpayers) but cannot be described as more efficient. Insofar as this is the case, the changes made are simply distributional, not productive; at best, any improvements in the competitive position of firms will be short-lived. Policies designed to cut employees' pay while raising labour input create strong disincentives for firms to compete on the basis of improved technology and marketing (Rubery *et al.*, 1987), a point illustrated by the overall low levels of investment in British manufacturing industry as a whole and in particular in the most deregulated sectors in the 1980s. At the end of the decade, as at the start of it, the British economy was characterised by relatively low pay and even lower productivity in international terms.

Unemployment and labour supply

Various supply-side measures, including training subsidies, government make-work schemes and changes to social security and employment law, aimed to cut employer's hiring costs and encourage the unemployed into the labour market. The value of unemployment benefits was cut and access limited at the same time as downwards pressure was put on wage levels in the lower ranges of the earnings hierarchy through the measures of labour market deregulation and privatisation. Taxation policy further widened the dispersion of pay. Between 1979 and 1988, for full-time workers the gap in pre-tax earnings between the highest and lowest deciles increased from 128% to 182% for women and from 138% to 194% for men. When taxation is taken into account together with rises in prices, the real increase for those in the highest decile was close to four times that of those in the lowest (Deakin and Wilkinson, 1991b, pp. 139–140).

Unemployment peaked in the summer of 1986 at over 11% of the labour force on the standard ILO definition and fell rapidly between 1987 and 1989 to reach a low of around 6% of the labour force, before starting to increase again in the middle of 1990. Even before this recent rise, Britain had a worse unemployment rate than Germany, Japan and the USA (Table 8.8). The size of the fall in the mid-1980s and its timing have been widely ascribed to the tightening of social security

Table 8.8. Unemployment rates in selected OECD countries 1980–1990.[a]

Country	1980	1985	1986	1987	1988	1989	1990
United Kingdom	6.4	11.2	11.2	10.3	8.5	7.1	6.9
France	6.3	10.2	10.4	10.5	10.0	9.4	9.0
Germany	2.9	7.2	6.4	6.2	6.2	5.6	5.1
Italy	7.5	9.6	10.5	10.0	11.0	10.9	9.9
Japan	2.0	2.6	2.8	2.8	2.5	2.3	2.1
United States	7.0	7.1	6.9	6.1	5.4	5.2	5.4
Total OECD 16[b]	5.1	7.8	7.7	7.3	6.7	6.2	6.0

[a]Source: *OECD Employment Outlook* (1991), Table 1.4. Percentage figures calculated using standard international (ILO) definition.
[b]Average of 16 leading OECD industrial nations.

administration brought about in 1986 by the Restart programme, under which the long-term unemployed were subject to regular monitoring by employment service officials to assess their availability for work. However, it is hard to give much credibility to this isolation of one factor, particularly when it is borne in mind that far more serious inroads were made into unemployment benefit through changes in legislation and administration both before and after the inception of Restart, without any visible effect on unemployment rates (Deakin and Wilkinson, 1991b). It should also be noted that unemployment benefit levels in relation to average wages are considerably lower in Britain than almost every other EC and OECD country, partly as a consequence of the abolition of the earnings-related component.

Despite the introduction in 1989 of a requirement that unemployed benefit recipients should be prepared to take up offers of part-time work after a 13-week waiting period, the use of part-time work as a route out of long-term unemployment remains limited. The part-time labour market is highly segmented by gender. Although there was a small increase in male part-time work in the 1980s, in 1988 over 83% of part-time workers were female, the majority of them married (Rubery, 1989). The normal flow into part-time work consists of married women returning to the labour market after a period of non-employment, usually associated with family responsibilities. Of the registered unemployed who are either looking for part-time work or say they are prepared to take it, the majority are again married women. A Department of Employment survey carried out in the spring of 1990 reported that two-thirds of unemployed men said that they would consider taking up a part-time job but that five-sixths would prefer a full-time job if one was available.

Although Britain had a superior record of employment growth in the 1980s to the rest of the EC, the difference was not substantial and predictions are for that growth to be reversed into 1992 (Table 8.9). The legal flexibility of employment protection legislation in Britain meant that employers were free to a much greater extent than elsewhere in the EC to offer jobs on a part-time or fixed-term basis. This does not, however, provide a convincing explanation for the growth of part-time and non-standard work in Britain. Much of this growth predates the 1980s measures of deregulation which were designed to encourage non-standard work. In addition, countries including France, Sweden and the Netherlands also saw considerable growth of part-time work in the 1980s at a time when part-time workers' employment rights were being confirmed and in some cases extended in those countries (Deakin, 1990). On the other hand, there are indications that high levels of taxation on part-time workers in Britain have encouraged a reduction in pay and hours below the thresholds set by legislation (Deakin and Wilkinson, 1991b), which suggests that the increase in part-time jobs

Table 8.9. Employment growth in selected OECD countries 1980–1992.[a]

Country	1980–1988	1989	1990	1991[b]	1992[b]
United Kingdom	0.4	3.1	1.5	−3.4	−1.6
France	−0.1	1.2	1.1	0.1	0.2
Germany	0.3	1.3	2.5	1.7	1.4
Italy	0.3	0.1	1.4	0.1	0.4
Japan	1.0	1.9	2.0	1.5	1.3
United States	1.8	2.0	0.5	−0.5	1.8
OECD Europe	0.5	1.6	1.6	−0.1	0.4
EEC	0.3	1.7	1.7	−0.1	0.3
Total OECD	1.1	1.8	1.3	0.0	0.3

[a]Source: *OECD Employment Outlook* (1991), Table 1.2. Figures are annual percentage rates of growth over previous period (1980–1988 averaged).
[b]Projected figures.

in the 1980s was accompanied by a deterioration in the terms and conditions on offer.

Training policy received a far higher profile in the 1980s but at the same time was subordinated to the wider aims of deregulation policies. The role of trade unions in the training infrastructure was marginalised with the abolition of the statutory Industry Training Boards, the winding up of the Manpower Services Commission and the devolution of resources to the voluntary TECs which are run almost exclusively by employers. Training subsidies, including the Youth Training Scheme allowance and payments under various short-lived youth employment schemes, were designed to set a low ceiling of 'more realistic levels of pay' to the wages and income of young workers. To similar effect was the removal of access to income support for the under-18s after 1988, in return for a guaranteed place on a training scheme. These policies, and the more general strategy of promoting low pay, can be seen as directly contradicting the government's efforts in other respects to raise awareness of the importance of training and to improve training quality.

The Growing Divide: Labour Market Policy and International Competitiveness

Evidence for the claimed link between labour law reforms and industrial relations performance remains elusive. Taking general indicators, the performance of the British labour market in the 1980s did not differ all that much from that of other OECD countries which avoided the widespread destruction of employment rights which the Thatcher governments undertook. Union membership rates and the incidence of strikes fell in nearly all countries outside Scandinavia, under the influence of high unemployment and recession. For a while in the mid-1980s Britain sustained a faster rate of employment growth and steeper decline in unemployment than most of its principal competitors; these trends were sharply reversed with the return of recession in 1990. The claims of an improvement in the industrial relations 'climate' sit uneasily alongside growing evidence of the harmful impact upon productivity and efficiency of policies of deregulation and labour intensification. From this point of view, the labour market policy of the Thatcher governments contributed to a dangerous loss of competitiveness at a time of growing internationalisation of product markets.

The argument that a high level of employment regulation in the past has been harmful to the competitiveness of the British economy has little or no empirical foundation. On the contrary: the long-term absence of effective labour market standards can be seen as a further aspect of the British economy's overdependence on cheap labour, which in turn is both cause and effect of its low levels of productivity and investment. The achievement of the Thatcher governments is to have institutionalised this dependence on low pay and labour exploitation across whole sectors of the economy.

British labour law regulation was historically weak by international standards and is now even weaker, to the extent that most of the basic employment rights which are guaranteed by law in other industrialised countries and incorporated into various international labour law treaties and conventions simply do not exist in Britain. This applies both to individual employment rights, such as rights to minimum terms and conditions in pay and hours and to protection from unjust dismissal, to collective or representational rights in the workplace, which in most EC countries take the form of a combination of enterprise committees and representative trade unions (Deakin, 1990). Similarly, in the area of social security, levels of unemployment compensation and income replacement benefits are not high by international standards.

Comparative evidence also points to the degree to which other systems have sought to develop labour market flexibility without resorting to the complete removal of labour standards (Deakin, 1991). In France, Germany and Italy limited derogations from employment protection legislation, which were necessary in order to promote the growth of part-time work and more flexible working-time arrangements, have been coupled with certain guarantees for part-time workers and a continuing role for collective bargaining in regulating the derogation process. In many cases legislation has been passed with the aim of extending the role of collective bargaining and employee representation in the workplace, as a means of enhancing flexibility in the application of labour law standards. While these measures have achieved only a limited degree of reintegration of the unemployed back into the labour market, they indicate the existence of a clear alternative strategy to out-and-out deregulation and individualisation of terms and conditions. Where they have been more successful is in promoting flexible forms of working time at the enterprise level. It could be argued from the experience of France and Belgium that the retention of collective representation and basic job guarantees is a prerequisite to the successful introduction of more advanced forms of flexibility involving annualisation of hours and multiskilling. In Britain, longer hours and overtime continue to be used in preference to the radical restructuring of the working week, although in enterprises where unions are strong enough to bargain for reduced working hours, as in the recent engineering dispute, this may be changing.

The British government's opposition to the harmonisation of social and employment rights within the European Community is based on its claim to have a superior record of tackling unemployment through deregulation. This claim is dubious at best. The inability of the Major government to accept the principle of qualified majority voting in social and employment matters and accede to the provisions of the EC Social Charter indicates how far out of line with international practice Britain has fallen.

Comment

Collective Rights

William Brown

The use of the law to reform the labour market was a central part of the economic programme of Mrs Thatcher's governments; it is certainly a key component in appraising the economic legacy of the 1980s. The experience of legislators in the British labour market has never been happy. Their laws have been dogged by perverse and unintended side-effects, and never more so than in the 1980s. A major reason has been that lawyers, whose main work has always been with the individualistic concerns of people and property, have found it difficult to understand collective interests and actions. They have long been baffled by the very private agglomerations of agreements that become established through collective bargaining, opaque to and largely impenetrable by the law. So far as individual labour law is concerned, a fundamental weakness was the dominant part played by the common law of the contract of employment. This has assisted deregulating legislation to undermine minimum standards of job and income security. For collective labour law, because the system of 'legal voluntarism' imposes no duty to bargain, union power rests upon the effectiveness of strike action. Unions were largely complacent about this in the post-War years; they were to discover that it made them highly vulnerable in the 1980s. However, because the sources of trade union power did not depend on a formal statutory underpinning of rights, the deregulation that was effective in eroding individual labour law protection would not work for collective labour law. Consequently, the government's collective labour law programme took the form of expanding rather than diminishing the role of law. The circumstances in which unions could take strike action without being in danger of suffering fines was steadily narrowed, and a variety of constraints were placed upon the internal government of trade unions, most notably obligations to ballot members.

As a dedicated Fabian I cannot help but admire the gradualist approach adopted by the 1979–1992 governments in these matters. What is hard to admire is that it was a gradualist approach not to greater equality but greater inequality. The approach was pragmatic: Mrs Thatcher once said that her government would pass an industrial relations law every 2 years 'until we get it right', and this they have done, with another promised for 1992. Their laws developed from events as they unfolded. They learnt from the Stockport Messenger dispute that it was possible (contrary to the folklore of the Pentonville Five) to paralyse a union without creating martyrs. They learnt from the miners' strike that those most zealous in using the law against unions were not the employers but the unions' own disaffected activists. Nor was the government too proud to repeal its own legislation, as it did with its procedures to create legal closed shops, solving the problem of the legislation's neglect by making all action to maintain a closed shop unlawful. The closed shop is a routine and uncontroversial issue of procedural tidiness for most employers. The government's constant tinkering with the legal status of the closed shop, in no less than four different acts in 10 years, shows clearly how keenly aware it was of the symbolic importance of labour legislation. Laws against witchcraft were long ago seen to be effective devices both for sustaining public belief in witches and for demonstrating governmental righteousness.

All this legislation adds up to the most intensive programme of labour law seen in recent years by any industrialised country (with the recent exception of New Zealand). Simon Deakin's chapter discusses the impact of it all upon collective bargaining; in so doing it is able to draw upon excellent research data, with a wealth of survey and case study material underpinning the sources used. The decline in strikes over the 1980s is explicable in many ways in addition to the legislation. The new laws weakened certain traditional forms of strike action, such as secondary, unofficial and 'wildcat' strikes and certain forms of picketing. However, paradoxically, other forms of action have been strengthened because of the increased use of strike ballots. The great majority of ballots go in favour of strikes and in almost all cases management then concedes without the strike taking place. Simon Deakin's chapter is rightly critical of some of the econometric studies that have ascribed to the new laws the reduction in union membership; structural change in the economy and unemployment have played a far more important part. It is, however, undeniable that the character of collective bargaining has changed substantially since 1979. The trade union movement has survived the legal onslaught surprisingly well but it has been sorely weakened by the decentralisation and fragmentation of bargaining that employers have themselves brought about, quite independently of any government action.

Perhaps there is always a tendency for analysts to overemphasise the impact of legal change in industrial relations matters. New laws seem so substantial and are accompanied by such an uproar but in practice it is employers who dictate the main agenda and pace of change. Especially in Britain, where the legal underpinning of the employment relationship is so weak, employers are sovereign. Because of this there is a great diversity and perversity of response to legal change. In this context perhaps more can be made of the role of government not as legislator but as actor and employer in its own right. However slight or perverse individual laws may have been, the industrial conflicts that the government initiated or supported during the 1980s had a profound demonstrative impact on the conduct of collective bargaining. In the first half of the decade the major struggles with unions were in the public sector—in the railways, water, coal, health, steel and education. Later the government encouraged private sector employers who did likewise—in newspapers, shipping, the docks and commercial television. Again, what powerful symbolism there is in government action in setting standards for the behaviour of employers.

Whether or not one is persuaded that the changed character of collective bargaining improved Britain's competitiveness depends upon how dynamic a view one takes of economic processes. The government's static analysis would see a weakened workforce as an inevitable facilitator of a more efficient labour market. The contrary dynamic argument would be that a higher level of minimum rights for employees and a more demanding trade union movement have the effect of forcing employers to manage their labour better and to invest more in both physical and human capital.

Mrs Thatcher's labour laws are mostly here to stay. For all the howls and forecasts of disaster that have accompanied the remorseless biennial advance of her legislation, we have to confront the notable fact that currently no likely replacement government is saying that it would find much to repeal. Is this just a reflection that the laws' impact (as opposed to the impact of her government's nonlegislative anti-union actions) has been slight? Or is it an indication of a deeper argument that she is in danger of winning by default? This deeper argument concerns the potentially fruitful role of the law in upholding collective rights and standards. Has not the neglect of collectivism gone too far? Labour law is far too important to be left to lawyers with their congenital failure to appreciate the importance of collective rights in a modern economy. Collective action by employers is needed to overcome the public goods problem that underlies Britain's training famine. Collective action by bargainers is needed to bring pay settlements into line with international competitive reality. New laws are needed to help both unions and employers to build productive labour market institutions. Perhaps the worst legacy of the Thatcher years has been that we seem to have forgotten that labour is most productive under institutions of community rather than of competition.

9

Inflation Policy and the Restructuring of Labour Markets

Jonathan Michie and Frank Wilkinson

> *Mr James Callaghan, Leader of the Opposition*— . . . will she tell us clearly whether increases in wages are a cause of inflation or not?
>
> *Mrs Thatcher*—Over a period the cause of increased inflation is increases in the money supply. Within money supply, there will be a different distribution both between the public sector and the private sector and within those sectors there will be increases in pay within the general money supply well beyond what are warranted, and they may come through in increases in particular products which will not necessarily affect the general price level.
>
> *Mr James Callaghan*—May I thank her for that reply and say that I did not understand a word of it.
>
> (Hansard, 3 July 1980)

The Thatcher Government of 1979 was elected on the promise of squeezing inflation out of the system. The policy instrument for doing this was to be control of the money supply. The record at first was at least consistent with the belief that the long-term goal of zero inflation could be achieved (Figure 9.1). But from mid-1983 the record deteriorated and, despite a dip in 1986, prices were on an upward trend until the end of 1990. Thatcher's premiership ended with inflation at around the same level as she inherited in 1979: the annual increase in the Retail Price Index stood at 10.3% when the first Thatcher government took office in May 1979, while when Mrs Thatcher left office in November 1990 it was 9.7%.

This chapter evaluates the government's anti-inflation policies since 1979. The first section reviews the theory and concludes that the belief that targeting money would eliminate inflation gave way to old-style policies of high interest rates and deflation combined with labour market policies to restrain wages. The availability of resources for increased real incomes is then analysed, with increased price mark-ups evident over much of the period but often marked-up on declining costs,

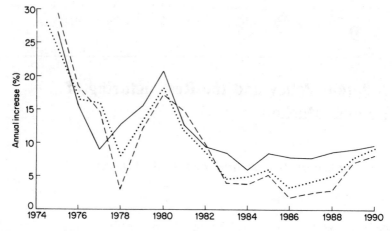

Figure 9.1. Annual increases in earnings (—), prices (····) and in prices and taxes (---) 1975–1990.

disguising inflationary effects. The impact of labour market policy on wage determination is then analysed. The implications of all this for the inflation record in the 1980s, and for the legacy left by the three Thatcher governments, are then considered.

Inflation: Theory and Practice

Monetary targets had been used prior to 1979; indeed, they were included in the IMF's 1976 loan conditions. However, prior to 1979, in neither theoretical nor policy areas was the monetarist explanation generally accepted as being adequate on its own, and the Callaghan government continued to rely on incomes policies as the main anti-inflationary device. Full acceptance by the government of monetarist theory and policy prescriptions came only in 1979, although even then these were pursued by means of controlling the public sector borrowing requirement; Friedman himself disowned the use of fiscal policy as the leading method of controlling the money supply and argued (before the House of Commons Treasury and Civil Services Committee) that the market should be left to determine the interest rate.

Policy developments under the Thatcher governments began with strict monetary targets that required public expenditure cuts. Within a year of Thatcher taking office exchange controls had been abolished, direct controls on the growth of bank deposits ('the corset') scrapped, reserve asset ratios abolished and the minimum lending rate consigned to virtual oblivion. Ironically, the original aim of the Thatcher governments to impose monetary control proved to be incompatible with the financial liberalisation which freed the banking system's money-creating potential.

Monetary control also proved difficult as inflation accelerated, generated by the second oil shock and fed by the switch from direct to indirect taxation. The tight credit policy exacerbated the cash-flow problem of firms as costs rose sharply. The consequences were two-fold: a rapid increase in bankruptcies and plant closures as firms cut back their operations, and a sharp increase in lending as banks supported their clients (and their own previous loans to their clients) so that the money supply increased by much more than the policy targets. Nevertheless there was a tight monetary squeeze in both 1979 and 1980. Interest rates rose sharply and this, combined with the beneficial balance of payment effects of North Sea oil and the popularity of the Thatcher policies with the international financial community, caused the sterling exchange rate to rise 19% above its 1978 level by 1980.

High interest rates, the growing competition from imports and reduced profitability of exports as the sterling exchange rate rose, reinforced the effect of the tight monetary squeeze on the level of activity and the overall level of employment fell by almost 8% between 1979 and 1982. Unemployment, which was 1.3 million in 1979, reached almost 3 million in 1982 and crossed that threshold in 1983. In face of the deepening recession, monetary constraints were relaxed. The money supply increased by around 19% in 1981 and 1982 (respectively 7% and 10.5% in real terms), interest rates fell in nominal terms but rose in real terms and the rise in the exchange rate was first checked and then reversed. The pace of inflation accelerated rapidly in 1979 and 1980 but then declined sharply with the downward pressure on domestic prices exercised by the high exchange rates and with the fall in commodity prices as the world recession intensified. Wage increases also moderated under the influence of sharply rising unemployment, direct government pressure in the public sector and the deceleration of the increase in retail prices, and this further contributed to a slowing of inflation.

However, bank lending to the private sector increased by 50% between 1981 and 1984 and by almost 200% from 1984–1988. In addition, the various forms of credit used to finance consumer expenditure increased two and a half times between 1981 and 1988. Consumer expenditure increased by almost 32% in real terms between 1981 and 1988, fuelled by a 21% increase in real disposable income and a fall in the personal savings ratio from 12.8% to 4.4%. The rapid growth in demand for consumer goods and the slow growth in domestic production combined to weaken the balance of payments. The current balance, which benefited from the import-saving and export-creating effects of North Sea oil and gas, and which had registered a surplus of more than £6 billion in 1981, was in deficit by £14.6 billion in 1988 and £20 billion in 1989, before the growing recession eased the pressure.

198 Jonathan Michie and Frank Wilkinson

The recovery from 1981 was based, then, on an increase in credit as monetary control was relaxed and a rise in disposable income as the pace of inflation slowed relative to the growth in money income. The depletion of the manufacturing base meant that the economy was increasingly supply-constrained and consequently unable to respond to the increase in home demand for consumer goods and for exports as, with rapidly growing productivity and the depreciation of sterling, the competitiveness of British manufactured goods improved. This supply shortage was not confined to finished consumer goods; the production infrastructure of intermediary and capital goods had been particularly eroded so that the increase in output and investment as manufacturing industry responded to the new market opportunities itself sucked in imports. The foreign exchange surplus that resulted from North Sea oil and gas shielded the economy from the balance of payments consequences of these developments until 1986 when declining oil prices and a fall in British oil production began to add to the growing balance of payments problem.

The policy response to the resulting crisis was to raise interest rates. The clearing banks' short-term rate, which had reached a low of 7.5% in May 1988, rose to 14% by the end of 1989. The declared purpose of the interest-rate policy was to cut private consumption and to support sterling. Nevertheless, consumer spending was 5% higher in the first half of 1989 than a year earlier, bank lending to the private sector rose by 30% and the depreciation of sterling added to the inflationary spiral. Despite its immediate demand-side failure, the tightening monetary squeeze had its supply-side success. The rate of increase in manufacturing output and productivity, which had been more than 6% in the first quarter of 1989, fell to around 3% in the third quarter and by the end of the year was stagnating. From the spring of 1991 the progressive policy squeeze impacted sharply on consumer demand and investment so that even the government was obliged to recognise the deepening recession and responded by continuing to lower interest rates.

Despite these reductions in interest rates, which had begun in 1990, July 1991 saw the weakest credit growth for 20 years with both sides of the banking system's balance sheet contracting, indicating a collapse in the demand for credit as well as in its supply. M4 declined by 0.4% in June 1991, the first fall since the series began in 1982, giving a year-on-year growth of 7.9%, the lowest since 1970; bank lending declined in June 1991 by £47 million.

Critics of monetarism

The failure to achieve the money supply targets from 1979 laid the basis for increasing criticism from nonmonetarists. In 1981 Desai published his *Testing Monetarism* in which he examined the major predictions of monetarism and found them to be invalid. Kaldor had continuously insisted that the money supply in modern economies is not under the control of central banks, but is determined by borrower demand for bank credit. Thus the money supply is credit-driven and the demand for bank credit is closely related to changes in business demand for working capital. Bank financing of *ex ante* net deficit spending in the economy permits aggregate demand to grow. This view became increasingly acceptable publicly. Dow and Saville, leading advisors to the Bank of England, argued in 1988 that money creation is an endogenous process determined partly by the price level, and not the other way round, and Goodhart (1989) pointed out that this direction of causation was more generally recognised than some opponents of monetarism supposed.

In 1983 the Bank of England published fierce academic criticisms of Friedman and Schwartz's historical analysis of the role of money (and by clear implication, criticism of the wilder claims which had previously been made for monetarism as an anti-inflationary policy). In his contribution, Professor Brown concluded thus:

> Do Friedman and Schwartz make their case that UK experience supports a simple quantity theory, with money supply controlling prices and output controlled by other factors entirely? In a word, no. First, strict truth of a simple quantity theory implies that velocity of circulation is constant (or changes only very slowly)—that nominal income varies in proportion to money stock, which we have seen . . . to be only loosely true over long periods, and over some very considerable periods not true at all. Second, price-changes have been as much imposed on the UK from outside, or by labour-market behaviour only very loosely connected with monetary conditions, as they have been caused by monetary changes within the country. Such correspondence as exists between money stock and money income is due perhaps as much to money supply responding to demands created by e.g. rises in import and/or export prices, as to UK prices rising after a creation of domestic credit. It *is* true . . . that output-growth shows no general, simple, connection with money-growth; it is affected by many factors, of which monetary *conditions* (a rather more complex matter than money-growth) provide only one. (Brown, 1983, p. 43.)

Hendry and Ericsson also refuted the historical relationship between money and prices claimed by Friedman, and in a revised version of their Bank of England paper stated that their findings were consistent with those reported by Desai (1981, especially Chapter 4), and that:

> The failure by Friedman and Schwartz to present statistical evidence pertinent to their main claims about the United Kingdom leaves those claims lacking in credibility. (Hendry and Ericsson, 1991, pp. 32–33.)

Responding for the first time to these criticisms, Friedman and Schwartz merely complained that Hendry and Ericsson:

> . . . use one equation from our book as a peg on which to hang an exposition of sophisticated econometric techniques. Insofar as their

empirical findings do bear on ours, they simply confirm some of our
principal results and contradict none. (Friedman and Schwartz, 1991,
p. 39.)

This defense was denied by the London Business School:

A number of recent articles have attempted to restore the use of a simple
measure of the money supply as an indicator of future price levels and
to re-establish a causal link from money to prices . . . we find . . . the
causality runs from prices to money—this result conforms well to the
work of Hendry and Ericsson . . . or Hall, Henry and Wilcox (1990)
. . . (Allen and Hall, 1991, p. 45.)

The policy fate of the theory that control of the money supply will
reduce the rate of inflation was sealed when John Major, then
Chancellor, told the Treasury Committee in 1989 that:

That used to be the theory . . . the Government may have followed
some time ago. It certainly has not been the theory that the Government
have followed during any period I have been in the Treasury. (Cited in
Johnson, 1991, p. 66.)

Nonmonetarist alternatives

The Phillip's curve apparently lost its explanatory value as from the
middle of the 1960s unemployment and inflation appeared to be directly
rather than inversely related. To explain this, monetarists broke
the link between labour market conditions and nominal wages by
hypothesising that money wage increases are determined by the rate of
increase of the money supply. Real wages, they argued, are determined
by supply and demand in the labour market so that unemployment is
essentially voluntary. Neo-Keynesian analysis incorporated elements of
monetarism, most notably the transformation of the Walrasian market-
clearing concept of a 'natural rate of unemployment' into the neo-
Keynesian idea of there being a 'non-accelerating inflation rate of
unemployment' which need not imply market clearing. The essence of
the neo-Keynesian analysis is that whilst involuntary unemployment is
a possibility, reducing it by increasing monetary demand depends on
money wage pressure; the faster the increase in wages, the higher will
be the level of unemployment associated with any increase in nominal
income. This focused attention on the relationship between unemployment and money wage increases, a tendency reinforced by the apparent
re-emergence of the Phillip's curve from the late 1970s.

One issue of major policy significance that arises from the nonmonetar-
ist debate on inflation is the theoretical perception of the process of
wage determination. Keynesians have traditionally held to the view that
the wage structure is institutionally determined and rigid so that a wage

increase in any one sector is rapidly transmitted into the general level of wage inflation by the restoration of customary differentials. Neo-Keynesians identify monopoly power of trade unions as the determining factor that drives wages faster than increases in productivity and hence generates inflation. From this perspective, an increase in the monopoly power of trade unions in the 1970s explains 'stagflation'—the coincidence of high unemployment and high inflation. Both Keynesian and neo-Keynesian approaches direct policy towards intervention in the wage-determining process by such measures as incomes policy or the weakening of trade unions.

In their analysis of the inflationary process the Cambridge Economic Policy Group focused attention on the interaction of price and wage setting. Firms mark-up on costs to restore profitability whilst workers target real wage levels which they attempt to establish and maintain in the face of erosion of living standards by inflation. Periods of accelerating inflation, both contemporary and historical, are identified as times when real disposable income from employment is eroded, whilst inflation tends to subside when real wages are rising; processes which are largely independent of the level of employment (Tarling and Wilkinson, 1977, 1982; Wilkinson, 1988). This idea, that inflation is related to 'real wage resistance', stood up well to econometric testing by Henry and Ormerod (1978). Rowthorn provided a synthesis of real wage targeting, a Phillip's curve relationship between unemployment and nominal wages and an active role for money, and located it within a 'conflict' model of inflation which had distinct Marxist overtones. He argued that both capital, in marking-up costs to form prices, and labour, in formulating wage claims, aspired to particular shares of the national income. When the shares demanded by labour and capital are greater than the income available for distribution, after allowing for the 'burdens' of taxation and the terms of trade, a price spiral results. The aspiration gap could be closed and inflationary pressures controlled, Rowthorn argued, by monetary means. A reduction in the money supply would increase unemployment and activate the reserve army of labour mechanism to reduce wage pressure, whilst intensified competition in the product market would squeeze profit margins. Thus, the weakening of workers in the labour market and of capital in the product market serves to bring aspirations more into line with income availability and reduces pressure on prices.

Outside monetarist circles then, with notable exceptions, students of inflation have retained an attachment to conditions in the labour market as an important determinant of inflation. Numerous explanations have been offered as to why this relationship should have changed and therefore be difficult simply to read off from the historical record. These include changes in the degree of trade union monopoly power, hysteresis modifications to the Phillip's curve, the changing relations between out-of-work benefits and earnings, the effect of long periods of joblessness on the ability of the unemployed to compete in the labour market, and the effects of technical and other changes on the relative power of insiders relative to outsiders.

What has to be explained for the recent past is indicated in Figure 9.1, where the solid, dotted and dashed lines trace the year-on-year percentage changes of, respectively, the indices of average earnings, retail prices and taxes and prices. The distance between the solid and dotted lines measures the annual increase in earnings after adjusting for consumer prices; the distance between the dotted and dashed lines measures the additional effect of changes in direct taxes. The total difference between the dashed and solid lines gives the percentage change in real disposable income from employment which is falling when the dashed line is above the solid line and increasing when it is below. Between 1974 and 1977 both prices and taxes grew faster than pay so that real disposable earnings fell sharply, and in 1981 and 1982 increased taxation more than cancelled out any increase in real pre-tax income. Otherwise the general tendency has been for earnings to increase more rapidly than retail prices and for the consequent increase in real wages to be further supplemented by reductions in direct taxes. The overall effect of the changes in earnings, prices and taxes was to reduce real disposable income by almost 10% between 1974 and 1977, increase it to 5.5% higher than its 1974 level by 1980 before lowering it by 2% from 1980 to 1982. The period after 1982 witnessed a sustained rise in average real disposable income from employment. The average annual rate was 3.6% and reached a peak of around 6% in 1986, with a sharp decline to less than 2% after 1987. By 1990 average real disposable income from employment was 33% higher than its 1982 level and 38.5% higher than in 1978, the last full year of the Labour government.

How these changes in the different earnings measures relate to unemployment is analysed in Figures 9.2–9.4 which relate unemployment to rates of change in nominal earnings, real earnings and net real earnings. Figure 9.2 gives the classic Phillip's curve relationship where the rate of money wage increases is inversely related to unemployment. However, this relationship underwent distinct changes. From 1974–1977 a 17.5 percentage point decline in the pace of wage inflation was associated with a 1.3 percentage point increase in the level of unemployment, whilst from 1980–1984 these changes were 12.3 and 5.6 percentage points respectively. From 1986 the rate of inflation began to decline and fell by 5.3 percentage points whilst the annual increase in earnings increased by 1.8 percentage points. Over the whole period, therefore, the relationship between unemployment and the increase in nominal income weakened so that from 1986 onward they appeared to be largely unrelated: the Phillip's curve had become horizontal.

Figure 9.3, which relates increases in real wages and levels of unemployment, is remarkable in that every possible type of relationship

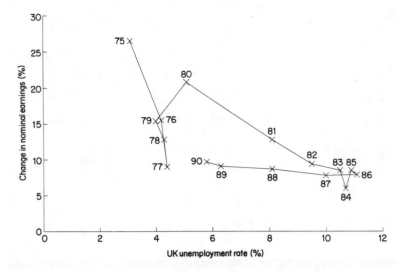

Figure 9.2. UK unemployment and percentage change in nominal earnings 1975–1990.

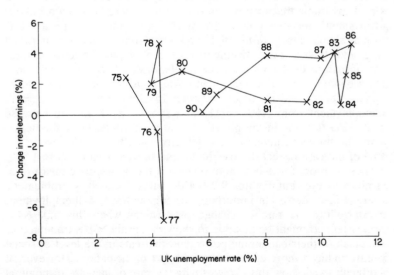

Figure 9.3. UK unemployment and percentage change in real earnings 1975–1990.

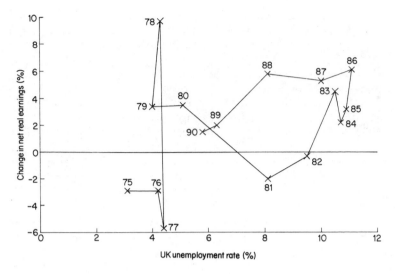

Figure 9.4. UK unemployment and percentage change in net real earnings 1975–1990.

is revealed. During 1976–1979 the 'real Phillip's curve' was vertical (it is perhaps ironic that this monetarist norm was produced by a Labour government's incomes policy). From 1980–1982 the curve resumed its normal shape, albeit rather flat, and after some indecision between 1982 and 1986 became distinctly backward-sloping. The backward-sloping nature of the Phillip's curve relationship becomes much more distinct in Figure 9.4 where unemployment is related to the rate of increase in net real earnings. Between 1981 and 1986 an increase in unemployment from 8.1% to 11.1% was associated with an increase from −2% to 6.1% in the growth of real net income. Over the next 4 years the level of unemployment fell from 11.1% to 5.8%, while the pace of increase in real disposable income slowed from 6.1% to 1.5%.

There is room for debate about which is the appropriate measure of earnings to use, but Figures 9.2–9.4 do suggest that it is problematic to argue in favour of an important role for the level of unemployment in controlling the rate of change of earnings when this link is so inconsistent. It might be possible to show that in the 1980s trade unions lost much of their bargaining power and that cuts in the level of social welfare induced more active labour market participation. However, it is difficult to see how this explains why the rate of increase of nominal earnings did not fall further under the growing weight of joblessness and poverty and why real earnings and especially net real earnings increased at such a historically high rate. One possible response to this is that at least a part of the reserve army of labour was demobilised from active to latent as unemployed workers lost their skills and work attitudes, and that for this and other reasons the 'insiders' retained their bargaining power. However, this hardly explains why the rate of increase in real earnings tended to rise whilst unemployment was rising and to fall whilst it was falling. There can be no objections to introducing new variables into models to help explain shifts in economic relations but it must cast doubt on the underlying theory if the package of supporting hypotheses has to be changed frequently.

Figures 9.1–9.4 do, however, lend support to the real-wage resistance hypothesis; as real disposable income began to rise continuously, the upward pressure on the rate of increase in wages subsided. What needs, then, to be asked is why real wages grew so fast in a period of high unemployment, when the Government had initiated a rolling programme of labour legislation designed to shift the balance of power in favour of capital and when membership of trade unions and the level of industrial militancy were both declining rapidly. In addressing this question it is necessary to consider, firstly, the availability of resources for increases in real income and, secondly, the impact of labour market policy on wage determination.

Income, distribution and real wage growth

Real wages can rise if the wage share in GDP increases, if productivity rises or if imports rise relative to exports. After-tax real income can also increase if taxation falls or if the burden of taxation is shifted from employment income. As a share in GDP, income from employment peaked at 69% in 1980; it was 67% in 1978. It then declined sharply to 64% in 1985 and remained around this level until 1988 before rising to 67% in 1990. Real GDP grew at 2.1% per year over the period 1978–1990 but population also increased so that *per capita* income grew at 1.9%. This increase was supplemented by the foreign sector. From 1978–1990 domestic expenditure increased at an annual average of 2.6% in real terms, 0.5% per year more than GDP, a difference accounted for by the growth in imports relative to exports. Part of this can be explained by favourable movements in the terms of trade. These can be measured by the unit value of exports expressed as a percentage of the unit value of imports, which was 83 (1985 = 100) in 1974, improved from 95 in 1978 to 103 in 1981, and worsened to 96 in 1986 before improving to 100 in 1990. The increase in the price of exports relative to imports, so that each unit of exports could 'buy' more imports, meant that the volume of imports could increase without worsening the current balance of payments. However, the current balance did worsen, from a positive 0.6% of GDP in 1978 to a negative 2.4% of GDP in 1990— an improvement on the 3.9% of the year before! This deterioration in the trade balance added to the resources available for distribution internally, but the consequent downward pressure on the exchange rate could be resisted only by generating inward capital flows by raising the interest rate.

The relative decline in import prices had two opposing effects on domestic industry. It had serious adverse consequences for those firms and industries which were directly competitive with imports but benefited those for which imported goods were inputs. This latter effect is explored in Table 9.1 which traces the changing prices of home sales of manufactured goods relative to, first, the prices of fuel and material inputs into manufacturing, and second, relative to the unit values of imports of semi-finished manufactures, of intermediate goods and of capital goods. Relative to manufacturing prices, fuel and material prices were stable in the early 1980s but declined sharply with the fall in oil prices in the late 1980s. Import prices declined sharply relative to home manufacturing prices to 1982, recovered somewhat as the pound depreciated to 1985, but moved downward again from that year onward. Over the period as a whole, relative to the price of manufactured goods, the price of fuel and material inputs and the price of imported intermediate goods fell more than 20% whilst for capital goods the decline was almost 30%. The decline in the relative prices of semi-finished manufactured goods was less dramatic but nevertheless they fell by 13%. The effect of the relative decline in import prices was dramatically to increase import penetration of the home market:

Table 9.1. Manufacturing, materials and fuels, and import prices 1978–1990.[a]

	Price of manufactured products (home sales)	Ratio to price of manufactured products of:			
		Prices of materials and fuels	Import unit values of:		
			Semi-finished manufactured goods	Intermediate goods	Capital goods
1978	100	100	100	100	100
1979	111	102	96	86	92
1980	126	97	90	78	85
1981	139	96	86	76	83
1982	149	96	87	76	83
1983	157	97	89	83	84
1984	166	100	92	85	83
1985	175	96	92	86	82
1986	183	85	90	83	81
1987	190	84	89	82	81
1988	198	83	86	79	74
1989	208	84	87	79	73
1990	221	79	85	79	71

[a]Source: *Monthly Digest of Statistics*.

between 1978 and 1989 imports rose from 26% to 36% of home demand (1989 is the last date for which these estimates are available because of the government's decision to stop collecting the necessary data). The increase in imports was particularly rapid for intermediate and capital goods, the volume of which was 3.5 times higher in 1990 than in 1978 compared with a 2.7 times increase in the volume of all imports.

The fact that import prices fell relative to manufacturing prices shows that the resulting cost advantages were not fully passed on. One of the notable features of the 1980s was the extent to which British industry took advantage of the slow growth of unit costs to raise margins rather than lower prices. When analysing this trend the Bank of England noted that 13 percentage points of the 36% increase in prices between 1982 and 1988 was explained by a growth in profit margins (Bank of England *Quarterly Bulletin*, May 1989, p. 229). The ability to widen margins also resulted from the slow growth of unit labour costs due to the rapid increase in labour productivity. Movements in labour costs are shown in Figure 9.5 in which the solid, dashed and dotted lines represent labour productivity (output per hour), product wages (weekly earnings deflated by manufacturing prices) and real unit wage costs (product wages per unit of output), respectively (annual percentage changes). The rate of increase in product wages was remarkably constant over 1978–1990, averaging 3.75% per year, whilst the rate of increase in productivity fluctuated cyclically but was higher in the early 1980s than in the later part of the decade. The combined effect of the changes in product wages and labour productivity was that unit labour costs fell in all years between 1981 and 1989 (except 1985) but rose in 1990. However, the trend in unit wage costs is clearly upwards.

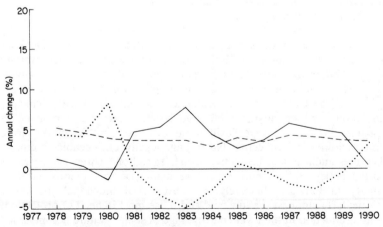

Figure 9.5. Percentage changes in UK manufacturing productivity, (—), product wages (---) and real unit wage costs (····) 1977–1990.

The ability of industry to 'capture' the benefits of favourable trends in the costs of nonlabour inputs and improvements in productivity by widening profit margins meant that it was possible for real earnings *and* profits to increase. Property and employment incomes also stood to benefit from the changing structure of taxation. Taxes as a proportion of national income increased from around 34% in 1978–1979 to almost 40% in 1981–1982 before declining to around 38% in 1990–1991. However, this apparent increase masks a switch in tax away from earned income towards expenditure. Between 1978 and 1990 the proportion of personal income and expenditure taxes accounted for by taxes on income fell from 59% to 47%. The net benefit of this change in the structure of tax is measured by the higher increases in the Retail Price Index (which includes the effect of increasing expenditure taxes) than in the Tax and Price Index (which includes the effect of both income and expenditure taxes) throughout the 1980s, as shown in Figure 9.1.

Increased productivity, improved terms of trade and the worsening trade balance provided the resource base for increases in real incomes. The ability of domestic industry to widen margins, despite the historically high increase in real product wages, allowed the share of profits to rise as a proportion of income, although this tendency was reversed as the economy moved into crisis in the late 1980s. The ability of industry to expropriate a more than proportionate share of the increase in resources was at the expense of both international competitiveness and domestic consumers, although the latter were shielded to the extent that they shared in increases in employment or property incomes. The shift in the burden of taxes from direct to indirect also worked to the advantage of property and employment incomes. The next section explores the impact of labour market policy on the distribution of the wage share.

Liberalisation of the labour market and the changing structure of earnings

Labour market policies are discussed in detail in Simon Deakin's chapter in this volume and Bob Rowthorn analyses the social welfare consequences of policy. This section explores the outcome of labour market deregulation and assesses the implications for the inflationary process. The Conservative governments brought about major changes in labour and employment law and social security in the name of encouraging greater wage flexibility and of liberating the market from the 'rigidities' of collective bargaining, legally enforceable minimum labour standards and protective social legislation. Three main strands in this policy can be identified: the weakening of trade unions and their ability to bargain effectively, the erosion of individual job rights particularly amongst the low-paid and those most in need of protection, and a reduction in the level and coverage of social welfare accompanied by a tightening up of the rules of eligibility and what officially constitutes 'genuinely seeking work', designed to coerce the unemployed into low-paid jobs.

The most notable success of these policies was their discriminatory effects. The position of those out of work was progressively worsened relative to those in employment, whilst pay and conditions of employment in the most disadvantaged labour market segments were subjected to the greatest relative degradation and increasingly detached from legal and social protection, with consequent exposure to greater degrees of exploitation. This latter tendency was compounded by trade union legislation which had its most marked detrimental effects where organisation was weakest by increasing the obstacles to establishing and maintaining effective collective bargaining and by encouraging employers to take legal action. The clearest indicator of the impact of labour market policy was the widening of wage differentials. This tendency is summarised in Table 9.2 which gives the annual increase at different points in the earnings distribution for men and women, manual and nonmanual workers. The general tendency has been for the earnings of nonmanual workers to grow more rapidly than those of manual workers, for the rate of increase to be slower lower down in the earnings distribution and for the earnings of part-time workers to grow less rapidly than the earnings of full-time workers. The rate of increase for the highest-earning decile of nonmanual workers was around 3% per year higher than for the lowest-earning decile of manual workers.

This change in the structure of earnings can be explained by three main factors. First, the jobs lost in manufacturing and in other nonservice sectors were concentrated mainly in the middle range of the overall earnings distribution. Second, the increase in employment was concentrated in sectors such as banking, insurance, finance and business

Table 9.2. Annual rates of growth of earnings at different points in the earnings distribution for manual and nonmanual workers 1979–1989.[a]

	Manual			Nonmanual		
	Men	Women		Men	Women	
		Full-time	Part-time		Full-time	Part-time
Highest decile	10.0	10.2	9.2	11.8	11.5	12.4
Upper quartile	9.7	9.6	9.0	11.2	11.8	10.9
Median	9.3	9.2	8.7	10.9	11.1	10.0
Lower quartile	9.0	9.0	8.4	10.5	10.5	9.5
Lowest decile	8.5	8.8	8.3	9.9	10.1	9.1

[a]Source: *New Earnings Survey* (1979, 1989).

services, where earnings are relatively high, and in hotel, catering and other such services, where earnings tend to be low. Third, earnings at the upper end of the distribution have grown relatively to those at the lower end since 1979. This is demonstrated in Table 9.3 which gives the rate of earnings increase for selected sectors for 1980–1990 (data for 1979 are not available on a comparable basis) and shows the extent to which the rate of increase in earnings has been slowest in sectors such as distribution and hotels and catering, where low-paid and part-time workers are concentrated.

The growing inequality of earned income can therefore be explained both by the restructuring of the labour force, with an increase in the relative importance of jobs at the two extremes of the earnings distribution, and by the differential rate of change in high- and low-level earnings. The former effect can be attributed to the restructuring of the economy in which the Thatcher governments' macroeconomic policy played a central role, and the latter can be attributed to the differential impact of labour market policy.

The impact of labour market policy on relative earnings

There is little evidence that employers in manufacturing have made extensive use of the new powers given to them by the law. Although there has been an increase in flexibility in the use of labour, this has been compensated for by increased wages (Brown and Wadhwani, 1990; Blanchflower, 1991). Consequently, although earnings in manufacturing grew relatively slowly as employment fell sharply between 1979 and 1981, from 1981–1990 average earnings in manufacturing increased by 8.9% on average per year compared with 8.0% in the rest of the economy. Information on occupational earnings from the *New Earnings Survey* reveals that between 1979 and 1990 manual earnings in a wide range of manufacturing occupations increased at annual rates of 9–9.5%

Table 9.3. Average annual rates of growth of earnings in selected sectors 1980–1990.[a]

Sector	Annual average rate of growth
Banking, finance and insurance	10.1
Manufacturing	9.5
Distribution and repairs	8.5
Hotels and catering	8.1
Whole economy	8.8

[a]Sources: *Employment Gazette* (April 1991); *Monthly Digest of Statistics* (November 1990).

whilst the increases for white-collar workers and foremen were in excess of 10%.

In banking, finance, insurance and related services the general trend has been towards a higher degree of industrial concentration and this has tended to increase the importance of the internal labour market in these sectors, resulting in higher pay, more organised promotion systems and greater job security. These changes, which originated in the 1970s, have been accompanied by a switch in recruitment towards graduate entry for professional and managerial grades. Consequently, the status and pay of such jobs has tended to increase, and the promotion paths of individuals recruited by traditional methods have been undermined. The more extensive use of graduate recruitment has also enhanced the status of accountants and related professions in the financial sector. This, and the market pressure from the rapid growth of financial and business services, has substantially improved their relative pay. Earnings for the occupational category including accountants and professionals in insurance and finance increased by 12% between 1979 and 1990.

The most dramatic changes in labour market organisation, however, are to be found in the public sector. The government engineered major job reductions, changes in the terms and conditions of employment, and labour restructuring in the then nationalised industries including coal, steel, the railways, postal services, airlines and automobile industries. Privatisation has continued this process. In other public sector areas, especially in local government, which has been subjected to a tight financial squeeze, the job security for 'core' professional and nonprofessional staff has been reduced with the increasing use of fixed-term and temporary contracts, particularly in education. The government response to the opposition from school teachers' unions was to impose a legal settlement to a protracted dispute over terms and conditions of employment and to scrap long-established bargaining machinery. However, the government's success in implementing its policy even in the public sector has been limited. In 1987 the Treasury concluded a long-term agreement with the Institute of Professional Civil Servants which provided for an annual pay review, regular pay comparability exercises, job evaluation and a national pay scale—all of which government ministers had argued strongly against. Nurses, civil servants, soldiers, policemen and judges also have pay review bodies which produce pay increases at least in line with the wage movements of comparable grades in the private sector. For professional and related occupations in education, welfare and health, earnings grew at an average annual rate of around 11% from 1979–1990.

The government was more successful in engineering a progressive erosion in the terms and conditions of employment of the low-paid in the public sector. The privatisation of an increasing proportion of central government, Local Authority and National Health Service services (including cleaning, catering and laundry), the scrapping of the

Fair Wage Resolution, and new legislation outlawing the insertion of
fair labour standard clauses in Local Authority contracts placed an
increasing number of low-paid public sector workers outside the scope
of collective bargaining. As a consequence there have been reductions
in pay, a shortening of the hours of part-time work and the elimination
of holiday and sickness pay and other fringe benefits. Where services
have not been privatised, workers have been obliged to accept an
intensification of work and worsened terms and conditions of employment under the threat of privatisation, or have been obliged to impose
similar cuts on themselves when formulating bids for their own jobs in
competitition with private contractors. The earnings increase of low-
paid public sector workers and those most affected by policy-induced
privatisation averaged not much more than 8% per year between 1979
and 1990.[11]

An important feature of the increasing privatisation of catering,
cleansing, refuse collection, laundry services and so on, has been a
rapid growth in the size of the firms that provide these services.
Profitability here depends almost exclusively on the ability to cut pay,
worsen working conditions, reduce hours (for example, to avoid social
security overheads and the need for meal breaks) and to intensify work.
The achievement of these objectives generates a large cash flow and,
as the scope for capital investment and innovation is small in many of
these services, this surplus has gone into the buying-up of small firms
so that the leading operators have increased several fold in size in a
very few years (Brosnan and Wilkinson, 1987). Thus, in contrast with
other sectors, where large firms tend to foster higher pay, improved
employment conditions and greater job security, in these sectors large
firms are pioneers in the driving down of labour standards. Much the
same process is at work in hotels, catering and retailing, all of which
have become increasingly concentrated in the hands of large chains who
pay low wages, adjust the size of the labour force and/or the hours
worked tightly to consumer 'traffic' and exclude temporary, casual and
usually part-time employees from nonwage employment benefits. Such
companies have internalised the polarisation between the primary and
secondary labour markets in that they are managed at the executive
level by elites—usually male—with very high pay and fringe-benefit
packages, supported by a nucleus of functional personnel, line managers
and supervisors with secure employment and promotion prospects.
However, this 'primary core' whose pay grew relatively rapidly over
the 1980s is small when compared with the bulk of the workforce which
is generally part-time, frequently on temporary or casual employment
contracts, low-paid and excluded from fringe benefits, and whose
relative pay has declined.

Such 'flexibility' in terms of pay and employment conditions has
nothing in common with a more efficient labour market generating
higher levels of employment; it represents managerial strategies designed

to reduce pay and employment and to intensify labour exploitation. As might be expected, such labour market policies require for their viability the appropriate labour supply conditions. These are provided by policy-induced high levels of unemployment, an exacerbation of the resulting family poverty by social security cuts, policies which provide various forms of direct and indirect subsidies for low-paid employment, and legislation which increases job insecurity by eroding individual employment rights and hinders a collective response by limiting the scope for trade union organisation and action (see Deakin and Wilkinson, 1991a, b). Paradoxically, policies designed to free enterprise and which are theoretically underpinned by arguments that they are necessary to generate full employment, depend for their effective implementation on continuous state intervention into the lives and protective agencies of the poorest in society and on high levels of unemployment.

The redistributive consequences of changing relative pay can be illustrated by reference to 'internal terms of trade': Table 9.4 presents ratios of average earnings in, first, the manufacturing sector and, second, the banking, finance and insurance sector to average earnings in the distribution and hotel and catering sectors combined. Thus by 1990 earnings in manufacturing were worth 9% more in terms of labour services in distribution and hotels and catering than they had been in 1980; for banking, finance and insurance the improvement was almost 17%. Provided that the changed relative pay is reflected in changing

Table 9.4. Shifting 'internal terms of trade' in manufacturing and in finance and insurance 1980–1990: ratio of wages to those in distribution, hotels and catering.[a]

Year	Manufacturing	Finance and insurance
1980	100.0	100.0
1981	100.9	101.9
1982	102.8	104.9
1983	103.4	105.4
1984	104.9	106.3
1985	106.8	107.6
1986	107.4	110.7
1987	107.9	114.0
1988	107.6	113.3
1989	107.9	114.9
1990	108.8	116.8

[a]Source: calculated from Monthly Earnings Index, *Department of Employment Gazette.*

relative prices and to the extent that the higher-paid consume the services of the lower-paid, the better-off benefit directly from the worsening relative pay of the worse-off. If the decreased relative pay of the lowest-paid is not transmitted into prices it 'trickles-up' the income scale in the form of profits, dividends and the enhanced stock market valuation of shares. Alternatively, lower real wage costs that result from intensified exploitation keep in existence obsolete equipment and products which should have been scrapped and replaced, and poor management which should have been reformed (or replaced).

Government policies had other redistributive consequences which were largely hidden and wholly regressive. The group of low-paid workers identified above as being directly and adversely affected by privatisation and government wage policy in the public sector had increases in earnings around 2% per year less than the average earnings for all occupations between 1979 and 1990. Thus whilst 190% was added to average earnings over these 11 years, the low-paid most affected by public policy benefited only to the extent of 140%. This 50 percentage point difference can be regarded as a levy on the lowest paid which allowed public services to be maintained at lower real costs and/or contributed to the profits of privatisation.

Implications for inflation

The governments' labour market policies since 1979, rather than improving the operation of the labour market, have tended to reinforce its rigidities, and the cost of adjustment has fallen on those least able to bear, and least able to resist, the imposition. As a consequence, inequalities of earnings and of job opportunities have increased. What implications have these policies had for inflation? The above measures might affect the rate of inflation via a number of routes, but most directly by influencing the rate of (nominal) wage increases or the level (or rate of growth) of productivity. Either of these effects would impact on unit labour costs and hence, with a given mark-up, on prices.

On the first effect, to the extent that the power of trade unions was weakened, wage rises might be expected to be lower than otherwise. The actual effects reflect the differential impact of government policies. While groups such as those working for firms bidding for contract cleaning have in some instances had their wage levels reduced, others have been able to continue to achieve substantial increases in both nominal and real wages. In certain sections of the economy, then, the government's labour market and other deregulatory measures (privatisation and contracting out) have reduced wage costs and hence, potentially, reduced the price of the relevant final consumer goods and services below what they would otherwise have been. However, the areas where this effect has occurred are in many cases labour-intensive with significant opportunities for productivity growth based on new technology; the worsening of terms and conditions of employment, and intensification of work effort, reduce the pressures for such technical change, thus losing potential long-term reductions in unit costs.

In other sectors of the economy where labour productivity has risen and/or where firms have benefited from reductions in the cost of material inputs, pay has increased so as to secure substantial real advances. Thus the two components to reducing unit labour costs have worked against each other: where the government has succeeded in reducing (increases in) pay this has often been at the expense of productivity; and where productivity has been enhanced, this has generally been taken out in profits and dividends[12] and to a lesser extent in wage earnings, rather than in lower prices.

By these means the economically powerful groups in society expropriated a more than proportionate share of the additional resources made available by the increase in productivity and the surplus from abroad. To this bounty were added the benefits of widening earnings differentials and the regressive fiscal redistribution secured by cuts in the higher rates of tax, the switch from direct to indirect taxes and reductions in social benefits. Enough of this reverse Robin-Hoodism percolated down to appease the well-organised and economically powerful in society, and changes in labour and employment law combined with manipulation of the social security system served to suppress resistance from the less powerful. Under these multiple pressures inflation subsided; the remaining question is, for how long?

Conclusions

The reduction in inflation up to 1986 did not follow the supposed monetarist textbook pattern. To the extent that the pursuit of monetarist policies did impact on inflation this was not due to a reduction in (the rate of growth of) the money supply producing a direct reduction in (the rate of growth of) prices, but rather the reverse: a good old-fashioned economic recession put downward pressure on prices and wages and it was this deflation which reduced the demand for money. However, not only did this policy have detrimental effects on output and employment, the impact of the resulting recession on inflation was never clear-cut. As for unemployment restraining wages and thus allowing a reduction in inflation, the process worked the other way round: the growth of real wages restrained pressure on nominal wage growth. The changes in industrial relations law acted not so much to prevent wage increases being won by trade union members, as to weaken trade union protection for groups of workers in certain sections of the economy. The contribution to restraining inflation from the growth of unemployment was more through weakening consumer demand and reducing the ability of firms to increase prices, than through reducing the rate of wage increases. Lower world commodity prices and the overvaluation of sterling by means of a policy of high exchange rates reduced import prices and to the extent that these were passed on, put downward pressure on home prices. The ability of industry to capture the benefits of lower import prices allowed real wages *and* profits to rise, reducing the 'conflict' element in inflation. This was also aided by the swing of internal terms of trade in favour of the more economically and politically powerful.

The question of whether the downward pressure on prices can be sustained depends importantly on what happens to real wages. In the short term the trend appears to be favourable. The solid line in Figure 9.6 shows the annual increase in net real earnings for each month from January 1990 to July 1991. This fell from more than 3% in January 1990 to −1% in October of that year. However, by July 1991 the rate of increase in net real earnings was again close to 3%. As before, in the 1980s, this cannot be explained by rising unemployment, which was fairly constant at around 5.7% until July 1990 before rising to 8.3% one year later. Nor can it be explained by the rate of increase in nominal earnings, which increased from an annual rate of 9.5% in January 1990 to 10% in July of that year before falling to 8.3% a year

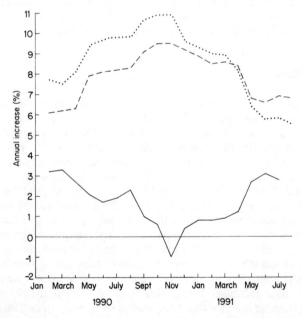

Figure 9.6. Earnings and retail prices January 1990–July 1991 (—, net real earnings; ····, retail prices including mortgage rate; ---, retail prices excluding mortgage rate).

later. The increase in net real earnings can be attributed mainly to the trend in retail prices and, as the dotted line in Figure 9.6 indicates, to the decline in mortgage rates from mid-1990.

However, the ability of the economy to sustain this rate of real wage advance must be seriously in question. It seems unlikely that, given the continuing current account deficit, interest rates can be continuously reduced, and the reduction in the current account deficit itself will be an important call on resources. If the pound was to be devalued within the Exchange Rate Mechanism, this would have the effect of reversing the favourable trend in import prices. Moreover, it seems unlikely that the 'productivity miracle' of the 1980s will be repeated. Much of this can be attributed to the heavy scrapping of obsolete equipment in the early 1980s and labour-saving, rather than capacity-expanding, investment in the late 1980s. The amount of capacity to scrap has fallen and the ability to save labour so as to increase overall productivity must fall as the proportion of employment in productive industry declines. Further, the trend in real interest rates is working against productive investment. The clearing bank's base rate, adjusted for increases in manufacturing prices, increased from 3.4% in 1979–1982 to 5.1% in 1983–1986 and to 7.1% in 1987–1990. The ability of the government to buy off inflationary pressure must therefore rest, to an important extent, on its ability to distribute yet more unequally a more slowly growing cake.

Acknowledgements

We are grateful to Andrew Glyn, Geoff Harcourt, Jane Humphries and Mike Kitson for their comments.

Comment

Demoralisation and Mobilisation

Roger Tarling

Has inflation been suppressed rather than cured? Despite its low level at the end of 1991, inflation has certainly not been cured. Yet perhaps some behaviour has changed in an irreversible way such that inflationary forces in the economy have been genuinely reduced rather than merely suppressed; in particular, the power of organisation within the labour market and the element of 'wage push', to use an old-fashioned expression, are weaker. The preceding chapter presents a picture of latent inflationary pressure at the end of 1991 as great as ever. I feel that its analysis, with which I agree entirely, perhaps allows for the view that some pressure has been reduced—but that no-one should feel proud about how this has been achieved or feel complacent about the consequences.

Government economic policy has been formed by monetarist ideology but implemented pragmatically using tangible policy instruments, primarily public expenditure and interest rates. The experience has led to a recognition that money is indeed endogenous. External terms of trade moved favourably and oil revenues were sustained for a while during the 1980s, giving a growth of real incomes which went largely into private consumption. This tended to hold down nominal wage growth in the manufacturing sector. However, within sectors and between sectors, real pay differentials increased. Combined with increased flexibility in the labour market, in both work organisation and job tenure, benefits of employment increased for some and diminished for others. Although much of this redistribution was the consequence of economic restructuring, it was enabled in part by rolling back the legislation on collective action and employee rights in the labour market. Thus those who lost out economically also lost some of the means of recovering their losses. Further, the rolling back of legislation, the diminution of welfare rights and the growth of means testing, have made it more difficult for people without employment to survive and remain in touch with the labour market. Employment and enterprise measures are geared towards those best able to benefit, and those left behind find it difficult to get into the programmes let alone find employment. The price of entry and cost of participation are high for those who lack their own resources.

All of the arguments for this scenario are in Michie and Wilkinson's chapter which establishes the demoralisation of sections of the workforce and particularly of those not in employment, whose lack of resources makes them less able to act in a resourceful or entrepreneurial way, and for whom it is more difficult now to mobilise to improve their situation than it was in the 1970s. Yet with the rise in individualism there has been less awareness and more acceptance of the levels of deprivation of others, and less public response to efforts to redress the balance, particularly because charity and self-help are seen to be an answer. More than before, part of the reason for the lack of action to help those suffering the deprivation is the inability of those on the receiving end to take action—even self-help—because they lack their own resources and cannot obtain other resources except at very high personal cost.

Without growth, what are the surviving mechanisms and processes for bringing about a redistribution of workers' claims and social welfare claims? Labour market policies in the UK are impotent in the face of no net additional job opportunities—they are effectively only work-sharing.

10

Changes in the Labour Market and the Psychological Health of the Nation

Brendan Burchell

The Thatcher years started with a dramatic and unprecedented rise in the rate of unemployment. Up to that point in post-War Britain any government that had allowed unemployment to approach the one million mark would have brought upon itself an intolerable level of criticism. Not only did the Thatcher administration allow unemployment to rise to well above the three million mark, but they also succeeded in convincing people that these high levels of unemployment were a new norm and not a case of mismanagement of the economy.

Whilst economists have concerned themselves greatly with the causes of unemployment, there is a void within the discipline when it comes to counting its cost to the individual. There may be good reasons why economists have not investigated the impact of an individual's economic life on their psychological health, but this omission is nevertheless one which needs to be rectified. It is argued in this chapter that the costs to the individual of unemployment (and other correlates of a downturn in the demand for labour) go far beyond the loss of a wage. If economic policy is to be determined (at least in part) by counting the costs and benefits to individuals in the nation, those aspects of well-being which are not so easily quantified should not be ignored simply because they are invisible in standard economic indicators. Although the arguments here are restricted to the labour market, it is not intended to infer that other aspects of Conservative policy have not also caused a large amount of psychological suffering—the alarming rise in house repossessions or increases in hospital waiting lists are obvious examples where individual suffering has been the direct outcome of government economic and public spending decisions. Increases in crime and the fear of crime are further examples of sources of increased anxiety amongst the population over the last 13 years.

The first section of this chapter addresses the nature of psychological well-being before discussing various sources of evidence concerning the psychological health of individuals in the workforce. The basis for the dependence of the individual on employment to maintain psychological well-being is then considered, before looking at more complex ways in which the labour market can affect psychological well-being.

Psychological Health and Illness; What Is It?

Psychological health and illness are both terms which are difficult to define but problems of definition have often been ignored with little cost to progress. It is probably more correct to consider psychological health and psychological illness as separate dimensions, in the same way that we might describe a person who took no physical exercise as being unhealthy but not ill. Being in good mental health is associated with being able to cope well with day-to-day life, and with the absence of negative feelings and emotions such as frustration, boredom, depressed mood and loneliness. Thus in most cases the common effects of unemployment could be described as a lowering of psychological health. The term 'mental illness', however, is more usually associated with psychiatric disorders such as clinical depression or schizophrenia.

Measurement of psychological health and illness

Psychological well-being can be measured in a number of different ways, depending largely upon the nature of the research. In survey research it is commonly assessed with the use of one of a number of well-validated batteries of questions; in employment research the most commonly used is the General Health Questionnaire (see Banks *et al.* (1980) for further details of this scale). These scales typically ask respondents to rate a number of questions about positive emotions (e.g. feeling confident and happy) and negative emotions (e.g. feeling worried or depressed), either in terms of severity or frequency of having those feelings. Alternatively, 'symptom checklists' can provide lists of stress-related symptoms (such as headaches, insomnia, panic attacks) and respondents record all those that they have experienced in a specified period. These scales can be administered face-to-face, in self-completion questionnaires or by telephone, and are typically used to create continuous dimensions of well-being, but in some cases a cut-off point is selected to divide the sample into those with abnormally high levels (potential psychiatric 'cases') from the rest.

A number of other techniques have also been used in some studies to measure the psychological health of the individual. Some have used physiological correlates of stress such as blood pressure, or analysis of blood or urine samples. Others have relied on detailed interviews with psychiatrists or records taken from general practitioners.

The other main method of measuring psychological health is through

indicators such as suicides, psychiatric admissions or mortality from
stress-related causes. It is assumed that as the aggregate level of mental
health of a group deteriorates, then the frequency of these very extreme
reactions will show a corresponding rise. These measures have the
advantage that, as well as being recorded in some large-scale surveys
(for example, the *Longitudinal Survey*), they are also available from
official statistical sources, and thus retrospective studies can be
performed by charting time-series of economic indicators against
indicators of mental health.

A final form of evidence is also worthy of mention: qualitative reports
of the experiences of individuals who suffer unemployment, redundancies
or other negative labour market experiences elicited from relatively
unstructured interviews. When people describe the nature of their own
psychological experiences in this way, what might be lost in lack in
rigour is compensated for in the richness of the data and the insights
into the ways in which individuals depend on employment.

Unemployment and Mental Health: the Evidence

It is generally accepted by the social scientist and layperson alike that
unemployment can be psychologically damaging. Arguments to the
contrary have occasionally been made, for instance by the extreme left
who see unemployment as a liberation from capitalist control, or from
the far right who have argued that the unemployed are content in their
idleness. There have even been academics who have suggested that in
recent times circumstances have changed and unemployment may be
seen as a welcome interlude of leisure to the individual; Garraty (1978)
argued that generous levels of benefits, combined with the widespread
knowledge that governments manipulate the level of unemployment as
one of the primary tools for controlling the economy, have removed
the poverty and stigma that were associated with unemployment in the
Great Depression. However, psychological and socioeconomic studies
have found that neither of these claims receives any significant support.

The rapid rise in unemployment in the 1970s and 1980s spawned
many psychological studies of the impact of unemployment. There have
recently been a number of excellent reviews of this literature (for
example Fryer and Payner, 1986; Feather, 1990), so this exercise is not
repeated here. Rather, an example of each of the main types of evidence
brought to bear on the relationship between unemployment and
psychological health is given.

Cross-sectional studies

The simplest type of evidence has involved the collection of an
indicator of psychological health from matched groups of employed and

unemployed individuals. For instance, Warr and Payne (1982) reported the results of interviews with a large random sample of adults in England, Scotland and Wales, in which respondents were asked about their feelings on the day prior to the survey. Six percent of men in jobs and 9% of employed females reported high levels of emotional strain, compared to 16% of unemployed men and 21% of unemployed women. This pattern of results has been replicated many times in Britain and elsewhere, and demonstrates conclusively that the psychological well-being of the unemployed is, on average, worse than among those with jobs at a particular point in time. This finding is, of course, open to alternative causal explanations—some unemployed individuals may have chronic low levels of psychological well-being which make it difficult for them to find work. It is also difficult to control for prior variables such as the social class, level of work ethic, and so on of employees and the unemployed using this research design.

Longitudinal studies

A superior design for determining the impact of unemployment on mental health is to follow the same individuals as they move into and out of employment. A number of studies have done this: for instance, Warr and Jackson (1985) and Payne and Jones (1987) reinterviewed men who were unemployed at the time of an earlier survey. Whilst those who remained unemployed at the time of the reinterview continued, on average, to have high levels of psychological distress, those who became re-employed in the time between interviews tended to improve in their psychological health.

The other logical possibility for a longitudinal design is to examine changes in psychological health associated with the inflow into unemployment. As the rate at which a representative sample of employees becomes unemployed is low, inflow studies have instead focused on plant closures and mass redundancies. However, findings from this type of study are typically confounded by the fact that the knowledge of impending unemployment is often as stressful as unemployment itself, if not more so.

Qualitative studies

A number of researchers have collected more detailed information about individuals' reactions to unemployment using less structured interviews. For instance, Fineman interviewed a number of white-collar workers who were made redundant in the late 1970s, and revisited them a couple of times later, during which time some became re-employed and some remained unemployed or alternated between temporary employment and unemployment (Fineman, 1983, 1987). By letting them relate their own narratives a more complex set of accounts emerged.

For instance, one feature that is not revealed in many quantitative studies is that a minority of individuals enjoy many features of unemployment, such as spending more time with their families or escaping from what was a stressful or unpleasant job. However, for most the experience of unemployment is not only very stressful but continues to affect their attitude to work long after re-employment. Furthermore, if that re-employment is into a job which is perceived as inferior to the job that they lost, for instance in the level of skill required or the prestige of the job, then that too can be a source of discontent.

Aggregate studies

A number of researchers have attempted to monitor the way in which the economy affects psychological health through time-series analysis. Brenner (1973) pioneered this field using data from New York State covering a period of up to 127 years. His main indicator of economic prosperity was the number of individuals employed in manufacturing, which he found predicted the number of psychiatric hospital admissions after a 2-year time lag. Brenner replicated this technique using British data and arrived at similar conclusions (Brenner, 1979).

However, these aggregate studies are problematic in interpretation, not only because of artifact in the measurement of indicators such as admissions and suicide rates, but also because they reveal little about the mechanisms which operate. Furthermore, by changing the specifications of the regression models, other researchers have shown that the models can be very unstable and that fluctuations in the economy may not be causing new cases of psychological problems so much as uncovering old ones. In the case of mortality there is also considerable variation in estimates of the strength of the relationship. Brenner's original estimate was that for every increase in unemployment of one million there would be an increase in mortality of 8000; other estimates using this technique have been as low as 3000. However, whatever the final regression estimates are, these studies still reveal little about the mechanisms by which employment and mental health are related. It is possible, for instance, that during times of high unemployment even those in work experience lower levels of psychological well-being. This question will be addressed after considering the mechanisms by which employment affects psychological well-being.

Why Does Unemployment Affect Psychological Well-being?

Several models have been put forward as to why unemployment is so damaging to an individual's psychological health, with much overlap between the various theories. Two of these theories are discussed here, chosen primarily for their wider applicability to labour market circumstances other than unemployment.

Environmental 'vitamins'

A number of psychological theories postulate that work provides a healthier environment for the individual and that the unemployed person, without the benefits which commonly accrue from such an environment, will suffer psychological ill-health. Warr (1987) provides a recent and very detailed example of such a theory but it is similar in its essential features to other influential models such as those advocated by Jahoda (1982). Warr proposed that certain features of the environment are necessary for psychological health in the same way that vitamins are essential for physical health. He listed nine such 'vitamins': opportunity for control; opportunity for skill use; externally generated goals; variety; environmental clarity; availability of money; physical security; opportunity for interpersonal contact; and valued social position (Warr, 1987, p. 2). The lack of an adequate level of any of these features will detract from the psychological well-being of an individual. Whilst Warr does not claim that each of his nine 'vitamins' has been tested and proven, he does cite an extensive number of studies that provide either support for or further understanding of the way in which the model may operate.

Personal agency

An alternative model to account for the psychological effects of unemployment portrays individuals as attempting to construct their own futures, rather than being passive recipients of 'vitamins' from their environment. Agency theory asserts that, rather than being primarily passive, individuals are active and striving, make decisions, initiate and plan, are future-oriented, purposeful and organise and structure their environments: in short, proactive rather than reactive. However, not all environments are conducive to those sorts of activities. It is the frustration of agency that causes poor well-being in unemployment. Unemployment is a threatening, inhibiting and restrictive environment characterised by inadequate resources, low social power and an uncertain future. Whilst this theory (or perhaps meta-theory) has received little attempt to test it directly, support comes from two types of observation.

Initial evidence (Fryer and Payne, 1984) came from very detailed case studies of 11 carefully selected individuals who were very well adapted to unemployment in most ways. These individuals had in common an ability to structure and fill their own lives and work towards goals which they set themselves. It was concluded that a small proportion of the population have the personal resources to continue to identify and pursue goals of personal significance outside normal paid employment, and thus protect their psychological health through such activity.

Further evidence of the nature of the psychological environment that allows men to be able to undergo periods without paid work but to avoid harmful psychological consequences comes from a study that compared groups of men from two factories faced with falling order books (McKenna and Fryer, 1984). One group were made redundant and the other group (following union negotiation) were laid off on a rolling basis. The data were collected in one period where one group of men, because of the coincidence of lay-off, holidays and maintenance shutdown, went for approximately 12 weeks without work. The two groups of men, redundant and laid-off, were thus both without work, claiming benefit and in other objective ways in a similar position. The groups differed greatly, though, in their adjustment to worklessness. The laid-off workers planned in advance how they would spend their spare time, for instance decorating their homes, repairing cars, gardening, taking up new sporting activities and going on holiday. They typically bought in the materials that they needed in advance of their lay-off, and were usually successful in carrying out their plans before their return to work. Five weeks after the lay-off these men were, if anything, slightly better in their perceived health than a control group of men who had remained at work in the factory.

By contrast, the men who had forcibly been made redundant had considerably worse perceived health. Because of relatively large redundancy payments they did not have immediate financial problems. However, they typically spent a lot of their days watching television and reported feeling bored. When interviewed it was their fear of uncertainty about their future that these men mentioned frequently as one of their main worries; they did not know whether they would be working or still unemployed in a few weeks time. The researchers concluded that it was the inability to plan for the future that caused the problems for the redundant group.

The Psychological Health of Employees and the Economically Inactive

The following section argues that it is not just the unemployed who have suffered in the British labour market over the past decade, but also those who have remained in work. A discussion of the extent to which that occurs inevitably as aggregate unemployment rises, or the extent to which some of the psychologically threatening changes in the labour market were brought about through government policy and legislation, is outside the scope of this chapter. However, it should be noted that the Thatcher government certainly did act to reduce the security of employment in several notable individual professions (for example, dockers and university lecturers) as well as more generally through changes in labour market regulation.

Not only do the theories of unemployment and psychological health described above go some way to help us to understand the nature of the psychological suffering of the unemployed, they also illuminate which other types of labour market phenomena could also give rise to psychological distress and which, although they might be less visible than unemployment, might be just as pervasive and threatening. Unfortunately, however, the psychological literature is small and fragmented by comparison to that relating to unemployment, reflecting psychologists' lack of concern for the nature of the labour market. Whilst there has been a considerable amount of interest in the effects of differing work environments on psychological functioning (and some attempts to use the same analytical tools to study that as to study unemployment, most noticeably Warr's 'vitamin' model), attempts to link those theoretical frameworks to conditions in the labour market have been almost nonexistent. Yet there is some provocative evidence to suggest that, as the aggregate level of unemployment increases, even the psychological well-being of employees decreases. Dooley *et al.* (1987) investigated the effect of the aggregate level of unemployment on the psychological health of employees and the unemployed in the US, using data collected between 1978 and 1982. They argued that if much of the anguish of the unemployed comes about because of their low relative position in society, then as the numbers of unemployed people increase, their plight will not seem to be so distinctively poor, and one might expect an attenuation in their low levels of well-being. However, the opposite was found to be the case; the psychological health of both employees and of the unemployed was found to vary inversely with the aggregate level of unemployment in their local labour market. The authors hypothesise that this may have been due to the higher perceived threat of unemployment amongst employees and lower levels of perceived opportunity for re-employment amongst the unemployed. An alternative explanation is that in periods of economic downturn the fiercer competition may force employers to adopt more stressful work regimes.

A study that comes close to understanding the link between economic recession and psychological health tested several models, each of which made different assumptions about the link between the economy, the experience of good and bad life events and psychological health (Catalano and Dooley, 1983). The three models were:

(1) economic contraction increases the incidence of undesirable job and financial events that, in turn, increase the incidence of illness and injury;

(2) economic change *per se* increases the incidence of undesirable job and financial events and therefore of illness and injury; and

(3) economic change *per se* increases the incidence of all job and financial events and therefore of illness and injury.

The best fit was found for the first model. Not surprisingly, however, for early attempts to understand complex phenomena, the pattern of results was not entirely straightforward. When tested on different socioeconomic groups the model fitted well only for the middle of the three groups. Studies that focus more narrowly on particular types of labour market phenomena have generally been more successful in arriving at results that were more readily interpretable.

The agency perspective suggests that unemployment is only one example of a position in the labour market that individuals find to be threatening to their sense of agency (and therefore to their psychological well-being). For instance, there is good evidence in the occupational psychology literature that job insecurity can, under many circumstances, be threatening to psychological health. If a perceived threat to job security is seen as threatening to one's whole future economic well-being then individual agency becomes difficult to assert, in a similar manner to the problems faced by the unemployed. Burchell (1989) and Burchell and Rubery (1990) found very low levels of psychological health amongst the insecure, casualised segments of the workforce. Furthermore, when unemployed men returned to work in insecure jobs, the improvement in their financial position was not matched by any improvement in their psychological health. However, men who returned to jobs which they perceived to be secure showed a considerable improvement in their psychological well-being.

Similarly, Fineman's (1983, 1987) qualitative surveys and follow-ups with white-collar males who had suffered redundancies (already referred to above) found some instances of men who seemed to cope better with unemployment than with work under very adverse labour market positions. Fineman also found that even long after a redundancy there is a legacy effect: for instance, some individuals continue to be almost obsessed with job security and care little about other aspects of their job (such as pay) long after re-employment.

Another example of individuals suffering a worst threat to their psychological health in employment than in unemployment comes from Kasl and Cobb's (1982) classic study of redundancy, where (using a number of physiological as well as self-report measures) they found that the threat or anticipation of unemployment was as harmful as unemployment itself; once the employees that they were studying had been given notice of redundancies, the period before the actual lay-off was, on average, more stressful than the unemployment that followed. However, like many studies of plant closures, Kasl and Cobb's research was conducted during times of relatively low levels of unemployment; Gordus *et al.* (1981) warned that plant closures that eject workers into sluggish labour markets may have much worse aftermaths.

A very different type of link between labour market conditions and psychological health was described by Elder and Caspi (1988). Using North American cohort studies started in the 1920s and 1930s, a link was found between the psychological well-being of children and the extent of the economic losses that their families suffered during the Great Depression, caused at least in part by worse parenting styles in cases of more extreme loss of family income. However, whilst that programme of research was unusual in the details collected from different sources (such as interviews with parents and health professionals), the exact nature of the economic causes and correlates of the loss of income were not recorded for analysis. Using British data from the 1980s, Burchell and Devereux (1987) also found evidence to suggest that parental unemployment affected children's economic value systems. Other studies have also shown that the influence of unemployment extends well beyond the claimant count. Moser *et al.* (1984) demonstrated convincingly, using the OPCS longitudinal study, that the wives of unemployed men also suffer increased levels of mortality. Fagin and Little (1984) found depression in the wives of unemployed men, particularly if they did not work themselves, and also found some evidence of psychological problems amongst their children, including disturbed feeding habits, minor gastrointestinal complaints, sleeping difficulties, proneness to accidents and behavioural disorders. These studies serve as a reminder that even those who are not in the workforce themselves will be victims of economic recession.

What are needed to understand the mechanisms involved in linking the labour market to psychological health are careful and detailed studies of the way in which the economic lives of individuals differ in times of economic recession from times of a healthier economy. However, these sorts of labour market phenomena need to be understood at a more detailed level than is currently the case, particularly in the psychological literature. For instance, redundancy and dismissal are discussed as being the normal precursors to unemployment, and threatening in themselves. However, recent studies of British labour markets have shown that this is a highly misleading stereotype of unemployment. In a study of the inflow into unemployment, Daniel (1990) found that only 37% of those who were working directly prior to their period of unemployment were made redundant, and a further 6% left because they came to the end of a fixed-term contract. Supporting this point that redundancy and unemployment are relatively autonomous problems, Burchell (1990) showed that involuntary job quits are fairly common (accounting for approximately 22% of all men's transitions between organisations, and 13% of women's transitions). Neither would they seem to be particularly traumatic in most cases; in 58% of cases for men, and 52% of cases for women, the next job after the involuntary quit was better paid (measured by self-report) than the one that they had left, and only 17% of the men's redundancies and

22% of the women's redundancies led to a reduction in pay. It seems to be the case that, for many employees, involuntary quits are the normal way that workers leave jobs, particularly in seasonal employment and in the construction industry, and in the majority of cases employees seem to be able to cope without economic (and presumably with little psychological) cost. However, focusing only on involuntary quits that also involve taking up another job at a lower rate of pay, there are large differences in those patterns between times of high unemployment and low unemployment. In the late 1960s until the late 1970s only about 2% of men's contiguous job changes were both involuntary and involved a loss in pay. However, from the late 1970s through to the mid-1980s there was a threefold increase in this rate (in line with the approximate threefold increase in unemployment) to around 6% (Burchell, 1990) (women's transitions between jobs during this period also suffered, but in more complex ways that reflect the larger numbers of women who leave jobs for domestic reasons).

Unfortunately, little is known about the psychological correlates of such transitions. Perhaps the study that has looked most directly at such issues was Ferman and Gardner's (1979) attempt to develop a theoretical framework which investigated the way in which unemployment had a knock-on effect throughout the workforce. There were many features of their analysis which made it unusual within the psychological literature—for instance, they considered both neoclassical and segmented models of the labour market (albeit rather simplistically). Using terms like 'skidding' and 'bumping', they considered mechanisms by which less-skilled workers may (or may not) be replaced by redundant, more highly skilled workers. While many of their assumptions about labour markets were inaccurate (for instance, that unemployment is usually preceded directly by dismissal or redundancy), they nevertheless made a start towards understanding more complex units of labour market behaviour and their psychological correlates. The most promising aspect of their work was their attempt to characterise different types of 'unemployment careers' and their psychological correlates. Six career types were identified, and three married men were interviewed from each group:

(1) those who had remained unemployed since losing their last job;
(2) those who had returned to their previous job after a lay-off;
(3) those who had found a new job and remained in it (this group experienced much anxiety, even after starting their new job—perhaps like Fineman's redundant men who continued to worry about job insecurity);
(4) those who had periodically moved in and out of work with the same employer (these men seemed to enjoy this pattern of employment, perhaps in a similar way to McKenna and Fryer's

sample discussed above who had been laid-off but used those periods without work constructively);

(5) those who had periodically moved in and out of work with one new employer (for some reason which is not made clear by the authors, these men did not receive supplementary or unemployment benefits so they suffered economic hardship and were forced to rely on casual or black-economy work but did not suffer from insecurity like some of the others); and

(6) those who had moved in and out of work with more than one employer (these men had the most chaotic and varied careers but reactions were mixed; as well as some very negative reactions, others were optimistic of finding the right job or 'striking it rich').

With such small sample sizes it would be reckless to attempt anything more than very tentative conclusions from these data, but they do give a flavour of the very different types of experiences of individuals in the same labour market, and the detrimental effects possible on psychological health even where there is little or no actual experience of unemployment. Recent data from British labour markets in the 1980s suggests that the last three patterns may be surprisingly common. Daniel's (1990) study of the inflow into unemployment was unusual inasmuch as it followed-up the sample long after they returned to work. For instance, of his sample who were initially unemployed for less than 5 weeks, the average period out of work for the 20 months following the start of their initial period of unemployment in May 1980 was nearly 6 months. Of all of those who had found work in 10 months or less, only one-third were in the same job in November 1981, and only two-thirds were still in any sort of paid work. The mean number of jobs in that 20-month period was 3.2. This study, combined with the psychological literature on job security, shows conclusively just how misleading a picture is painted by those who dismiss short spells of unemployment as 'frictional' and unproblematic—they typically occur repeatedly to the same individuals, and give them working lives which are (as has been argued above) as psychologically damaging as long-term unemployment.

From another perspective, a downturn in demand for labour could affect a number of Warr's 'vitamins' even for an individual who remains in continuous employment. For instance, individuals may feel a loss of control over their career when there is little opportunity to find employment with other firms, whereas in times of labour shortage employees would feel that they control their own career moves (even if that resulted in deciding to remain with their current employer).

Similarly, in times of high unemployment many individuals are forced into taking jobs that require the exercise of less skill than they consider that they were trained for, or are capable of. Over the past two decades there has been a considerable debate about skill underutilisation.

Bravemann (1974) hypothesised that new technologies were deskilling many jobs. Alternatively, O'Brien (1986) proposed that the increasing educational levels being achieved in many countries will lead to a situation whereby many of those who enter the labour market may not be able to find jobs that will exercise their abilities to the full. However, little attention has been paid to the role of unemployment in taking individuals out of skilled jobs and forcing them to accept less-skilled jobs, or to the psychological correlates of such phenomena.

What has been proven quite conclusively is that perceived skill underutilisation is both quite common and has a major impact on job satisfaction. In a random survey of Australian employees, O'Brien found that 38% of respondents reported that their jobs were underutilising their skills (and 30% reported that their jobs were more demanding of their skills than they desired). Furthermore, O'Brien's surveys on perceived skill utilisation, both with random samples of employees and with professions where deskilling has been a particular issue, found that the extent to which employees reported that their jobs allowed them to use their abilities, training and experience, and provided opportunities for learning new jobs, was more strongly associated with overall job satisfaction than was any other aspect of their jobs. O'Brien asserted that skill underutilisation may be one of the main causes of job-related strain amongst the workforce, although he had no direct evidence to support this except the fact that job satisfaction and the well-being of employees are generally considered to be closely linked. There is one other study that claims to have found a direct link between skill underutilisation and mental health: Kornhauser (1965) found that amongst a sample of North American automobile workers, skill underutilisation was associated strongly with mental health (measured as a composite of self-esteem, morale, sociability, hostility and life-satisfaction). However, Kornhauser's sample may have been too restricted to allow generalisation.

However, if the link between skill utilisation and psychological well-being were to prove valid, it would add to the mechanisms by which unemployment can indirectly affect the well-being of the workforce. There is considerable evidence that jobs following periods of unemployment may demand a lower level of skills than those preceding spells of unemployment. In an analysis of the *Social Change and Economic Life* work-histories dataset it was found, for individuals aged up to 40 and between the years 1967 and 1986, that 21% of job transitions involved a reduction in the Registrar General's skill level associated with the job. However, as can be seen from Table 10.1, there was a considerable difference between contiguous job shifts and changes between jobs that involved a gap of a month or more between leaving one job and starting the next. In cases of unemployment that lasted for one month or more, fully 30% of men and 32% of women were forced into taking jobs in a less-skilled category of the 6-point scale.

Table 10.1. Percentage of job transitions involving moves to less-skilled jobs by whether the transition was contiguous or involved a period without employment.

	Contiguous job transition	Gap of one month or more
Male	19% (5399)	30% (1079)
Female	20% (3701)	32% (2389)

Conclusions

It is clear from the evidence that the high levels of unemployment experienced in the 1980s brought about much misery and suffering for unemployed men and women and for their families. There are less data available to make the argument that employees also suffer lower levels of psychological well-being in times of high unemployment, owing to a dearth of British studies on the subject, but a considerable number of studies exist from a variety of countries and periods which, pieced together, tell a consistent story. The balance of evidence overwhelmingly suggests that the influence of unemployment has been felt very widely. Yet, perhaps partly due to the failure of psychologists and economists to emphasise sufficiently the widespread psychological damage inflicted by the Conservative government's labour market policies, we are now seeing these high levels of psychological damage being inflicted yet again on the nation. From a psychologist's perspective, I find it incredible that over the past year the government has been able to inflict the misery and damage caused by an extra million people out of work on the nation with so little outrage being expressed publicly by the opposition parties or the media.

The impact of this omission in the orthodox labour market literature has theoretical as well as policy implications. It has been argued here that an individual's position in the labour market will affect their psychological functioning, which will presumably, in turn, affect their labour market behaviour. So whilst job security can be argued from a neoclassical perspective to be an entirely negative influence introducing market inefficiencies (see for instance, Addison, 1988; Bellmann, 1988), the thoeretical underpinnings of such arguments flagrantly ignore the nature of peoples' reactions when faced with insecurity in their working lives. A realist perspective has the potential to rectify this theoretical deficiency, and perhaps to provide the way forward with labour market

policies that are more sympathetic to the human beings who provide
and reproduce the labour.

Comment

Public Welfare

Ray Jobling

There is ample evidence from psychological and sociological research
that the costs to individuals of unemployment go way beyond loss of
income. The impact in terms of damage to self-esteem and subjective
sense of well-being can be considerable. While aggregate studies have
been methodologically much more problematic, there are nevertheless
some indications that the psychological health of the whole population,
and not simply unemployed individuals (and their families), can be
affected. This is most evidently the case where there have been large
collective redundancies affecting particular industrial communities, for
example in the steel-making industries of the UK, USA, France and
elsewhere. However, it also seems that the wider community can be
affected. The stresses and strains of economic uncertainty, including
the threat of wide-scale unemployment, appear to elicit a response from
the population as a whole. Alongside all of this, the drive for greater
efficiency in production has led to an intensification of work for many
of those who are employed, coupled with terms of employment which
reduce security of tenure in their jobs. In some cases workers find
themselves working harder, under closer supervision and for less income,
and fearful of job loss. Some have argued that higher morbidity and
mortality from stress-related physical disease is the result. There may
be increased psychiatric morbidity, with increased suicide rates. Certainly
it seems to be the case that, worldwide, we resort to inpatient treatment
for psychiatric conditions far more readily and frequently during times
of economic recession and periods of high unemployment. Equally, the
data for prison and other custodial sentences show that there is a
perceived need to remove offenders from the community. Thus there
may be more crime, and more of particular crimes (e.g. burglary)

during recessions. It is also true that the offenders, if found guilty, are at greater risk of imprisonment.

The implications for 'welfare' spending are obvious. Recession and high unemployment involve a high price in many respects. Economists cannot therefore continue to ignore these implications of economic policies and programmes which produce unemployment, whether intentionally or as an unwanted side-effect. Moreover, it is notable that while in such circumstances the demand for remedial and support services grows significantly, welfare budgets have been put under ever stricter constraints with consequently much increased hardship.

The experience of the UK in recent years illustrates the problem. Economic and social inequality has intensified. Significant numbers of the population have felt increasingly insecure both socially and economically. In this sense 'citizenship' has been at least partly reduced or withdrawn, and in a 'structured' way. It is questionable whether the concern for improved public health increasingly voiced by the UK government over recent years, has been appropriately represented in decision-making over economic policy. Whereas in the immediate post-War years memories of the inter-War depression and all that went with it were fresh enough to condition policy choices to some extent, it may be that 50 years later economic research and analysis will have to be broadened and deepened to include attention to the psychosocial effects of public policy-making in a far more explicit, systematic and sensitive way than hitherto. Future governments which aspire to the improvement of public welfare, must be made aware of the issues raised by Dr Burchell in his discussion.

11

The Legacy for Women's Employment: Integration, Differentiation and Polarisation

Jane Humphries and Jill Rubery

This chapter explores the experience of women in employment during the second two governments of Margaret Thatcher. By the early 1980s it was already clear that the increase in women's participation achieved in the post World War II period would not be reversed by structural change or cyclical recession. Women had maintained, and indeed increased, their share of employment through the oil crises of the 1970s and through the sharp recession of the early 1980s (Rubery, 1988). Thus it was not in doubt that women would continue to increase their involvement in the labour market during the consumer boom of the later Thatcher years. However, the terms under which women were to participate in the 'recovery' depended on developments in the labour market and welfare system: developments that were clearly linked to a range of government policies.

The flow of women onto the labour market in these years might be seen as facilitating the government's policy of labour market deregulation. The terms and conditions of employment can be changed more readily for new entrants than for an established workforce. Women, who often work for 'component wages', less than sufficient to sustain themselves let alone a family, and who have limited access to unemployment benefit in their own right, are vulnerable to the expansion of low paid and unregulated employment. However, other trends were more favourable. The tightening labour market in the later 1980s, combined with the long term trends towards higher and more continuous labour market participation by women, and higher educational achievement, raised the possibility of improvements for women workers.

These conflicting tendencies resulted in both further integration of women into the wage economy and continued and even intensified differentiation between women's and men's employment. These trends are reconciled by the equally strong evidence of polarisation within the female labour force. These three tendencies—integration, differentiation and polarisation—are explored in relation to women's employment, pay, working-time and participation.

In the final part of the chapter we consider the extent to which these trends were determined by the political and economic policies pursued by the Thatcher governments. Contradictions among the policies themselves meant that their consequences were not always as intended. Moreover, the effects of policy were superimposed on longer-term changes in family structure and women's roles, which by the early 1980s had a momentum of their own and which interacted with policy initiatives, again with perhaps unintended social consequences. Intended or not, however, the increased integration, continued differentiation and exacerbated polarisation of women in paid work constitute a palpable legacy for British women.

Towards Greater Integration?

Increasing integration of women into the waged employment system implies a convergence in male and female participation patterns, entry of women into a wider range of employment areas, and convergence of the terms and conditions under which men and women are employed.

Participation patterns

Between 1983 and 1990 women's employment grew by close to 2 million, compared to only 1.36 million for men (Table 11.1). The expectation of increased absolute and relative employment of women in the 1980s was thus fulfilled. Expansion of employment can be fed by increases in population, increases in participation rates or by decreases in unemployment. Table 11.2 shows the increases in employment for men, women, and for married and unmarried women, over this period decomposed into these three effects.

The sources of employment growth differ dramatically by gender. For men, the participation rate actually declined over this period and all the increase in employment is explained by decreasing unemployment (58.3%) and rising population (41.9%). For women, over two-thirds of the much larger increase in employment was fed by an increasing participation rate, while declining unemployment contributed 16% of the increase and rising population 14.7%. For married women the role of increased participation was even more marked, accounting for 81.7% of the total increase in employment. This increase in participation is evident in the 6 percentage point rise in female participation between 1983 and 1990 and the 9.6 percentage point rise for married women, in contrast to the virtual stagnation of male participation rates during the same period. A major gap still exists between the participation rates of men and women (75.5% compared to 53.2%) but nearly 22%

Table 11.1. Private household population (000s) by economic status in Great Britain 1983–1990.[a]

	1983	1990	Change 1983–1990
All persons aged 16 and over	42308	43838	1530 (3.6%)
Economic activity rate	60.8%	64.0%	3.2% (5.3%)
Economically active	25740	28037	2297 (8.9%)
In employment	22829	26168	3339 (14.6%)
Unemployed	2910	1869	−1041 (−35.8%)
Men	20278	21121	842 (4.2%)
Economic activity rate	75.7%	75.5%	−0.2% (−0.3%)
Economically active	15343	15944	601 (3.9%)
In employment	13497	14855	1358 (9.1%)
Unemployed	1846	1089	−757 (−4.1%)
Women	22029	22717	688 (3.1%)
Economic activity rate	47.2%	53.2%	6.0% (12.7%)
Economically active	10398	12094	1696 (16.3%)
In employment	9333	11313	1980 (21.2%)
Unemployed	1065	780	−285 (−26.8%)
Married women	13620[b]	14018	398 (2.9%)
Economic activity rate	49%	58.6%	9.6% (19.6%)
Economically active	6741	8208	1467 (21.8%)
In employment	6231	7749	1518 (24.4%)
Unemployed	510	459	−51 (−10.0%)
Unmarried women	8409[b]	8699	290 (3.5%)
Economic activity rate	43%	44.7%	1.7% (4.0%)
Economically active	3656	3886	230 (6.3%)
In employment	3101	3564	463 (14.9%)
Unemployed	555	321	−234 (−42.2%)

[a]Source: *Labour Force Survey.*
[b]Calculated by the authors.

of the difference in participation rates observed at the start of the period had disappeared by 1990. Not all of the increase in participation can be considered evidence of changes in women's labour force attachment or commitment; in part, the higher participation rates in the boom reflect the presence of disguised unemployment in the recession, particularly for married women. Such a rapid increase in participation must, however, also indicate increasing integration of women into waged employment.

Most of the increase in women's overall participation came from the rise in the participation rates of married women, particularly those with dependent children. The participation rate for women with dependent

Table 11.2. Contributions to changes in employment by sex and marital status 1983–1990.[a]

	Change in employment (000s)	Percentage contributions			
		Change in population	Change in activity rate	Change in unemployment rate	Residual
All persons	3339	24.8%	39.5%	33.2%	2.5%
Men	1358	41.9%	−2.4%	58.3%	2.3%
Women	1980	14.7%	66.8%	16.0%	2.6%
Married women	1518	12.0%	81.7%	4.2%	2.1%
Unmarried women	463	23.1%	22.0%	52.9%	2.0%

[a]Source: calculated from Table 11.1.

children rose between 1983 and 1988 from 46% to 56%, compared to a rise from 65% to 72% for those with no dependent children (Table 11.3). Participation rates are still markedly lower for women with preschool dependent children and also decline with number of children, although this effect is less marked than that by age of youngest child, in contrast to the pattern in France (Rubery, 1988). However, the strongest increase in participation in the 1983–1990 period, from 24% to 36%, was recorded for women with a youngest child aged less than 5 years after a period of stability in participation rates for these women (Humphries and Rubery, 1991). Preschool children thus appear to have become less of a constraint on participation in the 1980s, even though there were no institutional developments in the form of improved child-care facilities or maternity leave that could provide an explanation for this change in behaviour. The much publicised career-break schemes came too late in this period and applied to too limited an employment sector to influence these overall figures. This reduction in the period of absence from the labour market after childbirth again suggests that participation is becoming a more continuous feature of women's lives and that there is thus a marked trend towards convergence with the pattern for male workers. Women still tend to take breaks from employment for childbirth but the breaks are shorter and wage work a more permanent feature of women's life-cycle pattern.

Integration into occupations, industries and employment forms

The 1980s also witnessed women's wider representation in all types of employment, whether defined by employment status, occupation or

Table 11.3. Percentages of women of working age working full time, part time and unemployed 1983–1988.[a]

	1983	1988
With dependent children		
Working full time	14	19
Working part time	32	37
All working	46	56
Unemployed	5	4
No dependent children		
Working full time	46	51
Working part time	18	21
All working	65	72
Unemployed	8	5
Totals		
Working full time	31	37
Working part time	25	28
All working	56	65
Unemployed	6	5

[a]Source: *General Household Survey*, Office of Population Censuses and Surveys, HMSO, 1988.

industry. Women's involvement in self-employment, traditionally a male preserve, increased rapidly over the period 1981–1987, even faster than the rate of increase for men in this expanding part of the employment system. In the boom years of 1987–1989, the share of women who were self-employed stabilised, possibly in response to good employment opportunities in direct employment. Consequently, by the end of the period the share of women in total self-employment was higher than in 1981 but the same as that found in 1983 just after the start of the upsurge in self-employment. Nevertheless, nearly 300 000 more women entered self-employment.

Another measure of integration could be considered to be the share of women engaged in full-time work. While the share of women engaged in part-time work rose over the period as a whole, from 1987 onwards the share of part-time work in total female employment actually declined slightly as female full-time employment rose (Humphries and Rubery, 1991). It was female full-time employment that had declined particularly in the earlier recession and this strong growth in full-time work can be seen as both a recovery from that position and as evidence of further involvement of women in the mainstream of the economy. Integration necessarily implies increasing female employment shares within industries and occupations. No less than one-quarter of the total increase in female employment between 1983 and 1990 can be attributed to increasing employment share, even in a period when the impact of deindustrialisation and strong growth in service sectors necessarily favoured the employment of women independent of any rise in women's share within industrial sectors. Out of 43 industries women's employment share rose in 35, stayed the same in one and declined in seven. Table 11.4 gives absolute numbers for selected industries (figures for all 43 industries, together with percentage shares of male and female employment, are given in Humphries and Rubery, 1991).

The tendency for women's share to rise seems to have been relatively independent of employment trends within the industries, since women's share increased in both declining and expanding sectors. Nor was women's employment share dependent on the growth of part-time employment. Industries divided almost equally between those with declining and those with increasing part-time employment shares, but women's employment share rose in industries both with and without rising part-time employment. However, where female employment shares declined this usually coincided with declines in part-time working.

Evidence of integration is equally strong in the occupational data: women's employment share increased in 10 out of 14 occupations over the period 1983–1990. The largest percentage rise in female employment share was in managerial occupations, again evidence of the erosion of traditional barriers to women's employment.

Pay and conditions

The main thrust towards better pay and conditions for women relative to men came in the early 1970s, under the dual influences of the *Equal Pay Act* and the general narrowing of differentials associated with inflation and flat-rate wage increases. After the mid-1970s women's pay relative to men's for full-time jobs tended to stabilise and even decline. It was not until the mid-1980s that there was again evidence of an improvement in women's relative pay for full-timers. Perhaps the most surprising aspect of this development was that it was in the opposite direction to the trend in differentials between other low-paid and high-paid groups. In the 1980s youth to adult wage differentials, manual to nonmanual differentials, and lowest-decile to highest-decile ratios all declined, indicating an increase in inequality. The only significant movement in the opposite direction was the narrowing of average female to male full-time earnings ratios (from 72% to 77% of male hourly earnings). These findings suggest that the gains that full-time women employees made in the early 1970s have been consolidated into the pay structure, unlike the similar advances made by all groups of low-paid workers, and that far from these advances being reversed by the tendencies towards greater inequality in pay in the 1980s, there is evidence of yet further narrowing.

Table 11.4. UK employees in selected industries, June 1983 and September 1989.[a]

Industry	Male		Female				Total		Percentage change in employment 1983–1989
	1983	1989	1983		1989		1983	1989	
			All	Part-time	All	Part-time			
All industries and services	11670.2	12073.5	8901.4	3775.9	10689.2	4572.8	20571.5	22762.7	10.7
Energy and water supply	556.4	376.1	82.8	15.9	79.4	14.3	639.1	455.5	−28.7
Electricity, gas, etc.	126.2	171.9	28.7	6.4	52.0	10.9	154.9	223.9	44.6
Chemical industry	235.8	231.4	96.6	16.8	104.9	15.5	332.4	336.4	1.2
Office machinery	58.9	57.7	22.1	2.3	24.6	2.0	81.0	82.3	1.6
Electrical and electronic engineering	407.6	383.5	197.1	32.2	192.7	26.8	604.7	576.2	−4.7
Motor vehicles and parts	262.3	224.2	33.6	3.5	31.9	3.4	295.9	256.1	−13.5

Other transport equipment	283.8	221.9	34.5	4.2	28.9	2.6	318.3	250.8	-21.2
Food, drink and tobacco	358.0	321.6	240.8	85.4	235.9	82.9	598.8	557.4	-6.9
Textiles	122.7	115.7	116.1	20.1	98.9	16.7	238.8	214.7	-10.1
Footwear and clothing	75.2	82.6	210.7	33.4	218.7	27.9	285.9	301.3	5.4
Construction	898.6	950.0	116.9	49.4	142.3	56.9	1015.4	1092.4	7.6
Distribution	1868.5	2164.9	2168.7	1218.2	2613.6	1510.0	4037.2	4778.6	18.4
Hotel and catering	322.9	437.2	625.9	430.1	803.2	551.3	948.8	1240.4	30.8
Transport and communications	1065.1	1057.7	260.9	53.4	318.1	74.1	1326.0	1375.8	3.8
Postal services and tele-communications	321.7	323.8	102.4	21.2	116.9	29.0	424.1	440.7	3.9
Banking, finance and insurance	954.2	1309.0	893.7	223.4	1375.7	324.7	1847.9	2684.7	45.3
Public administration and defence	835.3	815.3	717.3	217.5	749.5	226.7	1552.6	1564.8	0.8
Sanitary services	123.0	144.8	185.6	165.6	238.2	200.4	308.6	383.0	24.1
Education	512.3	528.0	1022.7	579.1	1177.9	648.9	1535.1	1705.9	11.1
Medical and health services	261.0	272.7	986.2	440.0	1188.0	570.1	1247.2	1460.7	17.1

aSource: *Census of Employment*.

Integration through Differentiation?

Women through the 1980s increased their commitment to paid work, moved into a wider range of occupations and industries, especially managerial jobs, and maintained and improved upon the gains in relative pay for full-timers achieved in the 1970s. This evidence does not, however, demonstrate that for the majority of women the experience of the 1980s was towards convergence instead of divergence or differentiation relative to men's labour market experience and behaviour. Indeed, the continuation and in some areas intensification of differentiation by gender was as much a feature of the 1980s as were integration and convergence. Again this differentiation can be illustrated under the headings of participation, employment distribution and terms and conditions of employment.

Participation

The convergence of participation rates described above to some extent gives a false impression of increasingly similar labour market behaviour for men and women. While engaging in paid work is indeed an increasingly continuous feature of women's lives, there is still a marked change in the pattern of labour market participation at and after childbirth. Most women still quit the labour market to have children and return to part-time jobs, often at lower skill levels than the jobs they had previously occupied as full-timers. This downgrading effect has been found to be both widespread and continuous, in the sense that women do not tend to recover their occupational position even after their children are no longer dependent. There is thus a discontinuity in the female labour supply: those women who have not had children effectively participate in different types of jobs from those who have had children, although there is a growing minority of women who do continue their careers over the childbirth period.

Differentiation by occupation, industry and employment form

Despite the trends described above for women to increase their share of even male-dominated occupations and industries in the 1980s, women's employment patterns are still more notable for their divergence from those of men. Men's involvement in part-time work grew along with women's in the 1980s but by the end of the decade it still accounted for only 5% of total direct employment for men, compared to over 43% for women. Moreover, where men were engaged in part-time work, over 40% of the jobs were considered temporary, compared to only around one-eighth of women's part-time jobs. Men were only significantly involved in part-time work in the younger and older age ranges, while in Britain part-time work for women constitutes a stable form of employment in which women of all ages participate.

The increase in women in self-employment in the 1980s also needs to be interpreted with care. While there is evidence that more women became independent entrepreneurs, there is also the likelihood that much of the increase in female self-employment has served to accentuate the differences in women's economic and social roles. In Britain no distinctions are made in statistics between the self-employed and family helpers and most people can be expected to define their status by their fiscal categorisation, which in Britain is likely to include family helpers, mainly women. Even where women are in independent self-employment there is some evidence to suggest that entry into self-employment is associated with women's specific participation patterns; recent data show that entry rates are particularly high when women have been out of the labour force for over a year (Rubery *et al.*, 1991). The explanations could include both difficulties in re-entering direct employment and the search for a more flexible work environment to match domestic commitments. Moreover, women often set up businesses in areas which are traditionally female (catering, hairdressing, etc.). While one-quarter of new jobs for women were created as a consequence of women increasing their share of employment within individual industries, over one-half of the new jobs (53%) for women between 1983 and 1990 can be attributed simply to the general expansion of employment (holding women's shares within individual industries and the shares of industries within total employment constant), and a further 18% can be attributed to the changing composition of industries which has favoured women's employment. Discounting the general expansion effect does suggest that the increasing share of women within occupations accounted for more employment growth in this period than the switch towards service sector industries (25% compared to 18% of total employment growth). Nevertheless, most of the increase in female participation is accounted for by growth in employment opportunities in areas where women were already employed.

The increasing shares of women within industries cannot necessarily be interpreted as evidence of declining gender segregation. In practice, women's employment shares have risen within some industries because of the maintenance of gender segregation. This effect is particularly apparent in the declining heavy industries where job losses have been concentrated on manual male jobs, so that the feminised clerical areas account for a higher share of the remaining employment. The occupational data provide strong support for a view that women are moving into an ever wider range of occupations and making inroads into high-level jobs: over one-half of the total increase in jobs for women over the 1983–1990 period occurred in management and professional categories. Against this development must be placed the trend towards even higher levels of feminisation in certain job areas.

A further one-third of the new jobs for women were located in the clerical area, where feminisation increased from 75% to nearly 78%. Moreover, within the managerial and professional categories there is evidence that certain occupational areas may be becoming effectively feminised, and new occupational divisions within professions are emerging where women tend to cluster in less prestigious areas. Thus the process of desegregation observed may lead to a new pattern of gender segregation where there are new feminised occupations within the managerial and professional areas to add to the traditional ones associated with education and health care.

Pay and conditions

The significance of the gains made by full-time women workers in terms of relative pay in the 1980s has to be set against four factors. The first is the continuation of low pay relative to men as the norm for women in Britain, as compared to other European Community member states (Rubery, 1991). Particularly striking in this respect is the very low ratio of earnings of nonmanual full-time female employees in industry relative to men (54% compared for example to 66% and 69% in Germany and Italy). Thus marginal improvements in no way suggest that the role of women as a low-paid labour force has been eroded significantly. Second, much of the improvement for full-timers has been captured by higher-paid women. Those at the lowest decile of the earnings distribution have seen their earnings remain static relative to male median earnings, while those at the top of the distribution, at the highest decile point, have enjoyed large relative gains. Third, even the gains in average pay are largely a consequence of the change in employment distribution towards higher-paid nonmanual work. Within the nonmanual and the manual categories women's relative pay has increased only marginally. Finally and most importantly, the experience of part-timers has been in directly the opposite direction to that of full-timers. Hourly pay rates fell relative to (female and male) full-timers' hourly pay. The consequence of including part-time pay in the estimate for average female hourly earnings is to reduce the overall gains in relative female to male pay ratios from around five percentage points to three percentage points (instead of the ratio rising from 72% to 77% it rose from 67% to 70%). The terms and conditions of part-time employees thus deteriorated significantly over the decade. These pay differentials must also be set alongside poor provision of fringe benefits for part-timers. The only area where there is some improvement in such provision is in pensions, under pressure from European law, but for most part-timers low pay is compounded by low provision of benefits.

Another area where there is little evidence of convergence is in actual working hours. A recent survey of working hours found not only that a large share of women work part time but that there were large differences in the number of hours committed to work between male full-timers and female full-timers (Marsh, 1991). These extra hours worked by men reflected longer basic working weeks, overtime and longer travelling times. To the extent that access to overtime opportunities can be considered a source of extra earnings, the continuation and indeed intensification of these differences in working-time patterns in the 1980s as overtime working rose could be considered further evidence of discrimination against women. Evidence does suggest that women are less likely to gain access to overtime and are less likely to be rewarded for overtime or unsocial hours at a premium rate, largely because premia are less common in private services (Horrell and Rubery, 1991). However, to the extent that men are required to work long hours, and increasingly to work unpaid overtime hours within salaried jobs, these conditions could be seen to be disadvantageous towards men and to present an effective barrier to families who wish to change the domestic division of labour. Whatever the interpretation, it is clear that convergence of working time between men and women would have to involve a significant cut in men's working time as it would not be feasible or socially desirable for all adults to be working these very long hours. What is still not clear is the extent to which requirements for very long working time over and above the standard working day represent effective barriers to further desegregation of employment.

Towards Polarisation?

The combined trends towards integration and continued differentiation do not necessarily imply a move towards polarisation or divergence within the female labour force. Integration could be based on women entering differentiated or sex-segregated employment, but on a permanent basis and with reasonable terms and conditions. However, many of the trends described above in fact reveal an underlying tendency towards increasing divergence in the experience of women in the labour market, a divergence that might be considered in many respects to amount to polarisation of the female labour force. Again we will examine these tendencies under our three subcategories.

Participation

Polarisation in participation patterns implies the emergence of distinct patterns of participation with very different consequences for the labour market experience of the women concerned. While such a hypothesis cannot be fully tested here there is evidence to imply the development of a significant minority of women who may escape from the dominant form of participation, namely discontinuity at childbirth followed by participation in part-time and low-grade work. Much higher participation rates are recorded for women with high-level qualifications and although there is still a decline in participation for such women with dependent children, the effect is much less dramatic than among less qualified women.

For those women with degree-level qualifications the participation rates of those with children under 4 years was 61% compared to 85% for all women with degrees. In contrast, for women with no qualifications at all, the rate for those with young children was only 30% compared to 61% overall. It is also notable that the share of women working full time was much higher for those with high-level qualifications (24% for those with degrees compared to 4% for those with no qualifications). These two factors imply the existence of an educated group of women who are more likely to continue working and to work full time over the childbirth period, thereby avoiding the downgrading effect of discontinuous and part-time work.

Inequality within the female labour force is also increasing by region. The South East saw the largest percentage rise in participation in the 1980s despite starting with the highest participation ratio. Moreover, more women were employed in higher-level occupations in the South East and earnings for women in the South East rose significantly relative to average female earnings, especially for full-timers.

There is therefore evidence of a minority of well-educated women in the South enjoying high and continuous participation in full-time work at relatively high earnings levels. What is perhaps most surprising is that this group has emerged without the development of a social infrastructure to facilitate women's involvement in full-time work; child-care provision has in fact been cut in the 1980s rather than extended, and is considerably poorer than the European average. It may be the case, therefore, that even these women are paying a heavy price for their careers in terms of total hours of work including domestic labour, and in terms of private child-care costs. Thus the escape from the downgrading effect of time out of the labour market and return to part-time work is not necessarily costless, and we do not know to what extent these patterns of high participation have been fuelled by financial needs, particularly in relation to housing costs in the South East. Nevertheless, taking the life-cycle as a whole, the groups that remain on career paths are likely to enjoy considerable advantages relative to those who opt for leaving the labour force and subsequently working part time, and these advantages are likely to continue to increase even when both groups of women no longer have dependent children.

Occupations, industries and employment status

The polarisation hypothesis is supported by the increase in women working full time, as entrepreneurs and most importantly by the entry of women into managerial and professional jobs. To the extent that it is these occupational areas where 'enlightened' schemes to facilitate career breaks and/or childcare will be first introduced, this polarisation could be expected to continue and intensify over the life-cycle. However, to the extent that the long working hours associated with male-related jobs are imposed on women within these occupations, women will not under current domestic arrangements be able to sustain these jobs over the childbirth period, possibly forcing them into lower-grade jobs or stimulating the development of lower tiers of jobs within the managerial and professional areas, with less status and pay but shorter or more flexible working hours. The skills shortage at the end of the 1980s did stimulate some employers to search for new means of attracting back or retaining highly qualified staff. The onset of recession seems to have dissipated this interest but not necessarily solved the problem for employers of how to retain the services of female management and professional trainees who are becoming an increasingly large proportion of total management resources. This increase in the recruitment of highly qualified women seems to have come upon firms effectively by chance, as a consequence of their policy of recruiting highly qualified labour, of which women make up an increasing share. Firms invest considerably in the training of this sector of the labour force and may still have to come to terms with the need to adjust their employment policies to reduce losses and subsequent skill shortages.

At the other end of the spectrum women are still moving into low-grade and low-status jobs. The recent moves to implement equal value have demonstrated that women's jobs have a generally higher skill and job content than is indicated by their relative pay. Nevertheless, a recent survey of individuals' perceptions of their jobs and job content found that part-time jobs appeared to be less skilled (taking into account a whole range of factors) than either female full-time or male full-time jobs. There has been little development in Britain of high-grade part-time jobs and this forced choice for women between working full time in a career job or part time in a low-skilled job is likely to increase the divergence in women's labour market experience, even for women starting with similar qualifications and occupational attainment. Polaris-ation can apply within, for example, the highly educated female labour force if one group follows the traditional female pattern of participation and the other emulates that of men.

Pay and conditions

The polarisation thesis is well supported by the evidence on trends in pay differentials. Not only have women at the top end of the earnings spectrum gained relative to those at the bottom, taking full-timers alone, but the 45% or so of women in part-time work have seen their earnings decrease in relative terms over the period. These changes in the extent of inequality in the female earnings distribution are related to changing labour market conditions in the 1980s: the deregulation and fragmentation of the labour market, the dismantling of labour standards through the disappearance of industry-level agreements, the use of subcontracting in the public sector, and the weakening of the Wages Councils. The development of individualised and performance-related pay also provides new possibilities for opening up inequalities between men and women, as this type of payment system is found frequently in male-dominated employment areas, particularly management jobs, and may also be influenced by discriminatory tendencies. Much of the progress that women have made through the use of the concept of equal pay for work of equal value in securing fairer rewards for their work, may be undermined by the progressive development of performance-related pay.

However, a complicating factor is that because of women's increasing entry into managerial grades, and because performance-related pay appears to be spreading down the job hierarchy, it is also likely that a minority of women will benefit or are already benefiting from these changes. Thus these developments provide a basis for polarisation among women in earnings opportunities as well as a potential source of further earnings inequality compared with men. These developments are particularly likely in the public sector where women are relatively well represented at all levels of the hierarchy. The experience of wage determination in the public sector over the past decade has been in any case to generate widely different outcomes for different groups of women workers, with those in ancillary and manual jobs faring the worst (Brown and Rowthorn, 1990). The move towards more performance-related pay in higher-level jobs, including the civil service, and the development of independent pay scales and systems for all parts of the public sector, including individual schools and hospitals, is likely to result in both wider and more chaotic systems of differentials in which some women will lose and some will gain; if, as seems probable, the losers will be those at the bottom of the hierarchy and the gainers those at the top, the impact will be increasing divergence of pay within the public sector. At the same time the relative decline of the public sector compared to the private sector seems set to continue, so that even though managerial and professional staff may be gaining relative to manual and clerical grades within the public sector, they may still be losing out relative to private sector managerial and professional staff. These trends will have a gender dimension as women are likely to continue to be better represented in professional jobs in public service than in the private sector.

Summary

The three characteristics of women's employment over the past decade, those of integration, differentiation and polarisation, were also evident in the 1970s; the experience of the 1980s has thus been to accentuate these trends such that by the end of the decade it had become almost essential to distinguish between groups of women workers, for example between managerial and professional and other occupations, and between full- and part-time work, when analysing the evolving position of women in the labour market. Given the identification of such tendencies in the earlier period it becomes important to question to what extent the patterns we have observed are evidence of relatively autonomous social and economic change (Humphries and Rubery, 1984), that is, relatively independent of the specific economic and social policies pursued during this decade.

Impact of Economic and Social Policies

The trends we have identified in women's employment find their origins in relatively long-term, and indeed relatively autonomous changes in women's relationship both to the wage and to the family economy. In the absence of the long-term trends towards greater financial independence for women, greater reliance on more than one wage to maintain standards of living, and more unstable and diverse family patterns, and without the influence of feminism on attitudes to women's labour market participation, it is unlikely that the 1980s would have seen such dramatic increases in participation or in the numbers of well-qualified women entering the labour market, and thereby breaking down some of the barriers to entry to high-level jobs.

Certainly these changes in women's labour force participation were not the intended consequences of government policy. Moreover, without the increasing reliance on extra income to maintain family living standards, there would not be the pool of women available for low-paid part-time jobs in service sector employment. Without these 'supply-side' changes in behaviour and attitude, employers would have had to meet their employment needs in different ways in the 1980s. However, these longer-term changes interacted with the social and economic conditions of the 1980s and in particular with the specific social and economic policies pursued by the Thatcher administrations. These policies can be divided into three areas: general economic policy, labour market policy and social and family policy.

The general economic policy can be characterised as one of deindustrialisation; maintenance of a production sector or balancing the current account were not part of government economic philosophy or indeed effective strategy in the 1980s. This policy necessarily affected male manufacturing workers most in the recession of the early 1980s, and when the consumer or credit-led boom came in the latter part of the decade it was the service sector, where women predominate, that experienced relative employment and output growth. Another aspect of the general economic strategy was the adoption of a 'low-tech' or cheap-labour policy as the route to employment growth, instead of the high-productivity, high-value-added route favoured by many European competitors. The expansion of low-paid, part-time and low-skilled jobs was thus consistent with the economic policy of the period. Despite government attempts to coerce the unemployed to take up such jobs, this employment sphere remained largely the preserve of female labour. It is also probably the case that the changing economic climate in the 1980s further intensified the economic need for many women to go out to work. This need arose first in the face of redundancy, short-time and lack of overtime in the early 1980s, but was further fuelled by the rise in house prices and other costs associated with the credit boom of the latter period.

The government's sustained policy of deregulating, fragmenting and individualising the labour market had a multidimensional effect on women's employment position. The decreasing level of pay for part-timers was consistent with the policy of dismantling or weakening protection for the least well-organised workers, through the abolition of the fair wages clause and the adoption of compulsory competitive tendering in the public sector, through the weakening of Wages Councils and the dissolution of many national-level agreements which were used as guidelines for pay setting in small firms. These same policies also provided the potential for increasing inequality within the female labour market and the tendency to polarisation. Some women improved their relative pay significantly over the decade but these tended to be the higher-paid workers who may have benefited further from the trend to company-level pay determination and individualised performance-related pay. Thus the divergence in women's participation patterns and occupational distributions which may be associated more with long-term trends for women to improve their qualifications, led to even greater divergence in pay differentials because of the tendency for pay in part-time work to be depressed and pay in the upper parts of the nonmanual hierarchy to rise significantly. It is also arguable that government policy towards education and training fuelled the increase in women in high-level jobs. Skill shortages created by the absence of a training policy undoubtedly eased the entry of women into nontraditional areas.

Women's employment experience over the last decade was necessarily also influenced by policy towards the public sector. Women predominate in the caring or community service areas. All aspects of public sector employment were subject to continuous and intense changes over the decade. These effects were felt not only in direct terms and conditions for those who remained within the public service and even more so for those re-employed by contractors, but also in the pace and quality of work. Reduction in standards of provision has a negative impact on job satisfaction and it is notable that much of the industrial action taken in the caring services over the decade both involved women and emphasised quality of service. Women were also affected by changes in the private services sector, towards greater emphasis on marketing, image and 'customer care'. These policies can again be seen as part of the labour market policy of moving towards closer individual indentification with the company. While women have been seen as particularly appropriate to promote a caring image, the tendency towards emphasis on personal skills is double-edged. It preserved and opened up job opportunities but at the same time provided new opportunities for gender segregation and stereotyping, and indeed for subordination of the individual to the company image.

The final area of policy which could be expected to interact with women's longer-term orientation to paid work is that of social policy, and in particular policy towards the family. It is in this area that policy could be argued to have inhibited rather than enhanced these long-term trends, as the 1980s were characterised by a move away from policies which provide social support for working mothers. It is surprising to see dramatic rises in the participation of women with young children at a time when there were almost no advances and some reversals in child-care provision. Estimates of potential labour supply suggest that even more women would participate if child care was more readily available and also that many would increase their hours. Nevertheless, increased child-care provision has not proved to be a precondition for increased participation amongst women with young dependent children. Only the most vulnerable groups, in particular lone mothers, have been unable to escape the impact of these social policies on participation rates. Caught between a means-tested benefit system and the absence of child-care facilities, participation rates of lone mothers have in fact fallen, against all other trends.

These family and social policies were espoused partly for economic reasons, to facilitate the cutting of public expenditure, but also to strengthen the Conservative Party's image as supporter of the traditional family. That their social policies do not fit easily with their labour market policies of encouraging the growth of low-paid and part-time jobs which women are most likely to fill does not seem to have given the Thatcher governments undue anxiety. It might even be argued that the lack of coherence or consistency between parts of the government's policy inhibited a critical analysis of the overall policy stance, and support for the traditional family has been a cloak used to disguise an economic and employment policy based on the increasing participation of mothers in low-paid work.

Conclusions

The key characteristic of the 1980s was rising inequality. This inequality arose out of the economic and social policies pursued by the successive Thatcher governments. Tax cuts for some were paid for by reductions in public provision and worsening conditions of work for those employed to provide basic social services. Labour market deregulation in the name of efficiency was used to justify and legitimate higher pay for the already well-off, and lower pay for those most in need of wage protection. Although women were not consciously singled out by policy-makers, many of these changes in the social and economic environment had a particularly disadvantageous impact on women; it is women who predominate in low-paid jobs, who both work in the public sector and rely on its provision to provide support in their domestic role.

However, it would be wrong to identify the 1980s as a period of negative progress for all women in their search for economic and social equality. Although again in no sense a deliberate aim of policy, a group of women have been on the winning side in terms of the rising inequality; these women have entered higher-status jobs, have made significant gains in pay and, if located in the South East, have often been in families where both wage earners have enjoyed rapidly rising rewards. It is no longer possible to ignore this element of the female labour force and to talk in general terms of the experience of women through the decade, as if there were no differences by class, educational level or indeed region. The legacy of the Thatcher years has thus been as much an increase in inequality in life chances for women as the continuation and intensification of the disadvantaged position of women compared with men. These tendencies towards polarisation were already present before Thatcher but were intensified by the greater inequalities that appeared in the labour market as a whole over the decade.

However, before we conclude that the category of 'women' as a labour force group is no longer valid, and that there is a need to differentiate by other measures of inequality in the labour market, it must be remembered that even those women who appear to have made progress over the decade did so within a social and institutional environment which could at best be considered hostile to women's advancement. Absence of child-care facilities, a working culture where long hours are expected of those interested in pursuing a career, weak equal opportunities legislation and maternity rights and continued discrimination against offering good jobs, either on a full- or part-time basis, to women returners, hardly provides a 'female-friendly' environment. The increasing share of career-orientated women thus occurred against the odds, and with undoubtedly high costs in terms of women's ability to combine career and family aspirations. It would be too simplistic to write off the more advantaged and educated women as having overcome their labour market disadvantage. Many currently advantaged women will still become disadvantaged, in labour market terms, at a subsequent point in their life-cycle if they are unable to maintain their career when they have children. The absence of consciously supportive social policies continues to threaten all women. Labour market disadvantage is thus still a general gender problem and not one that can be considered to be covered by problems of social class, skill or qualifications. Moreover, we have yet to see the full effects of women's rapid entry into higher-level jobs; new dimensions of gender segregation and gender stereotyping may be developing such that we will need to retain the dimension of gender in all areas of employment for the foreseeable future.

Comment

Cause for Optimism?

Francis Green

The free-market ideology and policies of the Conservative government's period of rule may be characterised as supporting a low-wage accumulation path for capital located in Britain. Many of the well-known policies of Thatcherism were directed at undermining wages—including the trade union legislation, the onslaught on the public sector and the tolerance of mass unemployment. In this context, the increasing participation of women in the economy—traditionally much lower paid than men—appears to fit well into this conception of the path of capital accumulation in 1980s Britain.

This is, however, far from a smooth path, and two contradictions have presented themselves with some urgency. First, the dual economic role that increasing numbers of women are coming to play conflicts with the ideology of the family and with social policies which call upon the more traditional caring and socialising role required of women in families. Second, because of the traditional segregation of the labour force, with women concentrated in relatively few occupations, the rising number of low-paid women can have only a limited impact on men's pay. These issues raise the question of whether those who wish to see greater overall equality between men and women at work can be optimistic about current trends.

The evidence is clear that, during the Thatcher period, more and more women participated in the paid economy (as indicated by Humphries and Rubery), despite a lack of policy commitment to child care. By the end of the decade, over 43% of the employed labour force were women. What is less well established is how far women have been integrated across all occupations, industries and types of work. A good way of gauging this is to calculate an 'index of segregation' (Tzannatos, 1990). This index ranges in principle from 0 (if the proportions of women were the same in every occupation) to 100 (if all women were working in just one occupation). If women are becoming more integrated, the index should fall over time. I calculated the index among 350 occupations in 1984 and 1989 using the *Labour Force Survey*: it declined slightly from 69.7 to 65.5 over this period, giving some small support to the hypothesis that segregation is on the decline. However, the period is too short to reach any conclusion about longer-term trends.

If women have increasingly been substituted for men because they cost less to employ, to what extent has this trend reduced their pay disadvantage by raising their pay relative to men? The answer is, not much if at all. From 1979–1990 the average hourly rate of full-time females as a proportion of that of males rose just from 70.4% to 71.3% for manual workers, and from 62.1% to 63.6% for nonmanual workers. These are minuscule shifts in over a decade. While some improvement occurred for the average woman owing to the shift from manual to nonmanual jobs, as indicated by Humphries and Rubery, taken together with the deteriorating position of part-time women it is hard to interpret these findings with any degree of optimism.

There is also another reason for pessimism in the failure of the education and training systems to integrate young women more widely across the labour force. There is evidence that, at least during the early and mid-1980s, female workers suffered discriminatory lack of access to training. More important, however, was the degree of segregation to be found in both private and government training schemes. The Youth Training Scheme, for example, tended to concentrate resources for young women on training in areas such as clerical work. In other words, much of the training reproduced existing segregation. Efforts to break into traditionally male areas of work were few and far between. Also worrying is the way in which the relatively new and skilled world of computing is beginning to be monopolised by boys in schools and later at work.

Training is an area where the government's policies worked specifically against the integration of women. Most notably the TOPS training programmes in the 1970s, with their open access, were of great benefit to women, and the training they received was not just of the low-level Youth Training Scheme kind: it included, for considerable numbers of women, substantive high-level skills training. The numbers on TOPS programmes were wound down through the 1980s and eventually TOPS was replaced in 1988 by ET, a system of low-skill training with access only for the long-term unemployed, with relatively few women.

All told I remain pessimistic about the prospects for women in the paid economy: they appear likely on current trends to remain a largely segregated part of the workforce and to remain low paid. A minimum wage law would undoubtedly be of benefit to many women; just as important is an education and training policy that maximises the opportunity for high-skill training and not just in what are traditionally women's areas of work.

PART IV

The Economic and Political Legacy

The Economic and Political Legacy

12

Government Spending and Taxation in the Thatcher Era

Bob Rowthorn

This chapter examines the legacy of the Thatcher government in the realm of public expenditure and taxation. It is not concerned primarily with macroeconomic management—although a few passing remarks are made on the subject—but with the impact of government expenditure and taxation policy on public services and the distribution of income. The chapter also discusses briefly how an alternative government during the 1980s might have behaved with regard to public expenditure, and what this would have meant for taxation. It concludes that under a Labour, or Heath-style Tory government the level of public expenditure would have risen significantly faster and that higher taxes would have been required to finance this growth. Even so, the share of taxes in GDP would still have been quite low by continental European standards.

The International Context

In 1969 the UK had the third highest ratio of government spending (including transfer payments) to GDP in the Western World and was surpassed only by the Netherlands and Sweden (Figure 12.1). The country now has one of the lowest ratios in the whole of Europe and the lowest in the European Community. Relative to GDP, government expenditure in the UK has actually fallen slightly since 1969. In every other Western country the ratio has risen substantially over this period. The picture is similar for taxes and other kinds of government revenue. The ratio of government revenue to GDP in the UK is now much the same as it was 20 years ago, whilst in most other countries there has been a large increase. At one time Britain was one of the most highly taxed of all OECD countries. This situation has changed dramatically, and the overall share of taxes is now well below that of most comparable European countries.

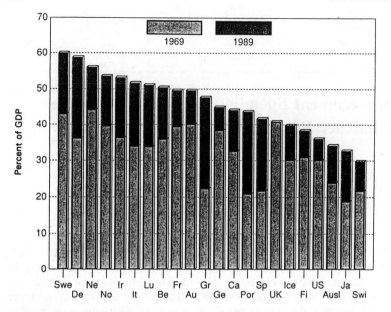

Figure 12.1. OECD general government outlays as a percentage of GDP 1969–1989.
Source: *OECD Economic Outlook.*

The transformation just described is entirely the result of developments which occurred under the Thatcher administration from around 1982 onwards. At that time, both government expenditure and revenue in the UK were almost exactly equal to the European Community average as a percentage of GDP; since then, the ratio of government expenditure to GDP has fallen sharply in the UK but has remained virtually constant in the rest of Europe (Figure 12.2). There is a similar contrast in the case of government revenue, which has fallen significantly as a percentage of GDP in the UK since 1982 but has remained roughly stable elsewhere in Europe.

Expenditure and Taxation in the Thatcher Era: An Overview

When the Thatcher administration took office in 1979, it faced two major problems in the sphere of public finance. First, there was a long-standing budget deficit which reflected the fact that public spending had been substantially greater than revenue throughout most of the previous decade (Figure 12.3). Second, the Tories had committed themselves before the election to measures that would make this deficit worse. They had promised to honour the findings of the Clegg Commission which recommended large pay rises for public employees,

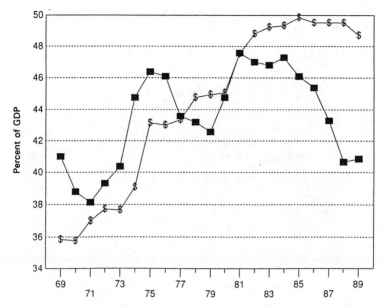

Figure 12.2. General government outlays in the European Community as a percentage of GDP 1969–1989: —$—, EC (excluding the UK); —■—, UK. Source: *OECD Economic Outlook*.

whose relative earnings had fallen well behind those in the market sector of the economy during the later 1970s. They had also promised to cut income taxes, not just for top earners but also for those lower down the scale. In addition, shortly after taking office, the Tories own anti-inflationary policies helped to provoke a severe economic slump which simultaneously reduced government revenue and increased expenditure on unemployment and other Social Security benefits.

Faced with this combination of an already large budget deficit, rising expenditure and a shrinking tax base, the Thatcher administration responded by raising indirect tax rates and levying new taxes. National Insurance contributions were raised, VAT was increased and special levies were placed on the North Sea oil companies who were enjoying huge profits at the time because of high world oil prices. These measures did not by any means eliminate the budget deficit but they did prevent it from mushrooming out of control.

It has been argued that the tax increases imposed in the early years of the Thatcher administration were unduly harsh (Maynard, 1988; Britton, 1991). Such large increases, it is claimed, exacerbated and helped to prolong the economic recession already underway. Moreover, from a fiscal point of view, they were not required. The government was in a relatively strong asset position and could have sustained a

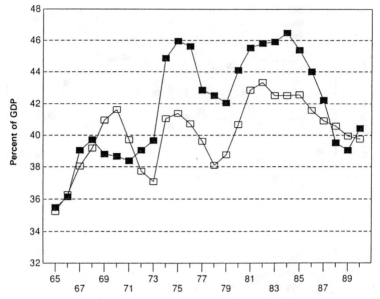

Figure 12.3. UK general government expenditure and revenue as a percentage of GDP 1965–1990: —■—, expenditure; —□—, revenue.
Source: *UK National Accounts.*

significantly greater deficit without immediate risk of a financial crisis. There is some truth in these claims. The slump would have been less severe if fiscal policy had been more expansionary, especially if this had been complemented by a more expansionary monetary policy. It is also true that the government was in a relatively strong asset position. Under the previous Labour administration, inflation had dramatically reduced both the real value of existing government debt and the real cost of new borrowing. As a result, despite large government deficits throughout most of the 1970s, net financial liabilities of the UK public sector had actually fallen in real terms during this period (Table 12.1). Indeed, these developments continued for a time under the new Thatcher administration which initially enjoyed the fiscal advantages of rapid inflation and negative real interest rates (Figure 12.4). By 1981, net public sector financial liabilities had fallen to about 35% of GDP, which is not unduly large by international standards. Moreover, the public sector had massive holdings of tangible assets in the form of dwellings, buildings, roads, railways, vehicles, plant and equipment. On paper, these were worth more than three times the value of the sector's financial liabilities. Part of these could have been sold to pay off some of the financial debt, as indeed actually happened in the course of time.

Thus, the government's asset position was fairly strong in the early

Table 12.1. UK public sector net financial liabilities 1975–1989.[a]

Year	£ billion	£ billion (1985 prices)[b]	Percentage of GDP
1975	45.9	127.9	43.4
1979	74.0	123.3	37.3
1981	88.9	111.4	34.9
1983	121.7	134.6	40.0
1987	141.4	130.1	33.6
1989	131.5	106.1	25.6

[a]Source: *UK National Accounts 1988, 1990.*
[b]Conversion to 1985 prices uses the GDP deflator.

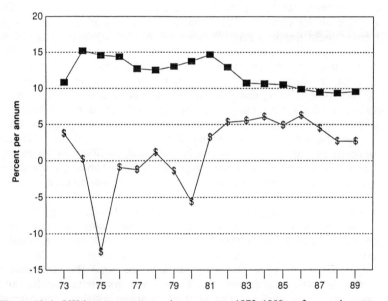

Figure 12.4. UK long-term pre-tax interest rates 1973–1989: —$—, real; —■—, nominal.
Source: *OECD Historical Statistics.*

1980s and the budget deficit could certainly have been larger without risk of an immediate financial crisis. However, there were underlying dangers in the situation, which in the medium term would eventually have forced the government to cut back the deficit quite severely. The ability of British governments to run a large deficit during the 1970s was predicated on the fact that rapid inflation made real interest rates,

266   *Bob Rowthorn*

and hence the real cost of government borrowing, negative. This happy
state of affairs could not last. The Thatcher government was pledged
to bring inflation down using monetary restraint as a central instrument.
Such a policy was followed by many OECD countries during the 1980s
and the result has been a universal and massive increase in real interest
rates. The turnaround in Britain came in 1981 and over the next 7 years
real rates of interest were in the region of 5–6%. Even allowing for
some tax clawback on government interest payments, real rates of
interest at this level make government borrowing extremely expensive.
They place severe constraints on fiscal policy and normally rule out a
'primary' deficit as a permanent instrument of policy (primary deficit
denotes budget deficit excluding net interest payments). For short
periods of time, in the depths of recession, governments may tide
themselves over by borrowing to finance their regular expenditures on
services and transfer payments, but most of the time they must finance
these expenditures out of their own revenue. Any other policy is likely
to cause an explosive growth of public debt culminating eventually in
a government financial crisis.[13]

When the UK moved into an era of high real interest rates in the
1980s, large budget deficits were no longer sustainable. There was no
need for the Tories to raise taxes as much as they did in the depths of
the recession in 1981, and the government deficit could certainly have
been larger for a time. However, this was only a temporary option and
in the longer term the government would have been forced to cut back
severely the scale of its borrowing. Whilst the timing of the Thatcher
administration in raising taxes can be criticised, its objective of greatly
reducing government borrowing was probably correct given the transition
to an era of high real interest rates in the UK and elsewhere.

Having dealt with the immediate budgetary situation by means of
selective tax increases, the Thatcher government then turned its attention
to longer-term issues. Its main objectives in the sphere of fiscal policy
were to reduce the overall rate of taxation from its new peak—especially
taxes on people with high incomes—and to eliminate the remaining
budget deficit, thereby removing entirely the need for government
borrowing. These objectives were pursued systematically for the
remainder of the decade. The method of achieving them was simple
enough. Government expenditure was held down by every politically
feasible means, and the additional tax revenue generated spontaneously
as the economy began to recover from the 1979–1981 slump was
channelled into tax cuts or used to reduce government borrowing. In
addition, land, council housing and nationalised industries were sold
off to raise money. Technically speaking, to reduce the need for overt
borrowing by selling assets does not represent a genuine improvement
in public sector finances, since it is merely operating on one side of the
balance sheet instead of another, by swapping assets for liabilities. This
is what Harold MacMillan was getting at when he accused the Thatcher

government of 'selling off the family silver'. Still, it was useful window-dressing which allowed the government to finance tax cuts at no apparent cost.

The Restraint of Government Expenditure

The measures used to contain expenditure affected many areas of government activity, although with varying severity. Margaret Thatcher and her ministers repeatedly claimed that her government was 'spending more real resources' on public services than ever before in British history. Although strictly speaking this claim was correct in its own terms, it was confusing on two counts. First, the use of the word 'real' was misleading. Second, although public spending on services was rising, its growth was inadequate compared both to need and to what the country could afford given the rapid growth of national output and income during the later years of the Thatcher administration.

The government's use of the term 'real resources' still causes confusion so let us examine what it means. This is best done by means of an example: it is highly artificial but it makes the point. Consider a school which employs only teachers and makes no use of either buildings or equipment. Suppose that teachers receive a pay increase which allows them to enjoy a 15% higher standard of living. At the same time, the number of teachers is cut by 10%. The combined effect of these changes is to increase total 'real' expenditure on teachers' salaries by 5% (15% − 10%). Faced with this situation, government ministers will claim that the 'real' resources devoted to education have been increased by 5%, even though the number of teachers employed has actually fallen by 10%. From the point of view of cost to the government, and ultimately the taxpayer, 'real' expenditure is what matters and ministers are right to take this into account. As far as quality of service is concerned, however, the volume of inputs is also of central importance (number of staff, materials, etc.). As we have just seen, the behaviour of this item may be quite different from that of 'real' expenditure as understood by the government. As a general rule, the volume of inputs into any government activity will rise more slowly than 'real' expenditure. Indeed, as the example shows, the volume of inputs may actually fall whilst 'real' expenditure is rising.

Table 12.2 shows what happened to government spending over the period 1979–1990. Information is provided for the government as a whole, and for health and education separately. For comparison, the behaviour of GDP is also shown. In current prices, general government consumption (expenditure on wages, salaries, materials, etc.) rose by 182.7% over the period, which is slightly more than the increase of 178.0% in GDP. The government procedure for converting these changes into 'real' terms is to deflate them by using the GDP implicit

Table 12.2. UK general government consumption 1979–1990.[a]

	Health[b]	Education[c]	All general government	GDP
Expenditure				
At current prices	308.1	244.5	282.7	278.0
In 'real' terms[d]	139.6	110.8	128.1	126.0
At constant 'own' prices[e]	113.7	99.5	113.6	126.0
Price indices				
GDP deflator	220.7	220.7	220.7	220.7
'Own' price deflator	270.9	245.7	248.8	220.7

[a]Source: *UK National Accounts*. All figures relative to 1979(=100).
[b]Refers to central government only.
[c]Refers to local government only.
[d]Expenditure at current prices deflated by the GDP deflator: this is the measure cited by the Thatcher government to indicate the real cost of government services.
[e]Expenditure at current prices deflated by the 'own' price deflator: this is the measure used in the *National Accounts* to indicate the volume of inputs used in providing government services.

price deflator. When this is done, it emerges that the 'real' growth of government consumption was 28.1% as compared to an increase of 26.0% in real GDP. These figures appear to support ministerial claims at the time that 'real' government expenditure on goods and services had risen faster than GDP. However, these claims ignore the fact that much of the 'real' growth in government expenditure was simply a reflection of increased wages and salaries for government employees. Although they have sometimes lagged behind those in the private sector, the real earnings of most government workers have risen substantially since 1979. This has pushed up the 'real' cost of government activities in addition to any increase that arises from genuine expansion in the scale of these activities. To eliminate this distortion, the official *National Accounts* use a quite different approach from that employed by government ministers. They measure the volume of inputs into government activities by number and type of employees, amount of materials purchased, etc. The resulting measure (line 3 of Table 12.2) indicates that the volume of current inputs used by the government rose by only 13.6% over the period 1979–1990. This is well under half of the figure indicated by the 'real resource' measure used by government ministers.

The contrast is especially striking in the case of education. The amount of 'real resources' devoted to education rose by 10.8% over the period 1979–1990. However, this rise was entirely explained by the increased salaries of teachers and other employees. When the effect of this factor is eliminated, the overall change in educational expenditure is actually negative (−0.5%). This virtually stationary overall figure reflects two offsetting factors. There has been a decline in the number of people employed in state education but at the same time an increase in the volume of inputs purchased from outside the sector.

An interesting feature is the relatively fast growth in expenditure on the National Health Service. Even after allowing for the distorting effect of wage and salary increases, the volume of inputs (employees, materials, etc.) used in this sector rose by 13.7% over the period 1979–1990. As will be seen below, this relatively favourable treatment of the NHS as compared to most other government services shows up in almost every indicator of expenditure.

Figures 12.5 and 12.6 plot the growth of government consumption since 1969, measured in 'own' prices. This measure eliminates the distorting effect of cost increases that arise from higher salaries and the like. It is the measure used in the *National Accounts* and provides a good indication of the volume of current inputs used in government activities. Between 1969 and 1979, government consumption, private consumption and GDP all rose by virtually the same amount. Over the 1980s as a whole, GDP growth was faster than previously but this

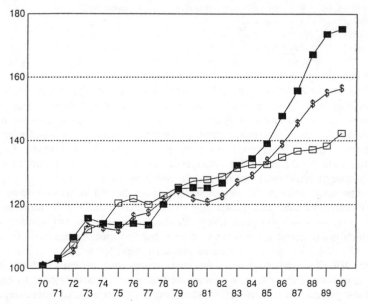

Figure 12.5. UK consumption and gross domestic product at constant 'own' prices 1970–1990: —$—, GDP; —■—, private consumption; —□—, government consumption.
Source: *UK National Accounts.*

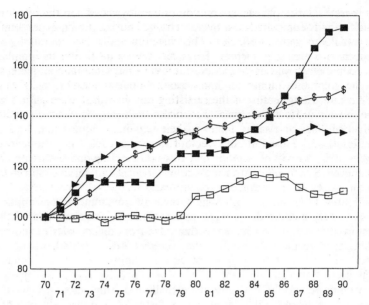

Figure 12.6. UK government and private consumption at constant 'own' prices 1970–1990: —■—, private consumption; —$—, public health; —▶—, public education; —□—, military.
Source: *UK National Accounts.*

improvement was not used to finance a more rapid expansion of government activities. On the contrary, the growth rate of government consumption declined, whilst private consumption accelerated dramatically. These Figures reveal two striking features of the later Thatcher period: severe restraint of public expenditure at a time of rapid output growth, and a massive boom in private consumers' expenditure. Even military expenditure, after a major build-up in the earlier part of the Thatcher period, was cut back quite severely in later years.

The restraint of public expenditure is also reflected in the behaviour of government employment. A study of 19 countries by OECD statisticians reveals that, over the period 1979–1989, the UK was the only country in which government employment actually fell in absolute numbers (Oxley *et al.*, 1990, Table 12). All other countries reported an increase, and in the OECD as a whole government employment rose by nearly 10% during this period. The picture is similar for the share of government in total employment. This share fell in three other countries—Australia, Japan and the US—but the decline was much greater in the UK. In most countries the government share of employment rose over the period 1979–1989, often by a considerable amount.

The effects of public expenditure restraint are also visible in the field of capital investment. Most types of public investment were either cut back or had their growth severely constrained during the 1980s. Amongst the worst hit were public housing, education and public infrastructure such as sewers, where there was little new construction and repairs were frequently neglected. The result was widespread and visible decay in some of these areas. In the case of housing, local councils were forced to sell-off many of their existing dwellings but were prevented from using more than a small fraction of the resulting income to build new dwellings or even to upgrade their remaining stock.

Figure 12.7 plots the behaviour of investment in some of the main areas of government activity and also in the business sector of the economy. From 1983 onwards there was a marked upswing in business investment (much of it in distribution and finance). Neither education nor public housing shared in this boom and throughout the entire period investment in these areas remained depressed. The chart also shows the relatively good treatment of the NHS; investment was inadequate

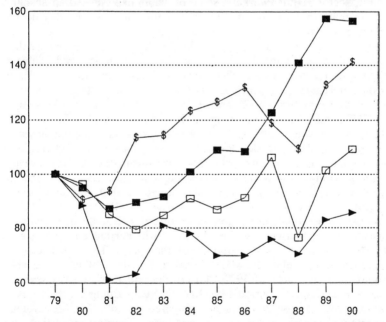

Figure 12.7. Gross domestic UK capital formation at constant 'own' prices 1979–1990. Business (—■—) includes all private sector and public corporations except for dwellings; public housing (—▶—) excludes transactions in land and existing dwellings; public health (—$—) and public education (—□—) figures are derived from current values deflated by the implicit price index for investment in public housing.
Source: *UK National Accounts*.

both in relation to need and to what the country could afford, but it fared noticeably better than other sectors such as public housing or education.

Perhaps the most contentious area of public expenditure during the 1980s was the pay of government employees (this topic is covered at length in Brown and Rowthorn, 1990). The policy of the government in this area was highly selective. In line with Thatcherite philosophy, top administrators, army generals, judges and the like received massive pay rises. Police and fire-fighters also did well because of pre-existing pay formulae that linked their earnings to the national average. These formulae were negotiated under the previous Labour administration and the Tories could theoretically have repudiated them but the resulting conflict would have been too costly. In particular, given their plans to confront the coal miners and other militant workers, the Tories were anxious to keep the police on their side. Others who did relatively well were health service professionals such as doctors and nurses, who obtained very large salary increases. At the other end of the scale were public sector manual workers, some of whom experienced an absolute fall in real earnings over the Thatcher period as a whole, despite the impressive growth in average earnings in the economy at large. For some of these unfortunates, the reduction in pay occurred whilst they were still employed in the public sector; for others, it occurred following their transfer to private subcontractors. These contrasts are clearly visible in Table 12.3 which shows the behaviour of real earnings of selected groups from 1972 onwards. Some public sector workers, such as NHS auxiliaries, were earning less in real terms in 1990 than in 1972! The unfavourable treatment of lower-grade workers in the public sector to some extent mirrors developments in the private sector, where there has been a general widening of differentials during the 1980s. However, even in comparison with similar workers in the private sector, the position of many lower-grade public sector employees deteriorated during this period.

Most professionals in the public sector did well under the Thatcher government, either because this was in line with current Tory philosophy or else because of public support for their case. The one exception were teachers of all kinds, who did uniformly badly. Following the large comparability awards of 1979–1981, the pay of teachers was severely restrained. Over the period 1981–1990 the real earnings of the average school teacher rose by 12% as compared to 26% for the average nonmanual worker in the economy at large. Teachers in further and higher education fared as badly or even worse.

Health and education

The two most important government services, both in terms of their cost and political significance, are undoubtedly health and education.

Table 12.3. Percentage earnings changes of selected groups 1972–1990.[a]

Group	Real earnings			Relative earnings[b]		
	1972–1980	1980–1981	1981–1990	1972–1980	1980–1981	1981–1990
Teachers	−10	12	12	−25	15	−8
Police	22	3	29	1	6	6
Nurses	18	11	24	−2	14	2
Armed forces	5	−2	3	−13	1	−16
NHS ancilliaries	2	−1	−7	−16	2	−24
Central government manual	−5	13	3	−21	17	−15
Local authority	1	−0	11	−16	3	−9
Town hall staff	−18	7	2	−32	10	−17
Civil servants	−0	6	3	−17	9	−15
Public nonmanual	1	7	12	−16	10	−9
Public manual	0	1	2	−17	4	−16
All public	1	6	10	−16	9	−10
Whole economy						
Nonmanual	17	−1	26	−2	2	3
Manual	21	−6	14	0	−3	−7
All workers	20	−3	22	0	0	0

[a]Sources: *National Institute Economic Review, New Earnings Survey.*
[b]Compared to average earnings.

These were the subject of bitter contention throughout the whole period of the Thatcher governments and remain so under the administration of John Major. Their treatment under the Tories presents an instructive contrast and shows clearly the influence of politics over government decision-making. On almost every indicator considered so far, be it investment, employment or the pay of professional staff, the NHS fared better than public education. Other indicators confirm this impression. Table 12.4 compares public expenditure on health and education within the European Community (Oxley *et al.*, 1990). Between 1979 and 1988 *per capita* expenditure on health by the UK government rose by 0.9% a year according to the measure shown in the Table. This was one of the lowest rates of growth in the European Community but at least it was an increase. In education, however, the OECD measure indicates a substantial fall in real expenditure per student in the UK as compared to an increase in most other European countries. Such a large reduction is surprising and conflicts with other evidence. Even so, it is consistent with the cinderella status of education under the Thatcher governments, both in comparison with other countries and with other public services.

Table 12.4. Education and Health: real *per capita* spending in the European Community (average annual rates of growth).[a]

Country	Education[b] 1980–1988	Health[c] 1979–1988
Belgium	4.3	2.3
Denmark	−1.4	0.8
France	1.9	3.7
Germany	4.8	1.3
Greece	0.8	6.0
Ireland	−0.8	−2.0
Italy	3.2	2.5
Netherlands	0.2	4.9
EC average (excluding UK)[d]	1.6	2.4
United Kingdom	−1.8	0.9

[a]Source: Oxley *et al.* (1990).
[b]Average spending per student.
[c]Spending per head of population covered by the public health insurance system.
[d]Unweighted average of 8 countries.

Table 12.5 shows what has happened to employment in the NHS since 1971. Up to 1979 there was rapid growth in most areas. Within the space of 8 years the number of general practitioners rose by more than 15%, the number of nurses and hospital doctors by approximately 30% and the number of clerical and 'professional and technical staff' by 50%. Amongst ancilliaries and other staff there was also some growth. Since 1979, growth in all but the last group has continued quite rapidly, although at a slower pace than during the spectacular expansion of the 1970s. The one exception is the category 'ancilliary and other staff', whose numbers directly employed in the NHS have fallen by one-third. These are the workers who have borne the brunt of the government's privatisation programme. Significantly, they are also the health workers who have fared worst in terms of pay. They are the hidden people, whose interests and contribution to the NHS have been largely forgotten in the vigorous, and partly successful, battle to defend the service. Many of them have lost their jobs in the NHS altogether, whilst others continue to work in the service but are now employed by private contractors under worse conditions than previously.

Table 12.6 shows what happened in state schools over the period 1971–1989. In the 1970s the number of teachers rose by almost 20%, with the result that class sizes in almost every type of state school fell dramatically. Since 1979 demographic factors have led to a considerable decline in the number of children attending state schools. This could

Table 12.5. Employment (000s) in the National Health Service 1971–1989.[a]

Sector	Great Britain		United Kingdom		
	1971	1975	1975	1979	1989
Regional and District Health Authorities					
Medical and dental (including locums)	33	39	43[b]	47	55
Nursery and midwifery (excluding agency staff)	344	406	420	449	509
Professional and technical	48	57	59	74	100
Administrative and clerical	79	106	109	122	149
Ancillary and other staff	248	256	266	272	187
Total	752	863	897	965	1000
Family Practitioner Services	44	47	48	52	602

[a]Source: *Social Trends*. Figures for family practitioner services are numbers, all other figures are full-time equivalents.
[b]Estimate.

Table 12.6. Selected education statistics for the public and private sectors 1971–1989.[a]

	1971	1981	1989
Public sector schools[b]			
Number of pupils (000s)	9472.8	9749.1	8272.9
Number of teachers (000s)	408.6	512.0	453.0
Pupil/teacher ratios			
Public sector schools:			
Nursery	26.6	21.5	21.6
Primary	27.1	22.3	21.9
Secondary	17.8	16.4	15.0
All public sector schools	23.2	19.0	18.3
Private schools	14.0	13.1	11.3
Special schools	10.5	7.4	6.1

[a]Sources: *Annual Abstract of Statistics, Social Trends*.
[b]Teachers and pupils are measured in full-time equivalents.

have provided the opportunity for further major reductions in class size. However, the government did not follow such a course. Instead, it cut the number of teachers by approximately 10%, with the result that average class sizes in both nursery and primary schools remained virtually constant. Average class size continued to fall in secondary schools but this may be largely a compositional effect that reflects the increasing proportion of children staying on at school in the sixth form. The experience of private schools provides an interesting contrast. The average class size has always been much lower in the private sector than in state schools but during the 1970s the gap was diminishing. During the 1980s, however, the gap widened once again as progress in the state sector was halted whilst class sizes continued to fall in the private sector.

The contrasting experience of health and education under the Thatcher administration highlights the role of politics in government decision-making. The relatively favourable treatment of the NHS during the 1980s is due to the enormous popular support this service enjoys and to the resulting political pressures on the government. Despite Margaret Thatcher's pledge that 'the National Health Service is safe in our hands', there is little doubt that her government would have privatised much of the NHS and starved the service of public funds, if such a course had been politically feasible. However, this was never a feasible option because of the vigorous defence of the NHS by doctors, nurses and other health employees who formed a united front to mobilise popular support for the service. They were not able to prevent reform of its operation but they were able to mobilise sufficient popular enthusiasm to ensure significant, if inadequate, growth in its funding.

In the case of education the situation was very different. Disunity and squabbling amongst the numerous trade unions and professional organisations in this sector allowed the government to deflect much popular discontent with the quality of education onto the teachers themselves. This allowed the government to restrain educational expenditure in a way which would have been very difficult if employees in the sector had presented a united front as had their counterparts in the NHS. Of course, this is not the only factor but it is certainly an important reason for the neglect of education under the Thatcher government.

Social Security benefits

Alongside its policy towards the public services, the Thatcher government also took a harsh line towards Social Security benefits. Entitlements to certain types of benefit were progressively reduced. Out of 38 significant changes in the rules governing entitlement to Social Security benefits available to the unemployed during 1979–1988, 23 were unfavourable to the unemployed and most of the rest were broadly neutral in their impact (Atkinson and Micklewright, 1989). The effect of these changes in coverage was to reduce the amount of Social Security payments to the unemployed by an estimated £510 million a year. The unemployed were not alone in having their entitlements reduced under the Thatcher government. The disadvantaged of almost every variety were affected by changes in the rules governing payments, for example the replacement of discretionary grants by loans for occasional items such as cookers and the like. Another area in which cuts occurred was the system of State Earnings Related Pensions (SERPs), which had been introduced by the preceding Labour government. The Thatcher government was hostile to them for both ideological and financial reasons. In 1986 the benefits offered by this scheme were reduced and financial inducements were given to people to contract out of the state scheme and adopt private alternatives (Atkinson, 1991).

Important as they were for the individuals affected, changes in the regulations governing benefit entitlements and the operation of SERPs were relatively small in terms of overall expenditure. The major cost-saving innovation in this area concerned the principles governing the uprating of Social Security benefits as a whole. Throughout the post-War period it had been an explicit policy of governments, Labour and Tory alike, that the fruits of economic growth should be widely dispersed in the population. Most Social Security benefits were systematically raised in line with real earnings, thereby increasing their real value as the economy grew richer (Atkinson, 1990). Indeed, under the 1970s Labour government a number of social benefits, such as Child Benefit and the basic old age pension, rose significantly faster than average earnings (Table 12.7).

The Thatcher government rejected this entire philosophy, and the previous link between benefit levels and national prosperity was almost completely broken. Instead of uprating benefits in line with average earnings, from 1979 onwards the vast bulk of them were increased only in line with inflation. The main exceptions were the Mobility Allowance and One-Parent benefit, whose real values rose by 12.2% and 8.0% respectively between the last Labour revision in November 1978 and the first post-Thatcher revision in 1991. Most other benefits remained roughly constant in real terms throughout this period. One exception was Child Benefit, which rose considerably in the early years of the Thatcher regime but then fell back again in real terms in the later part of the decade. After these ups and downs, the real value of Child Benefit for a two-child family in 1991 was virtually the same as in 1978.

Most social scientists agree that poverty in advanced societies is in large degree a relative matter. In the words of Donnison, former chairman of the Supplementary Benefit Commission, every age produces its own kind of poverty. Patterns of living change and yesterday's luxuries become today's necessities. This is not simply because peoples' aspirations for themselves and their families change. It is also because

278

Bob Rowthorn

Table 12.7. Selected UK Social Security benefits 1964–1991.[a]

Benefit	March 64	Nov. 69	Oct. 73	Nov. 78	Apr. 90	Apr. 91
Real purchasing power (November 1978 = 100)						
Basic Pension:						
Single	64.0	74.6	83.2	100.0	98.7	102.8
Couple	64.5	75.5	83.9	100.0	98.8	102.9
Basic Unemployment Benefit:						
Single adult	79.2	92.4	97.7	100.0	97.3	101.4
Child Benefit:						
1st child	0.0	0.0	0.0	100.0	99.2	106.1
2nd child	49.3	87.3	62.8	100.0	99.2	93.2
Two children	24.6	43.6	31.4	100.0	99.2	99.6
Average earnings	73.7	84.5	98.0	100.0	126.3	128.9
Relative value compared to average earnings (November 1978 = 100)						
Basic Pension:						
Single	86.7	88.3	84.9	100.0	78.2	79.8
Couple	87.5	89.4	85.6	100.0	78.2	79.8
Basic Unemployment Benefit:						
Single adult	107.4	109.3	99.7	100.0	77.1	78.6
Child Benefit:						
1st child	0.0	0.0	0.0	100.0	78.5	82.3
2nd child	66.8	103.3	64.1	100.0	78.5	72.3
Two children	33.4	51.7	32.0	100.0	78.5	77.3

[a]Sources: benefits: *UK Social Statistics*; retail prices: *Monthly Digest of Statistics*; average earnings: *Department of Employment Gazette* (and forerunners). The time intervals shown in this table span political administrations in the following order: Labour, Tory, Labour, Tory (Thatcher), Tory (Major).

their lives are interdependent, and higher incomes for some may reduce opportunities and living standards for others unless their incomes are raised to match. For example, rising incomes for the majority may lead to increased car use and the decay of public transport, severely reducing the mobility of those dependent on it. Such changes are reflected inadequately, if at all, in conventional price indices, and the use of such indices to measure the 'real' incomes of welfare dependents may conceal a significant decline in their standard of living. For a variety of reasons, therefore, it is misleading to judge the adequacy of benefits simply by looking at their so-called real value. What matters is their relative value as compared to the generality of incomes in society.

Under the Tories, the relative value of every major Social Security benefit fell substantially as compared to average earnings. The smallest relative decline was for the Mobility Allowance (−12.9%) and the largest for Child Benefit (−27.7% for the second and subsequent children). Most benefits fell by around 20% in relation to average earnings. This represents a remarkable reversal of the post-War consensus on the question of social benefits and shows clearly the radicalism of the Thatcher government in this area. In the case of Unemployment Benefits the policy of reducing their relative value had some immediate rationale. The theory was that such benefits increase unemployment by discouraging people from seeking work. There is little evidence that this was a major factor behind the high unemployment rates of the early 1980s but those responsible for government policy apparently thought it was (Atkinson *et al.* (1989) provide a good discussion of this). In the case of other Social Security benefits, the motives for reducing their relative value were mixed. One motive was to restrain government expenditure to make room for eventual tax cuts. In addition, Thatcher and many of her immediate circle were hostile to the so-called 'dependency culture' which they believed the entire system of social welfare encouraged.

Economic recovery

In addition to the effect of these deliberate measures, government expenditure and its ratio to GDP were influenced by developments in the economy at large. After the initial slump in 1979–1981, there was a prolonged economic expansion which lasted for almost a decade. This expansion was accompanied by rapid growth in the market sector of the economy. The result was a considerable fall in the amount paid out in unemployment-related benefits and a substantial rise in GDP, both of which helped to reduce the ratio of government expenditure to GDP. Thus, part of the decline in this ratio in the later years of the Thatcher administrations was a normal cyclical response to economic recovery. However, as will be seen below, economic recovery was not the main factor in reducing this ratio, and was quantitatively less important than the various expenditure restraints described previously.

Government Revenue

In the initial years of the Thatcher administration government revenue increased sharply and then, from the mid-1980s onwards, its share of GDP fell back again though not completely to its original level. Table 12.8 shows what happened to the main items of government revenue. Of the measures used to increase government revenue in the initial years, by far the most important were the increases in VAT and the special taxes levied on the profits of the oil companies, which had been inflated by the large rise in world oil prices in 1979. Between them

Table 12.8. UK government revenue 1979–1990.[a]

Source of revenue	Percentage of GDP			Change	
	1979	1984	1990	1979–1984	1984–1990
Taxes on income (excluding petroleum)	12.6	12.4	13.9	−0.1	1.4
Social Security contributions	5.9	7.0	6.3	1.1	−0.7
Taxes on expenditure (excluding petroleum)[b]	14.4	15.3	14.9	0.9	−0.3
Petroleum taxes	1.2	3.3	1.2	2.1	−2.1
Rent, etc.[c]	1.6	1.7	0.8	0.1	−0.9
Interest and dividends	1.7	1.6	1.2	−0.1	−0.4
Other revenue	1.4	1.3	1.5	−0.1	0.3
Total revenue	38.8	42.5	39.8	3.7	−2.7

[a]Source: *UK National Accounts*.
[b]Includes rates and community charge.
[c]Includes royalties and licence fees on oil and gas production.

these accounted for two-thirds of the additional revenue. Increased Social Security contributions were also a significant factor.

After this initial phase, the picture is quite complex. The top marginal rate of income tax was eventually reduced to 40% and the standard rate was gradually cut from 33% to 25%. Even so, the average share of income tax in GDP actually rose by quite a large amount between 1984 and 1990. This presumably reflects the failure of the government to increase tax thresholds in line with rising incomes. Apart from income tax, the share of other major kinds of revenue declined after 1984. Most striking is the case of petroleum, where special levies on oil company profits were rapidly phased out as world oil prices fell and these profits shrank. Also notable was the decline in government revenue in the form of rent, interest and dividends, all of which were adversely affected by the sale of public housing and nationalised industries.

Many countries reduced tax rates at the top end of the scale but the changes under the Thatcher government were more radical than elsewhere. In the 1970s, tax rates for the well-paid in the UK were relatively high by international standards. They are now amongst the lowest in the OECD group. Figure 12.8 shows the top marginal tax rates in force in 1988–1989 for this group. Out of 24 countries shown, only the US, Iceland and New Zealand had top rates below that of the UK. All North European countries, including France and Germany,

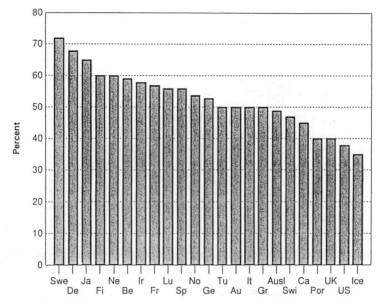

Figure 12.8. Top marginal OECD income tax rates (includes central and local taxes) 1988–1989.
Source: *Economies in Transition*, OECD, Paris, 1989.

had rates well in excess of Britain's. So, indeed, did Japan, where state and local tax rates combined produce a marginal tax rate of 65% on top incomes. The case of Japan throws an interesting light on the claim that low tax rates are required in the UK to encourage the highly paid to work harder, especially given the huge increases in pre-tax pay which many of them obtained under the Thatcher government.

Another persistent theme of the Thatcher government was that the British are a highly taxed nation and that the amount of tax paid by the average person is now at, or beyond, its upper limit. This is not supported by the evidence. Figure 12.9 compares the situation in a number of countries with regard to direct taxes and Social Security contributions (the latter, even when nominally levied on employers, are really a form of tax on labour and they should be included with direct taxes on workers' income to obtain a true picture of income tax rates). According to this table, the share of personal income taken by tax in the UK has been remarkably stable over the past decade and is low by international standards. Almost all European countries and, interestingly, Canada have a higher share of taxes in personal income than the UK. In some cases, the gap is very large. For example, when employers' Social Security contributions are included, the share of taxes in personal income in 1988 was 20% in the UK, compared to 25% in France, 27%

282 *Bob Rowthorn*

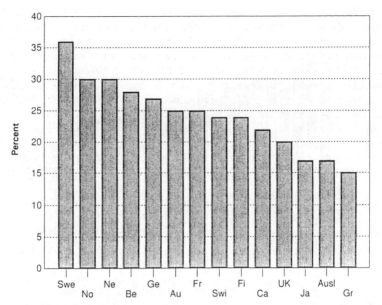

Figure 12.9. UK direct taxes and Social Security contributions as a percentage of personal income 1988 (includes employers' Social Security contributions). Source: *Economic Trends* (November 1990).

in Germany and over 30% in the Netherlands and Scandinavia. When employers' contributions are excluded France falls slightly below the UK but most other countries remain far above. As so often is the case, international comparisons reveal the shallow basis of politicians' claims.

Income Distribution

Under the Thatcher government income distribution became markedly more unequal, thus reversing the long post-War trend towards greater equality. This was partly the result of widening disparities in 'original' income in the form of wages, salaries, interest, dividends and the like. Many families and individuals were impoverished by the rise in unemployment, and amongst the employed workforce differentials increased considerably (see the chapter by Michie and Wilkinson). The latter development occurred in a number of countries during the 1980s but rarely on anything like the scale observed in the UK. At the top end of the distribution, upper managers and the like typically received salary increases well in excess of average earnings.

The above disparities in original income were intensified by the changes in benefits and taxation described earlier. When the Thatcher government took office, the UK was already an inegalitarian country with a great deal of poverty. By the time she left office the situation was considerably worse. Table 12.9 presents information from the *Luxemburg Income Study* which indicates the extent of poverty in a number of countries at the end of the 1970s, both before and after the impact of transfer payments in the form of taxes and benefits. The UK figures refer to 1979. Poverty is defined in this context as having an income less than or equal to half the median 'equivalised' income (i.e. adjusted to allow for variations in family type). According to this table, when taxes and benefits are taken into account, there was in general less poverty in the UK than in Canada or the US but significantly more than in Northern Europe. Moreover, the incidence of poverty varied

Table 12.9. Pre- and post-transfer economic distance poverty rates at the end of the 1970s.[a]

Country		Total (%)	Percentage of persons who are poor			
			Elderly families (%)	Single-parent families (%)	Two-parent families (%)	Other families (%)
Sweden	Pre-transfer	41.0	98.4	55.0	21.3	30.5
	Post-transfer	5.0	0.1	9.2	5.0	7.0
	Percentage reduction[b]	87.8	99.9	88.3	76.5	77.0
United Kingdom	Pre-transfer	27.9	78.6	56.3	17.6	12.8
	Post-transfer	8.8	18.1	29.1	6.5	4.1
	Percentage reduction	68.5	77.0	48.3	63.1	68.0
United States	Pre-transfer	27.3	72.0	58.5	16.0	15.4
	Post-transfer	16.9	20.5	51.7	12.9	9.8
	Percentage reduction	38.1	71.5	11.6	19.4	36.4
Canada	Pre-transfer	25.6	73.6	48.4	18.5	15.2
	Post-transfer	12.1	11.5	37.5	11.0	8.5
	Percentage reduction	52.7	84.4	22.5	40.5	44.1
West Germany	Pre-transfer	28.3	80.3	34.8	12.9	20.1
	Post-transfer	6.0	9.3	18.1	3.9	5.4
	Percentage reduction	78.8	88.4	47.1	69.8	73.1

[a]Source: Smeeding *et al.* (1990).
[b]Measured as (post-transfer − pre-transfer)/pre-transfer.

widely between groups, being concentrated at that time in the UK mainly on the elderly and single-parent families. This is a striking result considering the large increases in Child Benefit and state pensions implemented by the 1970s Labour government before the period covered by the table. Equally striking is the position of the elderly in the UK, amongst whom 18.1% were classified as poor. This is virtually the same as in the US at the time (20.5%), well above the figures for Canada (11.5%) and the continental European countries shown.

Unfortunately, the *Luxemburg Income Study* refers to the 1970s and provides no information about how UK experience under Thatcher compares to that of other countries during the 1980s.[14] However, it is still possible to see what happened within the UK itself. Table 12.10 presents information on 'disposable' (i.e. post-transfer) income taken from a special article in *Economic Trends*. It shows the percentages of various types of household that lie in the bottom quintile (20%) of the income distribution. It also shows how this quintile fared relative to the average person. In 1979 well over one-half of all retired households were in the bottom quintile, with an income less than 47% of the UK average. By 1988 this proportion had fallen to around two-fifths, which suggests that poverty amongst the elderly had declined. This is not surprising given the spread of occupational pensions, which augmented the income of many elderly people. However, it should also be noted that the income of the bottom quintile itself fell relative to the average. It is still the case that two-fifths of the retired population in 1988 had incomes less than or equal to 38% of the national average. Many of these were undoubtedly worse off in relative terms than in 1979. The evidence on single-parent families is even clearer: the proportion in the bottom quintile rose from 39% in 1979 to 52% in 1988. Since the

Table 12.10. Percentage of persons in households in bottom quintile of UK equivalised disposable income 1979–1988.[a]

Year	Retired households		Non-retired households				Income of bottom quintile as percentage of UK average
	1 adult	2 adults	1 adult	2 or more adults	1 adult with children	2 or more adults with children	
1979	57	54	12	4	39	10	47.0
1983	35	38	19	8	44	16	47.5
1988	39	40	19	6	52	13	38.0

[a]Source: *Economic Trends* (March 1991). Figures in this table refer to incomes adjusted for household size and composition.

bottom quintile itself fell back a long way relative to the average, this represents a serious impoverishment of single-parent families. This is not surprising given the relative decline in the value of Social Security benefits available to such families. The data also reveal a small reduction after 1983 in the extent of poverty amongst two-parent families. This is due partly to the decline in unemployment in the later part of the decade. It may also reflect the effect of a new benefit for low-income families, the Family Credit, which was introduced in 1988. Despite these improvements, however, the extent of poverty amongst two-parent families remains considerable.

Poverty in general increased markedly under the Thatcher government. Those already at the top end of the scale, by contrast, did extremely well. Table 12.11 compares the experience of the top and bottom quintiles of the income distribution. It shows how these groups

Table 12.11. Percentage shares of original, disposable and post-tax income by quintile groups of households 1979–1988.[a]

	1979	1983	1988
Equivalised original income[b]			
Bottom quintile	2.4	3.0	1.9
Top quintile	43	47	50
Equivalised gross income[c]			
Bottom quintile	8.5	8.5	7.1
Top quintile	37	39	43
Equivalised disposable income[d]			
Bottom quintile	9.4	9.5	7.6
Top quintile	36	38	42
Equivalised post-tax income[e]			
Bottom quintile	9.5	8.9	6.9
Top quintile	37	39	44
Ratios of equivalised income: top quintile/bottom quintile			
Original income	17.9	15.7	26.3
Gross income	4.4	4.6	6.1
Disposable income	3.8	4.0	5.5
Post-tax income	3.9	4.4	6.4

[a]Source as for Table 12.10. All figures in this table refer to income per head, equivalised to take into account the effect of different household type (i.e. number of children, adults).
[b]Income from property, work, gifts, etc.
[c]Original income plus social security benefits.
[d]Gross income less direct taxes and social security contributions.
[e]Disposable income less indirect taxes.

were affected by direct taxes, benefits and also indirect taxes such as VAT. When all these items are taken into account, the share of the bottom quintile in total income declined from 9.7% in 1979 to 6.9% in 1988. Most of this decline occurred in the long boom after 1983, when average earnings rose strongly and Social Security benefits fell behind. At the other end of the scale, the share of the top quintile rose from 37% in 1979 to 44% at the end of the period. Comparing the two groups, after all taxes and benefits are taken into account, the average income of the top quintile in 1979 was 3.9 times that of the bottom quintile. By 1988 it was 6.4 times as great. This is a remarkable increase in inequality which leaves a difficult legacy for any future Labour government to deal with. It also presents a severe challenge to any 'caring' Tory or coalition government.

Could Things Have Been Different?

It is now widely recognised that the Thatcher government's innovations in the sphere of taxation and benefits led to marked increases in both inequality and poverty. It is also recognised that public services and infrastructure were seriously neglected during this period. Most people, including many Tories, regret these developments. It is therefore an interesting question to ask how things might have been different. Suppose there had been a Labour government in office, or perhaps a Heath-style Tory government. What would have happened to government expenditure and, by implication, taxation under such a government? Any answer to such a question must, of course, be highly speculative. Even so, it is worth asking because it provides some indication of the true impact of the Thatcher administration on public expenditure. It also gives an indication of the scale of the problems she has bequeathed to her successors.

To give some idea of the relative importance of the various expenditure-saving measures implemented under the Thatcher government, I have made some rough calculations which are reported in Table 12.12. More sophisticated methods might produce somewhat different answers but the general picture is probably correct. They illustrate what government expenditure might have been at the start of the 1990s if a Labour, or Heath-style Tory government had been in power during the 1980s.

Total government expenditure in 1990 amounted to £223 billion. To see what this figure might have been under a more generous government, I have made the following assumptions:

- the volume of expenditure on nonmilitary public services grows at an extra 0.8% p.a. over the period 1979–1990 (as compared to actual growth under Thatcher); this figure includes capital investment;
- average pay in the public services is raised by 5% to make up for

Table 12.12. Hypothetical general government expenditure in 1990.[a]

	£ billion	Percentage of GDP
Actual expenditure	223	40.4
Additional expenditure		
Expansion of services	8	1.5
Restoration of relative pay in public sector	3	0.6
Restoration of relative value of Social Security benefits	8	1.5
Additional expenditure total	20	3.6
Grand total	242	44.0

[a]The assumptions underlying this table are described in the text; columns may not add because rounding errors.

the decline in relative earnings after 1981 (as compared to the market sector of the economy) (for some justification for this figure, see Brown and Rowthorn, 1990);

- expenditure on social benefits is raised by 15% to compensate for the massive decline in their relative value as compared to average earnings under the Thatcher governments and for restrictions in their coverage. This may be a rather conservative figure. To make an accurate estimate would require a careful examination of all the changes in entitlements and benefit levels which occurred under the Thatcher governments, and their combined effect would have to be estimated using a formal model of the tax and benefit system such as TAXMOD. This would be a time-consuming exercise which has not, to my knowledge, been done—although Atkinson and Micklewright (1989) made a partial assessment in the case of unemployment-related benefits.

The combined effect of the above items is to raise government expenditure in 1990 by approximately £20 billion. This indicates the kind of saving which the Thatcher squeeze on public spending achieved. Of this total, about one-half is due to the unlinking of Social Security benefits from average earnings, and most of the rest is due to the slow growth of public services. Restraining the pay of groups like teachers and public service manual workers caused considerable resentment but the sums of money involved were relatively small in comparison with the two major items.

The above calculations imply that, with an alternative government in office during the 1980s, public expenditure in 1990 might have been around 44% of GDP.[15] This is significantly greater than the actual share of 40.4% in 1990, and somewhat greater than the share when

Thatcher took office in 1979. It is interesting to ask what such additional expenditure would have meant for taxation and government revenue in general. The answer depends on what assumptions are made about government borrowing and proceeds from the privatisation of nationalised industries, council housing and the like. Given the high real interest rates ruling in the UK and elsewhere, it is inconceivable that government borrowing could have continued during the 1980s on anything like the scale observed during the 1970s. It is also likely that the scale of privatisation, and the funds thereby generated for the government, would have been much less under an alternative administration than under Thatcher. In view of these considerations, it seems inevitable that any extra expenditure undertaken by such an administration would have been financed entirely through higher taxes. Thus, given the expenditure programme outlined above, an additional tax revenue of some £20 billion a year would have been required. Let us consider where these taxes might have come from.

Where might the extra taxes have come from?

The additional tax revenue required to finance the additional expenditure could have been raised in many different ways. The following is a list of possible measures.

- *Higher taxes on the well-off.* Marginal tax rates at the top end of the scale were admittedly too high when the Thatcher government took office and some reduction was required. However, the huge cuts which the government made were unwarranted. An alternative government could have been less extreme.
- *Higher marginal tax rates for those on middle incomes.* As a result of changes under the Thatcher governments, the marginal income tax rate for people on middle incomes was reduced from 33% to 25%. There was no economic, or even political, necessity for a reduction of this magnitude.
- *Higher Social Security contributions.* By European standards, Social Security contributions in the UK are quite low. They were increased in the early 1980s but they could have been increased still further in the ensuing years. Employers' Social Security contributions were, and still are, especially low by European standards and could certainly have been raised. Moreover, the upper earnings limit on employees' contributions could have been eliminated, thereby raising more revenue from the well-paid.
- *Higher fuel taxes.* When world oil prices collapsed in the mid-1980s the profits of the oil companies fell sharply and the special taxes previously levied on these companies were eliminated. As a result, the price of oil to consumers fell in relation to the Retail Price Index in general. It fell even more in relation to the price of collective

transport such as buses and trains, whose costs rose steeply throughout the 1980s. Lower real oil prices had a knock-on effect on the price of other fuels. From an environmental point of view, it would have been an intelligent move to prevent this decline in fuel prices by raising the duty on oil and perhaps extending it to other fuels in the form of a carbon tax. The effect would have been to drive a wedge between domestic fuel prices and those on the world market. As world prices fell, the real cost of fuels to domestic consumers in the UK would have been kept artificially high or even increased. This would have stimulated energy saving, and also reduced pollution and congestion by discouraging the use of private cars. Interestingly, such a policy is currently under consideration by the European Community. The potential revenue from this source is considerable. For example, if the share of petroleum taxes in GDP had been kept at its 1984 level, the extra tax revenue in 1990 would have been £11 billion.

I have made no attempt to quantify the possible impact of most of the above measures but it is clear that together they could easily have raised the revenue required to finance the additional expenditure outlined previously. It must also be remembered that some of the expenditures would have been partly self-financing. Most Social Security benefits are taxable, as are the salaries of public sector workers. Increases in these items automatically generate a significant amount of government revenue even at existing tax rates. In addition, most of the people paying the extra taxes would have enjoyed better public services and higher Social Security benefits. Indeed, a majority of the population would probably have been better off under the alternative expenditure and taxation programme. A final point to note is that many of the tax changes described above are really foregone tax reductions rather than genuine increases. Since the early 1980s the share of government revenue in GDP has fallen almost continuously. If the tax cuts implemented during this period had been largely foregone, the additional taxes required to finance the alternative programme would be quite small. Given the large increase in real earnings which occurred during the 1980s (around 26%), a modest and gradual rise in the share of taxes would have been quite acceptable to most people. It would certainly have been more acceptable than the legacy of poverty and neglect.

Conclusions

We have seen what happened to government expenditure under the Thatcher government and examined how things might have been different. We have also seen how the UK has fallen behind comparable European countries during the 1980s. The scale of the present gap between the UK and these other countries is indicated by the following numbers. If the ratio of government revenue to GDP were raised to the German level, the UK government would now have an extra £20 billion a year to spend. With revenue increased to the French level the figure would be £40 billion, and with Scandinavian-style tax rates the additional revenue would be in the range £60–80 billion. It is sometimes argued that other European countries can afford such high levels of government expenditure because they are much richer than we are. The UK, it is said, is a relatively poor country and cannot afford such lavish expenditures. In reducing government expenditure and taxation, the Thatcher administration was merely recognising this unpleasant fact and reducing the share of government to what the economy could afford. This argument is not supported by the evidence. Britain is still a comparatively rich country: GDP *per capita* is greater than in Austria, Belgium, Italy and the Netherlands, and is only marginally less than in Denmark or France (latest OECD statistics; see Figure 12.10). It is only a few percentage points below that of West Germany alone and may well exceed that of unified Germany. All of these countries have levels of government expenditure well in excess of the UK's. In all of them, with the exception of Italy, taxes account for a greater share of GDP than is the case in Britain.

The contrast between the welfare state in Britain and continental

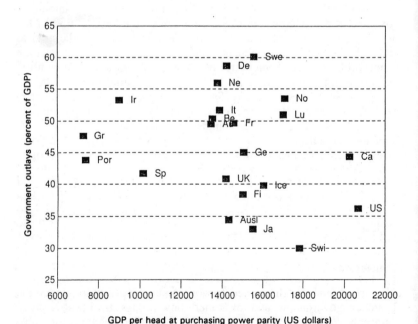

Figure 12.10. General UK government outlays and GDP per head in 1989. Source: *OECD Economic Outlook.*

Europe is not the result of British poverty, but of politics. It is the outcome of a deliberate policy of the Thatcher administration to hold down government spending and reduce taxes during the middle and late 1980s—at a time when the private sector of the economy was growing rapidly in the course of a prolonged economic recovery. Given the considerable rise in real incomes which occurred during this period, it would have been relatively painless and politically quite feasible to raise tax rates by the small amount needed at that time to put government finances on a sound footing and support a continental-style welfare state. For its own ideological reasons, the Thatcher government did just the opposite. The result was remarkable. In the early 1980s, the share of government expenditure in GDP was much the same in the UK as in the rest of the European Community. Within the space of just a few years, this share was dramatically reduced and a large gap was created between the UK and the rest of the Community.

Given the long-term process of social and economic convergence occurring in Western Europe, this gap is unlikely to be permanent. It is fairly certain that political and economic pressures will eventually force the UK to upgrade its welfare state to some common European norm, and this will require either a significant, overt rise in the share of taxes in national income, or else the use of alternative measures which are not officially classified as tax increases but whose economic effects are the same. For example, all employees (or their employers) might be legally required to subscribe to an approved private pension or health scheme. Government revenue from taxation could then be used to finance pensions and health treatment for those not covered by the compulsory private scheme. Such an alternative might be wasteful because of the large administration costs usually involved in private schemes, and its effects on employees (or their employers) would be economically equivalent to a new tax. However, it would have the cosmetic advantage of permitting an improvement in the welfare state without appearing to raise taxes.

Given the pressure to improve the welfare state, it seems only a matter of time before either taxes are significantly increased or some economically equivalent measures are implemented. How such a transformation will occur is a matter of speculation and is beyond the scope of the present chapter to consider. Suffice it to say that the process will not be easy. Neither of the two major parties is at present willing to advocate overt tax increases for the average voter, and it will require a considerable change in the political climate before they do so. Indeed, the Tories are still promising future cuts in income tax. A path which may tempt Labour in the coming years is some compulsory extension of private provision, with public funds used increasingly to bridge the gaps. Such a new partnership with the private sector would be inefficient and, on past experience, would create new inequalities of its own. However, it would be an obvious development for a party which genuinely wants to improve levels of provision in areas such as health, education and pensions but feels constrained to avoid overt tax increases for the average voter.

Two factors often mentioned in the present context are disarmament and economic growth. Military expenditure in the UK still absorbs some 4% of GDP and a drastic saving in this area could provide a significant part of the finance required to upgrade the welfare state. Fiscal pressures have already led to some reduction in military expenditure and further cuts have been officially announced. How much further these cuts should or will go is a matter of political judgement. My own view is that, whilst the potential 'peace dividend' is very large, it is unlikely to be realised on anything like the scale which its supporters advocate. Military expenditure cuts may provide useful savings in the coming years but they will not resolve the fiscal dilemma created by the need for increased expenditure in other directions. Whilst the potential 'peace dividend' is very large, it is unlikely to be realised in practice or anything like the scale which its supporters, including myself, advocate.

A similar observation applies to the so-called 'growth dividend'. Economic growth aids government finances in two ways: it creates employment thereby leading to reduced expenditure on unemployment-related benefits, and it increases national income thereby generating additional tax revenue. For these reasons, it has been argued that improvements in the welfare state can be financed in large measure from the proceeds of economic growth. The funds available from this source would be substantial if the long-term growth rate of the British economy could be significantly increased. These arguments have some force. However, they should be treated with caution. Raising the long-term growth rate will not be an easy matter and it would be unwise to rely on a dramatic improvement in this area. Moreover, economic growth creates its own problems for public finance. Growth is normally accompanied by higher incomes in the private sector of the economy. These increases have to be matched in the public services whose costs are thereby driven up. As the incomes of those in work rise, there is also pressure to raise social benefits to ensure that welfare dependents share in national prosperity. Thus, economic growth tends to drive up the cost of both government services and most welfare programmes. These additional costs absorb much of the additional tax revenue generated by growth, and its beneficial effects on government finances are much less than might appear at first sight.

Whilst military expenditure cuts and economic growth may ease the problem, they will not, in my opinion, resolve the fundamental dilemma of how to finance the expenditures required to upgrade the welfare state and make good the neglect of more than a decade. They will not eliminate the need for additional levies on the average voter, either in the form of overt tax increases or some economically equivalent measures which are not officially classified under the heading of taxes. This dilemma may be especially acute for a Labour government because of its more genuine commitment to the welfare state but it would also confront a future Tory government.

Acknowledgements

I should like to thank Andrew Glyn and Geoffrey Harcourt for their comments on the draft version of this chapter.

Comment

Government Policy and Company Profitability

Paul Ormerod

A key question underlying evaluations of the UK's economic perform-ance in the 1980s is as follows: quite simply, how could things have been different? There is a strong argument to suggest that the economic situation in Britain at the end of the 1970s was not sustainable: a major restructuring was essential. In its concrete historical form, this manifested itself primarily in the recession of 1980–1982, which involved a huge increase in unemployment and the scrapping of large amounts of capital stock in the manufacturing sector. How far reality could have been different depends upon how many parameters in the economic system we are allowed to vary.

The most important immediate problem at the end of the 1970s was the sharp fall in the share of profits in national income which had taken place in the 1974–1979 period. Figure 12A.1 plots the relevant profit share of non-oil companies over the period 1963–1979. The crisis of profitability first arose in 1974–1975 following the oil price shock, when the price of oil quadrupled. This represented a transfer of income from the West to the oil-producing countries of OPEC (the UK was still far from being self-sufficient in oil) so that the real income of the UK fell. Unfortunately, the labour force refused to recognise that a fall in real

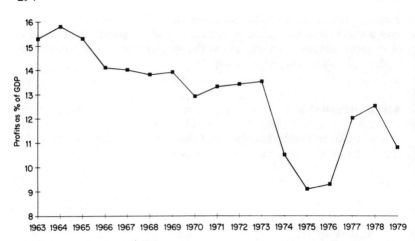

Figure 12A.1. Profits (net of stock appreciation) as a percentage of GDP 1963–1979.

wages was required because a portion of their living standards had been transferred to OPEC. They attempted to preserve real wage levels and in this they were successful. The consequences were two-fold: first, profits slumped and second, inflation rose dramatically as workers sought to defend real wages by seeking wage settlements in excess of the already high rate of inflation.

The response of industry to the profits crisis of 1975 was to save on labour costs by increasing unemployment almost three-fold to the then post-War record levels of one and a half million. This succeeded in bringing down inflation by curbing wage demands, in exactly the same way as did the 1980–1982 recession. A temporary revival of the profit share was made possible but as soon as unemployment stabilised it was once more under attack.

There was a further consequence of low profitability, whose effects have been felt in the longer term. Companies cut back investment, not simply in response to either weak demand for their products or a squeeze on liquidity, but also in response again to the fact that the prospect of earning profits was low. From the mid-1970s, there is a clear break in the trend rate of growth of the industrial capital stock of the UK. Since then to the present day, the capital stock has been inadequate to support full employment of the labour force. Evidence for this is seen in the CBI's capacity utilisation series: there is no trend whatsoever in this index over time. In other words, utilisation of capital stock has varied only cyclically. At the same time, however, unemployment—or underutilisation of the labour force—has risen from half a million to well over two million.

Profitability had to be restored to British industry at the end of the 1970s. If workers had suddenly become cooperative and had agreed to forgo real wage increases, the immediate need for the 1980–1982 recession would have disappeared. However, this is to postulate a change in behaviour which was beyond the imagination of commentators at the time. Even under this scenario, however, a major problem existed. A large increase in investment was required to make up the shortfall which had built up since 1974. This was compounded by the longer-term failure of management—hampered by the dominance of the City and of finance over industrial capital—to invest and to innovate on anything like an adequate scale. In short, much of the manufacturing capacity which was destroyed rapidly in the 1980–1982 period would have disappeared in any event over the 1980s as a whole, as the impact of global and in particular European competition intensified. Some restructuring would have been possible if worker cooperation had helped to restore profitability at the start of the 1980s but by itself this would have been insufficient.

There have been lasting benefits to the efficiency of the UK economy arising primarily from the 1979–1982 shock. Management have been more innovative and British firms are able to compete more effectively in world markets. This is demonstrated by the clear evidence which exists in support of the view that the elasticity of demand for British exports with respect to world trade has increased during the 1980s. However, major problems still exist with the British economy. To postulate that these—arising essentially from decades of neglect in investment in both physical and human capital—could have been solved by an alternative approach in the 1980s is to postulate wholesale changes in behaviour throughout the system. The fundamental defects of the cathartic approach of the 1980s are now becoming apparent. A more positive solution based upon cooperation and not conflict is now possible, with which the Thatcher approach has little or nothing in common.

13

Big Business, Small Business and the 'Enterprise Culture'

Alan Hughes

This chapter is concerned with the changing relative importance of self-employment and of small and large businesses in the UK. These are discussed in relation to the 'enterprise culture' which is deemed to have emerged in the course of the 1980s. First, government arguments spelling out the need to create an enterprise culture, the means to achieve it, and the role of self-employment and small firms in it are briefly reviewed using policy pronouncements as a guide. This is followed by a review of the evidence on the changing role of self-employment and of shifts in the shares of small and large businesses in the UK economy in the 1980s. This forms the basis for an interpretation of the 'enterprise culture' of the UK and its implications for UK supply-side policy.

The Enterprise Culture and Small Business Policy

> The vitality of our economy, the vitality of the country as a whole, and the vitality of individual towns and cities depends not upon large establishments, but upon the untidy undergrowth of small constantly adaptive competing businesses. . . No private wealth from small businesses, no widespread national wealth; no national wealth, no welfare. . . There is a close link between economic, social, cultural and political liberties, and at the heart of that link is the small businessman and the self-employed. (Sir Keith Joseph, *House of Commons Debate*, 1975.)

The links drawn by Sir Keith Joseph between self-employment, small-scale private enterprise, economic welfare and the political and social fabric of the country were in the course of the 1980s developed into a unifying theme in a variety of supply-side policy statements. An example is the White Paper that relaunched the Department of Trade and

Industry as 'DTI—The Department for Enterprise' (HMSO, 1988). This attributed the long-term industrial decline of the UK to a deep-rooted failure in the educational system which persistently disparaged money-making, business and profits, and failed to train people for work. This long-term failure, it argued, was reinforced in the post-War period by an increasingly corporatist approach to government policy intervention. Weakly managed big business and powerful unions, with the connivance of an interventionist state, protected vested interests in declining sectors and stifled new businesses and innovation in emergent sectors. The concomitant high rates of taxation to fund state subsidies exacerbated these problems by blunting incentives to take risks.

The White Paper argued that the key to government action to reverse these trends and increase prosperity lay in the creation of open markets, and in the focusing of policy on the needs of *individuals*: 'to champion all the people who make it happen, rather than just individual sectors, industries or companies'. Given a macroeconomic policy aimed at stable prices, open markets were to be achieved via competition policy, privatisation, deregulation and freedom of international trade. As far as individuals were concerned, reductions in individual or corporate taxes were required to strengthen incentives (such as the reduction in the 1980s in the 'small' companies' rate of corporation tax from 42%–25% in line with falls in the basic rate of income tax). Even so, individuals need 'positive encouragement to participate actively in the challenge of creating prosperity, if only to combat the past anti-enterprise bias of British culture'. This was to be achieved by bringing business and education closer together. Given open markets and the promotion of a culture of enterprise through the fiscal and educational systems, the remaining ingredient identified in the White Paper was information. The spread of best-practice information is especially important for small firms and individuals, who can only 'work efficiently in open markets if they have enough information about the opportunities and the problems to make reasoned business decisions'. Once information about the commercial success and relevance of new approaches has been provided, however, the 'normal operation of the market economy' can take over. It follows that the emphasis in government spending on the promotion of enterprise should switch away from sector- or company-specific near-to-market projects and towards collaborative noncompetitive research far from commercial exploitation. Equally, the White Paper argued that emphasis should be placed on technology transfer out of the science base and on the provision of consultancy services to raise the competitive ability of smaller businesses. Hence the Enterprise Initiative itself, launched in the aftermath of the 1988 White Paper, which provided support for businesses employing less than 500 workers seeking consultancy advice in key areas such as design, marketing and quality standards.

Similar themes that emphasise the need for a clearer articulation of business needs in education and training, the coordination of information flows and the promotion of self-help, can be traced in other policy initiatives with direct and indirect implications for small business promotion and self-employment. Insofar as competition policy was concerned, the emphasis on open markets was paramount. Thus under the so-called 'Tebbit doctrine' in force from the mid-1980s, mergers were to be referred for investigation by the Monopolies and Mergers Commission only if there was a potential anti-competitive effect involved. References on other grounds of public interest were in the main to be avoided. As few government inhibitions as possible were to be placed on the free play of takeovers in the market for corporate control:

> The government believe that there are considerable benefits from allowing freedom for exchange in corporate ownership and control through mergers and acquisitions. Generally, the market will be a better arbiter than Government of the prospects for the proposed transactions, and will ensure better use of assets, for the benefit of their owners and the economy as a whole. (HMSO, 1988, p. 7.)

Moreover, insofar as international takeovers were concerned, the government was keen to extend the benefits of takeover activity to the rest of the European Community and to secure a level playing-field for UK acquirers:

> The government is keen to secure the removal of unnecessary barriers to takeovers throughout the EC and to extend the benefits of open and efficient markets throughout the community. . . (John Redwood MP, DTI Minister for Corporate Affairs, HMSO, 1989.)

The emphasis on open markets and competition did not, however, produce any fundamental changes in either merger policy or restrictive trade practices (RTP) policy in the UK in the course of the 1980s. Although there were reviews of both, and major changes in RTP legislation were proposed which would have benefited smaller firms, no parliamentary time had been found by 1991 to implement them (for a fuller discussion of these potential RTP changes which would move the UK closer to EC practice and would ease collaborative arangements by small firms in certain areas such as research and development and specialisation, see Hughes, 1989).

Although these policy objectives and aims can be interpreted as a coherent whole, it would be misleading to treat the evolution of government policy towards industry, enterprise and the small business sector as part of a long-term, consistently articulated strategy. Between 1979 and 1990 no less than 12 ministers held the Trade and Industry brief (five of them between 1979 and 1983 when Trade and Industry were separate departments, and seven between 1983 and 1990 when they were joined together). Of these, it was Lord Young from 1987–1989 whose promotion of the 'enterprise culture' is most closely reflected in the 1988 White Paper discussed above. In the early 1980s in particular, the impact of the recession meant that the government was heavily involved in rescue operations that involved large public and private corporations. Moreover, in those years various forms of subsidy were introduced beyond those relevant to the promotion of information flows and advice. Thus conventional financial-market failure arguments made under the Labour Government by the Wilson Report in 1979, lay behind the Loan Guarantee Scheme of 1981, and the Business Expansion Schemes of 1983 onwards, and pressure of unemployment lay behind the Enterprise Allowance Scheme of 1983 which offered income support to those unemployed people who wished to become self-employed. Moreover, as discussed in the chapters by Martin and Tyler, and Moore, regional and urban support programmes were also inherited from the 1970s. There was, however, a shift away from the former towards the latter in the course of the decade. Regional support programmes continued to show the decline in real terms which had begun in the 1970s, whilst inner city and urban support programmes rose in real terms to outstrip regional expenditure by a substantial margin.

The shift towards an 'enterprise strategy' had the effect of reducing government expenditure on trade and industry (excluding the public corporations) by one-quarter in real terms between 1979–1980 and 1989–1990 (Johnson, 1991). The extent of support for small firms within this, and changes in it in the course of the 1980s, are harder to chart. This is partly because of the difficulty of evaluating the effect of tax concessions such as income tax relief under the Business Expansion Scheme and the 'small' firms' rate of corporation tax, and partly because support of small firms arose as part of wider schemes such as inner city policy. It has, however, been estimated that by 1988–1989 the value of tax relief was around £500 million and that additional central and Local Authority expenditure amounted to £510 million. Around £200 million of the latter was related to promoting start-ups via the Enterprise Allowance Scheme (Bannock and Albach, 1991). Table 13.1 suggests that by the mid- and late 1980s UK aid for small and medium-sized enterprises (SMEs) was, at 5.2%, an above-average proportion of overall aid for industry by EC standards. It is also clear that overall aid for industry in the UK, at 4.6% of GDP, was below the EC 10 average and below that of each of the six largest EC industrial economies.

A more detailed comparison with Germany for 1988–1989 is shown in Table 13.2. This focuses on expenditure and excludes the value of support from tax concessions that arose for instance from the Business Expansion Scheme and the existence of the 'small' firms' rate of corporation tax in the UK, as well as central and local government threshold and other tax concessions in Germany. Table 13.2 shows that UK expenditure in those years was moderate by comparison with contemporary support provided in Germany, especially in terms of loan guarantees and grants, and support for promotion of research and

Table 13.1. Industrial support and support for small and medium-sized enterprises in selected countries 1986.[a]

Country	Industrial support as a percentage of GDP 1986[b]	Support for small and medium-sized enterprises, as a percentage of industrial support 1986–1988[c]
Belgium	12.7	7.0
Italy	11.8	5.1
France	7.8	2.2
Germany	6.2	2.8
Netherlands	4.8	20.3
United Kingdom	4.6	5.2
EC 10	7.5	4.3

[a] Source: Ford and Suyker (1990), Tables 4 and 10, based on CEC (1989, 1990).
[b] Ratio of industrial subsidies to industrial GDP. The data are estimates of the grant equivalent of aid assistance provided, based on actual expenditures or appropriations. They are estimated on a before-tax basis, and include estimates of the aid element in new equity injections into companies as well as the inherent subsidy effect of 'soft loans' and the value of guarantee schemes covering loans and export credits.
[c] Based on the European Commission's allocation of the total industrial subsidy between support for Small and Medium-Sized Industries, Research and Development, the Environment, Sector and Regional Specific Support and General Support. There is a degree of overlap and arbitrariness in dividing subsidies between these categories.

development and technology. The differences in levels of expenditure on support remain even when differences in GDP between the countries or the relative size of their SME sector's contribution to GDP, are considered. Thus German support is estimated to amount to 0.25% of GDP, compared to 0.10% in the UK. Moreover, although Table 13.2 suggests that SME training support is higher in the UK, it omits the wide range of training provision which is subsidised or mandatory and carried out in Germany in collaboration with Chambers of Commerce and other official and trade bodies. Nevertheless, a shift of emphasis towards SMEs in UK policy was apparent in the 1980s.

The Changing Size Distribution of UK Business

Although the promotion of small enterprises and self-employment has come to be seen as an important element in government policy, tracking changes in their number and significance is far from straightforward. This is partly a matter of definitions. Estimates of the self-employed

Table 13.2. Support for small and medium-sized enterprises in the UK and Germany 1988–1989.[a]

Type of support	UK		Germany	
	£m	%	£m	%
Special regional assistance	108.5	21.2	167.1	9.1
Research and development, technology	10.0	2.0	375.2	20.3
Loans, grants and guarantees	3.8	0.7	1093.4	59.3
Start-up assistance	199.0	39.0	61.7	3.3
Training	110.0	21.5	81.5	4.4
Information and consultancy	77.9	15.3	64.7	3.5
Other	1.6	0.3	0.3	—
Total support	510.8	100.0	1843.9	100.0
Total support as percentage of GDP	—	0.10	—	0.25
SME activity as percentage of GDP	—	32.2	—	46.0

[a] Source: Bannock and Albach (1991).

come from a number of potential survey sources which use different definitions and yield varying estimates of the numbers involved. For firms, the notion of 'smallness' is notoriously imprecise so that arguments may occur about whether or not the self-employed—especially those with no employees—should count as small firms, or whether attention should be focused on 'microbusinesses' that employ less than 5 people, small businesses that employ less than 100 or 200 employees, or SMEs that employ less than 500. There is also the question of whether size is best measured in terms of assets, sales or market share rather than employment. In practice, the choice of size measure is limited by official statistics. In what follows, turnover and employment are used when the economy is discussed as a whole, supplemented by some data on net output for the manufacturing sector. Moreover, instead of focusing on one size band in the distribution, information is presented where possible on the whole distribution or major parts of it. Finally, insofar as the significance of small firms is to be interpreted in terms of their shares in employment or output in a particular sector, it is important to bear in mind the overall trends in employment and economic activity in that sector, and changes in that sector's importance in the economy as a whole. This is particularly so in the case of manufacturing.

Table 13.3 presents evidence on unemployment and self-employment in Britain and on the stock of businesses in the UK over the period 1979–1989. A rise in the number of self-employed is evident. There was a particularly rapid increase between 1983 and 1985 and again between 1987 and 1989, as unemployment first stabilised and then fell sharply. This increase of nearly 1¼ million self-employed between 1981

Table 13.3. Unemployment and self-employment in Britain; businesses registered for VAT in the UK; 1979–1989.[a]

Year	Self-employed as percentage of employed	Percentage unemployed	Self-employed (000s)	Percentage of self-employed employing others	Businesses registered for VAT (000s)[b]
1979[c]	7.4	3.9	1842	n.a.	1289
1981	9.2	8.0	2177	39	1337
1983	10.0	10.4	2295	39	1392
1985	11.4	10.8	2714	37	1441
1987	12.4	9.8	2996	35	1510
1989	13.2	6.0	3425	31	1662

[a] Sources: *Annual Abstract*, Daly (1990, 1991).
[b] The VAT data refer to estimates of the end-year stock of businesses. Variations in the numbers of registered businesses over time reflect upward shifts in the turnover threshold for registration which roughly doubled between 1980 and 1990, as well as growth in the numbers of businesses in existence.
[c] Data for self-employment for 1979 are from *Annual Abstract* and are probably underestimates compared with those for 1981 onwards based on Daly (1991).

and 1989 was higher than anything experienced in the previous two decades (Daly, 1991). It also outstripped the growth in total employment in the 1980s so that, as can be seen from Table 13.3, the proportion of the workforce in employment who were self-employed rose by four percentage points between 1981 and 1989. Table 13.3 also reveals that there was a contemporaneous increase in the number of UK businesses registered for VAT, by nearly 400 000 between the end of 1979 and the end of 1989. This too was a departure from the experience of the 1970s: there was relative stability in the number of registered businesses between 1974 (the year after the introduction of VAT) and 1979 (Ganguly, 1985). A number of features of this growth in self-employment and business formation are worth noting. The first is that the net changes each year, and over the period as a whole, represent differences between massive inflows into, and outflows from, the stocks of employment and businesses. Thus it has been estimated that between 1981 and 1989 3.3 million people entered self-employment and 2.1 million left via retirement, unemployment, moves back to employee status or other causes (Daly, 1991). Equally, the net change of 400 000 in the number of businesses registered for VAT represents the difference between 1.9 million registrations and 1.5 million deregistrations. These categories are not always the same as economic 'birth' and 'death' (for instance, around one-quarter of deregistrations are due to takeover). It is clear, however, that the world of enterprise is an extremely turbulent one.

Table 13.3 also reveals a low and falling proportion of the self-employed offering employment to others. In 1981 around 39% of the self-employed employed other workers; by 1989 this had fallen to 31%. As might be expected, the bulk of those with employment were very small-scale employers: the majority employed fewer than 5 workers and over 40% either 1 or 2 workers. Finally, an analysis of the industrial composition of self-employment shows a heavy concentration in agriculture, forestry and fishing, construction and the service industries. Within these sectors, banking and finance and other services (including business services) along with construction showed increases of over 100% in the number of self-employed between 1981 and 1989 (Daly, 1991).

Part of the explanation for the growth in self-employment is compositional. It reflects the substantial structural shifts that occurred in the distribution of economic activity in the 1980s. Whilst total industrial and service sector employment (including the self-employed) stood at around 24 million in both 1977 and 1987, service sector employment rose by 2.4 million, so that its share in the economy rose from 58% to 67%. Over one million of the increase in employment was located in banking, finance, insurance and business services. In the latter category, which includes market research, management consultancy, personnel and public relations, there was an increase of nearly 500 000 employees over the period 1982–1987. In the long term, service sector employment trends reflect growth in demand as income rises combined with a relatively low rate of productivity growth in the sector (Rowthorn and Wells, 1987). As for business service growth, a number of specific factors are also at work. In the recessionary years of the early 1980s, risk-spreading vertical disintegration by large industrial companies undoubtedly played a role. Moreover, the increasingly specialised nature of demands for business services and consumer services associated with changing production and information technology, and rising incomes, probably favoured the creation and survival of smaller firms in this sector (Keeble and Wever, 1986; Keeble, 1989). Changes occurred in UK input/output coefficients in the 1980s that reflected changes in intermediate demand patterns in manufacturing, construction, energy and services themselves, business services growth in particular being linked to demand from distribution, communications and transport (Barker, 1990). Whatever the relative strength of these effects, it is clear that part of the growth in self-employment reflected a shift in economic activity towards high self-employment sectors as well as an increase in the proportion of self-employed within them.

So far, only changes in the numbers of businesses and self-employed have been analysed. Part of the story of the enterprise culture depends, however, on changes in the share of activity for which small businesses account. In view of the high proportion of self-employed with no employees in the lowest size bands, and the high rates of exit and entry,

shifts in the employment and turnover size distribution of businesses
would be expected to be concentrated in the lowest size categories.
This is in fact the case. Only the very smallest turnover size bands in
the VAT data, with less than £100 000 turnover at 1985 prices, increased
their share of business between 1979 and 1987 (Hughes, 1989). This
trend towards the very small end of the size distribution is confirmed
by economy-wide data on the employment share of small businesses
summarised in Table 13.4. The numbers of businesses shown are
substantially higher than the VAT registration data in Table 13.2
because of the inclusion as separate businesses of estimates of the self-
employed who are not registered for VAT. This also accounts for the
more dramatic growth in businesses compared to the VAT data. It is
clear that firms employing between 3 and 20 people increased in
significance. Those employing 20–49 people, however, declined in
significance in terms of numbers and employment share. This result is
consistent with the reported poor 'job-generation' performance of this
cohort (Gallagher, Daly and Thomason, 1990). Studies of the job-
generation process which predate the 1980s show a similar picture, as
do studies for the USA. The job-generating performance of the smallest
firms is not therefore a singular feature of the UK economy of the
1980s (Storey and Johnson, 1987). All this is predicated on taking job-
generation studies at face value. In fact, none of the existing
studies for the 1980s provides well-specified estimations of size–growth
relationships. Where attempts have been made to recover estimates of
the size–growth relationship from published transition matrices, no
statistically significant relationship emerges (Hart, 1987). It is at present

Table 13.4. Changes in the employment size distribution of UK businesses
1979–1986.[a]

Employment size band	Number of businesses (000s)		Cumulative share of employment		Share of employment	
	1979	1986	1979	1986	1979	1986
1–2	1099	1579	6.6	9.7	6.6	9.7
3–5	319	473	12.4	18.6	5.9	8.9
6–10	179	190	19.1	25.8	6.7	7.2
11–19	109	140	26.7	35.9	7.6	10.0
20–49	46	44	33.6	42.6	6.9	6.7
50–99	16	20	38.9	49.5	5.3	6.9
100–199	15	14	49.1	59.4	10.2	9.9
200+	9	12	100.0	100.0	50.9	40.6
All	1791	2471	100.0	100.0	100.0	100.0

[a] Source: based on Bannock and Daly (1990).

not possible to tell to what extent the short-term employment gain estimates for the mid- and late 1980s are simply a statistical artefact as far as surviving firms are concerned. This is in the sense that firms temporarily displaced from their 'optimum' sizes may have a tendency to regress towards that optimum. At any time, 'large' firms will include many 'small' firms above their optimal 'small' size, and the opposite will be true for small firms. The result will be a negative relationship between size and growth which reveals very little by itself about the relative dynamism of small firms. There is also a deeper methodological issue at stake. Identifying the location of an employment increase (in say small firms, or the service industries) reveals very little by itself about the underlying dynamics of that change. Large employment gains in services do not, for instance, imply that policies to boost service industry activity would be appropriate. Those gains may depend crucially on high productivity and output growth in the tradeable goods sectors which have knock-on and multiplier effects on services. In a similar vein, the response of small firms' employment shares may be the result of changes in work organisation and competitive strategy by large firms, or the displacement of existing employment in established medium-sized businesses. All of this requires more detailed work on the complementarity and interrelatedness of large and small firms. What is apparent, however, is that the vast majority of the total employment growth in any cohort of small firms is accounted for by a very small number of fast growers (Storey and Johnson, 1987).

The changes of the shares of the smallest firms are reflected most dramatically in the growth of the service sector discussed above. The production industries experienced much less rapid growth. It is therefore worth looking at manufacturing as a separate sector. Table 13.5 divides the enterprises in UK manufacturing into four size classes according to levels of employment. The most obvious point to begin with is that this sector remains dominated by a very small number of large businesses which collectively produce three-fifths of total net output and provide slightly more than one-half of total manufacturing employment, yet account for less than 1% of total manufacturing enterprises. Conversely, the vast majority of businesses are small enterprises (96% of the total) which employ less than 100 individuals. These account for around one-fifth of national output and nearly one-quarter of total manufacturing employment.

It is also apparent from Table 13.5 that in all size classes but the smallest the total number of enterprises has been in decline since 1979. The increase in the total number of enterprises has thus been generated solely by increases within the smallest size class. A large part of the increase in number in the smallest size class occurred between 1983 and 1984. This, however, is a statistical artefact caused by a change in the business register in that year which increased the census coverage. In terms of the movement of output and employment shares, a number

Table 13.5. Number of enterprises and shares of output and employment by size of enterprise for UK manufacturing 1979–1988.[a]

Year	Total number of enterprises	Percentage share of:		
		Enterprises	Employment	Output
Size band 1–99				
1979	84229	93.9	17.5	14.6
1983	81474	94.8	22.0	18.0
1984	114186	95.8	23.4	18.8
1988	130396	96.3	24.3	18.6
Size band 100–499				
1979	4152	4.6	12.9	11.6
1988	3928	2.9	16.4	14.5
Size band 500–999				
1979	609	0.7	6.6	6.8
1988	506	0.4	7.2	7.0
Size band 1000+				
1979	751	0.8	63.0	67.0
1988	575	0.4	52.1	59.9

[a] Sources: ACOST (1990), Appendix A; *Annual Census of Production 1988*. There are substantial changes in the *Census* coverage between 1983 and 1984 which boost the recorded number of small enterprises (see text). In 1980 a revised definition of manufacturing was introduced so that 1979 is not strictly comparable with later years. The effect at this level of aggregation is relatively minor.

of significant changes are evident. The most striking of these relate to the smallest and the largest size groups of firms. The size class with less than 100 employees has progressively increased its share in total employment and net output since 1979. The largest size class in contrast has experienced a substantial decline in terms of employment and output shares. Within the two middle size classes the changes are less marked, although the numbers of enterprises and establishments have declined in both groups. Since 1979, the size class with 100–499 employees has substantially increased its share in employment and output. Enterprises with less than 500 employees now account for slightly more than one-third of manufacturing output and for 40% of total manufacturing employment.

It is important to note, however, that these are changing shares of a level of overall manufacturing activity which was lower at the end of the period than at the beginning. Table 13.6 shows indices of employment, net output and net output per head in constant prices for the four size categories of enterprise for the period 1979–1988. The

Table 13.6. Employment, net output and net output per head by size of enterprise for UK manufacturing 1979–1988.[a]

Employment size band	Employment (000s) 1979	Index of employment (1979 = 100)			Net output (£m at 1985 prices) 1979	Index of real net output (1979 = 100)			Net output per head (£000 at 1985 prices) 1979	Index of real net output per head (1979 = 100)		
		1983	1984	1988		1983	1984	1988		1983	1984	1988
1–99	1138	94.0	99.4	103.3	14597	106.8	114.4	135.9	12.8	113.5	115.1	131.6
100–499	835	83.9	95.3	95.1	11621	95.9	114.2	133.1	13.9	114.3	119.8	140.0
500–999	425	86.2	84.1	82.6	6799	98.2	92.9	110.6	16.0	113.9	110.6	134.0
1000+	4087	66.6	62.2	61.7	6706	79.2	78.2	95.3	16.4	118.9	125.7	154.5
Top 100 employers	2416	72.4	66.1	62.4	38885	88.6	84.3	100.9	16.1	122.4	127.5	161.8
All	6485	74.9	74.4	74.7	100078	86.4	88.7	106.7	15.4	115.4	119.1	142.8

[a] Source: *Census of Production*. Net output from the *Census of Production* deflated by the producer price index (1985 = 100) for all manufactured home sales (*Economic Trends Annual Supplement*, 1988; *Economic Trends*, January 1991).

growth in employment and output shares of the two smallest size groups was a result of the restoration of their employment levels to those of 1979 and of their output levels to beyond it, while the larger groups experienced a decline on both activity measures. For all groups, employment declined faster or rose less fast than output. The result was rising labour productivity. It is, however, apparent that the smallest size group declined in productivity relative to both the 100–499 and the 1000+ size categories. A number of possible explanations may be conjectured. First, large firms have shed inefficient plants and lines of business. We may then be witnessing a disequilibrium phenomenon. When the superior productivity performance of the large firms feeds through to their competitive performance, so small firms' share of activity may be squeezed again. Second, the externalisation of activities which are relatively labour-intensive by larger organisations may also have affected the relative spread of labour productivity between large and small firms. Third, these aggregate comparisons may reflect aggregation biases due to different changes in the shares of small firms across industries with differing productivity levels.

Part of the case for the emergence of an enterprise culture as reflected in the changing structure of employment and industry must rest on a break with the past. We have seen how this may be true in the case of the number and shares of the self-employed and the total number of business registrations. The case for a 1980s-based change in manufacturing is, however, weaker. Table 13.7 provides data on total

Table 13.7. Employment and output shares by size of enterprise in UK manufacturing 1935–1988.[a]

Year	Total employment (000s)	Employment (000s) in enterprises employing less than:		Employment share (%) of enterprises employing less than:		Net output share (%) of enterprises employing less than 200
		200	100	200	100	
1935	5409	2078	—	38.0	—	35.0
1963	7543	1543	—	20.1	13.9	16.9
1973	7268	1506	1109	20.7	17.2	17.1
1977	6883	1552	1175	22.5	17.1	18.7
1979	6485	1498	1138	23.1	17.5	19.5
1983	4859	1351	1069	27.8	22.0	22.8
1984	4828	1465	1130	30.3	23.4	24.7
1988	4843	1509	1175	31.2	24.3	24.1

[a] Source: Hughes (1991). The series are only roughly comparable over time because of changes in *Census* definitions and industrial coverage.

manufacturing employment and on employment shares in enterprises employing less than 100 and less than 200 employees, as well as the net output shares of these size groups for a run of years beginning in 1935. It is clear that the revival in employment shares began well before 1979. Moreover, as in the 1980s, the shift in shares in favour of small firms was the outcome of stability or decline in actual employment in the smallest firms combined with a collapse in overall manufacturing employment which had its origins in the 1960s but was massively accelerated in the 1970s and 1980s. The brunt of this was borne by the largest firms. The revival in net output share for small firms mirrors the employment share movements, though the recovery is less marked. Table 13.7 also reveals that shifts in favour of the smallest size classes slowed down in the second half of the 1980s. Whereas the share of those employing less than 200 rose by 4.7 percentage points during the recession between 1979 and 1983, it rose by only 0.8 percentage points over the next 5 years of relative expansion. The share of net output fell marginally.

Stability in shares at the bottom was accompanied by stability at the top. Between 1984 and 1988 the change in the average employment concentration ratio within manufacturing industries, from 41.8% to 41.4%, was negligible compared with the fall from 44.8% in 1980 to 43.5% in 1983 (the fall between 1983 and 1984 was due largely to the compositional effects of changes in the business register in those years; see Dunne and Hughes, 1991). This stabilisation of the relative fortunes of large firms coincided with the outbreak of a major wave of mergers. This was at first characterised by whales eating whales but soon generated a level of takeover activity which in terms of both values and numbers of companies acquired outstripped the previous UK post-War peak of 1969–1973 (Table 13.8).

If at the heart of an enterprise culture lies a free and open market in corporate control then at least in that respect the UK version cannot be found wanting. Whatever the merits of this market for the performance of large firms (for a sceptical review, see Hughes, 1990), the implications for small firms are worth discussing. Insofar as small firms are closely controlled by owner–managers, the arguments that takeovers exercise discipline against inefficient managers is inevitably weak. Selling out is a 'voluntary' affair by agreement, and the decision to sell is made by the owners who are usually also the key managers. Selling may meet the needs of the owners to secure adequate financial resources for innovation or restructuring of investment strategies. It is in these areas that failures of the capital market to supply the necessary funds are most prevalent. Selling may also provide an important 'exit route' by which entrepreneurs may realise capital gains on their investment in developing their businesses. This may therefore provide an important incentive to found and develop smaller businesses. Both of these arguments, however, depend for their strength upon failures

310   *Alan Hughes*

Table 13.8. Acquisitions and mergers by UK industrial and commercial companies 1969–1989.[a]

	Number	Expenditure (£m)	Expenditure in 1962 stock market prices (£m)
Annual averages			
1969–1973	1054	1483	832
1974–1981	509	1289	561
1982–1985	561	5005	914
1986–1989	1668	27049	2594
1986	1054	20105	2342
1987	1809	22511	2207
1988	1943	28383	2783
1989	1865	37196	3045

[a] Sources: *Business Monitor MQ7*; *Financial Statistics*.

of the capital market in the provision of finance. Measures which ameliorated these failures directly would reduce the need for large-firm/small-firm takeovers to fill the gap.

Conclusions

The 1980s saw substantial shifts in the number of self-employed and their share of the UK workforce. There were also substantial increases in the number of businesses registered for VAT, and in the share of the very smallest businesses in total employment. These changes were particularly notable in the service industries. Within manufacturing, the recovery of small firms' shares was accompanied by relatively stable employment in small firms and was heavily influenced by rationalisation and retrenchment in large firms. Moreover, although these changes were accelerated by the recession of 1980–1981 they had their origin before 1979 and were experienced in other countries with widely different policy regimes (Sengenberger, Loveman and Piore, 1990). The evidence of an emerging enterprise culture looks stronger for the services. Even here, however, some caution is necessary. First, part of the growth in small firms and self-employment in services reflected the deindustrialisation of the 1980s. Second, self-employment is pro-cyclical; when allowance is made for declining unemployment in the late 1980s, no time trend remains in econometric equations that explain upward movements in self-employment between 1983 and 1989. Third, direct tests using *British Social Attitude Survey* data concerning whether those in employment considered the self-employment option more seriously as the 1980s wore on, show little change. Finally, it is apparent that movements into self-employment occur for a wide variety of pull-and-push reasons which may have little to do with renewed entrepreneurial drive (Blanchflower and Oswald, 1991; Hakim, 1988). In this connection, two illustrative points may be made. When a distinction is drawn between the relatively small number of self-employed who employ others and the much larger number who do not, it turns out that the latter are more likely to have experienced spells of unemployment and are less likely to have parents with experience of small business. The reverse is true for those self-employed who do take on other workers. For them, the receipt of an inherited lump sum of over £5000 has a further positive effect whereas this makes no difference for the probability of becoming self-employed with no employees. These groups may therefore be responding to different aspects of the economic climate of the 1980s (Blanchflower and Oswald, 1990). Moreover, although employers cite the need to obtain special skills as a prime factor in choosing to use the services of the self-employed rather than in-house labour, they also show the desire to avoid excess labour capacity. In addition, changes in the use of the self-employed over time have also been influenced by the desire to benefit from the lower wage and non-wage costs of switching to self-employed labour. Employers' strategy as much as employee-based motivation is at work (McGregor and Sproull, 1991). Interpreting trends in small business and self-employment as symbols of 'enterprise' is not possible without a simultaneous evaluation of the strategy and power of larger businesses in relation to them.

Insofar as government policy towards industry in the 1980s was based on a coherent strategy, it emphasised the promotion of individual small-scale entrepreneurship, the opening up and deregulation of markets and the promotion of a change in attitude towards business and its needs. What was eschewed was any notion of sectoral industrial policy in which the state could play a developmental role beyond the blanket promotion of enterprise. The opportunity to modernise the UK economy in the face of underlying changes in technology and demand and in the organisation of corporations may, however, depend on more than this. The competitive advantage of nations is rarely comprehensive in nature but is focused on clusters of related industries. There is a growing realisation of the importance of industrial policy in the context of newly emerging industries, especially those with high-technology requirements. At a time of major structural change and in an economy which starts from a weak competitive position, reliance on individual enterprise alone may not be enough.

Comment

Enterprise Culture—Two Visions

Michael H. Best

Three observations of import to the idea of an enterprise culture are
emerging as more data are gathered on small firms in manufacturing:
first, the best-performing economies in the international marketplace
have a comparatively high proportion of employment in small firms;
second, small firms can be internationally competitive; and third, the
UK has a comparatively small proportion of employment in small firms.
Previously, the path to modernism, growth and balance of payments
success was defined in terms of dynamic big enterprises. In Eastern
Europe, the presumed identity of modern with big firms led to the
suppression of small and medium-sized firms and/or their lumping into
combines. Japan escaped the 'modern equals big' dictum: approximately
one-half of Japanese manufacturing employees have been in plants with
less than 100 employees throughout the century; the comparable ratio
for the US is roughly one-quarter. Alan Hughes' data suggest that the
comparable figure for the UK increased from 14% in 1963 to 17–18%
in the 1970s and reached nearly one-quarter in the mid-1980s. That
small firms in Italy and Western Germany can be internationally
competitive is painfully obvious to British managers in industries such
as footwear, knitwear, clothing, furniture and machine tools. Dynamic
small firms are part of the Japanese export success story as well: if
indirect and direct exports are taken into account, a Japanese government
study estimated that small and medium-sized firms hold a 40% share
of exports of manufactured goods (MITI, 1986, p. 41).

Claims about the potential dynamism of small firms are gaining
widespread acceptance. Increasingly, the controversy is between two
competing visions of the enterprise culture. The first is rooted in the
morality tale of the 'triumphant individual'. Here the concept of culture
is one of self-reliant individualism in a market free of interference; the
concept of enterprise is one of the business person operating his or her
small shop and competing against rivals who offer the same product or
service. The task for government is to remove barriers to free markets
and individual initiative. The second vision of an enterprise culture is
one of groups of small firms that cooperate locally in order to compete

internationally. Here culture is one of cooperation to enhance the productive capabilities of a group of firms (various forms of interfirm cooperation are examined in Best, 1991); the concept of enterprise is one of teamwork to enhance entrepreneurial enterprises, as distinct from individual entrepreneurship. The task of government here is to promote and support interfirm networks that sustain cooperation for the purpose of promoting international competitiveness.

The two visions highlight different aspects: the 'triumphant individual' vision focuses on firms; the cooperative vision identifies relations amongst firms. Examples of different types of firms and interfirm relations include: (1) independent local suppliers of noncomplex goods and services; (2) subcontractors of lead enterprises that pursue price-led competitive strategies (the subcontractor has no independent product design capabilities); (3) suppliers of lead enterprises that are pursuing product-led competitive strategies (with independent problem-solving capabilities that will increase their bargaining leverage with a range of buyers); (4) members of static industrial districts or communities of small firms that are not tied to large lead manufacturers; and (5) members of networked groups of mutually adjusting, continuously innovating, specialist enterprises which engage in complementary activities within entrepreneurial industrial districts.

While the data may not distinguish among types of interfirm relationship, competition in the international market place does. What stands out in the highly successful industrial districts of the Third Italy and Western Germany is the higher proportion of small enterprises in categories (3) and (5). A group of firms located within a region that has not developed institutions of interfirm cooperation (problem-solving and product development consultation, complementary specialisations, shared collective services such as skill upgrading and technology upgrading, joint marketing, etc.) is hard-pressed to compete against a similar group that has, for several reasons.

First, consultative networking relations amongst firms (as distinct from anonymous market relations) better enable small firms to develop distinctive competences; individual firms can specialise in one link in the production chain and cooperate with similar specialists to provide the other links. A single firm can internalise every business function and production activity but it cannot specialise in each. Second, a group of firms that specialise in specific activities has greater potential to achieve the production principle of flow and the technological improvements that result from focus and specialisation. Third, small firms that make up supplier networks managed by lead firms pursuing product-led strategies have greater opportunity to build problem-solving capabilities consistent with the goal of continuous improvement in products and processes, the hallmark of leading firms. In contrast, small subcontracting firms coordinated only by the market tend to be highly dependent and less capable of pursuing product-led competition. Fourth, networked groups of small firms have a superior capacity to adjust mutually to change. It is possible for a sector but not a single firm to pursue simultaneously distinct strategies and alternative technologies. Fifth, a group of cooperating firms is better placed to guide governmental policy in the direction of a strategic industrial policy which emphasises shaping the relationships amongst firms rather than promoting (or saving) individual firms. This distinguishes the industrial policy initiatives for small and medium-sized firms in the leading industrial nations from the 'enterprise culture' initiatives of the Thatcher period. For example, the Small and Medium Enterprise Modernisation Promotion Law passed in Japan in 1963 uses modernisation in the following sense:

> The modernisation of small and medium enterprises implies. . . the modernisation of management and facilities of individual small and medium businesses, but also extends to the modernisation of a small and medium enterprise sector as an entire system, which includes modernisation of relationships between individual enterprises. . . (MITI, 1986, p. 8.)

In short, the size distribution of firms alone does not capture the relationships amongst firms. It is the character of interfirm relationships which shapes opportunities for developing the enterprise capabilities of small firms. A small firm in an industrial district constituted by a range of collective services and a dense network of interfirm relations has opportunities not available to a similar firm located in a region without a similar institutional infrastructure. One task of government is to promote a culture of interfirm cooperation so that such networks and institutions can flourish against the erosion of community championed by the myth of the 'triumphant individual', a myth that undermines the social prerequisites to gaining competitive advantage in the international marketplace.

14

Industrial Prospects in the Light of Privatisation

Ben Fine and Clara Poletti

This chapter consists of three main sections. The first assesses the general significance of the privatisation programme under Thatcher. The next two examine some of its implications for the energy sector and the steel industry, respectively, before some final conclusions are drawn. The analysis is guided throughout by an antipathy to the new orthodoxy that has shot to prominence in the analysis of privatisation. This tends to suggest that the issue of public or private ownership as such is of secondary significance and that more important are the conditions governing regulation and competition. This stance, however, depends upon an overly static and microeconomic assessment of the sources of allocative and productive efficiency. It takes comparative advantage as given rather than rooting out its origins. Consequently, the inescapably poor performance of British industry over the long term is not confronted nor the agencies that are responsible for it, other than poor policy, poor management or poor incentive structures.

A second theme that runs through the chapter is to emphasise continuity and not just breaks in industrial policy consequent upon the privatisation programme. Continuity emerges in three ways: first, state microeconomic intervention remains substantial, despite the ideology of *laissez-faire*; second, policy still lacks coherence, coordination and long-term economic aims, other than to the advantage of large-scale private capital; and third, in this light, privatisation is itself the culmination of, not a break with, the experience of the past. This is not to argue that nothing has changed at all, only that some of the general weaknesses of the past have been reinforced as far as coherent industrial policy is concerned. Moreover, at a more detailed level, as is illustrated here for energy (conservation) and steel, the guarantee of the interests of particular private capitals has witnessed a continuity of policy at the expense of a more progressive industrial restructuring.

The Veil of Ignorance

Any analysis of privatisation as a component part of industrial policy in Britain must locate it in a broader understanding of the structural problems of the British economy. Within the major industrialised countries the UK can be characterised as suffering from low wages, low investment and low productivity. The agencies potentially involved in the process of restructuring the economy (labour, industrial capital, financial capital and the state) have been too fragmented to drive industrial change. There has not been an absence of extensive state intervention. However, the historical lack of coordination between policies both within and between sectors reflects the absence of a state able and willing to construct a strong interventionist system to provide industrial leadership. This has been coupled with the overseas orientation of a significant fraction of industrial capital and the short-term perspective of a highly dynamic capital market. It has led to a vicious circle where low wages are set to sustain a low-investment, low-productivity growth path.

It has been alleged that Thatcherism reversed this dismal picture and brought dynamism back to British industry. Since the 1979–1981 recession, labour productivity in British manufacturing industry has grown at an average rate of 5.4% (Haskel and Kay, 1990)—an exceptional result compared either to Britain's poor historical performance or to contemporary international standards. Even if less impressive, a similar upturn has occurred in GDP per person employed. Before the 1980s Britain's productivity growth rate lagged behind all the main industrialised countries other than the US. Over the period of recovery from the recession its performance has been exceeded only by that of Japan. Throughout the last decade even the gap in investment rates between Britain and other European countries has narrowed.

Attempts to explain the so-called 'Thatcher miracle' and to assess it from a long-term perspective have usually emphasised the shift from demand management to supply-side policies: lower direct taxation, privatisation, liberalisation and 'reformed' industrial relations. The Conservative Party's victory in the 1979 general election marked an important shift in its political rhetoric on the role of the state in the economy, from the concept of market failure to one of political failure. The antagonistic relationship between individual freedom and state intervention in society was the focal point around which the 1979 *Conservative Manifesto* developed. In its foreword Mrs Thatcher wrote:

> No one who has lived in this country during the last five years can fail to be aware of how the balance of our society has been increasingly tilted in favour of the State at the expense of individual freedom. This election may be the last chance we have to reverse that process, to restore the balance of power in favour of the people.

This threatening image of the state, and of its relationship with society, was used to give ideological legitimacy to the need 'to roll back the economic frontiers of the state'. The necessity to free the economy from the dead hand of the state and to enhance private initiative was the banner under which the break with previous pro-active industrial policies was justified. The industrial policy programme on which the Conservatives were elected in 1979—if there was any—was the microeconomic complement of their monetarist macroeconomic policy. Faith in the power of market forces to restructure industry and to create and pick 'winners' was opposed to the idea of managed reconstruction of the economy. The creation of winners, let alone the private sectors' ability to choose them, remained an unaddressed article of faith, at least in the realm of ideas.

Soon after the 1979 election, the government decided to merge the National Enterprise Board (NEB), a state holding company initially conceived as a major instrument of industrial reorganisation and rationalisation through public ownership, with the National Research Development Corporation (NRDC). Before September 1981 a large part of NEB's holdings were either transferred back to the private sector (Ferranti, ICL and Fairey) or liquidated (Alfred Herbert and British Tanners Products).

At the end of the 1970s public corporations in the UK accounted for nearly 8% of gross domestic product and employment. Services provided by local government and by the National Health Service accounted for a further important share of national product. By the end of the 1980s this picture had changed significantly. Nearly 50% of the 1979 state sector had been privatised and about 800 000 jobs moved from the public to the private sector. The privatisation programme involved sales of public sector housing, contracting-out of services such as hospital cleaning and refuse collection and the sale of public enterprises to the private sector. Since 1979 over one million publicly owned houses have been sold to the private sector. All the main public utilities (gas, water, electricity) have been privatised and by the end of 1991, flotations of British Rail, British Coal and London Transport were in the privatisation pipeline.

Our claim is that in many ways Thatcherism at the level of policy-making did not represent a break with the past. The impressive weight of the privatisation programme was the zenith of government's renunciation of strategic planning of British industry. What Thatcherism did was not to reduce economic intervention but to modify the institutional structure for intervention, transferring to different agencies the power to drive industrial change. Unsurprisingly, the consequence of this application of the supposed *laissez-faire* principle was, on the one hand, to concentrate power in the hands of fewer people and, on the other, to weaken the potential mechanisms of political control over that power.

Despite the ideological commitment to free market forces and the institutional reform realised over the 1980s, the government has hardly renounced its leading role in industrial intervention. Privatisation of British Telecom is a clear example. The transformation of British Telecom from a public to a private monopoly, with the introduction of a subordinate rival (Mercury), was a way of ensuring its survival as a national champion. The government's wish to protect the national market of information technology was reflected in the strategy adopted for the definition of international standards:

> A battle of standards is taking place, between Open Systems Interconnection on the one hand—the international standard accepted by AT&T, all the Japanese computer manufacturers and European manufacturers—and System Network Architecture (SNA), IBM's standard. . . The decision in 1984 by the British government to refuse permission for BT and IBM to develop VAN (Value Added Network) which would have SNA standards was taken on the grounds that it would have excluded all British manufacturers from the supply of equipment to customers. (Hills, 1986, p. 188.)

Another example was the government's decision to take a 40% stake in the privatised generating companies Powergen and National Power. This might be enough to expose those firms to political pressures but too little for the Government to direct them. Further, when in 1991 British Gas announced its intention to raise the price of gas supplied to new power station projects by 35%, Mr Kinnon (Director of Ofgas) required it to sign contracts at old prices. The main reason given was that four other power station projects could have collapsed if required to pay such a high price. It thus cannot be said that free market forces are shaping the gas and telecommunication industries. Intervention is extensive and discretionary, other than through regulation, however effective this might be, and even if veiled under an ideology of *laissez-faire*.

However, the channels through which industrial policy is being realised no longer have institutions explicitly directing it. New agencies have been created only to track or correct the inefficiencies associated with the shadow of market forces. The main effects have been a weakening of direct political control and a lack of transparency of policy. The most obvious example of this is provided by the various regulatory agencies which have wide discretion over the regimes of competition and regulation to be implemented. In the case of British Telecom:

> Parliament did not have an opportunity properly to consider some central elements of BT's license, which were not disclosed until after the 1984 Act was passed. (Vickers and Yarrow, 1988, p. 211.)

Regulation is, in effect, industrial policy by other means—but limited in scope, power and accountability. This 'half-way' reform has at once precluded the realisation of a coherent institutional system for the direction of industry. Further, this has led to fragmented state intervention in response to a variety of different interests. Even the privatisation programme, despite unifying ideological legitimation, has appeared to meet particular political needs at particular moments in time. There are certain common elements, such as shifting the balance of industrial relations—often achieved whilst corporations were still under public ownership—through redundancy, closure and change in management, or shifting the boundaries between different sectors of the economy, especially where they straddle the public–private enterprise divide (see Fine, 1990). At one extreme is information technology, for example, for which the earlier sectoral divisions between telecommunications and computing, and office equipment more generally, have increasingly been broken down. At the other extreme, in the contracting-out of public services, particular activities have been isolated and opened up for profitable exploitation. The steel industry falls somewhere between these two extremes.

Despite the lack of a consistent rationale behind this programme, privatisation has contributed to the restructuring of productive capital: the goal of privatisation provided greater short-term incentives to the government for more stringent monitoring and/or restructuring of firms. Substantial improvements in financial and technical performance were often achieved before the actual change of ownership. British Gas was privatised soon after it had completed a large capital expenditure programme for the construction of its gas transmission system. This represents an exception, in that the priority given by the government to short-term cost reduction and financial performance usually led to 'improved', more intensive use of existing inputs, instead of more profound restructuring. Drastic cuts of employment, changes in accounting practices and organisational reforms were the main source of improved performance.

The Water Companies, for example, were transferred to the private sector whilst in need of massive infrastructural investments to ensure quality of supplies. In order to guarantee the success of the share flotation, a partial restructuring of the industry was first realised. From 1980–1989 employment fell by 22% and, over the same period, output (water supply) increased by more than 6%. Another example of improvement in short-term performance comes from the electricity industry:

> The Area Boards were set performance aims which were intended to increase efficiency through setting targets for reducing controllable costs, i.e. salaries, goods, services, rents and insurances. These were met over the four year period to March 1988 by the Area Boards as a whole. . . This system of encouraging cost controls and improving productivity appears to have worked. . . There remains scope for further improvements in efficiency. . . However, as there has been discipline on costs in the

past, we do not expect radical change in the approach to cutting costs in the future. (James Capel, 1990, p. 17.)

A cause for concern is that these are all exhaustible sources of productivity gains and need to be balanced against long-term effects.

A number of studies indicate that the more important contributions to the productivity miracle came through labour-saving investments, reorganisation and improved management of existing inputs (see Bean and Symons, 1989; Craft, 1991; Haskel and Kay, 1990). It is not until the end of the decade that investment growth in manufacturing was able to compensate for the sharp deterioration of the capital stock that followed the 1979–1981 recession: 'Total productive capacity is now much the same as it was when Thatcher first came to office' (Rowthorn, 1989, p. 293). Moreover, other indicators suggest that regained productivity has not been associated with equivalent gains in Britain's rate of technological innovation. Expenditure on research and development as a proportion of GDP has fallen relative to the main OECD countries (Englander and Mittelstadt, 1988, Table 14). In his analysis of Britain's technological aspirations, Walker (1991) stresses how the growth of high-technology activity that did occur is actually explained by defence expenditure and foreign investments (mainly by American and Japanese firms) in electronics and other sectors.

Finally, the long-standing poor quality of the British education and training system, if anything, has worsened. Reported skill shortages, far from declining, reached a peak in 1987–1988. Haskel and Kay (1990) reported that in 1986 training expenditure per head by employers in Britain was significantly less than American and German standards. Steedman (1988) and Prais and Wagner (1988) stressed that the gap between the vocational skill levels of British workers and their French and German colleagues has widened.

What is more, privatisation has increased the degree of internationalisation of British industry. Multinational corporations have historically had an exceptionally strong presence and this has conditioned industry's interaction with the state, labour and finance. Over the last decade the pre-existing dependence of British manufacturing on foreign multinational corporations has strengthened. This further opening of the market to foreign capital is working in the direction of deepening British industry's structural problems. In the electricity industry, investment in the combined-cycle power plants which are expected to provide most of the additional generating capacity in the next decade, will be based on foreign technology (GE, Asea–Brown–Boveri, Siemens; see Walker, 1991) at the expense of UK power-station building capacity, which will waste away in the absence of alternative orders and direction.

Moreover, the power generators, linked until 1993 by a 3-year contract to British Coal, are planning to shift their demand from British to temporarily less expensive foreign coal. This is bound to have tremendous effects on the coal industry, and further knock-on effects in the location of power stations, the use of rail transport and on balance of payments problems.

Last but not least, the process of liberalisation is likely, if anything, to sharpen the coordination problem. At a microeconomic level, old issues such as the integration of scientific and technological communities, the shift from the traditional authoritarian managerial style to a consensus-building kind of organisation, or links among companies through a network of local institutions, have been eliminated from the political agenda. At a 'meso' level the effects of Thatcherism are likely to be even more destructive. The Government's claim of having no responsibility for the conduct of energy markets, or, until recently, for the definition of a system of transport, and so on into communications and environment, does not leave much hope for a progressive restructuring of productive capital.

Fundamental Shifts in Power

A striking example of hands-off policy has been the massive privatisation of the energy sector. The debate over the privatisation of the electricity supply industry has been characterised by a lack of historical perspective. Ten years of energy surplus and relative stability of international energy markets have been enough to narrow the debate to the trade-off between technical and allocative efficiency. It is in the name of this new economic imperative that in 1982 the then Secretary of State for Energy, Nigel Lawson, denied even the need for an energy policy (whilst preparations were well in hand for confrontation with the miners). The free-market rhetoric for energy was a big change from the previous command-and-control policy. This shift in paradigm took place in a contingently favourable macroeconomic environment which led to a widespread perception of energy as a traded commodity like any other. The policy implication was that private ownership of energy production was desirable as long as the regulatory system could enforce an efficient pricing policy.

The weakness of this line of reasoning emerges as soon as a historical dimension is introduced. A major lesson that can be drawn from the UK energy sector is the futility of searching for categorical judgements between public and private ownership. In interpreting the British experience it must be recognised that after World War II the character of state intervention in energy markets evolved in a context of rapidly changing macroeconomic conditions. In the post-War period a large proportion of the industry needed fast and massive reorganisation. The Labour government engaged in an important nationalisation programme which saw the creation of the National Coal Board (1947), the British Electricity Authority (1948) and the Gas Council (1949). One of the main effects of nationalisation in the electricity industry was to make it possible to finance large investment programmes. The number of power stations rose from only 30 in 1938 to approximately 230 between

322   *Ben Fine and Clara Poletti*

1948 and 1963, and electricity production increased by 232%. Moreover, continued extension of the high-voltage national grid allowed an increased coordination of production and distribution under the control of the British Electricity Authority.

The OPEC embargo at the beginning of 1973 turned international attention towards new issues such as conservation of energy, security of supply and environmental impact. The dramatic rise in crude oil prices worked as a warning of the possible military and political threats of excessive import dependence to world stability. The focus of national energy policies moved from investment to energy efficiency (reduction of energy input per unit of output) and diversity. This shift in the political agenda was clearly stated in the 1974 OECD report on future energy prospects:

> It was becoming already clear, more than two years ago, that the projected growth of energy demand in OECD area. . . was to put excessive pressure on relatively low cost supplies. . . creating the conditions of serious market disturbances, likely to have long term repercussions on the economic and social well-being of OECD countries. It appeared also that policy questions related to the energy market could no longer be regarded as purely sectoral issues, which could easily be isolated from more general economic, social and political considerations such as balance of payments equilibrium, the fight against inflation, growth and development policies and environmental matters. (OECD, 1974.)

By the end of the 1970s the emergence in the UK of large fiscal deficits led to the attachment of a greater priority to financial control on public corporations. The 1978 White Paper shifted the emphasis of policy objectives to profitability and cash-flow targets. A contextual relaxation of previous tensions on the balance of payments and international fuel markets over the 1980s facilitated this shift toward a more market-oriented approach to energy policy. It eventually culminated in the transfer of the gas and electricity industries to the private sector.

This brief historical overview gives an idea of the futility of examining the privatisation issue simply in terms of how the change in ownership has affected the internal performance of the electricity supply industry. A broader approach needs to be taken. A wide range of energy policy issues have been left aside in the discussion and ought to be considered, in order that continuities with the past can be highlighted as well as the more obvious breaks concerning forms of ownership.

Efficiency and energy conservation

There seems to be general agreement in the most recent literature that over the next decade emphasis will shift from competition and monopoly towards environmental issues. In the UK the electricity supply industry is the major contributor to the greenhouse effect and to acid rain. It also has many other adverse environmental impacts. Different generating technologies (coal, gas, nuclear, renewable) have different repercussions.

Pressing environmental constraints have strengthened the need for an integrated and consistent energy efficiency policy. However, government policy in the 1980s took an opposite direction in both demand- and supply-side interventions. On the demand side, shortly after the privatisation Bill was published the government announced a cut in the budget of the Energy Efficiency Office from £24.5 to £15 million. Figures compiled by ACE (Association for the Conservation of Energy) show that the market for energy conservation has dropped by 28% over the past 2 years:

> Energy conservation industries complain that the government has reduced financial support and promotion over recent years. In 1986–87 spending by the Energy Efficiency Office at the Department of Energy amounted to £26 million. In 1990 the budget dropped to £15m. This year, however, it is £42m and next year it should be £47.5m. (*Financial Times*, 16 May 1991.)

Nevertheless, ACE argues that these latest figures are misleadingly high because they include funding for a home energy efficiency scheme which the Department of Energy has taken over from the Department of Employment. The scheme, which will cost £27m this year and £30m the next, provides grants to low-income households for home insulation. When this sum is taken out the figures for promotion of energy saving remain nearly constant.

On the supply side, the extensive programme of privatisation has certainly not helped. Unless the negative externalities associated with energy production are taken into account in the way existing power stations are used and new capacity is planned, too many plants with high externality costs will be built. Private generators and suppliers do not have incentives to conserve energy. Private markets will fail to implement an optimal depletion policy as long as property rights over reserves are not properly defined and/or markets are not perfectly competitive. These problems were not faced by the 1988 Department of Environment White Paper:

> The longer term environmental concerns fell victim (like nuclear power) to electricity privatisation. The CO_2 and SO_2 problems created investor uncertainty about costs and voter uncertainty about future prices. In the interest of electricity privatisation, the Department of Energy therefore insisted on the insertion of a clause in the White Paper which put off any policy initiatives on price in the energy sector until after the next election. (Helm, 1991, pp. 11–12.)

Security of supply

Before privatisation, security of supply was ensured by placing on the Central Electricity Generating Board (CEGB) a statutory obligation to provide bulk supplies of electricity to the Area Boards. Distortionary effects of the CEGB obligation to supply were one of the main concerns in the White Paper. According to the government, this way of ensuring security of supply had important negative consequences:

> Because it (the CEGB) has to be sure of delivering electricity to meet its obligation, it has to own and control the grid, even though this discourages potential competition. Because it (the CEGB) has to meet its obligation, it naturally has to be able to recover the cost of doing so. At present the CEGB has an effective monopoly of supply and the Area Boards have little incentive to promote competition. The CEGB has a statutory duty to supply them and they effectively have to meet the CEGB's cost; there is therefore little point in encouraging other sources of supply. (*Privatising Electricity*, Department of Energy White Paper, February 1988.)

Once again, a very short-sighted competitive policy was favoured to the detriment of a longer-term view. The energy market is a capital-intensive sector which faces a highly cyclical demand. It is precisely the recognition of uncertainty that should play a major role in energy planning. Policies and strategies need to remain robust under a variety of alternative scenarios.

The possible imbalances may be exacerbated by the private sector's under-diversification of fuel choice. PowerGen and National Power, as a duopoly, have a clear incentive to follow the same strategy as far as fuel choice is concerned. In doing so they can avoid being isolated in case the fuel turns out to be uneconomic in the future. What the empirical evidence shows is indeed that the generation business is switching massively to new combined-cycle gas turbines (CCGTs). Almost all new capacity built in the 1990s will be gas-fired. Although this partly reflects shifts in technology and EC policy over the use of gas in electricity generation, it is also a product of short-termism in which the payback period for investment in generation must be quicker, if not more efficient over the long-term, particularly in the context of supply by any new entrant. More generally, the investment strategies of corporations in and around the electricity supply industry will become increasingly directed to financial performance rather than long-term industrial regeneration. Whilst past history should have taught us how dangerous a heavy dependence on one source of energy can be, even more than this is at stake in fuel and technology choices and the way those choices are made.

Vulnerability of the domestic energy market to fuel prices and exchange rate fluctuations will be further increased after the expiry of coal contracts in 1993. Until now domestic coal has provided a relatively more expensive, but secure source of energy. The generators have declared their intention to shift, after 1993, to cheaper foreign coal. The effect for the coal industry will be devastating and the irreversibility of pit closures means that we are getting into a 'one-way street'. Again, the 'market' solution seems to be far from optimal.

Steel Yourself for This

It has been argued that the legacy of the Thatcher years was both politically and institutionally to move even further out of reach the ability of the state to intervene to establish or support the development of 'economies of scope'. The steel industry is a clear example, where state intervention, instead of pursuing coherent long-term policy, has operated predominantly to ensure the profitability of the private sector. Privatisation was the ultimate expression of this line of action.

At a global level, the early 1970s proved something of a watershed for the steel industry. The uninterrupted expansion of the post-War boom came to an abrupt halt and was drastically reversed even as large-scale and long-gestating capacity was still being laid down for what were anticipated to be expanding markets, domestically protected for the major producers. Production fell by 20% in the EEC and the US in 1975, and by 13% in Japan. In 1974, world production had stood at over 700 million tonnes and planned new capacity totalled 240 million tonnes. In addition, the NICs were also significantly increasing capacity to serve their own domestic markets as well as mounting a challenge in shrinking export markets (for accounts of the industry at a world level, see Goldberg, 1986; Yachir, 1988; Hudson and Sadler, 1989; EIU, 1990; UN, 1990; OECD, 1990).

In the UK, the steel industry was subject to renationalisation by the Labour government in 1967, following the attempt less than 20 years earlier when the post-War Labour government's attempt to nationalise what was a profitable and strategic industry was essentially thwarted.[16] The opposition to renationalisation was muted, given the failure of the private sector to gear itself up for large-scale, capital-intensive, high-productivity mass production of bulk steel. Crucial to this lack of opposition, however, was the provision for generous compensation for the assets taken into public ownership[17] and the leaving of the major part of special and finished steels in private hands—these were and continued to be profitable. Bryer *et al.* (1982, p. 43) sum up the situation:

> The steel industry in 1966 was in a financial mess. The industry's leaders finally accepted that the only way out of this mess was to obtain public finance (although they hoped to avoid full nationalisation. . .). Given the Labour Party's historic commitment to the nationalisation of steel, the Government was only too happy to provide the money when the time came.

Here then lay the major sectoral cleavage—between bulk and (a variety of) specialised steel products. The newly renationalised British Steel embarked upon a programme of large-scale mass production even as world demand for steel was soon to embark upon its precipitous decline. This might be considered to have been more bad luck than bad timing. However, the division between public and private ownership along the lines of basic and specialised steels laid the foundation for the public sector to work in such a way as to guarantee the profitability of the private sector. Productivity of (publicly owned) bulk steel was to be subordinated to that of (privately owned) special steels.

The 1970s proved to be a decade of adjustment. British Steel adopted a strategy of both closing a major part of its existing capacity and of investing in new capacity at previously underutilised coastal sites so that advantage could more readily be taken of higher-grade imported ore. This strategy's commercial viability depended upon a continual expansion of demand for steel in the second half of the 1970s. When this failed to materialise, in part due to the poor quality of British output as far as export markets were concerned, the imposition of cash limits on British Steel in the late 1970s entailed an even faster pace of closures in order that investment in new capacity could be funded. The workforce had to be run down and plant closed in order that new plant could be financed. Thus, in current prices, annual average capital expenditure rose from £193 million in 1973–1974 to £392 million in 1975–1980 before dropping to £150 million in 1981–1984. By the early 1980s, the major programme of (re)construction had been completed even if the programme of destruction still had some way to run. Thus, whilst the industry's employment fell from 250 000 to 120 000 between 1971 and 1981, with output dropping from 24.7 million tonnes to 11.9 million tonnes (the latter partly affected by strike action), the workforce fell to 52 000 by 1988 with output increasing to almost 15 million tonnes.

For Bryer *et al.* (1982) British Steel's strategy was faulted from the outset, and not just in retrospect in the light of the collapse in global and domestic steel demand (although these were not entirely exogenous). The idea that the UK industry could follow the previously successful Japanese strategy is shown to have been predictably erroneous because cheap iron ore was no longer available, export markets were limited, even domestic markets were less secure with entry to the EEC, there was no complementary industrial strategy (for which mutually supportive expansion across a swathe of domestic industry would have proved beneficial)[18] and there was liable to be limited commitment to such a strategy over the long term (for which 20 years at least seemed necessary). This raises the issue of why the strategy was adopted. Although managerial incompetence and self-interest are not to be ruled out, it must also be observed how powerfully the strategy conformed to the interests of the (fattening) rump occupied by the private sector.

Effectively, the public sector, through massive losses and hence subsidy, totalling £1619 million between 1967–1968 and 1979–1980, had borne the cost of adjustment for the UK industry whilst sustaining the specialised private sector through provision of its basic input. Or, to put it another way, as elsewhere in the world, British Steel had restructured domestic industry in the face of global excess capacity and changing technological imperatives (on which, see later), but it had done so without the financial support that could have been provided by its retaining the subsector that was least subject to depressed world conditions.[19]

However, this is not simply a matter of British Steel taking the rap and functioning to provide the private sector with bulk steel as its major raw material input. The private sector also produced limited but growing quantities of bulk steel of its own and, consequently, had both a guaranteed market for its own output and a guaranteed source of supply for whatever it was short of, given the excess capacity of British Steel. Thus, denied the major part of specialised steels, the public sector suffered the dual burden of limited access to the profitable subsector of its business and to its associated market for bulk steel as an input in conditions of excess capacity. British Steel was more the private steel firms' supplier than their competitor (Abromeit, 1986, p. 226).

Nor is it simply a matter of redistribution of rewards and losses as between the public and the private sector. One of the implications of the role played by British Steel was that it should not embark upon investments in the increasingly globally popular minimills which were not only much smaller than integrated bulk production plants, as their name suggests, but were also dependent upon recycling of scrap. This technology was essentially reserved for the private sector which, nonetheless, adopted it only to a limited extent given the overwhelming weight of capacity available to British Steel. Thus, a structure of the industry evolved in which British Steel's new capacity displaced its old in the provision of bulk steel, the private sector employed this to manufacture special steels, and neither the public nor the private sector developed minimills[20] which were elsewhere one of the major innovations in reducing costs and in responding more flexibly to uncertain demand (see UN, 1990, p. 63).

This somewhat lengthy account provides the necessary background for understanding developments in the 1980s which ultimately led to the reprivatisation of British Steel in November 1988. The lead up to, and the preparations for, privatisation reflected the continuing commitment to use the public sector to promote the private sector. If the 1970s were to provide the core investments to restructure the production of bulk steel, the 1980s were to witness the explicit use of that base for restructuring to private advantage in the production of specialised steels.

A major mechanism for doing this was the Phoenix programme which ran from 1981–1986, in which the government forced British Steel into 12 joint ventures with the private sector and in which British Steel itself was only allowed a majority share in just one of these ventures.[21] Effectively, joint assets were pooled and supplemented by investment through British Steel with the aid of government subsidy. As Cockerill (1989, p. 3) put it:

> BSC was instructed by the government to prepare proposals to eliminate areas of overlap between itself and the private sector.

The mechanism was to be through the Phoenix joint ventures with the following guidelines, in principle: British Steel should not have majority equity ownership or control; the new ventures should be free-standing companies without recourse to parent guarantees; the new ventures should be viable commercially from the outset (i.e. with low financial gearing and relief from obligations incurred prior to foundation); working capital requirements were to be channelled through British Steel; the finance required should be significantly less than would be required to finance British Steel's business if it remained in the public sector; and the valuation of assets should reflect their contribution to the new ventures (Cockerill, 1989, p. 4). Cockerill's overall assessment is that:

> The Government, in pursuing the joint venture policy, used BSC as a catalyst to instigate change and as a channel to supply public funds to the private sector. . . The clear beneficiaries have been the private sector partners in the joint ventures, which have been able to transfer loss-making assets from their balance sheets to those of the joint ventures. (Cockerill, 1989, p. 20.)[22]

With this restructuring, effected over a 20-year period, British Steel was itself ready for return to the private sector. Since privatisation, as previously occurred for the private companies, and quite apart from Phoenix, the industry has been subject to further restructuring through mergers and acquisitions.

Perhaps it is worth dwelling on an (American) outsider's view of the policies that have seen this triumphal return of the private sector. Abromeit (1986, pp. 289–290), following a detailed study of the steel industry, assessed the performance of the nationalised industries as showing a general 'lack of purpose and objectives' both individually and as a whole; a lack of long-term development concepts; a lack of coordination of their policies; a lack of economic efficiency and of economic and social performance control; too many short-term interventions; excessive financial control, leading (*inter alia*) to the Treasury gaining a preeminent role without being a real partner of the boards; a general 'blurring of responsibilities' between the boards and all those concerned with them; and finally, a similar general lack of expertise in the controllers. Here are identified some of the more long-standing weaknesses in the making of British industrial policy more generally, to which might be added the limited influence of organised labour on policy[23] and the peculiarly distant relationship between finance and industry. These features are not, however, without a logic. As has been shown, the persistent theme is of the use of the public sector to sustain private sector profitability. Are the associated weaknesses in economic performance liable to be rectified in the future as British Steel and its erstwhile competitors and partners increasingly engage in similarly ambiguous relations with their European, or even non-European, counterparts?

The prospects are not optimistic for the simple reason that, from the analysis presented, the UK industry still lies far behind those of other countries for which diversification within and out of the steel industry has long been a response to the critical restructuring of the 1970s. As NEDO (1986, p. 11) cautiously confessed:

> It may require diversification to capitalise on technology and skills acquired in steelmaking as, for example, the Japanese major steel companies are doing.

Hudson and Sadler (1989, p. 23) are more forthright, and the experience they describe has been repeated in other countries:

> All the major companies have diversified into the manufacture of silicon wafers for the electronics industry. Kawasaki Steel anticipates that its non-steel business, centred on electronics, will generate 40 per cent of its income by the end of the century (compared to 20 per cent in 1985), while Nippon Steel estimates that electronics will provide 20 per cent of its turnover by 1995.

Consequently, there is not only a lack of coherence and integration currently in industrial policy-making, there have also been two lost decades as the industry's main producer has only juggled around in its role in bulk and specialised steelmaking. It should have provided the initial basis for diversifying and specialising in both specialised steel and minimills as well as into other sectors of the economy, rather than retreating into the shell of bulk production in order to provide for a small-scale but heavily dependent private sector. Truly a case of the tail wagging the dog.

Conclusions

This is not the place to assess the implications of world events for Britain's industrial prospects. However, the single European market, the opening up of the East European economies and the continuing emergence of the NICs expose the UK to intensified competition from a variety of sources. It is the ultimate contention of this chapter that the increasingly global role of Britain's financial institutions and of the multinational corporations that operate from and within the UK may well benefit substantially from this restructuring of the world economy.

However, the prospects for industry located in Britain are correspondingly bleak as a relatively skilled, disciplined and compliant workforce serves as a low-wage assembly point within the European region. Such is the legacy of Thatcher and her Tory successors. However, the programme of a prospective Labour government offers solutions that are little different from those offered in the past; the only difference is that they were more strongly pursued then in what were arguably more favourable conditions—only to fail. They can hardly be expected to work in the future. Britain's problem remains the creation, not the picking, of winners. This is less a matter of policy as of restructuring the exercise of economic and political power.

Comment

The Industrial Policy Legacy

Malcolm Sawyer

During the 1960s and 1970s there were some hesitant attempts, generally by Labour governments, to halt Britain's relative economic decline through industrial policies which could be labelled corporatist or tripartite. These included the National Plan (1965–1966), the Industrial Reorganisation Corporation (1966–1970) and the Industrial Strategy and Sector Working Parties (1975–1979). These policies involved to some degree the state adopting a developmental role with a strategic view on the future evolution of the economy and the involvement of enterprises, unions and government. The policies were generally operated on a small scale in comparison with the magnitude of the problem (see Sawyer, 1991a, for the detailed arguments concerning this aspect of industrial strategy). The Thatcher goverment (and to a lesser degree the Heath government) was particularly hostile to these policies and reversed them as quickly as possible.

I would argue that there were two important constraints on the successful implementation of such policies. The first is the general absence of an entrepreneurial and developmental outlook by the civil service and the disbelief by business that there is a developmental role for government in industrial affairs. The second is that the intellectual and cultural environment was antipathic to such policies. In particular, orthodox economic analysis, with its emphasis on static efficiency and with the role of government seen in terms of regulation (widely interpreted so as to include anything from control over profit levels to enforced changes of industrial structure), cannot comprehend the need for a developmental role for the state. The purpose of government policy is seen as the correction of 'market failure': widespread government intervention may be advocated if there is a perception of extensive 'market failure' though it became commonplace in the 1980s to argue that such failure has to be compared with 'government failure'. The regulatory approach to industrial policy, in which there is an arms-length relationship between government and industry, has generally characterised British and American policy, and we will use the label 'Anglo-Saxon approach' (Sawyer, 1991b).

The policy towards industry pursued by the Thatcher and Major governments gradually changed and evolved, with—as would be expected—a number of inconsistencies. It is useful to highlight three particular aspects. The first has been the privatisation programme, particularly of public utilities. Successive governments had sought for ways to monitor the public utilities, and one impact of privatisation has been the use of arms-length regulators such as Oftel and Ofgas to impose control over price increases in the public utilities. Whilst at one level this represents a distinct shift in policy, at another level it represents a continuity of policy in that it seeks to find ways to regulate natural monopolies. The second aspect is the influence of the ideas of Austrian economists (notably those of Hayek on Thatcher and Joseph), where private ownership is seen as important for productive efficiency and the major barriers to competition are viewed as those erected by government (rather than by dominant firms).

The third, and most important, aspect is the declared acceptance of market solutions. Market solutions involve some, but not others, in the decision-making process. This is clearest in merger policy, where 'let the market decide' means that the shareholders of the company make the decision, without any input from workers, consumers or government. This approach involves no role for government other than encouragement of the operation of markets and competition. It denies any role to government in the support and development of the industrial base or in the consideration of production in the formulation of fiscal and monetary policies. Further, it does not recognise any need for government to adopt a strategic position on industrial development (for example, to recognise that some sectors, often high-technology ones, are important for future prosperity).

The industrial policies of the 1980s can be seen as the full application of the Anglo-Saxon model, with a particular emphasis on the benefits of competition and the market. One response to the use of the Anglo-

Saxon model (and its failure to provide the promised industrial regeneration) has been a search for more socially acceptable and workable alternatives. This has led to increasing interest over the past decade in the industrial policies pursued in successful market economies, notably Japan, Germany and Korea. There are continuing debates over the precise nature of industrial policies in these countries, and over which features of those policies and the societies concerned have been important for economic success. There are also many features of those policies which are thoroughly undesirable. However, it is clear that they do not involve notions of leaving everything to the market; those governments do involve themselves in industrial development.

The mainstream economics approach has counterposed markets and government, the role of government being to regulate and restrain markets. The developmental view sees the possibility that markets and governments might operate in a complementary manner:

> The first element in a successful industrial policy is a creative use and shaping of the market. Industrial policy fails when it overrides or ignores the market and is based upon the presumption that plans and markets are alternative means of economic coordination. The purpose is not to substitute the plan for the market but to shape and use markets. . . effective policy towards industry depends upon breaking with the plan or market dichotomy that informs conventional economic theory and is taken for granted by policy-makers guided by that theory. (Best, 1991.)

Conservative politicians often claim that they are uniquely qualified to run a market economy. However, the experience of the 1980s and of other market economies suggests that blind faith in market forces is not the route to a successful market economy. There is now some appreciation of the developmental role of the state, though this is largely confined to academics and some disgruntled industrialists. The effect of Thatcherite policies has been to make the implementation of such a role more difficult. The two constraints identified above were intensified by the policies of the 1980s: the privatisation of public utilities has limited government policy in these areas to regulation, and there has been an undermining of institutions such as NEDO which were associated with previous developmental-style policies.

15

The Development of Labour Policy, 1979–92

John Eatwell

The government which takes office after the 1992 General Election will face economic problems more severe than any faced by an incoming government since 1945. The deterioration in the overall competitive performance of the economy over the past 13 years is illustrated by the fact that, despite the severity of the recession, Britain's current account deficit is still likely to reach £6 billion in 1991. Any recovery will, in these circumstances, be associated with a sharp deterioration in the external accounts. Britain's growth rate is therefore severely constrained, and with that constraint goes the prospect of cumulative decline as slow growth discourages and inhibits investment, which in turn leads to a further deterioration in competitiveness.

Moreover, over the past 13 years there has been substantial consumption of national productive assets. The exploitation of North Sea oil resources has not been associated with an equivalent accumulation of productive assets.[24] Social infrastructure, including school buildings, hospital buildings and equipment, and substantial parts of the rail network, has been allowed to deteriorate. The resources which should have been used to (at least) maintain capital intact have instead been used to expand consumption.

The run-down of the asset base of the economy has been exacerbated by the fact that investment has been heavily biased against export-earning sectors. Investment in manufacturing has not increased at all since 1979. The share of national product devoted to investment in commercially viable research and development has been cut. Whilst there has been a significant expansion of investment in the financial sector, this has not resulted in an expansion of Britain's share in the world markets for financial services.[25]

Investment in human capital, in education and training, has also been significantly inferior (both as a share of national product and in absolute terms) to that in most of our major competitors. In an era in which competitive success is more than ever associated with skill, quality and

technological sophistication, the lack of investment in people will place
Britain at a severe competitive disadvantage.

Labour Party Policy

It is against this background that the current economic policies of the
Labour Party have been formulated. The objective of those policies is
the attainment of a sustained increase in the volume of investment—
investment in capacity, in people, in ideas and in infrastructure. This
is necessary both to make up the deterioration in Britain's productive
capacity which has occurred over the past 13 years, and to lay the
foundations for the steady expansion in competitive output which is
necessary if high levels of employment are to be maintained.

The stress on the need for investment and production, rather than
social consumption and redistribution, does not imply the abandonment
of egalitarian goals. Indeed, Labour's policies on, for example, access
to flexible education and training, and on opportunities for women, are
based on the premise that there is no contradiction between equality
and efficiency. However, there is no doubt that there has been a change
of emphasis, with the needs of industry to the fore. That change has
been brought about by the very clear fact that the condition of the
British economy is such that a major reconstruction must be the first
priority.

However, it is not only the emphasis of Labour's economic policy
which has changed; the content of policy has also changed since Neil
Kinnock became Leader of the Labour Party in 1983. Some of the
changes are only now coming to fruition, and like any good policy
framework, the economic policy of the Labour Party has the potential
to evolve yet further, particularly in the light of changing circumstances.
The most significant broad changes in current Labour Party thinking
away from what was previously typical have been as follows.

(1) Abandonment of the idea that short-term macroeconomic manage-
    ment is the key to the maintenance of full employment. It is argued
    in effect that it is no longer possible to have Keynesianism in one
    country, and hence fine-tuning should be replaced by a search for
    macroeconomic stability as a framework for long-term investment.
    Stability is defined as a stable exchange rate, stable interest rates
    at levels no higher than those of Britain's principal competitors,
    and low inflation.
(2) Replacement of hostility towards the European Community, in
    which the EC was seen as an inhibition upon Labour's policies,
    with an enthusiasm for the EC as an arena within which Labour's
    objectives can best be attained. This extends beyond environmental
    issues and the Social Charter to the industrial potential for Britain

of the move toward Monetary Union, and the need to pursue policies at an EC level which would sustain expansion and employment throughout the Community.

(3) Abandonment of the idea that nationalisation of an industry is necessarily the way to achieve efficiency, and its replacement by the proposition that regulation may achieve the same results.

(4) Replacement of the idea that industrial policy should involve the government in making tactical managerial decisions, with the proposition that the state should provide the 'well-springs' of growth—skills, research and development, infrastructure—within a broad strategy of accumulation.

(5) A shift from discretion toward rules, that is, from the politicisation of tactics to the politicisation of strategy. Economic reform should be essentially institutional reform, creating a framework within which social objectives can be attained, rather than attempting to impose social objectives on an inappropriate framework.

These broad changes have, of course, been manifest in particular policies such as support for ERM entry, plans for an integrated and flexible education and training system, the development of new methods for making high-quality research and design more readily available to small and medium-sized companies, new ideas for the financing of major transport investments, and so on. However, in this chapter I concentrate on the broad sweep of policies outlined in the list above and attempt to identify the major influences that led to the changes.

Influences

Economic policy does not develop in a vacuum. Nor does the theory of economic policy. The *General Theory* is a product of the 1930s and it is difficult to imagine that book being written at any other time. In the same way, the changes in Labour Party policy are necessarily a product of the experiences of the past decade. However, Labour's policy also bears the mark of a fundamental proposition which has not changed. That is the proposition that, left to itself, a market economy is inefficient. This inefficiency may be expressed in terms of externalities, or more general market failures of the type identified by Keynes and associated with the process of accumulation. In either case there is a potential for government policy to produce greater efficiency. The problem of policy formation then becomes that of constructing the right sort of policy which is efficient and which most nearly achieves social goals, and this will undoubtedly be affected by the circumstances of the time.

In the light of the events of the past 13 years it might be expected that the content of Labour's economic policy has been shaped by: (1)

the changed 'material' circumstances of the economy, ranging from the discovery and production of North Sea oil to the greater economic integration of the UK within the EC; (2) changes in the economy brought about by Conservative policy, such as the privatisation of major public-sector companies, capital depreciation within the public services (school buildings, hospitals, council houses, transport infrastructure, etc.), the size of the overall tax burden (3 percentage points up since 1979), the composition of the taxation system and the deregulation of domestic and international finance; (3) the perceived success or failure of the economic policies of previous Labour governments; (4) changes in the accepted parameters of economic debate, for example, the widespread hostility which the Conservatives have managed to instill towards public borrowing; and finally, (5) the acceptance and/or absorption of Conservative ideas. Of these five potential sources of influence, the last has, I believe, been of virtually no significance.[26]

Of greatest significance, of course, have been the changes in the material and organisational circumstances of the economy. This is clearly the case with respect to the changes in European policy—if Britain were not closely integrated into Europe then economic policies might be implemented on a national scale which are now better pursued within an EC context. Similarly, the privatisation of the major utilities has led Labour to develop its policies on the regulation of utilities. The rise in the average tax burden suggests that any increase in taxation on the majority of tax-payers would be inefficient.[27] The serious run-down in social infrastructure means that the expansion of social and public services which Labour desires must be preceded by a period of restoration. Whilst commitment and intentions are unwavering, extravagant promises are out.

There is no doubt, too, that the presentation of Labour's policy has been affected by the extreme conservatism (with a small 'c') of economic debate in Britain today. This is particularly true on the question of government borrowing. The government accounts today combine capital and current transactions in a manner which is not only misleading but which would be illegal in the case of a public company. Nonetheless, the Public Sector Borrowing Requirement has acquired a symbolic significance quite out of proportion to its economic meaning. Labour has attacked this confusion, arguing that public accounts should differentiate between current and capital spending, and that while Labour will not borrow to fund the expansion of public consumption, proper accounting and economic efficiency would allow the expansion of borrowing, where appropriate, to fund public investment.

However, these practical matters are only part of what I believe to be a wider and more important change in Labour Party thinking. I would characterise that change as a turn toward the core ideas of European social democracy, and away from a peculiarly British version of 'socialism'—a turn away from the Anglo-American model of the market economy, towards the more efficient European model.

Anglo-American and European Models

There are, broadly speaking, two distinct models of market economy (the classical exposition of the differences between the Anglo-American and European models, and the consequences for the content of economic policy, is Andrew Shonfield's *Modern Capitalism*, Oxford University Press, 1965). The Anglo-American model is based essentially on the view of markets promoted within orthodox neoclassical theory—i.e. that competitive markets allocate given resources efficiently (at least, Pareto-efficiently). The model is essentially static and, in policy terms, results in considerable emphasis on the role of free financial markets in securing the efficient allocation of material resources. The model is essentially a late nineteenth-century rationalisation of *laissez-faire* (and is analytically quite distinct from the case for *laissez-faire* advanced by Smith and Ricardo, which was associated with the dynamics of accumulation, not the statics of allocation).

The European model derives from a fusion of socialist ideas with an acknowledgement of the dynamic potential of markets. The efficiency of markets is to be found not in the static theorems of allocative efficiency but in the dynamic potential for change which is stimulated by market competition. As a dynamic force, markets can be both constructive and destructive. It is therefore necessary to create a framework of institutions within which the benefits of market competition can be enjoyed and the negative aspects minimised. European social democracy has, since its origins in the work of 'revisionist' theorists at the turn of the century, been based on three propositions: the promotion of a democratic (parliamentary) road to socialism, the rule of law, and the dynamic potential of the mixed economy. The intellectual and political enemy of social democracy was communism.

The Anglo-American and European models have had a great effect on their democratic rivals. The right-wing, free-market theory of the Anglo-American model produced a democratic socialism which saw the role of the state in the economy predominantly in terms of *ownership* and the direct control of economic activity. Only by public ownership of the means of production could social objectives be achieved in a competitive market-place. Otherwise, the imperatives of competition would force any company to obey the market's rules. In this context, 'state intervention' means direct involvement of the state in industrial management.

The European social democratic analysis of markets has likewise had a great effect on its rivals. The parties of the right have developed notions of the 'social responsibility' of the state which go beyond considerations of social welfare and included the acceptance of responsibility within the process of accumulation. Erhart's conception of the 'social–market' economy was not, as the British SDP tried to pretend, simply a free market plus social welfare. It was a (right-wing) model of the responsibilities of the state within the operation of the economy.

West European social democratic parties have placed far less emphasis on ownership than has been the case in Britain. Instead they have concentrated on developing institutions and structures of state intervention which have reinforced the role of markets as an engine of accumulation and change. In this context, 'state intervention' is less likely to imply direct involvement in industrial management: the state sets the framework, the private sector does the management. The difference between the British and the European conceptions of socialism finds an echo in the short-termism, long-termism debate. Starting from the Anglo-American theory of markets, there can be no such thing as short-termism.[28] Starting from a European view of markets, there is a clear rationale for the development of institutions which reinforce the process of accumulation. These will tend to be institutions which are today identified as reinforcing long-termism.[29]

Of course, actual practice has not fallen into the neat divide I have suggested. Over the past 30 years there have been persistent attempts in the UK to adopt ideas from the more successful West European economies. However, these have, until now, still been couched within the terms of the Anglo-American model. For its part, the European model has been affected by the dominance of the fashion for deregulation, although this has involved a rethinking of the institutions which sustain accumulation, rather than adoption of the static allocation model.

Changes within Labour Party Policy

This shift towards the European definition of socialism, away from the sort of socialist policy which was coloured by an acceptance of the Anglo-American view of competition and markets, derives not from the failures of the past 13 years, but from the longer-term decline in British economic performance. The successful application of 'European' policies will, of course, depend upon the development of a British variation on the European theme. It is no good trying to transplant institutions from France or Germany, and expecting them to flourish within a British environment which, if not hostile, is indifferent. However, past experience of such transplants does suggest that British versions will need to be far-ranging, and certainly not piecemeal.

An important concrete change in the conduct of economic policy will be a steady shift towards rules rather than discretion. This will mean that the policy role of the Secretary of State will not be the daily exercise of his or her discretionary powers, but instead the design of a long-term framework of institutional 'rules' within which both public and private sectors must operate. An example might be competition policy. If competition policy is to stimulate a positive approach to long-term investment within the industrial sector, then there must be confidence that that policy will be operated consistently in a way which reinforces the long-term. The declaration that the Secretary of State is to pursue such a policy, abandoning the Tebbit doctrine and replacing it with a discretionary long-term approach, may not, in itself, be enough to achieve the desired change in behaviour. An explicit change in the legal rules that shape competition policy might have a greater long-term effect.

Similar changes might be appropriate in the legal framework that defines the relationship between finance and industry, in the development of consumer rights, and in environmental policy. The industrial relations proposals of the Labour Party are also built on the premise that efficiency is best served by a clearly defined set of rules, rather than discretionary beer and sandwiches.

Another important policy change is the shift in the emphasis of economic policy from attempts to persuade companies that they should invest long-term, towards the creation of an economic environment within which companies would wish to invest long-term. This is indicated both by the emphasis on macroeconomic and financial stability[30] and by the commitment to ensure that investment expands in the 'well-springs' of economic growth—education and training, research, design and infrastructure.

Of course, policy will develop in the light of experience. However, the fundamental shift has been made towards the European version of democratic socialism, using the dynamics of the market to achieve social ends. If European experience is anything to go by, this will in due course lead to significant changes in the social responsibility of the economic policies of the Conservative Party. My interpretation of the changes in the policy stance of the Labour Party should not be taken to suggest that there was a single conscious decision to shift towards the European model. There was not. What occurred was first, the commitment in Neil Kinnock's very first speech as Leader of the Labour Party in October 1983, to develop policies which made productive efficiency the foundation not only of economic strength but also of the expansion of social policy; and second, the steady accumulation of policy changes which stemmed from Kinnock's initial stand. The new stance is the logical outcome of the approach to economics enunciated in that first speech.

Comment

An Agenda for the 1990s

Will Hutton

A generous interpretation of the Labour Party's economic policy is that it amounts to a serious attempt at reindustrialisation around European social market principles: not only the right policy, but radical for both the Labour Party and the country. A more critical view is that this is no more than a rationalisation of where the party has found itself as a result of a decade of temporising and tactical withdrawals, and that even if it were the right policy it is shot through with inconsistencies—notably its attitude towards wage bargaining and the lack of a worked-out position towards the City. On balance I tend to the more generous view, although not without important reservations about the coherence of the whole package.

Although it is fashionable on both the right and left to decry Labour's moderation and abandonment of the old Alternative Economic Strategy approach as 'unprincipled', the criticism is disingenuous—and from the left, naive. The right-wing argument is tinged with regret that Labour has not locked itself into a world of economic impossibilism, while the left ignore the immense conservatism of the culture and mores in which Labour has to sell itself; and to label workability and practicality as an intellectual retreat is poor economics and even worse politics.

Britain is a very conservative country. In particular, the assumption that public borrowing is always bad is almost hysterical. While it is true that international commitments undoubtedly constrain policy, the enthusiasm to insist that there are no other alternatives but breathtaking austerity and nonintervention is excessive—and tribute to the success of City pundits and Tory economic spokesmen alike in defining what is 'sound' and what is not. Yet this is the background against which non-Conservative parties have to operate and, when out of power, to have their policies judged. It is to the credit of the Labour team that they have managed to put together a policy mix which is both credible with the financial markets and yet distinctively purposeful in its approach to managing the market economy: there is little doubt that the emphasis on industrial policy, extensive training and research and development would mark a decisive break with the recent past.

Equally, it is heartening that one of the two main parties is no longer looking to the US as an economic model, and is beginning to copy some of the best elements in mainstream European thinking and economic institutions. The commitment to European Monetary Union does imply a wholesale Europeanisation of, for example, the ramshackle approach to education and training; the Tory idea that this should be organised voluntarily along US lines is doomed to failure. Without compulsion, the incentives in the system are not to train but to pay more for recruits that others have invested in and developed. Labour policy at least addresses this fundamental weakness in the government's position.

However, despite the worthiness of the aims and genuinely radical nature of some of the policy proposals, the retreat from macroeconomic policy has surely gone too far. While it is plainly impossible for Labour openly to advocate devaluation—and indeed any exchange rate adjustment could now take place only in the context of a wider European realignment—the commitment to hold today's parities is developing into a major totem of policy. Sterling, however, is overvalued by anything up to 20% on the calculations of 'full equilibrium exchange rate' provided by John Williamson at the Institute for International Economics in Washington, and the disinflation implied to win back lost competitiveness means that the whole of the next Parliament will be dogged by the economy growing at below its already low capacity and unemployment rising inexorably if gradually through 3 million.

This is an unnecessarily high price to pay for European monetary integration: to force the UK to have lower-than-average European inflation in order to win competitiveness is surely excessive. Could we not settle for the European inflation average and some economic growth, even if that does imply, say, a 10% or 12.5% devaluation within a general realignment? At the moment it is doubtful whether the Labour team in office would even dare to press for an exchange rate realignment in case this was interpreted as a fall from the grace of financial orthodoxy; and while credibility is important, Labour has more than once this century hung itself on the cross of defending an indefensible exchange rate. I have a profound sense of foreboding that history may be about to repeat itself.

Equally, fiscal policy will become more and not less important as the only means of managing the economy in a world in which the exchange rate and interest rate are pre-set. Here some indication of the rules by which borrowing would be judged would be welcome: 'trust me to be prudent' is not very convincing in the long run from either Nigel Lawson or John Smith. Is Labour in favour of balancing the budget over the economic cycle? Of a national debt to GDP target? Or of getting away with what it can?

As for the City of London, short-termism and Britain's deal-making culture, these should be major targets of any government with the zeal to reform our ailing supply-side. Yet the failings of British financial institutions have received little policy attention or serious interest from Labour economic spokesmen—at least in part because, unlike training, this area is something of a black box. This is a major policy deficiency.

As for the labour market, the silence about possible initiatives to improve the nominal wage/unemployment trade-off is deafening. British wage growth must match the European average for long-term success inside the ERM, and if pay settlements are not at least to be coordinated then the only alternative is to allow the market to work as at present. Is Labour's intention really to leave the institutions of wage bargaining unreformed and continue with the policy of pay decentralisation? Politically, of course, these issues are uncomfortable but as the Tories have no worthwhile position, there has been little cost to Labour in leaving policy vague if generally well-intentioned—and to keep down specific pledges as hostages to fortune. That does not make them any less important.

Perhaps the largest vacuum is over the nature of the very state and democratic institutions Labour will inherit. Not only is the machinery of government imbued with the same conservative ideology as the City, but a British government that wants to manage a market economy along the lines of Europe's social market needs better and more diverse instruments than are available under British Parliamentary absolutism. Decentralised government and independent agencies and watchdogs are a very minimum, and they cannot be invented without constitutional change. Labour has a programme for just such radical change, but does it appreciate how essential it is for its economic policy? Or does it just want its own turn at those absolutist levers? Mr Kinnock could head a reforming government to match Attlee—or he could go the same way as Ramsay Mcdonald. He and his Party deserve the benefit of the doubt, but only just.

Notes

1 This is quite apart from the fact, discussed in Chapter 12, that the figures quoted in support of the government's claim are quite inappropriate.
2 There may be some justification for the claim that in certain types of manufacturing, 'hidden' unemployment (in the shape of superfluous people on the payroll) has become 'visible': for manufacturing as a whole, output per head has risen by more than the historic norm. However, the policies which produced this led also to very disappointing output figures. Good productivity figures which lengthen the dole queues rather than raise GDP are of little value; and the poor industrial base which exists in 1991, largely as a result of those policies, is one of the worst features of the legacy which the next Government will inherit.
3 The resultant closures of plants—sometimes accompanied by the export of second-hand machinery—may be regarded as the originating cause of our weakening industrial base. Some plants were obsolete, but many good ones were sacrificed to financial exigencies, and new investment was very feeble.
4 The action needed has to have two components. Putting it crudely, one is to raise the level of saving (whether government or private) as a fraction of GDP; the other is to increase the competitive power of British producers so as to secure a rise in exports or a reduction in imports. Since most measures to secure the first will tend to lower the level of activity in the UK the second is the more urgent, since it would also tend to raise activity to a more satisfactory level.
5 A disagreement had occurred in 1984 between Lawson and the Bank of England over whether Johnson-Matthey Bankers should be rescued. The Bank decided that to allow failure was too risky, given the fragility of the international banking system in the wake of the world debt crisis. Lawson, not having been fully informed of all the detail, was left publicly to defend the Bank's decision, which involved some partial loss of taxpayers' money. This may account for some of his sensitivity on the issue of substituting public for private debt. However, in a broader perspective, Lawson was simply doing what neo-Marxists describe as acting against the interest of particular sections of the capitalist class (in this case foolish bankers), as part of the defence of the capitalist order in general (Brewer, 1980, pp. 14–15).
6 Our judgement contrasts with the more optimistic views of the City's future

prospects found in Davis and Latter (1989) and Grilli (1989). Our view finds support in several of the contributions in Budd and Whimster (1992).

7 This would be equal to the proportionate change in the profit rate except that profits are deflated by the consumer price index (for comparison with real wages) rather than investment goods prices; moreover, the estimated growth of the capital stock makes no allowance for extra scrapping which may have occurred in the early 1980s, or for the slower rise in net than in gross stock in a period of slow accumulation.

8 The basic idea of the decomposition is that the wage share is increased when real wages rise faster than productivity adjusted for the (usually faster) increases in consumer prices relative to manufacturing prices.

9 The lack of a cross-sectional relationship between investment growth and profitability growth after 1979 is consistent with the erratic relationship between the two variables over time within individual countries (see Bhaskar and Glyn (1992) for a survey of the evidence and recent estimates).

10 The basic source is *OECD National Accounts* Vol. II, supplemented by *EC National Accounts*. An important problem with the data is that the finance sector's investment includes assets leased out to other sectors, which exaggerates levels and growth rates of investment within the sector.

11 These estimates are based on a weighted average of the earnings of hospital porters, caretakers, road sweepers, refuse collectors and dustmen, home and domestic helps, maids, hospital ward orderlies, school helpers and school supervisors' assistants and other cleaners, taken from the *New Earnings Survey* for 1979 and 1990 (using the sample numbers as weights and including full- and part-time workers).

12 'Among appropriations, dividend payments rose by 17% in 1990, a lower growth rate than in the preceding two years (27% in 1989 and 33% in 1988), but one that was still surprisingly rapid. The dividend payout ratio, defined as the ratio of dividend payments to total income after deducting tax and interest payments, rose to 56% in the fourth quarter of 1990 and 64% in the first quarter of this year. . . Such a level of dividend payments is not only high by historical standards but exceptional given the current downturn in company profitability.' (*Bank of England Quarterly Bulletin*, August 1991, p. 364.)

13 The dynamics of public debt depend primarily on the relationship between the real interest rate (i) and the growth rate (g). If $(i-g)$ is strongly negative, as it was in the UK during most of the 1970s, the government can maintain a large primary deficit without provoking an explosion in public debt. The situation is different if $(i-g)$ is positive, as it was for most of the 1980s. Under these conditions, the financial situation of a government which borrows is extremely precarious and even a small primary deficit may lead to a rapid explosion in public debt. This was the danger facing the Thatcher government following the transition to a regime of high real interest rates.

14 O'Higgins and Jenkins (1989) and Boltho (1992) provide evidence on poverty in OECD countries, but only up to the mid-1980s. This is of limited use in the present context, since much of the impact of tax and benefit changes on income distribution in the UK has occurred more recently.

15 This assumes hypothetical GDP in 1990 equals actual GDP. The economy might have grown faster under an alternative government, but it is unlikely that the difference would have been great. The main difference would probably have been a smoother growth path. The structure of the economy, and its long term viability, would also have been different. Output growth

would have been more balanced, with faster growth in manufacturing and less in non-tradeable services like distribution and domestic finance. This would have meant a stronger balance of payments.

16 See McEachern (1980). The industry was strategic after the war, in the context of a steel shortage, in that it determined what capital investments could be made.

17 See Bryer *et al.* (1982) who argue that, after adjustments, overcompensation of £342 million was paid, or 17%.

18 Thus, steel, (coking) coal, cars and water could have been expanded together rather than subject to mutual decline; see Beynon *et al.* (1986) and Hudson and Sadler (1987).

19 As an index of the effect on the workforce both of reduced capacity and increasing productivity on a world scale, employment fell between 1974 and 1989 from over 2 million to just over 1 million.

20 The UK was limited to three (private) minimills (see NEDO, 1986).

21 For details of Phoenix, see Cockerill (1989, pp. 32–33); NEDO (1986); Dudley and Richardson (1990); and Sadler (1990).

22 See also Sadler (1990, p. 48). Above all, though, the Phoenix ventures represented a means of reintroducing private capital into the industry. By 1987, this had been accomplished: British Steel was confined to bulk steel production and the preliminary reorganisation of ownership was virtually complete.

23 For the lack of influence of trade unions over steel restructuring, other than concerning the pace and conditions of closure, see Bryer *et al.* (1982) and Hudson and Sadler (1989).

24 The accumulation of overseas assets which has been the counterpart of oil-funded current account surpluses has clearly not produced a flow of revenues sufficient to offset the deterioration in other parts of the current account.

25 Between 1979 and 1989, fixed investment (at 1985 prices) in the British economy grew by 45% but investment in manufacturing grew by only 12.8%, and has since fallen by 18% below the 1989 'peak'. At the same time, investment in transport and communication grew by 39.7%. In stark contrast, investment in distribution grew by 60.8%, and in banking, finance, insurance and business services by 320.3%. In broader terms, having started the decade roughly equal, by 1989 investment in services was running at roughly twice the rate of investment in industry (all figures from *UK National Accounts 1991*, Table 13.7 and Central Statistical Office).

26 In this discussion of economic policy I am not considering industrial relations policy, an area in which it is clear that some of the legal changes introduced by the Conservatives would be preserved by the Labour Party. However, the present position of the Labour Party on industrial relations sits well with other aspects of Labour's new framework of economic policy which are certainly not derived from positions taken by the Conservative government.

27 The current size of the tax burden is also part of the rationale for the emphasis placed by the Labour Party on the need to enhance competitive production. Without that improvement, either social and public services will deteriorate or the tax burden will rise or (most likely) both. A sustained increase in productivity and an expansion of industrial production is necessary if the tax burden is to be reduced without cutting public services.

28 If factors are perfectly mobile, Samuelson's 'myopic decision rule' applies. If not, then markets would develop to eliminate the intertemporal rents which arise from immobilities.

29 There is, of course, another side of the coin. Hayek's interpretation of the dynamics of markets suggests that social efficiency is attained only when all institutions are subordinated to the market.

30 Financial stability will require some re-regulation of the financial sector to control the growth of credit and hence the growth of broad money. An effective policy for monetary stability requires other instruments in addition to short-term interest rates.

References

Abromeit, H. (1986). *British Steel: An Industry Between the State and the Private Sector*. New York: St Martin's Press.

ACOST (1989). *Defence R&D: A National Resource*. London: Advisory Council on Science and Technology/HMSO.

ACOST (1990). *The Enterprise Challenge: Overcoming Barriers to Growth in Small Firms*. London; HMSO.

Addison, J.T. (1988). 'The demand for workers and hours and the effects of job security policies: theories and evidence'. In: R.A. Hart (ed.), *Employment, Unemployment and Labour Utilisation*. Cambridge, MA: Unwin Hyman.

Allen, C. and Hall, S. (1991). 'Money as a potential anchor for the price level: a critique of the P* approach'. In: London Business School, *Economic Outlook 1990–1994*. Aldershot: Gower, pp. 45–49.

Anthony, I., Allebeck, A.C. and Wulf, H. (1990). *West European Arms Production*, SIPRI.

Armstrong, P., Glyn, A. and Harrison, J. (1991). *Capitalism Since 1945*. Oxford: Blackwell.

Atkinson, A.B. (1990). *A National Minimum? A History of Ambiguity in the Determination of Benefit Scales in Britain*. STICERD Working Paper 47. London: London School of Economics.

Atkinson, A.B. (1991). *The Development of State Pensions in the United Kingdom*. STICERD Working Paper 58. London: London School of Economics.

Atkinson, A.B. and Mickelwright, J. (1989). 'Turning the screw: benefits for the unemployed, 1979–1988'. In: A.B. Atkinson (ed.), *Poverty and Social Security*. Hemel Hempstead: Harvester Wheatsheaf.

Atkinson, A.B., Gomulka, J., Mickelwright, J. and Rau, N. (1989). 'Unemployment Benefit, duration and incentives in Britain. In: A.B. Atkinson (ed.), *Poverty and Social Security*. Hemel Hempstead: Harvester Wheatsheaf.

Audit Commission (1989). *Urban Regeneration and Economic Development: The Local Government Dimension*. London: HMSO.

Audit Commission (1991). *The Urban Regeneration Experience*. Audit Commission Occasional Paper 17. London: HMSO.

Auerbach, S. (1991). *Legislating for Conflict*. Oxford: Clarendon Press.

Bailey, R. and Kelly, J. (1990). 'An index measure of trade union density', *British Journal of Industrial Relations*, **28**: 267–70.

Banks, M.H., Clegg, C.W., Jackson, P.R., Kemp, N.J., Stafford, E.M. and Wall, T.D. (1980). 'The use of the General Health Questionnaire as an indicator of mental health in occupational studies', *Journal of Occupational Studies*, **53**: 187–94.

Bannock, G. and Albach, H., eds (1991). *Small Business Policy in Europe: Britain, Germany and the European Commission*. London: Anglo-German Foundation.

Bannock, G. and Daly, M. (1990). 'Size distribution of UK firms', *Employment Gazette* (May 1990): 255–8.

Barker, T. (1990). 'Sources of structural change for the UK service industries 1979–84', *Economic Systems Research*, **2**: 173–83.

Barker, T., Dunne, P. and Smith, R. (1991). 'Measuring the peace dividend in the United Kingdom', *Journal of Peace Research*, **28**: 345–58.

Bean, C. and Symons, J. (1989). 'Ten years of Mrs T'. In: NBER, *Macroeconomic Annual 1989*. Cambridge, MA: MIT Press, pp. 13–61.

Beaumont, R. and Harris, I. (1991). 'Trade union recognition and employment contraction', *British Journal of Industrial Relations*, **29**: 49–58.

Begg, I.G. and Moore, B.C. (1990). 'The future economic role of urban systems'. In: D. Cadman and G. Payne (eds), *The Living City*. London: Routledge.

Begg, I.G., Moore, B.C. and Rhodes, J. (1986). 'Economic and social change in urban Britain and the inner cities'. In: V.A. Hausner (ed.), *Critical Issues in Urban Economic Development, Vol. I*. Oxford: Clarendon Press, pp. 10–39.

Bellmann, L. (1988). 'Employment-at-will, job security and work incentives'. In: R.A. Hart (ed.), *Employment, Unemployment and Labour Utilisation*. Cambridge, MA: Unwin Hyman.

Best, M.H. (1991). *The New Competition: Institutions of Industrial Restructuring*. Cambridge: Polity Press.

Beynon, H., Hudson, R. and Sadler, D. (1986). 'Nationalised industry policies and the destruction of communities', *Capital and Class*, **29**: 27–57.

Bhaskar, V. and Glyn, A. (1992). 'Investment and profits: evidence from the OECD countries'. In: J. Epstein and H. Gintis (eds), *The Political Economy of Investment, Saving and Finance*. Oxford: Oxford University Press (forthcoming).

Bird, D., Stevens, M. and Yates, A. (1991). 'Membership of trade unions in 1989', *Employment Gazette*, **99**: 337–43.

Blanchflower, D.G. (1991). 'Fear, unemployment and pay flexibility', *Economic Journal*, **101**: 483–96.

Blanchflower, D.G. and Oswald, A. (1990). *What Makes a Young Entrepreneur*, London School of Economics Centre for Labour Economics Discussion Paper 373. London: LSE.

Blanchflower, D.G. and Oswald, A. (1991). *Self-Employment and Mrs Thatcher's Enterprise Culture*, London School of Economics Centre for Labour Economics Discussion Paper 30. London: LSE.

Boltho, A. (1992). 'Macroeconomic trends and household welfare in the industrialised economies since the first oil shock'. In: G.A. Cornia (ed.), *Child Poverty in Industrialised Countries*. London: Macmillan (forthcoming).

Bravemann, H. (1974). *Labour and Monopoly Capital*. New York: Monthly Review Press.

Brenner, M.H. (1973). *Mental Illness and the Economy*. Cambridge, MA: Harvard University Press.

Brenner, M.H. (1979). 'Mortality and the national economy: a review and the experience of England and Wales 1936–76'. *Lancet*, **2**: 568–73.

Brewer, A. (1980). *Marxist Theories of Imperialism*. London: Routledge and Kegan Paul.

Britton, A.J.C. (1991). *Macroeconomic Policy in Britain 1974–87*. Cambridge: Cambridge University Press.

Brosnan, P. and Wilkinson, F. (1987). 'A national statutory minimum wage and economic efficiency', *Contributions to Political Economy*, **7**: 1–48.

Brown, A.J. (1983). 'Friedman and Schwartz on the United Kingdom'. In: *Monetary Trends in the United Kingdom*. Bank of England Panel Paper 22. London: Bank of England, pp. 9–43.

Brown, W. and Rowthorn, B. (1990). *A Public Services Pay Policy*. Fabian Tract S42. London: Fabian Society.

Brown, W. and Wadhwani, S. (1990). 'The economic effects of industrial relations legislation since 1979'. *National Institute Economic Review*, **131**: 57–70.

Bryer, R., Brignall, T. and Maunders, A. (1982). *Accounting for British Steel: A Financial Analysis of the Failure of the British Steel Corporation, 1967–1980, And Who Was to Blame*. Aldershot: Gower.

Budd, L. and Whimster, S., eds (1992). *Global Finance and Urban Living: the Case of London*. London: Routledge.

Burchell, B.J. (1989). *The Effects of Labour Market Position, Job Insecurity and Unemployment on Psychological Health*. SCELI Working Paper 19. Oxford: Nuffield College.

Burchell, B.J. (1990). 'Job quality over a lifetime: a new way of analyzing labour markets through data derived from work histories', Paper presented to the XIIth International Working Party on Labour Market Segmentation, Trento, Italy.

Burchell, B.J. and Devereux, J. (1987). 'The influence of father's unemployment on the values of schoolchildren', *Youth and Policy*, **21**: 36–41.

Burchell, B.J. and Rubery, J. (1990). 'An empirical investigation into the segmentation of the labour supply', *Work, Employment and Society* **4**: 551–75.

Cameron, G.C., Moore, B., Nichols, D., Rhodes, J. and Tyler, P., eds (1990). *Cambridge Regional Economic Review*. Cambridge: Department of Land Economy.

Catalano, R.A. and Dooley, D. (1983). 'Health effects of economic instability: a test of economic stress hypothesis', *Journal of Health and Social Behaviour*, **24**: 46–60.

Central Statistical Office (1990). *Regional Trends*. London: HMSO.

CEC (1989). *First Survey on State Aids in the European Community*. Brussels: Office for Official Publications of the European Communities, Commission of the European Communities.

CEC (1990). *Second Survey on State Aids in the European Community in Manufacturing and Certain Other Sectors*. Brussels: Office for Official Publications of the European Communities, Commission of the European Communities.

Cockerill, A. (1989). *Phoenix from the Ashes: Joint Ventures in the Privatisation of the British Steel Industry*. Working Paper 176. Manchester: University of Manchester Business School.

Craft, N.F.R. (1991). *Productivity Performance in the UK in Historical and International Perspective*. Discussion Paper 103. Southampton: University of Southampton.

Daly, M. (1990). 'The 1980s: a decade of growth in enterprise: data on VAT registrations and deregistrations', *Employment Gazette* (November 1990): 553.

Daly, M. (1991). 'The 1980s: a decade of growth in enterprise: self employment data from the Labour Force Survey', *Employment Gazette* (March 1991): 109–34.

Daniel, W.W. (1990). *The Unemployed Flow*. London: Policy Studies Institute.

Davis, E.P. and Latter, A.R. (1989). 'London as an International Financial Centre', *Bank of England Quarterly Bulletin* (November 1989): 516–28.

Deakin, S. (1986). 'Labour law and the developing employment relationship in the UK', *Cambridge Journal of Economics*, **10**: 225–46.

Deakin, S. (1990). 'The floor of rights in European labour law', *New Zealand Journal of Industrial Relations*, **15**: 219–40.

Deakin, S. (1991). 'Legal change and labour market restructuring in western Europe and the US', *New Zealand Journal of Industrial Relations*, **16**: 109–25.

Deakin, S. and Wilkinson, F. (1991a). *The Economics of Employment Rights*. London: Institute of Employment Rights.

Deakin, S. and Wilkinson, F. (1991b). 'Labour law, social security and economic inequality', *Cambridge Journal of Economics*, **15**: 125–48.

Department of Trade and Industry (1983). *Regional Industrial Development*. Cmnd 9111. London: HMSO.

Desai, M. (1981). *Testing Monetarism*. London: Frances Pinter.

Docklands Consultative Committee (1988). *Urban Development Corporations, Six Years in London's Docklands*. London: LDDC.

Dooley, D., Rook, K. and Catalano, R. (1987). 'Job and non-job stressors and their moderators', *Journal of Occupational Psychology*, **60**: 115–32.

Dow, J.C.R. and Saville, I.D. (1988). *A Critique of Monetary Policy. Theory and British Experience*. Oxford: Clarendon Press.

Driver, C. and Morton, D. (1992). *Investment, Expectations and Uncertainty*. Oxford: Blackwell.

Dudley, G. and Richardson, J. (1990). *Politics and British Steel in Britain, 1967–1988*. Aldershot: Gower.

Dunne, P. (1990). 'The political economy of military expenditure: an introduction', *Cambridge Journal of Economics*, **14**: 395–404.

Dunne, P. and Hughes, A. (1991). *The Changing Structure of Competitive Industry in the 1980s*. Cambridge: Small Business Research Centre, Department of Applied Economics.

Edgerton, D. (1991). 'Liberal militarism and the British State', *New Left Review*, **185**: 138–69.

EIU (1990). *World Steel Forecasts: Consumption, Production and Trade for 33 Countries to 1995*. London: Economists' Intelligence Unit.

Elder, G.H. Jnr. and Caspi, A. (1988). 'Economic stress in lives: developmental perspectives', *Journal of Social Issues*, **44**: 25–45.

Englander, A.S. and Mittelstadt, A. (1988). 'Total factor productivity: macroeconomic and structural aspects of slowdown', *OECD Economic Studies*, **10**: 7–56.

Evans, S. (1990). 'Free labour markets and economic performance: evidence from the construction industry', *Work, Employment and Society*, **4**: 239–52.

Ewing, K. (1989). *Britain and the ILO*. London: Institute of Employment Rights.

Fagin, L. and Little, M. (1984). *The Forsaken Families*. Harmondsworth: Penguin.

Feather, N.T. (1990). *The Psychological Impact of Unemployment*. New York: Springer.

Feinstein, C. and Matthews, R. (1990). 'The growth of output and productivity in the 1980s', *National Institute Economic Review*, **133**: 78–90.

Ferman, L.A. and Gardner, J. (1979). 'Economic deprivation, social mobility and mental health'. In: L.A. Ferman and J.P. Gordus (eds), *Mental Health and the Economy*. Michigan: Upjohn Institute.

Fine, B. (1990). *The Coal Question: Political Economy and Industrial Changes from the Nineteenth Century to the Present Day*. London: Routledge.

Fineman, S. (1983). *White Collar Unemployment: Impact and Stress*. Chichester: Wiley.

Fineman, S. (1987). 'Back to employment: wounds and wisdoms'. In: D. Fryer and P. Ullah (eds), *Unemployed People: Social and Psychological Perspectives*. Milton Keynes: Open University Press, pp. 268–84.

Fontanel, J. and Smith, R.P. (1991). 'A European Defence Union?', *Economic Policy*, **6**: 393–424.

Ford, R. and Suyker, W. (1990). 'Industrial studies in the OECD economies', *OECD Economic Studies*, **15**: 37–81.

Friedman, M. and Schwartz, A.J. (1991). 'Alternative approaches to analyzing economic data', *American Economic Review*, **81**: 39–49.

Fryer, D.M. and Payne, R.L. (1984). 'Proactivity in unemployment: findings and implications', *Leisure Studies*, **3**: 273–95.

Fryer, D.M. and Payne, R.L. (1986). 'Being unemployed: a review of the literature on the psychological experience of unemployment'. In: C.L. Cooper and I. Robertson (eds), *International Review of Industrial and Organisational Psychology*. Chichester: Wiley and Sons, Vol. 1, pp. 235–78.

Gallagher, C.C., Daly, M. and Thomason, J. (1990). 'The growth of UK companies 1985–87 and their contribution to job generation', *Employment Gazette* (February 1990): 92–8.

Ganguly, P. (1985). *UK Small Business Statistics and International Comparisons*, London: Harper and Row.

Garraty, J.A. (1978). *Unemployment in History: Economic Thought and Public Policy*. New York: Harper and Row.

Glyn, A. (1988). 'Colliery results and closures after the 1984–85 coal dispute', *Oxford Bulletin of Economics and Statistics*, **50**: 161–73.

Glyn, A. and Rowthorn, R. (1988). 'European unemployment: corporatism and structural change', *American Economic Review, Papers and Proceedings*, **78**: 194–99.

Glyn, A., Hughes, A., Lipietz, A. and Singh, A. (1990). 'The rise and fall of the Golden Age'. In: S. Marglin and J. Schor (eds), *The Golden Age of Capitalism*. Oxford: Clarendon Press, pp. 39–125.

Goldberg, W. (ed.) (1986). *Ailing Steel: The Transoceanic Quarrel*. Aldershot: Gower.

Goodhart, C. (1989). 'Has Moore become too horizontal', *Journal of Post-Keynesian Economics*, **12**: 29–34.

Gordus, J.P., Jarley, P. and Ferman, L.A. (1981). *Plant Closings and Economic Dislocation*. Michigan: Upjohn Institute.

Green, F. (ed.) (1989). *The Restructuring of the UK Economy*. London: Harvester Wheatsheaf.

Griffith-Jones, S. (1991). 'International financial markets: a case of market failure'. In C. Colclough and J. Manor (eds), *States or Markets? Neo-Liberalism and the Development Policy Debate*. Oxford: Clarendon Press.

Griffith-Jones, S. and Gottschalk, R. (1991). 'Is there still a Latin American debt crisis?'. Mimeo. Brighton: Institute of Development Studies.

Grilli, V. (1989). 'Europe 1992: Issues and Prospects for the Financial Markets'. *Economic Policy*, **4**: 387–421.

Hakim, C. (1988). 'Self-Employment in Britain. A Review of recent trends and current issues', *Work, Employment and Society*, **2**: 421–50.

Hall, S.G., Henry, S.G.B. and Wilcox, J.B. (1990). 'The long-run determination of UK monetary aggregates'. In: S.G.B. Henry and K.D. Patterson (eds), *Economic Modelling at the Bank of England*. London: Chapman and Hall.

Hart, P.E. (1987). 'Small firms and jobs', *National Institute Economic Review*, **121**: 60–3.

Haskel, J. and Kay, J.A. (1990). 'Productivity in British industry under Mrs Thatcher'. In: T. Congdon *et al.*, (eds), *The State of the Economy*. London: Institute for Economic Affairs.

Helm, D. (1991). 'The assessment: energy policy', *Oxford Review of Economic Policy*, **7**: 1–16.

Hendry, D.F. and Ericsson, N.R. (1983). 'Assertion without empirical basis: an econometric appraisal of Friedman and Schwartz'. In: *Monetary Trends in the United Kingdom*. Bank of England Panel Paper 22. London: Bank of England, pp. 45–101.

Hendry, D.F. and Ericsson, N.R. (1991). 'An econometric analysis of UK money demand in *Monetary Trends in the United States and the United Kingdom* by Milton Friedman and Anna J. Schwartz', *American Economic Review*, **81**: 8–38.

Henry, S.G.B. and Ormerod, P.A. (1978). 'Incomes policy and wage inflation: empirical evidence for the UK 1961–1977', *National Institute Economic Review*, **85**: 31–9.

Hilditch, P. (1990). 'Defence procurement and employment: the case of UK shipbuilding', *Cambridge Journal of Economics*, **14**: 453–68.

Hills, J. (1986). *Deregulating Telecoms*. London: Frances Pinter.

HMSO (1988). *DTI—The Department for Enterprise*. Cmnd 278. London: HMSO.

HMSO (1989). *Barriers to Takeovers in the European Community: A Study by Coopers and Lybrend for the DTI*. **1**, London: HMSO.

Horrell, S. and Rubery, J. (1991). *Employers' Working-Time Policies and Women's Employment*. Equal Opportunities Commission Research Series. London: HMSO.

House of Commons (1990). *International Debt Strategy. Third Report from the Treasury and Civil Service Committee*, Session 1989–90. London: HMSO.

House of Commons Treasury and Civil Service Committee (1980). *Memoranda on Monetary Policy, Session 1979–80*. London: HMSO.

Hudson, R. and Sadler, D. (1987). 'Manufactured in the UK? Special steels, motor vehicles and the politics of industrial decline', *Capital and Class,* **32**: 55–82.

Hudson, R. and Sadler, D. (1989). *The International Steel Industry: Restructuring, State Policies and Localities*. London: Routledge.

Hughes, A. (1989). 'Small firms, merger activity and competition policy'. In: J. Barber, S. Metcalfe and M. Porteous (eds), *Barriers to Growth in Small Firms*. London: Routledge.

Hughes, A. (1990). 'The impact of merger: a survey of empirical evidence for the UK'. In: J. Fairburn and J.A. Kay (eds), *Mergers and Merger Policy*. Oxford: Oxford University Press.

Hughes, A. (1991). 'UK small businesses in the 1980s: continuity and change', *Regional Studies*, **25**: 471–8.

Humphries, J. and Rubery, J. (1984). 'The reconstitution of the supply side of the labour market: the relative autonomy of social reproduction', *Cambridge Journal of Economics*, **8**: 331–46.

Humphries, J. and Rubery, J. (1991). 'Position of women in the labour market in Britain'. Study for *Women in Employment Project: 1989–1990 Programme* of the European Commission.

IPMS, MSF, T&G (1990). *The New Industrial Challenge*. London.

Jahoda, M. (1982). *Employment and Unemployment: A Social-Psychological Analysis*. Cambridge: Cambridge University Press.

James Capel & Co. Ltd. (1990). *The New Electricity Companies in England and Wales*.

Johnson, C. (1991). *The Economy Under Mrs Thatcher, 1979–1990*. Harmondsworth: Penguin.

Kaldor, N. (1986). *The Scourge of Monetarism* (2nd edn). Oxford: Oxford University Press.

Kaldor, N. (1989). *Further Essays on Economic Theory and Policy*. London: Duckworth.

Kasl, S.V. and Cobb, S. (1982). 'Variability of stress effects among men experiencing job loss'. In: L. Goldberger and S. Breznitz (eds), *Handbook of Stress: Theoretical and Clinical Aspects*. New York: Free Press, pp. 445–65.

Keeble, D.E. (1989). *Small Firms, New Firms and Uneven Regional Development in the UK*. Working Paper 2. Cambridge: Small Business Research Centre, Department of Applied Economics.

Keeble, D.E. (1990). 'New firms and regional economic development: experience and impact in the 1980s'. In: G.C. Cameron, B. Moore, D. Nichols, J. Rhodes and P. Tyler (eds), *Cambridge Regional Economic Review*. Cambridge: Department of Land Economy, pp. 62–71.

Keeble, D.E. and Wever, E. (1986). 'Introduction'. In: D.E. Keeble and E. Wever (eds), *New Firms and Regional Development in Europe*. London: Croom Helm, pp. 1–14.

Keegan, W. (1989). *Mr Lawson's Gamble*. London: Hodder and Stoughton.

Kelly, J. (1990). 'British trade unionism 1979–1989: changes, continuity and contradictions', *Work, Employment and Society*, Special issue, May: 29–65.

Kolodziej, E. (1987). *Making and Marketing Arms: The French Experience*. Princeton, NJ: Princeton University Press.

Kornhauser, A.K. (1965). *Mental Health of the Industrial Worker*. New York: Wiley.

Landesmann, M. and Snell, A. (1989). 'The consequences of Mrs Thatcher for UK manufacturing exports', *Economic Journal*, **99**: 1–27.

Lawless, P. (1988). 'Enterprise Board: evolution and critique', *Planning Outlook*, **31**: 13–18.

Layard, R. and Nickell, S. (1987). 'The labour market'. In: R. Dornbusch and R. Layard (eds), *The Performance of the British Economy*. Oxford: Oxford University Press.

Lovering, J. (1990). 'Military expenditure and the restructuring of capitalism: the military industry in Britain', *Cambridge Journal of Economics*, **14**: 453–67.

Lovering, J. (1991). 'The British defence industry in the 1990s: a labour market perspective', *Industrial Relations Journal* **22**: 103–16.

Marcel, M. and Palma, J.G. (1988). 'Third World debt and its effects on the British economy: a Southern view of economic mismanagement in the North', *Cambridge Journal of Economics*, **12**, 361–400.

Marsh, C. (1991). *Hours of Work of Men and Women in Britain*. Equal Opportunities Commission Research Series. London: HMSO.

Martin, R.L. (1985). 'Monetarism masquerading as regional policy: the government's new system of Regional Aid', *Regional Studies*, **19**: 379–88.

Martin, R.L. (1988). 'The political economy of Britain's North–South divide', *Transactions of the Institute of British Geographers*, **13**: 389–418.

Martin, R.L. (1992). 'Has the British economy been transformed? Critical reflections on the policies of the Thatcher era'. In: P. Cloke (ed.), *Policy and Change in Thatcher's Britain*. Oxford: Pergamon, Chap. 7.

Martin, R.L. and Tyler, P. (1990). 'Real wage variation in Great Britain'. In: G.C. Cameron, B. Moore, D. Nichols, J. Rhodes and P. Tyler (eds), *Cambridge Regional Economic Review*. Cambridge: Department of Land Economy.

Mason, C. (1991). 'New firm formation and growth'. In: R.L. Martin and P. Townroe (eds), *Regional Development in the 1990s: The British Isles in Transition*. London: Jessica Kingsley.

Maynard, G. (1988). *The Economy Under Mrs Thatcher*. Oxford: Blackwell.

McCombie, J.S.L. and Thirlwall, A.P. (1992). *Economic Growth and the Balance of Payments Constraint*. London: Macmillan (forthcoming).

McEachern, D. (1980). *A Class Against Itself: Power in the Nationalisation of the British Steel Industry*. Cambridge: Cambridge University Press.

McGregor, J. and Sproull, C. (1991). *Employer Labour Use Strategies: Analysis of a National Survey*. Department of Employment Research Paper, **83**. London: HMSO.

McKenna, S.P. and Fryer, D.M. (1984). 'Perceived health during lay-off and early unemployment', *Occupational Health*, **36**: 201–6.

Metcalf, D. (1989). 'Water notes dry up: the impact of the Donovan reform proposal and Thatcherism at work on labour productivity in British manufacturing industry', *British Journal of Industrial Relations*, **27**: 1–31.

MITI (1986). *Outline of the Small and Medium Enterprises Policies of the Japanese Government*. Tokyo: Small and Medium Enterprise Agency, MITI in cooperation with the Japan Small Business Corporation.

Monopolies and Mergers Commission (1986). *GEC PLC and Plessey PLC, A Report on the Proposed Merger*. Cmnd 9867. London: HMSO.

Monopolies and Mergers Commission (1989). *GEC PLC, Siemens AG and Plessey PLC, A Report on the Proposed Merger*. Cmnd 676. London: HMSO.

Monopolies and Mergers Commission (1991). *British Aerospace PLC and Thomson-CSF SA, A Report on the Proposed Merger*. Cmnd 1416. London: HMSO.

Moore, B.C., Rhodes, J. and Tyler, P. (1986). *The Effects of Regional Economic Policy*. London: Department of Trade and Industry/HMSO.

Moser, K.A., Fox, A.J. and Jones, D.R. (1984). 'Unemployment and mortality in the OPCS Longitudinal Survey', *Lancet*, **2**: 1324–9.

National Audit Office (1991). *Ministry of Defence: Initiatives in Defence Procurement*. London: HMSO.

Nolan, P. (1989). 'Walking on water? Performance and industrial relations under Thatcher', *Industrial Relations Journal*, **20**: 81–92.

NEDO (1986). *Steel in the World Market and the UK Steel Industry*. London: National Economic Development Office.

O'Brien, G.E. (1986). *Psychology of Work and Unemployment*. Chichester: Wiley.

OECD (1974). *Energy Prospects to 1985*. Paris: Organisation for Economic Cooperation and Development.

OECD (1990). *The Steel Market in 1989 and the Outlook for 1990*. Paris: Organisation for Economic Cooperation and Development.

O'Higgins, M. and Jenkins, S. (1989). 'Poverty in Europe'. Paper presented to a seminar on Poverty Statistics in the European Community at the Erasmus University, Rotterdam, 24–26 October 1989.

Oulton, N. (1990). 'Labour productivity in UK manufacturing in the 1970s and 1980s', *National Institute Economic Review*, **132**: 71–91.

Oxley, H., Maher, M., Martin, J.P. and Nicoletti, G. (1990). *The Public Sector: Issues for the 1990s*. OECD Department of Economics and Statistics, Working Paper 90. Paris: Organisation for Economic Cooperation and Development.

PA Cambridge Economic Consultants (1987). *An Evaluation of the Enterprise Zone Experiment*. London: Department of the Environment, Inner-Cities Directorate/HMSO.

PA Cambridge Economic Consultants (1991). *An Evaluation of the Government's Inner City Task Force*. London: Department of Trade and Industry/HMSO.

Panić, M. (1982). 'Monetarism in an open economy', *Lloyds Bank Review*, **145**: 36–47.

Panić, M. (1991). 'The impact of multinationals on national economic policies'. In: B. Burgenmeier and J.L. Mucchielli (eds), *Multinationals and Europe 1992*. London: Routledge.

Payne, R.L. and Jones, J.G. (1987). 'Social class and re-employment: changes in health and perceived financial circumstances', *Journal of Occupational Behaviour*, **8**: 175–84.

Posner, M.V. and Steer, A. (1979). 'Price competitiveness and performance in manufacturing industry'. In: F. Blackaby (ed.), *De-industrialisation*. London: Heinemann.

Prais, S. and Wagner, K. (1988). 'Productivity and management: the training of foremen in Britain and Germany', *National Institute Economic Review*, **123**: 34–47.

Riley, B. (1991). 'The long view', *Financial Times* (3 August 1991).

Robson, B.T. (1988). *Those Inner Cities: reconciling the social and economic aims of urban policy*. Oxford: Clarendon Press.

Roger, P. (1991). 'Overcoming the barriers to US–French arms cooperation', *Armed Forces Journal International* (January 1991): 32.

Rowthorn, B. (1989). 'The Thatcher revolution'. In: Green, F. (ed.), *The Restructuring of the UK Economy*. London: Harvester Wheatsheaf, pp. 281–98.

Rowthorn, R.E. (1977). 'Conflict, inflation and money', *Cambridge Journal of Economics*, 1: 215–39.

Rowthorn, R.E. and Wells, J. (1987). *Deindustrialization and Foreign Trade*. Cambridge: Cambridge University Press.

Rubery, J., ed. (1988). *Women and Recession*. London: Routledge and Kegan Paul.

Rubery, J. (1989). 'Precarious forms of work in the United Kingdom'. In: G. and J. Rodgers (eds), *Precarious Jobs in Labour Market Regulation*. Geneva: International Institute for Labour Studies.

Rubery, J. (1991). 'Equal pay and institutional systems of pay determination; a comparative study'. Study for the *Women in Employment Project: 1989–1990 Programme* of the European Commission.

Rubery, J., Earnshaw, J. and Burchell, B. (1991). 'New forms and patterns of employment: the role of self-employment in Britain'. Report for the Zentrum fur Europaisches Rechtspolitik, Bremen.

Rubery, J., Tarling, R. and Wilkinson, F. (1987). 'Flexibility, marketing and the organisation of production', *Labour and Society*, 12: 131–51.

Sadler, D. (1990). 'Privatising British Steel: the politics of production and place', *Area*, 22: 47–55.

Sawyer, M. (1991a). 'Industrial policy'. In: M. Artis and D. Cobham (eds), *Labour's Economic Policies, 1974–79*. Manchester: Manchester University Press.

Sawyer, M. (1991b). *On the Nature and Role of Industrial Policy*. Discussion Paper. Leeds: University of Leeds, School of Business and Economic Studies.

Schor, J. (1990). *Financial Openness and National Autonomy*. Discussion Paper 1523. Cambridge, MA: Harvard Institute of Economic Research.

Schwarz, J.A. (1990). 'Baruch, the New Deal and the origins of the military and industrial complex'. In: R. Higgs (ed.), *Arms, Politics and the Economy*. New York: Holmes and Meier.

Sengenberger, W., Loveman, G.W. and Piore, M.J., eds (1990). *The Re-emergence of Small Enterprises*. Geneva: International Institute for Labour Studies.

Singh, A. (1990). 'Southern competition, labour standards and industrial development in the North and the South'. In: *Labour Standards and Development in the Global Economy*. Washington, DC: US Department of Labour, pp. 239–64.

Smeeding, T.M., Rainwater, L., Rein, M., Hauser, R. and Schaber, G. (1990). 'Income poverty in seven countries: initial estimates from the LIS database'. In: T.M. Smeeding, M. O'Higgins and L. Rainwater (eds), *Poverty, Inequality and Income Distribution in Comparative Perspective*. Hemel Hempstead: Harvester Wheatsheaf.

Smith, R.P. (1977). 'Military expenditure and capitalism', *Cambridge Journal of Economics*, 1: 61–76.

Smith, R.P. (1983). 'Aspects of militarism', *Capital and Class*, 19: 17–30.

Smith, R.P. (1990). 'Defence procurement and industrial structure in the UK', *International Journal of Industrial Organisation*, 8: 185–205.

Stark, T. (1989). 'The changing distribution of income under Mrs Thatcher'. In: F. Green (ed.), *The Restructuring of the British Economy*. Hemel Hempstead: Harvester Wheatsheaf.

Steedman, H. (1988). 'Vocational training in France and Britain: mechanical and electrical craftsmen', *National Institute Economic Review*, **126**: 57–70.

Storey, D.J. and Johnson, S. (1987). *Job Generation and Labour Market Change*. London: Macmillan.

Tarling, R. and Wilkinson, F. (1977). 'The Social Contract: post-war incomes policies and their inflationary impact', *Cambridge Journal of Economics*, **1**: 395–414.

Tarling, R. and Wilkinson, F. (1982). 'The movement of real wages and the development of collective bargaining in the period 1855 to 1920', *Contributions to Political Economy*, **1**: 1–23.

Taylor, T. and Hayward, K. (1989). *The UK Defence Industrial Base: Development and Future Policy Options*. London: Brassey's.

Toye, J. (1991). 'The aid and trade provision of the British aid programme'. In: A. Bose and P. Burnell (eds), *Britain's Overseas Aid Since 1979*. Manchester: Manchester University Press.

Turnbull, P. (1991). 'Labour market deregulation and economic performance: the case of Britain's docks', *Work, Employment and Society*, **5**: 17–35.

Turner, D. (1988). *Does the UK Face a Balance of Payments Constraint on Growth? A Quantitative Analysis Using the LBS and NIESR Models*. Discussion Paper 16. Warwick: ESRC Macroeconomic Modelling Bureau, University of Warwick.

Tzannatos, Z. (1990). 'Employment segregation: can we measure it and what does the measure mean?' *British Journal of Industrial Relations*, **28**: 105–11.

UN (1990). *The Steel Market in 1989*. New York: United Nations.

Vickers, J. and Yarrow, G. (1988). *Privatization: an Economic Analysis*. London: MIT Press.

Walker, W. (1991). 'From leader to follower: Britain's dwindling technological aspirations'. SPRU Mimeo. University of Sussex.

Warr, P. (1987). *Work, Unemployment and Mental Health*. Oxford: Clarendon Press.

Warr, P. and Jackson, P.R. (1985). 'Factors affecting the psychological impact of prolonged unemployment and re-employment', *Psychological Medicine*, **15**: 795–807.

Warr, P. and Payne, R.L. (1982). 'Experiences of strain and pleasure amongst British adults', *Social Science and Medicine*, **16**: 1691–7.

Wilkinson, F. (1987). 'Deregulation, structured labour markets and unemployment'. In: P. Pedersen and R. Lund (eds), *Unemployment: Theory, Policy and Structure*. Berlin: de Gruyter.

Wilkinson, F. (1988). 'Real wages, effective demand and economic development', *Cambridge Journal of Economics*, **12**: 180–91.

World Bank (1985). *World Development Report 1985*. Washington, DC: World Bank.

Yachir, F. (1988). *The World Steel Industry Today*. London: Zed Books.

Index

accumulation xix, 255, 335, 337–338
ACOST 99, 109
advanced capitalist countries *see* OECD
aerospace 63
   see also British Aerospace
Africa 25, 32, 34–35
   see also Southern Africa, sub-Saharan
      Africa
aggregate demand 16, 61–2
agriculture 84–85, 303
aid 2, 29–36
Anglo-American 'special relationship' 11,
   23, 31
Argentina 12, 25, 27–28
arms contracts 12, 20, 31, 33
Asia 2, 25
Atkinson, A.B. 277, 279, 287
Audit Commission 125, 132, 139
Australia 29, 177, 232
Austria 29, 177, 290
Austrian economists 331

Baker Plan 23–25
balance of payments xvii–xviii, xxii–xxiii,
   1–3, 60–74, 197, 205, 208, 217,
   251, 312, 320, 333
   constraint 69
banks xxii, 11, 15, 21, 32, 37, 40–41, 44,
   196–9, 217
   Bank of England 20, 40–3, 48, 199,
      207
   banking, finance and insurance sector
      210–211, 213, 242–243, 303
   central 14, 199
   minimum lending rate 196
      see also interest rates
   reserve asset ratios 196
   see also finance, financial institutions
bankruptcies 3, 197
   see also insolvencies
bargaining power 204–5
   see also collective bargaining, trade
      unions
Begg, Iain 3, 116, 137, 139

Belgium 29, 78–9, 85, 274, 290, 300
benefits *see* welfare payments
Best, Michael 5, 312–313, 332
Big Bang *see* financial deregulation
BL 96, 108
Bolivia 25, 27–28
BP 96
Brady Plan 23–25, 28, 32
Brazil 25, 27–28
Bretton Woods 15, 41
British Aerospace 96–7, 101–5, 107–8,
   112
British Coal 317, 320
   see also coal mining
British Empire 38–9
British Shipbuilders 96, 101
British Steel Corporation 106–7, 326–329
British Telecom 318
Brittan, Samuel 66–7, 73
Brosnan, P. 212
Brown, A.J. 199
Brown, William 4, 191, 210, 250, 272,
   287
Burchell, Brendan 4, 220, 228–230, 235
business services *see* services

Callaghan, James 195
   Callaghan government 3, 94, 196
      see also Labour governments
Cambridge Economic Policy Group 201
Canada 29, 85, 177, 283–284
capacity utilisation 69, 90, 294
capital 37, 56, 65, 201, 205, 255, 309–310,
   315, 321, 333
   accumulation *see* accumulation
   flows 18, 34, 64–5, 206
   goods 198, 206–7
   market 316
   scrapping 61, 88, 214, 217, 293
   stock 3, 64, 85–90, 293–294, 320
   working xx
   see also capacity utilisation, capitalism
capitalism 2, 50
Carlin, Wendy 88

Carribean 25, 28
central banks *see* banks
chemicals 63
child benefit xvii, 277–279, 284
child-care 239, 248–249, 253–254, 256
Chile 25, 27–28
Chisholm, Michael 4, 168
CIA 2
City of London 2, 6–7, 37–59, 295, 340–342
Clegg Commission 262
Coakley, Jerry 2, 37, 58
coal mining 79, 82–4, 324–325
  see also British Coal
Cold War 2, 13, 24
  'New Cold War' 91
collective bargaining 208–209, 211–212
  see also bargaining power, trade unions
Columbia 25, 27–28
commodity prices *see* prices
comparative advantage 315
competition 52, 92–3, 201, 315, 331
  nonprice 70–72
  policy 297–298, 339
  see also market forces
competitiveness 3–4, 6, 60, 190, 198, 208, 297, 312–314, 333, 341
concentration 211, 309, 317
  see also monopolisation
conflict 5, 201, 216, 295
conservation 315, 322–323
Conservative Party 12, 253, 316–317
  Conservative Government *see* Heath, Major, Thatcher
  Conservative policy 336
  Conservative politicians 332
construction 37, 242–243, 271, 303
consumers 77, 82–3, 186, 208, 331
  consumer demand 215
  consumer goods 197–8, 214
consumption xviii, xxiii, 138, 197–8, 218, 269–270, 333–334
cooperation 4–5, 295, 313–314
coordination 315–316, 321–322, 328
corporatism 57, 297, 330–332
costs 195, 201, 207–8, 214–5
  cost accounting 4
  see also prices
Coutts, Ken 3, 60, 85
credit xx–xxi, 52, 65, 198–9
  boom 87, 252
  see also Lawson boom
  regulation of 14, 41, 197
  see also debt, money supply, mortgages

Deakin, Simon 4, 77, 173–4, 176, 187–8, 190, 192–3, 208, 213

debt xxii–xxiii, 2, 52, 62, 65–6
  government 264, 266
  Third World crisis 11–12, 15–36
  trap 18
  see also credit, mortgages
defence conversion 3, 110–114
defence firms 3
defence industry 91–114
  see also military spending
deflation 195, 215
deindustrialisation 74, 113, 115, 241, 251, 310
demand management 14, 316
  see also aggregate demand, fiscal policy
denationalisation *see* privatisation
Denmark 29, 177, 274, 290
depreciation 18, 70, 206
  see also devaluation, sterling
deregulation 4, 34–35, 186, 214, 297, 311, 338
  see also financial deregulation, labour market deregulation
Desai, Meghnad 198–199
Deutschmark 38, 43
devaluation 64, 69–71, 341
  see also depreciation
developing countries *see* Thirld World
developmental institutions 6, 311, 330–332
differentials 201, 209, 215, 218, 241, 246, 249–250, 252, 272, 282
discrimination 209, 250, 254, 256
distribution of income xvii, 3, 88, 90, 205, 217, 261, 282–286
distribution sector 84–5, 210, 213–210, 242–243, 271, 303
diversification *see* defence conversion
dividend payments 3, 77, 80, 86, 214–215, 282
Donovan Report 174
Driver, Ciaran 3, 88, 90
Dunne, Paul 3, 91–2, 112–114, 309

earnings *see* wages
Eatwell, John 6, 333
economic growth *see* growth
Economic and Monetary Union 3, 41, 43, 54, 65–7, 73–4, 335, 341
economic planning *see* planning
economic power 6, 330
economic regeneration 3, 138–139, 332
  see also industrial regeneration, restructuring
economic restructuring *see* restructuring
economies of scale 99
economies of scope 325

Ecuador 25, 27–28
education 5, 67, 129, 211, 242–243, 252,
        256–257, 267–269, 271–276, 292,
        297–298, 320, 333–335, 341
efficiency 321, 328, 331, 334–335
    allocative 315, 321, 337
    productive 315, 331, 339
Eisenhower, Dwight 13, 92, 108
electricity supply industry 83, 317–318,
        320–321
employment xix–xxi, 14, 34, 60, 79–82,
        88, 197, 201, 236–245, 301–310,
        312, 317
    see also full employment, unemploy-
        ment, women's employment
energy 6, 37, 84, 242–243, 315, 321–324
    see also electricity supply industry,
        North Sea oil, prices
enterprise 6, 158, 160–161, 218–219
    culture 5, 61, 296–314
    Enterprise Boards 125
    Enterprise Initiative 297
    entrepreneurs 245, 248
environment 110, 115, 130, 133–6, 289,
        321–323, 334, 339
equal pay 250
    Equal Pay Act 241
    see also wages
eurodollars 39
Europe 25, 79, 81, 88–9, 98–9
European Community 2, 6–7, 38, 41, 53,
        74, 141, 169, 191, 246, 261–263,
        273–274, 289, 291, 298, 334–336
    European Commission 134
    Treaty of Rome 74
European Monetary System *see*
        Exchange Rate Mechanism
European Monetary Union *see* Economic
        and Monetary Union
exchange controls 18, 40, 44, 57, 196
Exchange Rate Mechanism xxi, 43, 59,
        71, 217, 335
exchange rates xvii, xxi, 14–15, 18, 197,
        205, 341
    floating 14, 39, 41, 70
    stability 14, 43
    see also Exchange Rate Mechanism,
        sterling
expectations xx, 89
    see also uncertainty
exploitation 209, 213–214
exports xxii–xxiii, 62–4, 114, 197–8, 205
    see also Balance of Payments
externalities 72, 109, 169, 308, 323, 335

Faber, Mike 33

Falklands/Malvinas 12, 31, 93, 95
Federal Reserve Board *see* US monetary
        policy
Ferranti 96, 317
finance 2, 37–59, 295, 320, 329
    see also financial sector, money
financial capital 316
financial deregulation xxi–xxii, 38–59,
        197
financial institutions 342
    see also banks, international financial
        institutions
financial sector 2, 37, 77, 84, 89, 211,
        271, 333
    see also banks, financial institutions,
        services
Fine, Ben 5, 315, 319
Finland 29, 177
fiscal policy 15–16, 69, 74, 196, 264, 331,
        341
    fine tuning 14
    see also demand management
flexibility 210, 218, 249
    see also deregulation
France 6, 29, 79, 93, 107, 177, 179–181,
        234, 239, 274, 290, 300, 320
Friedman, Milton 196, 199–200
fuel prices *see* prices
full employment 14, 34, 72, 174, 213,
        294, 334

GEC 96–101, 103–4, 112
Germany 6, 21–22, 29, 54, 81, 102, 174,
        177, 179–81, 187, 274, 283, 290,
        299–301, 312–313, 320, 332
Glyn, Andrew 3, 34, 77, 81–2, 88, 217,
        293
Godley, Wynne 3, 60, 85
Goodhart, Charles 199
    Goodhart's law 15
government spending *see* public
        expenditure
Greece 177, 274
Green, Francis 5, 111, 255
Griffith-Jones, Stephany 17, 24, 28, 33
growth xviii–xx, 2, 7, 34–36, 60, 68–70,
        88–90, 140, 292, 312, 316, 333,
        341
Gulf States 12
Gulf War xviii, 91, 93

Harcourt, G.C. 217, 293
Harland & Wolff 96
Harris, Laurence 2, 37, 58

health 5, 67, 267–268, 292
  see also National Health Service, private health schemes
Heath, Edward 1
  Heath government 330
  Heath-style Tory government 261, 286
Hilferding 54
Holland *see* Netherlands
Horrell, Sarah 186, 247
hotels and catering 210–213, 242–243
House of Commons Treasury and Civil Services Committee *see* Treasury
housing 38, 65, 115, 123–4, 129–136, 141, 271–272
  homelessness 3
  market xxii, 121, 156, 252
  repossessions 52, 220
  sale of public 51–52, 266, 271, 280, 288, 317
  see also mortgages
Howe, Geoffrey 13–14, 21, 42
Hughes, Alan 5, 77, 296, 304, 308–309, 312
Humphries, Jane 5, 217, 236, 239–241, 251, 256
Hutton, Will 6, 340
hysteresis 81, 201

ICL 317
ideology 11, 255, 315–319
imperialism *see* British Empire
imports xxii–xxiii, 62–4, 197, 205–7
  price of 206, 216
  see also Balance of Payments
incentives 16, 61, 297, 315, 319, 341
income distribution *see* distribution of income
income tax *see* taxation
incomes policies 1, 14, 196, 201, 204
industrial capital 6, 295, 316
industrial policy 5–6, 92–3, 106, 109–111, 147, 311, 314, 315–321, 326, 328–329, 330–332, 335, 340
industrial regeneration 40, 56
  see also economic regeneration, reindustrialisation, restructuring
industrial relations legislation 4, 61, 173–194, 205, 208–209, 215, 255
  see also trade unions
industry 37–40, 311, 315, 329, 334
inequality 5, 52, 210, 235, 241, 248, 250, 252, 254, 286, 291
inflation xvii, xx–xxi, 4, 13–16, 31, 34–35, 42, 61–2, 67, 70–2, 195–219, 241, 264–266, 341
information technology 318–319

infrastructure 3, 7, 115, 121, 123, 129, 132, 136, 138, 141, 198, 271, 314, 333–335
inner cities 3–4, 115–139, 299
  Action for Cities 116, 123–4, 129–30
  Enterprise Zones 123, 125–8, 130–1, 133–4
  Urban Development Corporations 123, 126–9, 132–3
  Urban Programme 122–4, 126–131, 133
  see also Enterprise Boards, local government, Rate Support Grant
innovation 297, 309, 313, 320
insecurity 4, 235
insiders 202, 205
insolvencies 52, 65
  see also bankruptcies
institutions 200, 254, 313–314, 317–319, 321, 325, 335, 337–339
insurance companies 40, 44, 50–1
interest rates xxi, 15–21, 31, 34, 38, 43, 61, 65, 68, 74, 195–8, 206, 217, 218, 264–266, 341
international competitiveness *see* competitiveness
international financial institutions (IFIs) 18, 23, 29–31, 34
  see also banks, International Monetary Fund, World Bank
International Labour Organisation 176, 187
International Monetary Fund (IMF) 1, 17, 20, 23–25, 34–35, 196
  see also international financial institutions
international trade *see* trade
internationalisation 37–9, 99, 101–5, 190, 320, 329
investment xviii, xxii, 3, 6–7, 64, 69–70, 74, 77, 88–90, 198, 271, 294, 316, 320, 333
Ireland 29, 177, 274
  Northern Ireland 93, 141, 158–61
Italy 29, 73, 102, 107, 177, 179, 274, 290, 300, 312–313

Japan 2, 29, 45–7, 79, 85, 177, 187, 281, 312, 314, 316, 332
  Japanese capital 53, 153, 320
  Japanese trade surplus 21
Jobling, Ray 4, 234
Joseph, Sir Keith 296, 331

Kaldor 14, 198

Keeble, David 160, 303
Keegan, William 14
Kemp–Roth 16
Keynes 22, 335
Keynesian 6, 14, 34, 74, 144, 200–201
  instruments 41–2
  Keynesianism 334
  neo-Keynesian 200–201
Kitson, Mike 217
Korea *see* South Korea

labour 201, 316, 320, 328
  intensification 4, 173, 212–215, 234
  process 90
labour market 4, 113, 117, 141, 173,
        191, 195–6, 199–205, 208–217,
        218–219, 222, 226–229, 233,
        236–255
  deregulation 208–210, 236, 252, 254
  see also industrial relations legislation,
        trade unions
Labour 57, 291, 330, 333–342
  Labour government 1, 3, 93–6, 202,
        204, 261, 264, 272, 277, 284,
        286, 293, 299, 321, 325, 330
  Labour Party 6, 114
  see also Callaghan, Wilson
laissez-faire 315, 317–318
  see also market forces, supply side
Landesmann, Michael 63, 72
Latin America 15, 23–25, 28, 34–35
Lawson, Nigel 13–14, 22–25, 42–3, 62,
        65, 321, 341
  Lawson boom 43, 69, 156
LDCs *see* Third World
local government 4, 116–138, 183,
        211–212, 271, 299, 317
  see also inner cities
London Business School 70, 200
Lovering, John 3, 99, 111–113
low pay 4, 6, 189–90, 208–214, 236, 241,
        246, 251–254, 257, 316

Macmillan, Harold 13, 266
macroeconomic policy 6, 14, 35, 41–2,
        46, 61, 114, 138, 174, 210, 261,
        297, 317, 334, 341
Major, John 25, 62, 93, 200
  the Major government 191, 273, 331
manufacturing 3, 6, 37–9, 42–3, 58, 61,
        63, 69–71, 77–90, 114, 118, 198,
        209–210, 252, 293, 301, 305, 310,
        312, 316, 320, 333
margins 207–8
  see also mark-up
markets 200, 331–332, 335, 338

market failure 109, 138, 168–169, 299,
        316, 331, 335
market forces 1, 3, 6, 14, 20, 35, 87,
        92–3, 112, 114, 140, 297, 313,
        317–318
  see also deregulation, *laissez faire*,
        monetarism
mark-up 195, 201, 214
  see also margins, prices
Marr, Ana 33
Martin, Ron 4, 140, 143, 146, 154, 161,
        168, 299
Marxist 201
material prices *see* prices
McCombie, John 3, 68, 71
McKendry, Ian 33
means test xvii–xviii, 218, 253
medium term financial strategy xxi, 42,
        56, 58, 61
mergers 298, 309–310
  merger policy 331
  see also Monopolies and Mergers Com-
        mission, takeovers
Mexico 11–12, 17, 20–21, 25, 27–28, 31
Michie, Jonathan 4, 195, 219, 282
microeconomic policies 61, 315, 317, 321
  see also supply side
Middle East 12, 25
military industrial complex 91–3, 105,
        108–9, 111–3
military spending 1, 3, 5, 7, 16, 20, 94–6,
        110–111, 270, 292, 320
  see also arms contracts, defence con-
        version, defence firms, defence
        industry, peace dividend
minimum wage 5, 257
mining *see* coal mining
Mitterrand 24, 73
monetarism xxi, 4, 13–16, 31, 34, 38,
        174, 196, 198–200, 215, 218, 317
  see also monetary policy
monetary policy 2, 57–9, 62, 69, 264, 331
  monetary targets xxi, 38, 42, 58, 61,
        196–7
  see also medium term financial strat-
        egy, US monetary policy
money xxii, 2, 14, 37, 195–201, 218
  quantity theory of 42, 199
  supply of xx, 13–14, 195–201, 215
  velocity of circulation 199
  see also credit, monetarism
Monopolies and Mergers Commission
        97–8, 105, 107, 298
monopolisation 101
  see also concentration, mergers, natu-
        ral monopolies

Monroe Doctrine 24
Moore, Barry 3, 114, 138–9, 141, 163, 299
moral hazard 108
Morocco 23–25, 27–28
mortgages xxii, 46, 51–2, 216–217
multinationals 44, 99, 105, 320, 329

NAIRU 81, 200
National Audit Office 51, 97
National Economic Development Office 329, 332
National Enterprise Board 317
National Health Service 211, 269–276, 317
National Insurance contributions 263, 280–282, 288
national minimum wage *see* minimum wage
nationalisation *see* public ownership
NATO 94–5, 112
natural monopolies 331
natural rate of unemployment 200
see also NAIRU
neoclassical theory 337
Netherlands 29, 177, 180–1, 261, 274, 290, 300
networks 5, 313–314, 321
New Deal 92
new international economic order 29, 34
new technology 37
see also technical change
New Zealand 24, 29, 33, 177
NIESR model 70
Nigeria 23–25, 27–28
nonprice competition *see* competition
North America 2, 229
see also United States
North Sea oil xviii–xix, 3, 6–7, 24, 62, 113, 197–8, 263, 333, 336
see also oil and gas sector
Northern Ireland *see* Ireland
'North–South' divide 4, 140, 153, 162
Norway 29, 79, 177, 180–1

OECD 2–3, 6, 15, 18, 25, 33–36, 82, 179, 261–266, 270, 273, 280–281, 290
Development Assistance Committee (DAC) 29
oil and gas sector 85
price xix, 15, 18, 20, 29, 31, 35, 198, 206, 263, 279, 288, 322
revenues 69, 218, 280
1973 shock 11, 15, 39, 236, 293
second shock 197, 236
see also North Sea oil, OPEC

oligopolistic markets 70
OPEC 24, 293–294, 322
see also oil and gas sector
Ormerod, Paul 5, 201, 293
output xix–xxi, 1, 3, 6, 14, 66, 77–82, 199, 301
overseas investment 6–7, 316

PA Cambridge Economic Consultants 133
Panić, Mića 2, 57–8
participation rates *see* women's employment
part-time work 175, 188, 209–210, 212, 240–241, 244, 246, 249, 250–254
pay *see* wages
peace dividend 111, 292
see also defence conversion, military spending
pension funds 40, 44, 50–1
pensions 5, 38, 246, 277–278, 284, 291–292
personal consumption *see* consumption
Peru 25, 27–28
pharmaceuticals 63
Philippines 23–25, 27–28
Phillips curve 200–204
planning 92, 110–111
Plaza Agreement 24
Poletti, Clara 5, 315
pollution xvii, 289
poverty 3, 137, 204, 213, 277, 283–286, 289, 291
prices xxi, 3, 195–6, 199–202, 206–8, 214–7, 331
commodity 15, 17–19, 34–35, 197, 216
fuel and material 2, 206
see also inflation, oil price
private health schemes 5, 291
privatisation 6, 34–35, 41, 49–53, 92, 106–108, 211–212, 214, 274, 288, 297, 315–328, 331–332, 336
productivity xviii–xx, 1, 3–4, 6, 61, 70, 77–90, 198, 201, 205, 214–215, 217, 303, 305, 308, 316, 320
profits 3, 5, 77, 79–86, 197, 201, 214–216, 293–295, 297
protectionism 21–22
psychological health 4, 220–235
public expenditure 14, 218, 220, 261–292
cuts 196, 253
public ownership 38, 91, 106–111, 315, 317–322, 325–329, 335, 337
see also privatisation
public procurement 93, 111

public sector borrowing requirement 14, 49, 196, 336
public services 7, 121–2
    see also welfare
public utilities 331–332, 336

Rate Support Grant 125, 128
    see also inner cities
Reagan 13, 16, 31, 34, 36, 91
    governments 2, 15–16
    Reaganomics 18
recession 197–8, 215, 235, 252, 263, 266, 293–294, 299, 303, 310, 316, 320, 333
Reddaway, Brian xvii, 1–2
redundancy 3, 158, 223, 228, 234, 252, 319
regional policies 4, 98, 110–111, 116, 128, 140, 146–8, 153, 167, 299–301
    regional development corporations 4, 169
regional problems 3–4, 66–7, 73–4, 140–70
regulation 315, 318, 321, 331–332, 335–336
reindustrialisation 6, 340
research and development 7, 64, 96, 99, 298–301, 320, 333, 335, 340
reserve army of labour 201, 204
    see also unemployment
restructuring 3, 99, 105, 112–214, 210–211, 218, 293, 295, 309, 315–317, 319, 321, 327, 330
Rhodesia *see* Zimbabwe
Ricardo 18, 337
Rolls Royce 96, 104
Rowthorn, Bob 5, 7, 81, 83, 87–8, 201, 208, 250, 261, 272, 287, 303, 320
Royal Ordnance 96, 101, 106, 108
Rubery, Jill 5, 186–188, 228, 236, 239–241, 245–7, 251, 256

Saudi Arabia 12, 101, 113
saving xxii–xxiii, 38, 66, 74, 197
Sawyer, Malcolm 6, 330–331
Scandinavia 290
Scotland 116, 125, 131, 141, 144, 158–160, 223
self-employment 5, 61, 158–62, 240, 245, 296–303, 308, 310–311
services 37, 43, 58, 77, 138, 209–211, 241, 251, 303, 305, 310
    financial and business 37, 43, 79, 84–87, 139, 209–211, 303
    see also banks, finance
share prices 77, 80, 87, 214

shareholders 82, 331
shareholding 50, 186
Short Brothers 96
short-termism 6–7, 56, 316, 324, 338, 341
Singapore 2, 12
Singer, Hans 33
Singh, Ajit 2, 33–34
single currency *see* Economic and Monetary Union
small firms 5, 61, 160–161, 212, 252, 296–314
Smith, Ron 3, 91–2, 99, 101, 105, 109, 112–114
Snell, A. 63, 72
social democracy 113, 337–338
social ownership *see* public ownership
social policies 3, 5, 208
    see also welfare
social security benefits *see* welfare payments
social security contributions 281, 288
socialism 337–339
socialist countries 44
    collapse of 2, 29
sociological research 4, 234
South Korea 2, 107, 332
Southern Africa 30
Spain 177
speculation 18, 72
stagflation 35, 201
State, the 6, 91, 99, 105, 311, 317, 325, 330, 338
    British 37, 73, 92, 316, 320
statutory national minimum wage *see* minimum wage
steel 6, 106–7, 315, 319, 325–329
    see also British Steel Corporation
sterling xxii, 198
    overvaluation of 15, 42–3, 59, 197, 216, 341
    see also exchange rate
stock exchanges 40–41, 45–9
sub-Saharan Africa (SSA) 24, 28
supply side 15–16, 34, 62, 64, 67, 146, 174, 187, 251, 316
    see also laissez faire, monetarism
Sweden 6, 29, 86, 177, 179, 261, 283
Switzerland 29, 177

takeovers 90, 309
    see also mergers
Tarling, Roger 4, 201, 218
taxation xvii–xviii, 5, 14–18, 38, 61, 187, 196–7, 201–5, 208, 215, 261–293, 297, 299, 316, 336

income tax xvii–xviii, xxi, 208, 263, 280–281, 288

tax cuts 17, 215, 254, 266, 279, 291

tax revenue 14, 16, 280

technical change 202

technical progress xviii, 70

telecommunications *see* British Telecom, information technology

terms of trade 18, 34, 201, 205, 208, 218
internal 213

Thatcher, Margaret xvii–xix, 1, 6, 12–16, 20, 25, 30–31, 33–34, 36–43, 50, 137, 195, 315, 331
Thatcher governments 2–4, 11, 14–18, 37, 49, 53, 57–9, 68, 77–9, 87, 91–8, 140, 146–7, 168, 173, 191–2, 195–8, 210, 220, 236–237, 251, 253–254, 261–267, 270–291, 325, 330–331
'Thatcher miracle' xix, 74, 316
Thatcherism 91–114, 153, 255, 316–317, 321
Thatcherite ideology xx, 49
Thatcherite policies 5, 332

Third World 2, 12, 15–21, 39, 44

Thirlwall, Tony 3, 68, 71

Toye, John 2, 11, 30, 33–34

trade 2, 71, 295, 297
traded goods sector 5–6
see also Balance of Payments, competitiveness

trade unions 2, 35, 97, 173–84, 192–3, 201, 204, 214–215, 297
see also bargaining power, collective bargaining, industrial relations legislation, wage bargainers

training 5, 7, 64, 130, 133, 136, 138, 174, 182, 187, 189, 194, 249, 252, 256–257, 297–298, 300, 320, 333–335, 340–341

transport 67, 84, 129, 136, 242–243, 288–289, 320

Treasury 20–21, 131, 211, 328
and Civil Services Committee 196

Turner, David 70–72

Tyler, Peter 4, 140, 143, 154, 168, 299

uncertainty 3, 90, 108, 234, 324
see also expectations

unemployment xx–xxii, 1, 4, 7, 34–35, 42, 58, 60–2, 66–9, 115–121, 132–7, 141, 167, 197, 200–205, 215–6, 220, 222–235, 237–240, 255, 282, 285, 293–294, 301–302, 310–311, 341

unemployment benefits 187, 263, 276–279
see also employment

United States 2, 11–13, 29, 31–33, 72–3, 85–6, 98, 112, 131, 174, 177, 179, 187, 234, 283, 304, 312, 316, 341
budget deficit 16–17, 21, 32
capital 53, 320
Congress 2
monetary policy 16–18, 31
trade deficit 17
see also North America

urban policy *see* inner cities

Uruguay 25, 27–28

utilities *see* public utilities

VAT xx, 15–16, 263, 279, 286, 302, 304

Venezuela 27–28

Verdoorn effect 70

wages 4, 6, 77, 153–6, 166, 195–197, 208, 236, 241, 282
Fair Wage Resolution 175, 212
wage bargainers xx–xxi, 154
wage restraint 195, 255
Wages Councils 154, 182–3, 250, 252
see also Clegg Commission, differentials, equal pay, incomes policies, low pay, minimum wage

Warwick University Macroeconomic Modelling Bureau 70

welfare 5, 208, 211–213, 218–219, 234–235, 292, 338
payments xvii–xviii, 67, 201, 204, 215, 276–279, 285–289, 292
state 290–293
see also social policies

Wells, John 6, 303

West Germany *see* Germany

Wheeler, Joyce 111

Widdicombe Committee Report 125

Wilkinson, Frank 4, 174, 187–8, 195, 201, 212–213, 219, 282

Wilson, Harold 1
Wilson government 13
see also Labour governments
Wilson Report 299

women's employment 5, 180, 188, 209, 236–257
participation rates 81, 236–239, 244, 247–249, 251

World Bank 2, 17, 23, 34–35
see also international financial institutions

Yugoslavia 23–25, 27–28

Zimbabwe 12, 31